Art of
Judgement

For my parents

Art of Judgement

Howard Caygill

Basil Blackwell

Copyright © Howard Caygill 1989

First published 1989

Basil Blackwell Ltd
108 Cowley Road, Oxford, OX4 1JF, UK

Basil Blackwell, Inc.
3 Cambridge Center
Cambridge, Massachusetts 02142, USA

British Library Cataloguing in Publication Data

A CIP catalogue record for this book is available
from the British Library.

Library of Congress Cataloging in Publication Data
Caygill, Howard
    Art of judgement / Howard Caygill
        p. cm.
    Bibliography: p.
    Includes index.
    ISBN 0-631-16596-7:
    1. Judgment (Aesthetics) 2. Kant, Immanuel, 1724-1804. Kritik
    der Urteilskraft. 3. Aesthetics. I. Title.
    BH301.JBC39 1989
    111'.85—dc20   89-31494
                                                         CIP

Typeset in 11 on 12 pt Ehrhardt
by Photo-graphics, Honiton, Devon
Printed in Great Britain by T.J. Press (Padstow) Ltd

Contents

Part II
4 Judgement before the Critique

5 The Critique of Judgement-Power

Acknowledgements

This book would not have been written without my friends Gillian Rose and Greg Bright.

The clarifications offered by Jay Bernstein and Garbis Kortian at the end and the beginning of the project were crucial, as were the innumerable contributions of friends and colleagues in Oxford, Brighton, and Berlin. My thanks to them all.

The basic research for this book was carried out under an SSRC (UK) quota award at the University of Sussex. Additional research for chapter 3 in Göttingen was supported by the British Academy, whose subsequent award of a Postdoctoral Fellowship at Wolfson College, Oxford gave me the conditions necessary to complete and bring the work to publication. I wish to record my thanks to these institutions for their support.

Preface

A striking feature of recent theoretical debate in the humanities and social sciences is the emergence of judgement as the issue through which the disciplines discover and deliberate their limits. As the first text to take judgement as its explicit theme, Kant's *Critique of Judgement-Power* is central to this debate, and its authority is acknowledged by thinkers as diverse as Arendt, Derrida, Habermas, and Lyotard. But while the third *Critique* is used to reflect on the limits of judgement in politics, art, and philosophy, its own judgement on these issues is not trusted. The text is taken to exemplify the failure of the ambition to unify freedom and necessity, and to suffer the limits of judgement-power as aporia. Yet this distrust underestimates the *Critique* which, far from being limited by the difficulties of judgement, strives to explore these difficult limits in the medium of tradition. It is as a consciously aporetic analysis of the limits of judgement that the work is still able to challenge the boundaries of contemporary thinking.

List of Plates

The Aporia of Judgement

> If one were able to apprehend what sort of a secret power it is that makes judging possible, then one would be able to untie the knot. My current view is that this power or ability [to judge] can be none other than the capacity of inner sense to make its own representations into objects of its thoughts. This capacity cannot be derived from any other, it is fundamental in the proper sense, and can, I hold, only belong to a rational being. The entire higher faculty of knowledge rests on this power.
>
> Kant, *The False Subtlety of the Four Syllogistic Figures*

Kant regarded the power of judgement as a secret power, concealed in its sources – a hidden art giving rise to tangles, knots and riddles. Yet this concealed power underlies the systems of theoretical, practical, and aesthetic judgements analysed in the three *Critiques*. The difficulties involved in giving a secret power philosophical exposition are suffered and worked through in all of Kant's texts, but most of all in the *Critique of Judgement-Power*, where the power itself is judged, and where concealment reveals itself.

Kant manifests the power of judgement through a rehearsal of its tangles, knots and riddles. He is able to do so because the secret power has left traces of its activity in the competing and disputed 'claims' that constitute its history. Judgement can come to self-knowledge through instituting a tribunal to judge – according to its own law – its heritage of disputes and quarrels. But how can judgement so legislate without contributing another knot to an already tangled history?

In the first Preface to the *Critique of Pure Reason* Kant is confident that this can be accomplished through an interrogation of the 'faculty of reason in general' isolated from its embodiment in 'books and systems'. The tribunal examines the metaphysical questions over which reason has 'fallen out' with itself and finds them to be misunderstandings. However, this procedure supposes not only that the disputed questions are before the tribunal – reason has *already* fallen out with itself over them – but that the 'principles' by which it judges them are already given too. In the name of 'reason in general' Kant refuses both the tangled history of judgement and the recognition that all current and future judgements must be implicated in it.[1]

In the course of the first Preface the laws by which judgement judges itself become principles through which it discriminates between the conflicting claims of its history. We shall see that this move from conceiving judgement as the execution of a law to the discrimination of differences is not without its own tangled history. Meanwhile, if we move to the Preface of the third *Critique*, we find that the critical tribunal has set itself a different task. Faced with the 'riddle' of the pleasure evoked by judgement's recourse to itself for its own principle, the tribunal in the person of Kant hopes 'that the great difficulty of unravelling a problem by nature so entangled [*welches die Natur so verwickelt hat*] may serve as an excuse for a certain amount of hardly avoidable obscurity in its solution, provided that the accuracy of our statement of the principle is proved with all requisite clearness.' Here it is admitted, in open court, that the difficulty of the problem has implications for philosophical procedure. The outcome of unravelling the problem is not a clear solution – the revelation of a principle, as in the first *Critique* – but a statement or report of its difficulty.

The emphasis on stating a difficulty rather than resolving it places Kant's *Critique of Judgement-Power* within the tradition of aporetic philosophy. In the terms of this tradition, the task of the third *Critique* is a clear statement of the aporia, or difficulty, of judgement. The most celebrated example of aporia in philosophy is the embarrassing perplexity evoked in the interlocuter during the Socratic dialogue. In transforming Socrates' aporetic practice into a method, Aristotle makes it both an interpretative strategy for reading the history of philosophy, and the object of that history itself.[2] The first sense is exemplified by *Of the Heavens* (279b, 7–12):

> But first let us start with a review of the theories of other thinkers; for the proofs of a theory are difficulties [*aporiai*] for the contrary theory. Besides, those who have first heard the pleas of our adversaries will be more likely to credit the

assertions which we are going to make. We shall be less open to the charge of procuring judgement by default. To give a satisfactory decision as to the truth it is necessary to be rather an arbitrator than a party to the dispute.

The philosopher is here cast as an arbiter between the conflicting accounts of an issue, and not as a party to the dispute. It is apparent that Kant's procedure laid out in the Preface is in many respects as old as philosophy itself.

Aporia is for Aristotle not only the interpretative predicament of philosophy, but also its fate. This, the second sense of Aristotelean aporetic, is exemplified by Aristotle's celebrated claim that he, and not the Platonists, was true heir to the Socratic method. For him, Socratic definition does not separate universals as transcendent forms from their individual embodiments, but gives an aporetic statement of their relation. By granting existence to the universals, the Platonists foreclosed on the ontological aporia of universal and singular being which is the proper object of philosophy. Philosophical definition must state this aporia as precisely as possible, as is exemplified in the following sentence from the *Metaphysics* (1087a, 10–15): 'The statement that all knowledge is universal, so that the principles of things must also be universal and not separate substances, presents indeed, of all the points we have mentioned, the greatest difficulty, but yet the statement is in a sense true, although in a sense it is not.' This truth can only be appreciated if the difficulty is stated clearly, but this clear statement by no means solves the difficulty.

Kant's preference for an accurate statement of the entangled problem of the principle of judgement over its solution is comparable in ethos to Aristotle's desire to state clearly the ontological aporia. This is even the case with the critical tribunal in the first *Critique*, which would act as an arbiter in identifying and resolving reason's differences with itself. Furthermore, the third *Critique* also follows Aristotelean procedure in stating the difficulty in terms of opposed positions revealed in the history of philosophy. This procedure was suppressed in the first two *Critiques*, but acknowledged in the third; here, both the subject matter and its exposition is aporetic.

The 'entangled problem' of the principle of judgement is not confined to the special case of aesthetic judgements of taste in the third *Critique*. The theoretical philosophy of the *Critique of Pure Reason* derives the system of judgements from judgement-power but concedes that this power cannot itself be spoken; similarly in the *Critique of Practical Reason*, where judgement-power cannot be stated apart from its system of judgements. All three critical works offer 'canons' for the guidance of judgement, but in none of them does Kant venture 'doctrinal' or 'dogmatic' definitions of the power itself.

In the first *Critique* the aporia of judgement manifests itself in two related guises. The first is in the difference between judgement's subsumptive and discriminative modes, and has already been encountered in the procedure of the critical tribunal. Judgement-power is capable 'of subsuming under rules; that is, to distinguish whether something stands under a given rule (*casus datae legis*) or not' (1781/1787, A132/B171). But how can judgement give itself a rule for distinguishing whether or not something stands under a rule, or whether it can be made to do so? It cannot do so, in 'general logic', which is concerned only with the form of concepts, because 'if it sought to give general instructions how we are to subsume under these rules, that is, to distinguish whether something does or does not come under them, that could only be by means of another rule. This in its turn, for the very reason that it is a rule, again demands guidance from judgement' (A133/B172).

We return to the problem of how the critical tribunal can justify the 'principles' by which it differentiates between cases before it brings them before the law. Here the exercise of judgement is found always to presuppose judgement: its discriminations require rules, and its rules require discriminations.

Judgement-power underlies and exceeds its distribution in terms of discrimination and subsumption. It evokes a similar aporia in transcendental logic, where it is deemed to give rules for its own application: 'although general logic can supply no rules for judgement-power, the situation is entirely different in transcendental logic' (A80/B106). The power of judgement informs the division of concept and intuition; it is the common principle which founds the possibility of their unity:

> Without sensibility no object would be given to us, without understanding no object would be thought. Thoughts without content are empty, intuitions without concepts are blind. It is, therefore, just as necessary to make our concepts sensible, that is, to add the object to them in intuition, as to make our intuitions intelligible, that is, to bring them under concepts. These two powers or capacities cannot exchange their functions. The understanding can intuit nothing, the senses can think nothing. Only through their union can knowledge arise.
>
> (A51/B75)

The union of sensible and intelligible is achieved through judgement-power, but this achievement requires that the power be imputed paradoxical properties, acting as the means of exchange between two qualitatively distinct faculties.

Nowhere in the *Critique of Pure Reason* does Kant specify judgement except in terms of its operation. In the 'Analytic of Principles' he restricts himself to developing a 'critique to guard against errors of judgement-power' (A135/B174). The power in itself is not open to philosophical understanding, something Kant admits in the 'Schematism' chapter of the 'Analytic of Principles'. Schematism offers a 'transcendental doctrine of judgement-power' through which may be achieved 'the *subsumption* of intuitions under pure concepts, the application of a category to appearances' (A137/B176). Kant first introduces judgement in the imperative voice and then lists its contradictory properties:

> Obviously *there must be* some third thing, which is homogeneous on the one hand with the category, and on the other hand with the appearance, and which thus makes the application of the former to the latter possible. This mediating representation must be pure, that is, void of all empirical content, and yet at the same time, while it must in one respect be *intellectual*, it must in another be *sensible*.
>
> (A138/B177, first emphasis mine)

The 'third thing' which exchanges between the intellectual and the sensible has the properties of both; it is the 'entangled principle' upon which all knowledge depends but which cannot itself be thought; it is 'an art concealed in the depths of the human soul, whose true workings nature ever painfully keeps us from having unveiled before our eyes' (A142/B181). The principle of judgement then, which is called upon to found the possibility of objective knowledge, possesses contradictory properties and is unthinkable: in other words, the *Critique of Pure Reason* is founded upon an aporia.

The aporia of judgement is also central to the *Critique of Practical Reason*, as is apparent in the discussion of the 'typic' where Kant confesses that 'The judgement of pure practical reason, therefore, is subject to the same difficulties as that of the pure theoretical, though the latter had a means of escape' (1788b; p. 68; p. 70). Yet practical reason finds its own way out of these difficulties by postulating the understanding as mediating between the universal and the individual through a 'rule of judgement' in which natural law becomes the typic of practical judgement. But the power of judgement itself, although the same for practical as for theoretical judgement, remains 'concealed in the depths of the human soul'.

In the *Critique of Judgement-Power* Kant opts to admit judgement's difficulty rather than plot an escape from it. His Preface alerts the reader that a clear statement is preferred over an 'obscure solution' to the peculiar principle of judgement. However, this preference has been passed over by many of Kant's readers, who have opted either to embrace or to reject the 'obscurity of the solution', a common response to aporetic texts.[3] In the case of the third *Critique*, the reception oscillates between panoramic and microscopic extremes: some readers see it as the unification of freedom and necessity – the 'crowning phase' of the critical philosophy – while others see it as a candidate for dismemberment and analytical dissection.[4]

Recent French accounts of the third *Critique* have formally restored the aporetic character of the text. The readings of Lyotard and Derrida rub themselves against the aporetic grain of the text, but take its aporia as symptomatic and not thematic. The *Critique* is found to register Kant's failure to bring pleasure under judgement, and its aporias are seen as the collapse of this venture. By attempting to name a principle which would unify judgement and pleasure, the text fails and falls into aporia. For Lyotard, the feeling of the beautiful 'escapes being mastered by concept and will. It extends itself underneath and beyond their intrigues and their closure ... It is a region of resistance to institutions and establishments ...' (p. 15). The topic eludes the logical apparatus with which Kant tries to capture it, evoking aporia and casting logic into confusion.

Derrida's reading, too, sees the *Critique* as the violent framing of beauty within the table of logical judgements (quality, quantity, relation, modality) – 'a transportation which is not without its problems and artful violence: a *logical* frame is transposed and forced in to be imposed on a *nonlogical* structure' (1978, p. 69). The frame has been 'hastily imported', it 'fits badly'; moreover, it 'artificially constrains' a discourse that threatens to 'overflow' its limits. Derrida's deconstruction of the third *Critique* shows how the table of logical judgements undoes itself in venturing to frame beauty; but perhaps the text is more radical than this allows. It may turn out that the violence of framing is directed toward exposing other histories of violence more artfully concealed in the apparently 'nonlogical' structure of beauty itself.

Regarding the 'categorical frame' imposed on the experience of the beautiful, Derrida asks 'where does this frame come from? Who supplies it? Who constructs it, where is it imported from?' (p. 68). He answers that it comes from the analytic of concepts in the first

Critique. Kant, it seems, takes this frame and applies it to the experience of the beautiful; but where does this experience come from? The experience itself turns out to be already framed. It is not that he applies a frame and brings beauty under judgement, but he uses the frame to discover through beauty other violations of the beautiful which indicate an aporia of judgement. The *Critique of Judgement-Power* begins with the aporia of judgement as manifest in tradition, and uses aporetic procedures to present and exceed it; aporia is at issue in this text, it is not its fate.

It is because the 'principle' of judgement is so obviously confused in the case of pleasure in the beautiful, because these kinds of judgements mark a limit of judgement itself, that Kant can use them to expose the way judgement conceals itself. One of the main means of concealment employed in the first two *Critiques* is to deny it its history, to consider it in formal terms. If it is stripped of its tangled history, judgement remains a hidden art. But if its tangled history is presented – 'stated' – as a tangled history, then the knot, or aporia, is itself framed, and brought to judgement. It is this history of judgement, tangled in other histories of metaphysics, politics, pleasure, law and production, which the third *Critique* tries to bring before itself.

These histories are presented in terms of two traditions of judgement: aesthetic and taste. In a footnote to the 'Transcendental Aesthetic' of the *Critique of Pure Reason* Kant distinguishes between German claims for a science of aesthetics which 'originated in the abortive attempt made by Baumgarten, that admirable analytical thinker, to bring the critical treatment of the beautiful under rational principles, and so raise its rules to the rank of a science' and 'what others call the critique of taste' (A21/B36). The 'others' in question are not the Italian and French critics who first developed the discourse of taste, and with whose works Kant was unfamiliar, but the British philosophers whose writings on taste were extremely fashionable in mid eighteenth-century Germany. The two traditions form the subject matter of the *Critique of Judgement-Power*, whose first heading is '*Das Geschmacksurteil ist ästhetisch*' – 'The Judgement of Taste is Aesthetic'.

The traditions of taste and aesthetic are set within distinct experiences of modernity which represent the different ways in which production and legislation, and civil society and the state, were brought into relation in the early modern period. The two traditions bear the scars of these different but related histories to the third *Critique*. Together they embody the aporia of judgement in its logical, political and aesthetic aspects. Kant's examination of them in the *Critique* allows the history of the aporia of judgement to come forward and point beyond its forced unifications to different relations of law and production. In the guise of a statement of the aporia of the aesthetic judgement of taste, the third *Critique* offers a meditation on the metaphysical and political crises of modernity.

The examination of the 'concealed sources' of the aporia of judgement undertaken in this book is divided into two parts. The first part examines what is characteristically modern about the aporia of judgement, and how it informs the histories of taste and aesthetic. The detailed reconstruction of the two traditions frames them within distinct intellectual and political responses to modernity, and gives historical substance to the names 'taste' and 'aesthetic' which are deployed in the *Critique of Judgement-Power*.

Chapter 1 traces the emergence of the problem of judgement in the early modern period and its violent resolution by Hobbes. Chapters 2 and 3 locate the development of the discourses of taste and aesthetic within those of 'civil society' and the 'police-state'. In both cases a different aspect of the aporia becomes manifest, and it is this difference which permits Kant to discern 'a bias of judgement' from within judgement. Kant's interrogation of the traditions is presented in the second part of the book. Chapter 4 traces Kant's appropriation of them in the pre-critical writings and his discovery of the bias of judgement, while chapter 5 records their aporetic examination in the third *Critique*. The final section, 'Beyond Judgement', reflects on the implications of the recognition of the formal and substantive aporia in the *Critique of Judgement-Power* for the understanding of judgement, and the attempt to think beyond it.

Part I

1

Beauty under Judgement

The Difficulty of Beauty

They grasped that reason can only see into what it produces through its own projection, that it leads with principles of judgement according to constant laws, not allowing itself to dangle on nature's reins, but insisting that nature answer its questions.

Kant, *Critique of Pure Reason*

Socrates' conclusion to his gruelling interrogation of Hippias – 'Now at least I see what they mean when they say "All beauty is difficult"'[1] – is echoed by Kant in the Preface to the *Critique of Judgement-Power*. There he admits that he has not solved the 'riddle' of the judgement of beauty, but is satisfied with the 'accurate statement' of its difficulty. But the peculiar difficulties of aesthetic judgement point beyond beauty to those of judgement in general. The latter arise from the alignment of freedom, production, and judgement evoked by Kant in his claim that reason has insight only into what it produces according to its own principles of judgement. The difficulty of beauty may offer a privileged standpoint from which to survey the difficulties of judgement in general.

Our difficulty with beauty is inseparable from those difficulties of judgement which represent a specifically modern predicament and which are the outcome of a history of repression and misrecognition. So much is apparent if we contrast the modern obsession with judgement in its theoretical, practical, and aesthetic modes, with a pre-modern philosophy such as Aquinas's where neither the knowing and acting subject nor its judgements are of particular interest. Aquinas's speculative and practical philosophy rests on the notion of an objective proportion, while modern philosophy departs from the judgements of an autonomous subject. For Aquinas speculative philosophy is the knowing of proportion, and practical philosophy the production of things and actions according to it:

> Note, however, that a thing is referred differently to the practical intellect than it is to the speculative intellect. Since the practical intellect causes things, it is a measure of what it causes. But, since the speculative intellect is receptive in regard to things, it is, in a certain sense, moved by things and consequently measured by them. It is clear, therefore, that, as is said in the *Metaphysics*, natural things from which our intellect gets its scientific knowledge measure our intellect. Yet these things are themselves measured by the divine intellect, in which are all created things – just as all works of art find their origin in the intellect of an artist. The divine intellect, therefore measures and is not measured; a natural thing both measures and is measured; but our intellect is measured, and measures only artefacts, not natural things.
>
> (1256–9; vol. I, p. 11)

The human intellect is here placed in the unfamiliar role – unfamiliar at least for modern philosophy – of being measured; it is not in the active role of measuring and judging. Aquinas's subdivision of speculative knowledge into categorial and transcendental departments is apparently more familiar – Kant after all wrote a transcendental philosophy – but it too turns out to be something quite different. For Aquinas, categorial knowledge is accomplished through the determinations or measures established in Being by the divine intellect: 'being is narrowed down in the ten categories, each of which adds something to being – not, of course, an accident or difference which is outside the essence of being, but a definite manner of being which is founded upon the very existence of the thing' (vol. III, pp. 5–6). Categorial knowledge determines according to the objective proportion of Being in which it partakes. Transcendental knowledge, knowledge beyond the categories – Being, Unity, Truth, Goodness, and Beauty – adds an 'intelligible aspect' to categorial determination. Unity adds the aspect of indivisibility to Being; Truth adequates categorial knowledge to the measure of Being; Goodness equates the achievement of an end to proportion; while Beauty consists in the pleasure of contemplating due proportion. Transcendental knowledge, in other words, establishes the conditions for the coherent exercise of categorial determination.

Aquinas's hierarchy of knowledge is the opposite of the modern one, whose apex is the self-conscious and active *cogito* of the subject. For Aquinas, the divine intellect measures but is not measured; Being is measured and measures; the human intellect is measured, and, Aquinas adds for consistency, can also measure its artefacts. The distance between his and our hierarchy is brought out in his thought experiment on the nature of truth. Imagine the fate of truth following the extinction first of the human intellect, and then of both human and divine intellects:

> In a natural thing, truth is found especially in the first [with respect to its conformity with the divine intellect], rather than in the second [with respect to its conformity with a human intellect] sense; for its reference to the divine intellect comes before its reference to a human intellect. Even if there were no human intellects, things could be said to be there because of their relation to the divine intellect. But if, by an impossible supposition, both intellects did not exist and things did not continue to exist, then the essentials of truth would in no way remain.
>
> (vol. I, p. 11)

Truth would survive the first catastrophe but not the second. What is inconceivable to Aquinas, less conceivable even than the extinction of both divine and human intellects, is the constitution of truth by the human intellect alone. Such a view of truth was subsequently proposed by his nominalist critics, who defined truth as the agreement of individuals created by God with universals established by man. The freedom of the human intellect to create its own universals and perform acts of judgement according to them was central to Renaissance humanism, which transformed Aquinas's objective proportion into a subjective proportion constituted by human activity. The humanists inverted Aquinas's priority of speculative over practical philosophy and dissolved the objective order of proportionality into subjectivity. What is with Aquinas a residual category of little intrinsic interest – human artifice measuring its own products – had within a century and a half become central to human self-understanding.

The new emphasis on subjectivity led to a revised understanding of the character of transcendence. While Aquinas and Kant might agree that transcendental knowledge is by definition beyond categorial knowledge, they would seek transcendence in different places. For Aquinas categorial determination is achieved by virtue of the transcendent relation to objective proportion, while for Kant, judgement depends on the transcendental productive and legislative activity of the subject. Medieval transcendental philosophy rested on objective proportion, while the modern version is founded on a complex alignment of freedom, production, and judgement.

The transition to a modern transcendental philosophy is evident in the writings of Pico della Mirandola (1463–94). His surviving texts show the infusion of scholasticism with a new concept of human subjectivity and freedom. The human subject is free to produce its own order and proportion, but against the resistance of matter, described in the *Oration on Human Dignity* (1486) as the 'excrementary and filthy parts of the lower world' (p. 224). The new emphasis on human freedom brings with it a notion of matter and the flesh as obstacles to the establishment of order and proportion. Unlike Aquinas's view of practical activity as the production of objects out of a matter irradiated with divine proportion, Pico's free production is defined against matter, as freedom *from* the material world.

Aquinas's proportioned harmony of divinity, being, and human activity makes way in Pico to the 'grievous and more than civil wars of the spirit' (p. 231). The wars of the spirit are provoked by Pico's substitution of an alignment of freedom, production, and judgement for objective proportion. The substitution is apparent in his report of God's instructions to Adam, which completely inverts Aquinas's version of the place allotted to human beings in creation:

> Thou, constrained by no limits, in accordance with thy own free will, in whose hand we have placed thee, shalt ordain for thyself the limits of thy nature. We have set thee at the world's centre that thou mayest from thence more easily observe whatever is in the world. We have made thee neither of heaven nor of earth, neither mortal nor immortal, so that with freedom of choice and honour, as though the maker and moulder of thyself, thou mayest fashion thyself in whatever shape thou shalt prefer. Thou shalt have the power to degenerate into the lower forms of life, which are brutish. Thou shalt have the power out of thy soul's judgement, to be reborn into the higher forms, which are divine.
>
> (pp. 224–5)

Human freedom is autonomous and productive: the activity of self-limitation involved in 'ordaining for thyself the limits of thy nature', is presented in terms of 'making and moulding'. This productive legislation is identified with the 'power of thy soul's judgement', whose exercise Pico subsequently describes as 'transcendental'.

The activities of self-limitation and 'making and moulding' which comprise the 'power of judgement' mediate a series of dichotomies: these are, in the *Oration*, heaven and earth, mortality and immortality; in *Of Being and Unity* (1492) 'senses and reason', 'unity and dispersion', and 'spirit and flesh'. However, the mediation of these dichotomies presupposes a ground of agreement between their terms, for without an underlying order, such as Thomist proportionality, the terms of the dichotomy remain irreconcilable. The main difficulty which faced philosophical modernity lay in thinking the production of such an order, or in Pico's terms, in showing how the 'setting of limits' (autonomy or self-legislation) is also a 'making and moulding' (a productive activity). The notion of a productive activity which proportions itself constituted Pico's redefinition of the transcendental. Pico calls this activity the 'bond of virtue', and explicates it in terms of the fourfold transcendence of Being, Truth, Unity, and Goodness, although it is 'Unity' which is given precedence over the others:

> For we are not one and integrated if we do not link together with a bond of virtue our senses, which incline to earth, and our reason, which tends to heavenly things; this is rather to have two principles ruling in us in turn, so that, while today we follow God by the law of the spirit, and tomorrow Baal by the law of the flesh, our inner realm is divided and as it were laid waste.
>
> (1492, p. 34)

The alignment of autonomy and production in the 'bond of virtue' is thought in terms of judgement, in terms of the unification of a manifold. Instead of a proportioned order which gives both identity and difference their due, difference is figured as a threat to unity, one which must be bound. Pico's last words in *Of Being and Unity* are that unity is life, difference is death.

Kant inherits Pico's dichotomy in his 'transcendental distinction' of sensibility and reason, but is aware of the difficulties to which it gives rise. If the poles of a dichotomy are irreconcilable, then there is no point in speaking about binding them. But if they are reconcilable, then they imply an order which exceeds their opposition. The 'bond of virtue' or its equivalent has to be thought to transcend the dichotomy of sensibility and reason. The unity of reason and the diversity of sensibility – the poles of judgement – are already implicated in an order that transcends judgement. Pico, too, seems to recognize this when he employs the traditional vocabulary of transcendental philosophy to describe the bond of virtue, but in the end he privileges unity over goodness and truth.

Pico's notion of human freedom inverts Aquinas's hierarchy of proportion wherein God measures, Being is measured and measures, and human intellect is measured and can only measure its own artefacts. Pico's God has delegated to human freedom the responsibility for measurement; and since the human intellect can only measure its own products, it must consider itself and Being as if they were its creations. A complex relation of legislation and production succeeds the old transcendental philosophy. Speculative philosophy in Aquinas's sense – the contemplation of the divine proportionality of Being – succumbs to the judgement of Being according to an artificial measure. The practical philosophy in which production is ordered according to objective proportion is succeeded by one in which freedom is ordered according to human laws. In both cases the relation of identity and difference is definitive: legislation and production meet where difference is vanquished by identity. Only in beauty, Aquinas's fifth transcendental, is proportion preserved. Beauty becomes the bad conscience of judgement, and the work of art the site of a privileged relation of legislation and production, one which points beyond the violent opposition of identity and difference.

The difficult relation of production and legislation is manifest in the distinction of invention and judgement which pervades early modern theoretical philosophy.[2] Invention produces the objects of perception which are to be ordered by judgement. However, the distinction between the two activities is nominal, since bringing forth objects in invention presupposes an ordering principle in judgement. In Arnauld's *Port Royal Logic* (1662) the four divisions of Conception, Judgement, Reasoning, and Ordering are subordinated to the 'principal task', which is 'to train the judgement, rendering it as exact as we can' (p. 7). Judgement is extended to include not only its three proper functions, but also conception (invention or sensibility). Kant's later unification of invention and judgement in the 'Aesthetic' and 'Analytic' of the 'Transcendental Logic' of the first *Critique* follows this tradition. It is judgement which must give content to the empty concept and bring light to the blind material of the intuition; in other words, it must be both inventive and estimative, producing objects for judgement.

A similar role for judgement emerges in the shift in the emphasis of early-modern practical philosophy from natural law to natural rights. Natural rights theory was preoccupied with the project of constituting an order of property and sovereignty out of natural freedom. This was a complete departure from traditional practical philosophy whose summit was the doctrine of virtue. In Aquinas's practical philosophy virtue is the *habitus* which realizes an objective proportion through action:

> And therefore, since virtue is the principle of some kind of operation, there must pre-exist in the operator in respect of virtue some corresponding disposition. Now virtue causes an ordered operation. Therefore virtue itself is an ordered disposition of the soul, in so far as, namely, the powers of the soul are in some way ordered to one another, and to that which is outside.
>
> (1266–73, II/I, q. 55, a. 2)

Virtue is the ordered disposition of the soul which is proportioned to 'that which is outside'. In rights theory, the ordered disposition of virtue is translated into the exercise of judgement; its paradigm is the creation of individual rights and their orderly unification. However, as with the distinction of reason and sensibility, there must be a conformity between individual rights and their unity in judgement, for there would otherwise be no possibility of unification. In rights theory this prior conformity is continually disavowed in favour of such contraries as unity and dispersal, universal and particular.

But what again of the fifth transcendental, of beauty? In Aristotle, the three main divisions of episteme are the theoretical, the practical, and the productive. Modern philosophy inherited the first two divisions, but transformed productive knowledge into the philosophy of art. It is preoccupied, even obsessed with beauty and art, and for definite reasons. We shall see that the productive legislation of theoretical and practical philosophy was habitually thought in terms of judgement, in terms of unifying a manifold. In beauty a different relation is figured, one which exceeds unity and diversity. This relation is signalled by pleasure, which points to a relation of production and legislation that transcends the violent unifications of judgement. Beauty and pleasure haunt the career of judgement, testifying to a transcendence which it has usurped.

The difficulty of beauty emerges with the crises of judgement. Whenever diversity is to be unified, beauty appears with a promise of a different order. And it must appear for judgement to take place at all, for without it the unification of diversity is undisguised violence. Yet it cannot be allowed to linger without throwing the legitimacy of judgement into question. The trope of admitting beauty as an autonomous production only for as long as it enables judgement to take place, and then retracting it, characterizes the modern traditions of beauty and judgement represented by the theories of taste and aesthetic. They show that the difficulty of beauty under judgement is both metaphysical and political. It is on the basis of these traditions that Kant set out to confront beauty and judgement in the third *Critique*. He is content, he says in the Preface, with an 'accurate statement' – and, like Socrates, to 'see what they mean when they say "all beauty is difficult".'

The Matter, Forme and Power of a Commonwealth

> Signs (of reproduction) (In respect of time and being in them) are marks (horses, false coins) reminders (omens) or figurative marks. SYMBOL (of the) intellect. (analogy) parables and allegories. Symbolic (tropes) of God. Schematism of the understanding (mystical signs of a secret revelation. Theosophist.)
> Leviathan: Hobbes's symbol for a state, whose soul is the prince. Symbolic writing of the egyptians: snakes, bees.
>
> Kant, *Reflection* 1486

Hobbes's use of the terms 'matter', 'forme', and 'power' in the subtitle to *Leviathan* underlines his fusion of rights theory with a notion of productive judgement. He elaborated this position against the scholastic principles of 'invisible species' or 'substantial form', whose postulation of a form or objective proportion prior to matter he saw as a philosophical error fraught with grievous theoretical and practical consequences. In open revolt against scholasticism, he developed a demonstrative system of philosophy which, beginning with 'body', proceeded to analyse 'man' and then the 'citizen'. The onset of civil war provoked him to reverse his intended order of composition. He published *De Cive* in 1642 and then the remaining parts, *De Corpore* and *De Homine*, in 1655 and 1657. However, the notion of productive judgement, although not formally enunciated before the later works, already informs his early political philosophy.

The philosophical background and the political occasion of Hobbes's political philosophy are inseparable. The *Elements of Law* of 1640 and *De Cive* ventured to settle the 'questions concerning the rights of Dominion, and the obedience due from Subjects, the true forerunners of an approaching War' (Hobbes 1642a; p. 35). When in *Behemoth* (1680) and the *Dialogue Between a Philosopher and a Student of the Common Laws of England* (1681) he lifted the self-denying ordinance of *De Cive* 'not to dispute the laws of any government in special' (p. 37) he argued that the claims made against the sovereign on the grounds of natural law were among the major causes of the civil war. He saw natural law theory as a political consequence of the theoretical error of substantial form. The metaphysical postulate of a form or proportion prior to matter supported a view of natural law as a ground for social unity prior to the contract of sovereignty. It was this conviction which lay at the heart of the 'boyling hot' questions of dominion and sovereignty which were settled on the battlefield; for if a contract among the members of civil society preceded the contract with the sovereign, then sovereignty was divided between society and state and open to negotiation through arms.

In place of an objective proportion or form, Hobbes proposes to think of form as artifice. He impiously compares the productive legislation which 'makes', 'sets together', and 'unites' a commonwealth with God's creation of the world: 'the *Pacts and Covenants*, by which the parts of this Body Politique were at first made, set together, and united, resemble that *Fiat*, or *Let us make man*, pronounced by God in the Creation' (1651, pp. 81–2). The paradigm for this productive legislation is the production of a work of art. However, for Hobbes the work of art does not evince a harmony between its parts, but a unification of diversity: there can be no relation between the parts outside of their relation to the whole. Hobbes theorizes this unification in terms of illusion and misrecognition. The avowal and disavowal of mutual recognition is stated in terms of the optical illusion characteristic of anamorphic art. The paradigm of illusory unity of the parts employed in this art form is definitive for Hobbes's understanding of *Leviathan* as a work of art.

The decisive moment in the development of Hobbes's philosophy came during the conversations he held with Galileo and Mersenne while accompanying his pupils on the Grand Tour in 1637. It is well known that Hobbes's materialist philosophy of motion was inspired by Galileo, but the importance of his interest in optics, stimulated by Mersenne and his circle at the Monastery of the Minims in Paris, has been underestimated.[3] Hobbes considered the results of his work in optics to be as significant as those achieved in his political philosophy, and concluded his *A Minute or First Draught of the Optiques* (written in 1646) with the claim: 'I shall deserve the reputation of having been ye first to lay ye ground of two sciences, this of optiques, ye most curious, and ye other of naturall justice, which i have done in my booke de Cive, ye most profitable of all other' (1646). The optics is divided into two sections: the first on optical theory, the second on catoptrics, a division akin to Mersenne's own posthumously published *L'Optique et la Catoptrique*. The influence of the optical experiments of the Mersenne circle on his philosophy was as great as that of Galilean physics: if Galileo may be said to have given Hobbes the matter of his philosophy, then the optical experiments of the Mersenne circle gave him its form.

The members of the Mersenne circle were preoccupied with the exploration of the physical and metaphysical implications of catoptrics, and during their researches in the 1630s brought together the illusionistic properties of reflection disclosed by catoptrics with anamorphic art. The result was the new art form of the catoptric anamorph. Anamorphic art in general exploits the distortion of perspective in such a way that a different image appears in a picture according to the position of the spectator.[4] The researches of the Mersenne circle overcame the necessity for the spectator to change position with an optical device which shifted perspective by reflection (thus 'catoptric'). The use of such a device 'is comparable to the effect of an automaton causing pictures to arise directly out of a confused tangle' (Baltrusaitis 1977, p. 131). The catoptric device became a metaphor for creative perception and was seen by the Mersenne circle as opening the possibility of a synthetic geometry in which the subject's perception produces the perceived object. The illusory resolution of the catoptric anamorph seemed emblematic of the unity of invention and judgement.

Traces of this interest in catoptric art are discernible throughout Hobbes's philosophy, most obviously in his praise of the poet in the *Answer to D'Avenant* (1650):

> I believe, Sir, you have seen a curious kind of perspective, where he that looks through a short hollow pipe upon a picture containing divers figures, sees none of those that are there painted, but some one person made up of their parts, conveyed to the eye by the artificial cutting of a glass. I find in my imagination an effect not unlike it, from your Poem.
>
> (1650, p. 451)

Here the catoptric anamorph is used as a metaphor for the production of unity out of diversity in the work of art. It also serves as a metaphor for civilization, which is described as the inventive work of 'fancy' guided by the precepts of judgement; for 'All that is beautiful or defensible in building; or marvellous in engines and instruments of motion . . . and whatsoever distinguisheth the civility of Europe, from the barbarity of the American savages; is the workmanship of fancy, but guided in the precepts of true philosophy' (pp. 449–50).[5] The image of the divers figures 'becoming some one person' is employed in the frontispiece to *Leviathan* which Hobbes designed at about the same time as he wrote the above passage (dated 10 January 1650). The most astonishing feature of the engraving (reproduced in part in plate 1) is the way Leviathan is figured in terms of individuals united into a single body through their gaze at its face.[6]

Unlike Vico in the Introduction to his *New Science*, Hobbes did not explicitly discuss the allegory of his engraving. However, analysis of the lower section of the engraving has shown it to be remarkably close to the contents of the book, especially the 'Civil and Ecclesiastical' parts. This is true also of the figure looming over the landscape in the upper half of the engraving, which has a subtle figurative relation to the 'Matter, Forme and Power' of the commonwealth. Most discussion of the giant figure has focused on the identity of the face: is it Cromwell, Charles I or II or even Hobbes himself? But speculations on its identity are largely irrelevant, since what is essential about this face – 'which had to be generalized a little for iconic purposes' (Brown 1978, p. 34) – is that it is a *mask*. The interpretation of the face as a mask agrees with an important step in Hobbes's argument about the constitution of the body politic, namely the discussion of personification, a concept which Hobbes introduces in *De Homine* in terms of the theatrical mask. It will be seen that the mask or the person performs an analogous role to the catoptric anamorph in the work of art, unifying 'divers figures' into 'some one person'. The individuals or 'matter' in the state of nature are united through the 'power' of sovereignty into the 'forme' of a commonwealth.

The unification of a manifold does not follow a given proportion, but is produced. Hobbes explores this complex view of the relationship of form and matter in the recently discovered *Thomas White's De Mundo Examined* of 1642. Here he develops a distinction between *ens* and *imaginatio* (which he also calls 'fictions', 'orders', and 'mind-pictures'), and argues from it that matter and form are bound by the power of 'fluxion'. In one suggestive passage, which anticipates Hobbes's later image of the body politic, he uses the relationship of matter, form, and fluxion to compare the continuity of the state with the life of an individual. After raising the topos of identity and difference – was Jason's Argo the same ship on its departure as on its return? – Hobbes continues:

> Likewise if one asks: 'Is a man, when old or young, the same being, *ens*, or matter, in number?' it is clear that, because of the continual casting of [existing] body-tissue and the acquisition

of new, it is not the same material [that endures], and hence
not the same body; yet because of the unbroken nature of the
flux by which matter decays and is replaced, he is always the
same man. The same must be said of the commonwealth.
When any citizen dies, the material of the state is not the
same, i.e., the state is not the same *ens*. Yet the uninterrupted
degree [*ordo*] and motion of government that signalise a state
ensure, while they remain as one, that the state is the same in
number.

(Hobbes, 1642b; p. 141)

In the context of insisting that order or form is neither an accident
of matter nor its preformation, but the product of imagination,
Hobbes identifies life with order, and order with a continually
produced unity; death is the dispersal following the inability to
reproduce unity. The consequences of the identification of life and
unity are drawn out in *Leviathan*. Here, however, the main point is
that form is produced, a view which Hobbes employs in his critique
of Descartes's definition of space and extension wherein he claims:
'the existence of space depends not on the existence of body, but on
the imaginative faculty' (p. 42). His epistemological position is neither
empiricist, nor a priorist, but rests on the production of form: matter
is moulded and form produced by the power of fluxion. *Thomas
White's De Mundo Examined* marks Hobbes's development toward a
trichotomous view of the relation of matter and form, individual and
universal as contraries united by power.

Hobbes's location of power between matter and form informs his
definitions of the procedures of philosophy in *De Cive* and *De Corpore*.
He wrote in the 'Epistle Dedicatory' to the earlier text that it is
through philosophy that 'a way is open'd to us, which we travel from
the contemplation of particular things to the inferences or results of
universal action' (1642a, p. 25). In *De Corpore*, the 'way' between
particular and universal is presented in terms of the cause or
generation of the object: 'Philosophy is such knowledge of effects or
appearances, as we acquire by true ratiocination from the knowledge
we have first of their causes or generation: And again, of such causes
or generations as may be from knowing first their effects' (1655,
p. 3). The emphasis in this definition lies less on form and matter
than on the power 'generation or cause' which binds them. This
emphasis is also apparent in Hobbes's example of the 'philosophical'
definition of a circle as the 'circumduction of a body'. Instead of
giving a formal definition such as 'a line each of whose points are
equidistant from a given point' he defines a circle thus:

a body carried about, retaining always the same length, applies itself first to one *radius*, then to another, to a third, a fourth, and successively to all; and, therefore, the same length, from the same point, toucheth the circumference in every part thereof, which is as much as to say, as all the *radii* are equal. We know, therefore, that from such generation proceeds a figure, from whose one middle point all the extreme points are reached unto by equal *radii*.

(p. 6)

Here the formal definition of a circle gives way to a description of its production. Similarly in the political philosophy of *Leviathan*, the philosophical definition describes how the matter of individuals in the state of nature is configured into a commonwealth through the power of sovereignty. Here Hobbes brings to rights philosophy an uncompromisingly modern account of the production of the relation between universal and individual which has little to do with either the Platonic or Aristotelean traditions.

In this philosophy production is taken to consist in the unification of a manifold. Unity and dispersion stand opposed to each other, and there can be no thought of a harmony or proportion betweeen them. The consequences for political theory are extremely stark:

For in a multitude not yet reduc'd into one Person . . . there remaines that same *state of nature* in which *all things belong to all men*; and there is no place for *Meum & Tuum*, which is call'd Dominion, and *Propriety*, by reason that that security is not yet extant which we have declar'd above to be necessarily requisite for the practise of the *Naturall Laws*.

(1642a, p. 91)

Natural laws are themselves unable to guarantee their own observance, and so it is necessary for the multitude to unify themselves. The question then arises of how they may be 'reduced into one person'. The question is clearly put, if obscurely answered, in the *Elements of Law*. In the state of nature not even the simplest contract would be honoured unless 'there shall be such power coercive over both the parties, as shall deprive them of their private judgements on this point; then may such covenants be effectual; seeing he that performeth first shall have no reasonable cause to doubt the performance of the other, that may be compelled thereunto' (1640, p. 78). Humans unlike bees do not possess a *habitus* which might incline them to live peacefully in society, for 'natural concord such as is amongst those creatures is the work of God by the way of nature; but concord amongst men is artificial, and by way of covenant' (p. 102). There is no natural law which might guarantee a peaceful society prior to the institution of the artificial covenant. Hobbes consistently regards this artificial concord as the unification of the multitude into a person: 'This union so made, is that which men call now-a-days a *body politic* or civil society; and the Greeks call it *polis*, that is to say, a city; which may be defined to be a multitude of men, united as one person by a common power, for the common peace, defence, and benefit' (p. 104). Yet at this stage the way in which unity is produced remains obscure, for apart from the violent unification of conquest and compulsion, there is only the 'arbitrary institution of many men assembled together, which is like a creation out of nothing by human wit' (p. 108). But the paradoxical formulations of 'arbitrary institution' (what does it mean for an institution to be arbitrary?) and 'creation out of nothing' indicate a difficulty in conceiving how individuals without 'natural concord' are nevertheless able to unify themselves artificially.

In the early 1640s Hobbes had not yet developed a proper understanding of the process by which the 'multitude' became a 'person'. As in his early definition of philosophy, he could not see how a scatter of individuals or particulars could produce a universal. This problem is finally addressed in his later discussions of personification: the final chapter of *De Homine*, 'Of Artificial Man', and chapter 16 of *Leviathan*, 'Of Persons, Authors, and Things Personated', both of which concern the transition from the state of nature to artificial society. In these chapters Hobbes describes the production of political form (personification) as the process by which the matter of dispersed individuals is united into a sovereign person through the power of their collected authorities.

When describing the production of the commonwealth 'out of nothing' Hobbes relies heavily on theatrical metaphors, claiming in his account of personification in *De Homine* that 'such artifices are no less necessary in the state than in the theatre' (1657, p. 83). We shall see Hobbes finds in the theatre the same logic of illusion he found in catoptric art. In the theatre the audience produce the spectacle by its gaze, and are united by it into an audience. Should their gaze turn away from the spectacle and toward each other, then the illusion on stage would be destroyed along with their unity as an audience. The unification of diversity follows from individuals in the audience producing the illusion which constitutes them as an audience.

We may witness this phenomenon in the *Leviathan* frontispiece, which unites both theatocratic and catoptric metaphors. The reader is given a theatrical *adventus* to the text by being shown the production of the commonwealth, the instant when discrete individuals are transformed into one body.[7] The image of *Leviathan* is captured at the moment when the 'short hollow pipe' of the catoptric anamorph transforms the 'divers figures' into 'some one person'. But what is happening in the body itself? If we surrender the superior viewpoint of the reader/viewer and descend among the 'divers figures', mingle with the audience, we find ourselves implicated in the production of the commonwealth. Here the illusory effect of the catoptric anamorph described in the *Answer to D'Avenant* is achieved by means of theatrical illusion. The individuals, all gazing in rapt silence at the mask, at this moment constitute the spectacle which constitutes them as a single body or audience. In terms of political philosophy, they are at the moment when they renounce their authorities to the sovereign person and are reconstituted as subjects.

Before prosecuting this theatocratic reading of Hobbes through a study of his account of personification, there arises the problem of why the citizens in the *Leviathan* engraving have not doffed their hats. The vast majority of the citizens are covered, and, in the arms of the great body, some are even *kneeling* with their hats on. This is odd given the importance Hobbes attached to the 'civill honouring of the person' (1651, p. 677) and his amusement at the 'rusticity' of the man 'ignorant of the Ceremonies of Court' (p. 694). He carefully distinguishes the baring of the head before majesty from idolatry: 'To be uncovered, before a man of Power and Authority, or before the Throne of a Prince ... is to worship that man, or Prince with Civill Worship; as being a signe, not of honouring the stoole or place, but the Person; and is not idolatry' (p. 670, see also p. 667). Why then, in the presence of the Sovereign, do the members of the commonwealth fail to dispense with their headgear? One explanation involves the 'rusticity' of Hobbes or his engraver, another is that Hobbes meant the citizens to be represented as 'insolent schismatics', both of which seem unlikely. A third explanation is conceivable: the one occasion when a crowd might stand before a king without uncovering is when they are in the theatre watching an actor represent a king.

The view that the face of the person of Leviathan upon which the multitude gaze is a mask is supported by Hobbes's own etymology of the word 'person' in *De Homine*:

What the Greeks called *prosopon* the Latins sometimes call man's *facies* (face) or *os* (countenance), and sometimes his *persona* (mask): *facies* if they wished to indicate the true man, *persona* if an artificial one, such as comedy and tragedy were accustomed to have in the theatre. For in the theatre it was understood that the actor himself did not speak, but someone else, for example, Agamemnon, namely the actor playing the part of Agamemnon in a false face who was, for that time, Agamemnon; nevertheless, afterwards he was also understood without his false face, namely being acknowledged as the actor himself rather than the person he had been playing.

(1657; p. 83)

The persona is the theatrical mask through which the words of another are represented; but not only represented, for while the actor was behind the mask he was Agamemnon, his words Agamemnon's: after the performance the mask returns to being a mask and the actor to being an actor. The constitution of the person of *Leviathan* in the engraving marks an analogous performance. The gaze of the individual citizens, their acknowledgement of the mask, simultaneously gives it reality and constitutes them as a body or audience.[8] But this gaze is unidirectional since the audience do not recognize each other; and should the gaze be distracted, then the body of the audience will revert to its original elements.

Hobbes does not immediately draw such conclusions from his etymology of person in *De Homine,* but cautiously builds up to them by extending the idea of theatrical representation to social relations:

on account of commercial dealings and contracts between men not actually present, such artifices are no less necessary in the state than in the theatre. Moreover, because the concept of person is of use in civil affairs, it can be defined as follows: *a person is he to whom the words or actions of men are attributed, either his own or another's*: if his own, the person is *natural*; if another's, it is *artificial*.

(p. 83)

Here, in order to ensure the continuity over space and time of a legal subject, Hobbes personifies even the *facies* or 'true man'. In order to engage in contracts even the 'true man' must be defined as a legal subject or person of the law, since otherwise there would be no perdurable legal subject. Without this artifice the 'true man' Jason, on returning from his voyage, would have been able to evade obligations contracted before his departure in the Argo by claiming that he was not the same Jason (see also 1642b, p. 143). The physical individual must be represented as a legal subject with a perdurable identity, and this is the work of the 'power coercive' mentioned in the *Elements of Law*. If the person represents themself as such, they are a 'natural person'; if, however, the person represents themself through another person, the latter becomes an 'artificial person'.

For social life to be possible, individuals must represent themselves as persons – must accept the legal form of personality; but where does this form originate and what is the source of its authority? Hobbes answers this question by developing the idea of an artificial personality in which, like the actor in the mask of Agamemnon, the words of another may be represented. He extends the idea of the artificial person from one person representing the words of another to one person representing the words of many others: 'just as the same actor can play different persons at different times, so any one man can represent many' (1657, p. 83). This passage transforms the paradox of identity and difference (one and many) over time – 'the same actor can play different persons at different times' – to identity and difference in space – 'so any one man can represent many', i.e. simultaneously – precisely the shift which stimulated the optical speculations of the Mersenne circle. How is the simultaneous representation of the many in one achieved? The answer lies in the power of the authority which sustains the representation.

The distinction between the person that represents another individual and the person that represents a multitude of individuals involves the distinction between *dominium* and *imperium*. The first involves a one to one relationship between author and person, while the second is a many to one relationship between authors and their person. The notion that a proportioned relation need not involve unification of a multitude is not considered. In the first case the individual author is directly responsible for acts committed by his artificial person, he owns the words in the mouth of the person. However, the representation of a multitude of authors in a single person corresponds to political rule or *imperium*. Instead of giving their person his script, the multitude give him the authority to improvise; and once they have done so they cannot walk out on his performance. The quantitative shift from individual to collective authorship results in a qualitative change in the relationship of the authors to their person. The person constituted by their collective authority becomes a single author which represents its authors as persons. It is this reconstitution of the original authors as person or subjects which makes it self-contradictory for them to complain about, or resist, the actions of their person:

> Not only can a single man bear the person of a single man, but one man can also bear many, and many, one. For if many men agree that, whatsoever be done by one man or group out

of the many, they themselves will hold it as an action of each and every one of them, each and every one will be author of the actions that the man or group may take; and therefore he cannot complain of any of their actions without complaining of himself.

(p. 85)

Hobbes plays on the sense in which 'any man or group' is both author and person; as authors of the sovereign person they cannot complain about actions which affect them as persons or subjects of the sovereign. In authorizing a single person the multitude have created a mortal god which rules over them and claims to have created them as *its* persons or subjects. The mask of the sovereign in the frontispiece does not acknowledge its body; as a mortal god it cannot return the gaze of its creatures, for this would be to acknowledge that they are also its creators.

In *Leviathan* Hobbes emphasizes the distinction between the representation of one author by one person and of many authors by one person. He intensifies his critique of the natural law argument that obligation exists prior to the authorization of a sovereign:

A Multitude of men, are made *One* Person, when they are by one man, or one Person, Represented; so that it be done with the consent of every one of that Multitude in particular. For it is the Unity of the Representer, not the Unity of the Represented that makes the person *One*, and it is the Representer that beareth the Person, and but one Person; and *Unity*, cannot otherwise be understood in Multitude.

(1651; p. 220)

There is no unity before the constitution of the sovereign person; if there was it would mean that the relation of author to person is one to one, and the sovereign simply the mouthpiece of society. This argument is related to his critique of that 'vain philosophy' of scholasticism, especially the 'jargon' of 'certaine essences separated from Bodies, which they call Abstract Essences, and Substantial Forms' (p. 689). For Hobbes, such philosophical doctrine along with its natural law corollary poses a threat to the life of the commonwealth:

this doctrine of *Separated Essences*, built on the Vain Philosophy of Aristotle, would fright them from Obeying the Laws of their Countrey, with empty names; as men fright Birds from the

Corn with an empty doublet, a hat, and a crooked stick. For it is upon this ground, that when a man is dead and buried, they say his Soule (that is his Life) can walk separated from his Body, and is seen by night amongst the graves.

(p. 691)

The scorn for the doctrine that the soul exists apart from the body follows from Hobbes's application of the metaphor of body and soul to the body politic. In his critique of Bellarmine in Part III of *Leviathan* Hobbes disputes the point that

the Members of every Commonwealth, as of a naturall Body, depend one of another: it is true, they cohaere together; but they depend onely on the Soveraign, which is the Soul of the Commonwealth; which failing, the Common-wealth is dissolved into a Civill war, no one man so much as cohaering to another, for want of a common Dependance on a known Soveraign; Just as the Members of the Naturall Body dissolve into Earth, for want of a Soul to hold them together.

(p. 602)

The soul which unifies the body cannot exist apart from the body, nor the body apart from the soul. The soul is the 'life' or 'power' which keeps the material of the body informed; or in terms of the *Thomas White* commentary, it is the fluxion which keeps *ens* and *ordo* together. There is no coherence between the parts of the body or commonwealth apart from the unification through the soul or sovereignty, and this maintains the form of the body; it cannot exist without the body nor the body without it. Yet the soul or sovereignty is here considered as unity and life, against which diversity figures death.

The body politic cannot exist without the soul or power of sovereignty since its members do not 'cohaere' without it. There is no form or 'cohaesion' prior to matter; matter, form, and power are inseparable. Hobbes most strenuously denies the existence of a ground for social unity, an innate sociability or moral sense, prior to the constitution of the sovereign person. The inescapable conclusion is that there is no realm of moral activity apart from the law; there are no inalienable natural rights based on a source of obligation preceding the establishment of the commonwealth. The common-wealth can only be created through the complete surrender by each individual author of all natural rights; if any rights are reserved, the sovereign person is in a one-to-one relation of *dominium* with its author, which results in divided sovereignty. In this case the sovereign's power will be insufficient to reconstitute the 'matter' of the multitude into the form of legal relations.

In this case the choice of how far to be obliged to the sovereign is left to the judgement of the individual, which places the burden of order back onto the same rules of reason which were incapable of guaranteeing security in the original state of nature. As a result, the individual surrenders to the sovereign its individual judgement concerning the law. It is an error in political philosophy to permit 'a Private man, without the Authority of the Common-wealth, that is to say, without permission from the Representant thereof, to Interpret the Law by his own Spirit ... [because] in the Power of making Laws, is comprehended also the Power of Explaining them when there is need' (pp. 700–1). Since legal personality and law were created by the sovereign, the sovereign knows best what they may mean. The claim that the producer has the best understanding of their product is another testimony to Hobbes's philosophical modernity.

The account of personification accords with Hobbes's requirement that a philosophical explanation give an account of the production of its object. In it the three factors of matter, form, and power are united in a manner that avoids privileging substantial form over matter. Just as the continual interplay of matter (*ens*) and form (*ordo*) in the physical body are united by the soul or life (*fluxion*), so the continual process of citizens (matter) surrendering their authority to the sovereign and being reconstituted as persons (form) defines sovereignty or power as the soul of the commonwealth (see Schmitt, 1938). The commonwealth is being continually re-created by the acknowledgement of the *imperium* of the sovereign and the ordering of the citizens as persons. The moments of producing the sovereign and then surrendering to its judgement are inseparable. Hobbes proposes the continual production of matter and form in place of the objective proportions of substantial form and natural law. The Thomist *habitus* is replaced by the artificial soul of sovereignty. In the engraving of Leviathan the natural bodies of the citizens, their *ens* or matter, are transformed, through the rapt gaze at their person/ author, into the form of the artificial body; the whole process sustained by the concentration of the dispersed powers of their individual authorizations into the single power of sovereignty: 'by Art is created that great *Leviathan* called a *Common-wealth*, or *State*, (in latine *Civitas*) which is but an Artificiall Man; though of greater stature and strength than the Naturall, for whose protection and defence it was intended; and in which, the *Soveraignty* is an Artificiall *Soul*, as giving life and motion to the whole body' (p. 81). Life is the constantly produced unification of matter into form: the moment or event of transition from matter to form through power represented in the frontispiece is the only reality. If the process of production is interrupted, if power is insufficient to inform and unify matter, then matter will disintegrate into chaos, civil war and death.

The threat of dissolution hanging over the commonwealth points to the fragility of the illusion which founds it. Hobbes can only think of productive legislation in terms of unity and dispersal, and can only figure this unification through artistic illusion. The unity of the sovereign person is produced, but its production is disowned: *Leviathan* is an artifact, but it is also a god; created and creative. In Hobbes the moments of creator/created which produce the commonwealth are unified only in illusion: productive legislation is disowned. Kant will later call this activity 'realization and restriction', and it is noteworthy that in his stream of consciousness on signs and symbols he turns from the 'schematism of the understanding' – which he characterized as 'realization and restriction' – to the soul of *Leviathan*.

A Certain Beauty of Order

Those Philosophers who derive the principle of morality out of inner actions are of two sorts.

1 Some derive it from pure concepts of truth, such as Cumberland and others of the English,

2 others, however, out of the concept of perfection, which is what Wolff does.

Kant, Lectures on Moral Philosophy

'But why use such crooked paths when we may walk the straight and level road?' demanded Pufendorf. Both he and Cumberland abandoned Hobbes to his refractory paths of 'Matter, Forme and Power' only to find that their straight and level road forked into two branches. This was in their respective Hobbes critiques *De Jure Naturae et Gentium* and *De Legibus Naturae*, both published in 1672. Both texts reject Hobbes's productive legislation in favour of a relation of matter and form; but while both find a pattern for this relation in beauty, and imagine a beautiful society as its practical realization, both shun the responsibility of freedom to limit and make itself. Reason as the realm of legislation and form, and sensibility as the bringing forth of objects or matter, are not recognized in their mutual implication, but are divided for the sake of their violent reconciliation.

Although the two works have many similarities,[9] they differ in the ways in which they prosecute the reconciliation of sense and reason. The difference may be attributed to the complicated settings from which they emerged. Such complications were already evident in Hobbes's texts, which are beset by the alarms and excursions of civil war. The impurities which form and complicate Cumberland and Pufendorf's texts are different, the one pointing to a theory of civil society, the other to a theory of the police-state. Yet both texts share a critical posture towards Hobbes. Cumberland's hostile attitude toward the crooked paths of Hobbes's philosophy is indicated in the full title of his work: *A Philosophical Inquiry into the Laws of Nature, in which their Form, chief Heads, Order, Promulgations, and Obligation, are deduced from the Nature of Things: also the elements of Mr Hobbes's Philosophy, as well Moral as Civil, are considered and refuted.* The advertised refutation of Hobbes rested on the impossibility of establishing a natural right without presupposing a law of nature: 'the nature of this right cannot be so distinctly understood, unless the knowledge of the law of nature be first supposed' (Cumberland 1672, p. 76). It is impossible for individuals to claim rights without prior knowledge of a law which would order those rights; the dispersion of individual rights presupposes a prior unification in a natural law. This is 'the standard of virtue and society' and is derived 'from the nature of all things' (p. 36); but when speaking of the nature of things, Cumberland does not mean the Galilean nature of ceaseless motion, but one in which matter is subordinated to form.

The problem arises of how this form – the nature of things – is translated into a natural law which determines human action. Here Cumberland equivocates between action issuing from the rational knowledge of the law, and action according to the promptings of sentiment. The laws of nature are, in Cumberland's opening definition, 'certain propositions of unchangeable truth, which direct our voluntary actions, about choosing good and refusing evil; and impose an obligation to external actions, even without civil laws, and laying aside all consideration of those compacts which constitute civil government' (p. 39). The laws of nature are rational propositions which *direct* through the reason and *impose* through the sentiment. The exercise of sentiment is accorded the properties of reason when the rational standard of 'virtue and society' is actualized through the sentiment of benevolence: 'The greatest benevolence of every rational agent towards all, forms the happiest state of every, and of all the benevolent, as far as it is in their power; and is necessarily requisite to the happiest state which they can attain, and therefore the common good is the supreme law' (p. 41).

The equivocation of reason and sentiment, exposed in those propositions which both direct and impose, structures the *Laws of Nature*. It is restated in the definition of the law of nature in the crucial chapter 'Of the Law of Nature, and its Obligation':

> The law of nature is a proposition proposed to the observation of, or impressed upon, the mind, with sufficient clearness, by the nature of things, from the will of their first cause, which points out that possible action of a rational agent, which will chiefly promote the common good, and by which only the entire happiness of particular persons can be obtained.
>
> (p. 189)

Once again, the law of nature is a proposition which is both *proposed* to, and *impressed* upon the mind by the will of the first cause, which 'points out' which action will promote the common good.

At stake in this equivocation is the problem of judgement, expressed in the relation between reason and sentiment. The conformity of reason and sentiment is achieved through God's will, since what God wills is rational, and the rational being is one that acts in accord with God's will. However, God's will proposes to reason, but disposes through sentiments. His will ensures that reason and sentiment are conformable, so transferring the responsibility for good judgement to providence. As a result, moral response takes the place of political judgement. For Cumberland, the state is peripheral to social order: divinely framed sentiments of property and commerce ensure the equivalence of the common good and individual happiness. In this, as in many other respects, his work anticipates the topoi of eighteenth-century moral philosophy and political economy: it justifies a moral civil society through a natural law which is prior to the state and which manifests divine providence through sentiments of benevolence, private property in things and labour, and commerce (see Viner, 1973; pp. 65 8).

Cumberland is the source of the tendency to intellectualize the senses which was endemic to British eighteenth-century thought. But although he and his followers refused the notion of productive legislation – the setting of limits which was also a fashioning and a making – they nevertheless suffered its aporias. For them reason could not be legislative, because this granted excessive power to the state; but nor could sensibility, since this valorized activities perceived as base. The civil society which this theory justified is like a work of art in being regular without being legislated or produced. The hand which both made and apportioned the fruits of its making was invisible.

Pufendorf[10] also set out to criticize Hobbes, but arrived at different conclusions to Cumberland. Like his contemporary, he too saw natural law as resting on the nature of things, but for him it only indicated possible courses of action to reason; the 'impression on the senses' came from elsewhere: 'this reason in a state of nature has a common, and, furthermore, an abiding, and uniform standard of judgement, namely, the nature of things, which offers a free and distinct service in pointing out general rules for living' (1672, p. 172).

In Cumberland the invisible hand of God is imperative, its finger indicates to the *sentiments* what must be done; in Pufendorf the nature of things shows *reason* what ought to be done. It is the advocate of civilization through the production of such institutions as 'speech, ownership of property, value, sovereignty of command', which contribute 'to the grace and tranquility of mankind' (p. 454). For Pufendorf the equation of grace and tranquility is axiomatic:

> It is not the perfection of this world of nature, as is the case with physical entities, but it is the perfection in a distinctive way of the life of man, in so far as it was capable of a certain beauty of order above that in the life of beasts, as also the production of a pleasing harmony in a thing so changeable as the human mind.
>
> (p. 5)

Human perfection consists in producing a harmony in the mind through a harmony in society, or a 'certain beauty of order'.

The ability to produce a beautiful order derives from the faculty of judgement, which forms 'the dignity of man's nature, and that excellence of his in which he surpasses other creatures', and which 'requires that his actions be made to conform to a definite rule, without which there can be no recognition of order, seemliness and beauty' (p. 148). Here Pufendorf is unclear about how a universal rule may be conformed to an individual action or thing: he simply says they must be 'made to conform'. But is conformity *produced* or *imposed* in this making to conform? Pufendorf tries both alternatives. In the first of them, judgement is the reflexive activity which produces the conformity of universal and individual:

> This end the soul attains chiefly by its power to proceed from known principles to unknown, and to decide what is suitable for it and what is not, to form universal ideas through induction,

to devise signs by which the ideas of the mind can be imparted to others, to understand numbers, weights, and measures, and compare them, to understand and observe their order and its meaning, to excite, repress, or allay affections, to remember a multitude of things, and to call them back, as it were, for the eye to gaze upon, to turn its sight upon itself and to recollect its own dictates and compare them with its actions, from which recollection and comparison the force of conscience comes.

(p. 149)

This splendid vision of human reflexivity unites the production of institutions with self-reflection through them. The sentence may be divided into a series of tropes. The first considers deduction – the move from known to unknown principles – and induction, which are united in the devising of signs for communication. This movement develops into one which encompasses the understanding of number, weights and measures, their comparison, and then the renewed understanding of their order and meaning which follows from the comparison. There follows the excitement, repression, and allaying of affections which develops into the recalling to the eye of a multitude of things, the turning of sight upon itself, and, through this turning, a recollection of dictates and a renewed comparison.

The conformity of rule and action or thing is based on a complex movement of bringing forth, reflecting on the manner of bringing forth, and then bringing forth anew. This recollection and comparison constitutes conscience, or the ability to judge 'what is suitable and what is not'. The movement encompasses both knowledge and affect, so the judgement of what is fitting for a human being has neither exclusively rational nor sensible sources. The movement of producing a thing or an action, reflecting on the means of production, and then producing anew is analogous to the excitation, repression, and allaying of an affection. This movement of production and reflection gives rise to the conformity which a thing or an action has to a rule: in other words, conformity is produced.

Pufendorf's account of judgement at this point anticipates many aspects of Kant's later position. Judgement itself is only possible by virtue of a reflexive movement – 'realization and restriction' – which produces both the objects to be judged and the law by which they are judged. However, Pufendorf is unable to sustain this position. The reflective movement which constituted conformity quickly dissolves into its separate elements: rule and action are forced to conform. Yet this violent conformity is still considered to be beautiful, but this option only remains open because of the ambiguity of phrases such as 'graceful tranquility', the 'beauty of order', and a 'seemly order'. Is beauty orderly, or is order beautiful? On the first account conformity is orderly because it is beautiful; on the second it is beautiful because it is orderly.

The shift in the priority of beauty and order is apparent in Pufendorf's discussion of the institution of language, but even here some ambiguity persists. Pufendorf does not yet follow Hobbes in reducing diversity to unity, although he will do so eventually. The cacophony of diverse tongues in the state of nature must be *guided* into a 'marvellous orderliness' and, as an afterthought, 'beauty':

> Now the more voices there are, the more dreadful and unpleasant the sound in the ear, unless they unite in harmony. In the same way the greatest confusion would have prevailed among men, were not their dissimilarity of customs and appetites reduced to a seemly order through laws. And yet this variety in another way yields man a remarkable grace and reward, since out of it, if properly guided, a marvellous orderliness and beauty may arise, which could not possibly have come from complete uniformity.
>
> (p. 151)

In contrast to the first account, beauty cannot now be produced autonomously through self-reflection. The diversity of tongues ('trumpets of sedition') have to be 'properly guided', which is something they cannot be trusted to do for themselves. The movement of reflection described above in terms of human agency in general is now divided between state and civil society. Instead of beauty and order being assured by the free reflection of individuals, the state reflects for them 'by thrusting in [their] face the immediate evil which will await [them] upon their attacking another' (p. 967). 'Surely everyone realises' that the state must assume the responsibility for judgement, because that capacity is not equally distributed? Behind this thought is the fear that the multitude may be deceived by false idols, led astray by bad tunes:

> But very few are blessed with ability enough to be able of their own power to see what is for the permanent advantage of mankind in general and of individuals and to be willing to persist in that knowledge. So many in their dulness are imposed upon by gross error posing as reason. The majority are led by the violence of their passions wherever their lust or a false idea of their advantage may take them. In such a medley of

opinions and fancies what sure peace and concord can there be. But since reason alone, as it is found in individual men, is unable to compose such great differences, some sort of agreement of opinions must be sought by a different course.

(p. 964)

The different course is the establishment of sovereignty. The agreement is less a harmony than a silencing of the diverse voices of society. Towards the end of *The Law of Nature and the Nations* Pufendorf writes that since a society is

made up of many physical persons, each of whom has his own will and inclination, and since these wills cannot be physically compounded into one, or combined into a perpetual harmony, it follows that the one will in a state is produced in the following fashion: All the persons in the state submit their will to that of one man, or of a counsel, in whom the supreme sovereignty has been vested.

(p. 1101)

The agreement of opinions in this state is only achieved through the submission of diversity to unity. When beauty defined order, self-reflection, diversity, and harmony prevailed; but when order defines beauty, there is submission, unity, and silence.

The two texts of 1672 contributed to the emergence of distinct traditions of thought in Britain and Germany. Through his influence on Shaftesbury, Cumberland contributed to founding the theory of civil society in Britain; while Pufendorf, through Wolff, contributed to that of the police-state in Germany. In the former, the harmony of civil society was theorized as the providential disposition of the senses, while in the latter the common welfare was achieved through the legislation of the enlightened sovereign. But both traditions experienced considerable difficulty in equating their accounts of judgement with the claims of beauty. The theory of civil society was haunted by the problem of taste, while the theory of the police-state formed the matrix for the emergence of aesthetics. For both of them, beauty was the crisis-point of judgement since it exceeded judgement. In working through the difficulty with beauty the traditions dissolved themselves: the one into political economy, the other into the philosophy of history. Neither of them can be said to have found out what was difficult about beauty, although they provided indispensable evidence for Kant when he set himself to confronting beauty and judgement in the third *Critique*.

2

Taste and Civil Society

Taste and the *je ne sais quoi*

Taste is the capacity for judging the conformity of the power of imagination in its freedom with the legitimacy of the understanding.

Kant, *Reflection* 510

Taste conceived as a 'faculty of judgement' is the precipitate of taste conceived as an activity. This emerges in the *OED*'s etymology of the word taste from the Old French *tast* 'touching, touch' and the Italian *tasto* 'a feeling, a touch, a trial, a taste'.[1] Two points of particular interest follow from this derivation. The first is the original active and investigative connotation of taste; it was the activity of feeling or testing and not a passive faculty that tested or felt. The second is the difference between the meanings of taste and aesthetic: both terms denote activities of feeling, touching, and seeing, but while taste produces its own content and gives itself law, aesthetic receives content and law from without.

The transformation of taste into a faculty which mediates between subject and object gives rise to some specific difficulties. The formative aspect of taste as an activity producing its own content and giving itself laws – taste as autopoetic and autonomous – is repressed when it is transformed into a faculty. Yet traces of this repressed activity persist in the exercise of the faculty, and emerge as the difficulties involved in thinking the acquisition of the faculty, its application by the subject, and the peculiar conformity it has with its objects. However, the most important trace of the reduction of taste to a faculty is the persistent and ineluctable relation of the judgement of taste and pleasure.

The influential writings of the Spanish Jesuit, Baltasar Gracian

(1601–58) exemplify the difficulties accompanying the reformulation of the activity of taste into a faculty. Like Hobbes, who saw productive judgement as the creation of illusion, Gracian resolved the formative moment of taste into the production of appearance. In the *Oraculo Manual Y Arte De Prudencia* (1647) taste finds itself between reticence and dissemblance, applying judgement to the shaping of appearances. It is an unknowable faculty, present in the subject in an inexplicable way, and exercised intuitively. The object of its formative activity is the subject as appearance, the prudent one 'who realises that he is being observed, or will be observed' (1647; § 297). Much of the pathos of Gracian's writing arises from the necessity of the prudent to dissemble, to represent themselves as appearance, to 'Cultivate a happy spontaneity'. But what if the object of taste is not the subject itself, but a different object? A similar conclusion follows: the object exists only as appearance, only in so far as it has been produced by taste. And yet this formative activity of taste cannot know itself; it is only discernible through the pleasures of producing and manipulating appearances.

Gracian's courtly scepticism persists in the French theory of taste which emerged in the second third of the seventeenth century. The French theorists narrowed his view of taste as an art of judgement into a concern with the judgement of art (Saisselin, 1970). The adaptation of taste to art was a gesture of aristocratic dissent against the Royal Academy. In place of the conformity of judgement to publicly licensed rules, critics appealed to the *je ne sais quoi* in which the judgement of the work of art was largely a 'matter of taste'. The French critics embraced the difficulties surrounding the possession, application, and object of the faculty of taste as sceptical aporias. We have a faculty of taste, but how we come by it is unclear; we apply it, but how we do so is unclear; it is congruent with objects, but why it is so remains unclear. The *je ne sais quoi* is an admission of the inexplicability of the workings of taste following its restriction to a faculty. The history of taste in the eighteenth century may be seen as the gradual recovery of its formative aspect through the exploration of the difficulties posed in accounting for pleasure.

The British development of the theory of taste was from the beginning characterized by an idiosyncratic appropriation of the French model. It is distinguished by its revaluation of the *je ne sais quoi* into the necessary ignorance of the workings of providence. This position is inseparable from the tendency of late seventeenth-century British scepticism to draw activist political conclusions from theoretical scepticism. The *je ne sais quoi* did not justify the apathy and political indifference of a defeated *fronde*, but assumed positive content as a spur to activity. This is apparent in Locke's *An Essay Concerning Human Understanding* (1690), where the premiss that our finite understandings can never hope to gain insight into God's providence does not lead to passivity or renunciation of the world. The very limitation of our understanding is part of His providence, for we have been given the ability to make certain discriminations without knowing their grounds:

> For our faculties being suited not to the full extent of being, nor to a perfect, clear, comprehensive knowledge of things free from all doubt and scruple, but to the preservation of us in whom they are, and accommodated to the use of life: they serve to our purpose well enough if they will but give us certain notice of those things which are convenient or inconvenient to us.
>
> (1690; p. 343)

Scepticism does not paralyse the judgement, since it is possible to discriminate with certainty between the convenience or inconvenience of a particular course of action. This discrimination is an intuition or a sense whose validity is secured by providence.

The notion of a providential congruence between our imperfect judgement and self-preservation underlies Locke's account of political judgement in the *Essay*. The emphasis on discrimination leads to the extremely violent view of judgement as the choice between two alternatives:

> We are forced to determine ourselves on the one side or other. The conduct of our lives and the management of our great concerns will not bear delay: for those depend, for the most part, on the determination of our judgement in points wherein we are not capable of certain and demonstrative knowledge, and wherein it is necessary for us to embrace the one side or the other.
>
> (p. 359)

The distinction between convenience and inconvenience becomes the necessity to embrace one 'side' or the other in 'great concerns' which brook no 'delay'. The sentiments of this passage are much closer to those of the oligarchy who risked the 1688 Revolution than to the natural rights justification of revolt developed by Locke in the *Two Treatises on Government*. The confused debate surrounding the nature of the 'Revolution Principles' after 1688 showed that no positive programme united the forces of the Revolution, least of all one of natural rights. The decision to act was not rationally grounded but, as in Locke's case, was legitimated by a providentially guided judgement. Kant shrewdly recognized this emphasis on discrimination without a concept as a 'sensualization' of the differential 'concepts of reflection' (1781; A271/B327), and saw it as a one-sided restriction of a proper art of judgement. The violence which necessarily accompanied this restriction became apparent in Locke's successors.

The British theory of taste which emerged from the matrix of scepticism, providential argument and 'Revolution Principles' was shaped by very specific political and intellectual circumstances. These emerge when the accounts of the pleasures of art characteristic of the early legitimation crisis of the regime are compared with those following its stabilization through the fiscal and political 'Financial Revolution'. The difference emerged in the role theorists gave to art in the promotion of the virtues appropriate to civil society. The change in the conception of civil society at the beginning of the eighteenth century was accompanied by a change in the understanding of the pleasures of art.

It was never the intention of William's regime to create the conditions for a 'civil society' apart from the state. The emergence of civil society was largely the accident of an oligarchy anxious to limit executive power combined with the successful mobilization of public credit for the finance of foreign military and commercial adventures.[2] Indeed, an important aspect of William's early domestic policy was the disciplining of civil society through a 'Reformation of Manners' or 'Moral Revolution'. This policy, initiated after 1688, was a diluted version of continental 'police-state' measures, and although unsuccessful, this was not due to any lack of legislative commitment: 'If Acts of Parliament and orders of justices of the peace could create a moral paradise, England would have been one by 1700' (Bahlman 1957, p. 22). Unlike the continental monarchs, William had neither the bureaucratic apparatus nor the standing army required to apply his police measures; the enforcement of the 'Reformation of Manners' was left to private individuals banding together into 'Societies for the Reformation of Manners' or to the inconsistent enthusiasm of individual JPs. But this was not the main reason for the failure of the policy; by the beginning of the new century, such direct measures of social control were unnecessary.[3] The burden of legitimation shifted toward the establishment of an autonomous civil society in which the moral policing of society by the state was considered unnecessary for the establishment of 'throne, religion, happiness and peace'.[4]

The transition from moral revolution to civil society is reflected in the fortunes of the most important theorist of art of the late seventeenth century – John Dennis (1657–1729), *the* Critick. His reputation was a notable casualty of the change in the structure of legitimacy. His writings span from 1692 to 1729, but by the beginning of the new century he had become a distinctly unfashionable, rather comic figure. And although his arguments resembled those of the new theories of taste and civil society, there are important differences of emphasis. Like the theorists of taste, Dennis identified natural law with providential design, but unlike them he saw the design as mediated either through the rules of art or through the legislation of the state. He had no conception of an immediate 'taste' or 'moral sense' valid apart from the rules of art or the direct agency of the state.

Dennis consciously aligned the 'Reformation of Modern Poetry' with the 'Reformation of Manners': the pleasures evoked by properly regulated arts would contribute to soothing the 'jarring passions' of the 'rebellious English'. For him as for Pufendorf, natural law is mediated through the institutions of art, religion and the state; it is not disclosed immediately to the individual. This view of the relationship of natural law to civil society was appropriate for the time of 'Moral Revolution' which sought to discipline society by institutional means, but became irrelevant after the consolidation of the state through the development of the mechanisms of public credit. The internal mediation of natural law prefigured in Cumberland's text – where providence spoke directly to the conscience of each citizen – was more appropriate to an increasingly autonomous public sphere. The burden of legitimation shifted from the inculcation of piety and virtue from without, to the moral justification of civil society from within, a shift which was registered in the equation of commerce and virtue (Dickinson 1977, p. 125; Hirschmann 1977, *passim*).

Dennis's Horatian view that art contributes to social control by instructing through delight was superseded by the theory of taste. Instead of regarding art as a means for moralizing civil society, the theory of taste saw it as representing the same natural law which directed individual moral judgement. Individual judgement was not ordered by the institutional representation of natural law, but by an intuition or inner sense of it. The axioms of Cumberland's critique of Hobbes reappear in the philosophy of Shaftesbury and his successors. Beauty and order were expressions of a providential natural law mediated through the senses of beauty and obligation. The mediating term, the *sense* of beauty and virtue, was the pleasure of 'taste'.

The British writers saw taste as a faculty, and so fell prey to many of the difficulties surrounding the faculty of taste. These difficulties were complicated by the providential foundation of the British theory of taste, which made the question of how the faculty of taste is given to a subject critical. The chronic equivocation over whether taste was sensible or ideal issues from this complication. As with Locke, providence does not direct individual judgement through reason, but nevertheless determines it according to rational ends. The individual judgement is a sentiment or an inclination to which providence accords the properties of an idea. Shaftesbury, Hutcheson, Kames, and Burke all maintained that the prompting of providence is experienced with the immediacy of a sense; in their writings the 'rational sense' of taste is distributed among a number of discrete senses, including a 'sense of beauty', a 'sense of virtue', a 'sense of contract', and even a 'sense of property'. Individuals behave affectively, according to sentiment, but providence ensures that the sum of their actions realizes the common good. In this way the freedom and autonomy of the individual at the level of sense is reconciled with the lawlike characteristics of universality and necessity at the level of idea. The price of this solution was the disembodiment of taste; it became an intangible medium of exchange between the rational will of providence and the irrational individual sentiment.

The disembodiment of taste affected its relationship to its objects. Instead of seeing in it a formative activity involving legislation and production, the British theorists interpret the activity of taste as the work of providence. They devolve the responsibility for self-legislation – the ordering of civil society – upon providence, and violently exclude its productive moment. Shaftesbury renders production immaterial by regarding it as the issue of the *je ne sais quoi*; his notion of a providential ordering of civil society and his dematerialization of production were attacked by Mandeville in the *Fable of the Bees*. In defending Shaftesbury, Hutcheson excludes production altogether, placing it outside the operations of taste and subjecting it to entirely different laws. The 'benevolent philosopher' considered the moral sense insufficient to ensure labour discipline, and went so far as to advocate slavery for the 'slothful'. In both cases the giving of the law and the production of its objects are relegated to the *je ne sais quoi*; the formative activity of taste is rendered unthinkable.

Hume and Smith's writings represent attempts to rethink the *je ne sais quoi*. Hume sought to specify the relation between individual and universal without resort to providence. His argument in the *Treatise* that individual moral responses and responses to the beautiful are related through 'reflected sympathy' points to a rediscovery of the formative aspect of taste. He later abandoned this project in favour of a sceptical admission that the relation of individual response and universal standard is 'obscure'. However, on the basis of the *Treatise*, Adam Smith rediscovered the formative aspect of taste, and initiated the transition from the theory of taste and civil society to political economy. He absorbed Mandeville's critique of taste which emphasized need, desire and production, and attempted to unify not only virtue and commerce, but virtue, commerce, and production. His political economy restored the formative aspect of taste by setting out the relation of production and legislation. Production was the suppressed premiss in the theories of taste and civil society, the *je ne sais quoi* which repeatedly undermined their attempts to unify virtue and commerce. And while it is the case that Smith acknowledges the *je ne sais quoi* as both a process of exchange and a labour process, his attempt to know it did not escape providential notions such as the invisible hand and metaphysical proportionalities between production and circulation.

Smith's invisible hand is an apt image for the task of unifying virtue and commerce mounted by the theory of taste. The hand holding the scales, the traditional emblem of justice, is in the act both of weighing the two sides of the case and of giving the law by which it is to be judged. With the disembodiment of taste in the eighteenth century the activity of the investigative and adjudicative hand is dematerialized into the invisible hand of providence. The moments of invention and judgement underlying taste are separated. The surrender of Hobbes's citizens to the judgement of their own creation becomes the surrender to the judgement of providence and the *je ne sais quoi*: the sovereignty of the mask is exchanged for that of the invisible hand.

Whig Hellenism

> the second system derived from inner subjective grounds, is the system of the moral sense, which has nothing philosophical about it at all. In recent times it is particularly notable in the English Shaftesbury and Hutcheson. It won't catch on so much in Germany, and for this one has Wolff to thank.
>
> Kant, *Lectures on Moral Philosophy*

The parameters of the British theory of taste and civil society were defined by the writings of Anthony Ashley Cooper, Lord Shaftesbury (1671–1713). The rhapsodic and dialogical form of his texts liberated philosophy from the learned tome, and anticipated the textual practices employed by enlightenment writers to take philosophy out of the schools and into civil society.[5] They also set the agenda for the synthesis of commerce and virtue which occupied British social philosophers during the eighteenth century. In the collection of essays *Characteristics of Men, Manners, Opinions, Times* (1711), Shaftesbury justified the 'Revolution Principles' with a philosophy of taste. He followed his tutor Locke in regarding judgement as discrimination, but stated its providential validation in terms of the teleological Platonism of the Cambridge Platonists. More than Locke's, his writings exemplify what Kant later identified as an 'amphiboly', identifying not only sense and idea, but extending this equation to individual interest and universal end. The repression concealed in this identification was exposed by Bernard Mandeville (1670–1733) in his *Fable of the Bees*. Mandeville claimed that Shaftesbury's equations of sense and idea, interest and end, and commerce and virtue could only be maintained through violence and deception. His claim was amply borne out by the subsequent defences of Shaftesbury's position, and was eventually conceded by Smith in the *Wealth of Nations*.

Shaftesbury's correspondence collected in the *Philosophical Regimen* (1900)[6] frames his moral and metaphysical theories within a definite political setting. While continuing the family's Whig politics of limited monarchy, protestant succession, and the liberty of subjects under law, he was not of the generation of 1688 who considered commerce necessarily injurious to virtue. Shaftesbury's commitment to the 'Revolution Principles', his 'zeal for the Revolution, and for that principle which effected it' (written on the back of a letter to Lord Marlborough dated 10 April 1702; 1900, p. 311) is distinguishable from the vulgar 'enthusiasm' of the moral reformers; he preferred the equation of virtue and beauty over that of virtue and piety. Both virtue and beauty rested on a providential *telos* which ensured the realization of a 'beautiful order'.

Shaftesbury defends this position in his outline of the three possible approaches to practical philosophy in the essay 'The Picture of Cebes': one that

> establishes a providence disposing all things in the most beautiful order, and giving to man a capacity to attend to its laws and to follow them; another that attributes the disposition of things to atoms and chance and that makes the pursuit of pleasure its end, and that which takes neither way, but judges things not to be all comprehensible, and therefore suspends opinion entirely.

> (1914, p. 87)

Shaftesbury does not reject the Epicurean and Sceptical positions out of hand (positions he later attributed to Hobbes and Locke), but considers their tenets inadequate as foundations for virtue. For him, three elements are necessary for such a foundation: (i) a *providence* which disposes 'all things' into (ii) a *beautiful order*, and which gives to human beings (iii) a *capacity* to recognize and to act according to that order. This is close to Cumberland's view of natural law as the providential disposition of the parts of social life into an harmonious whole. But Shaftesbury, unlike Cumberland, sees providence and order as a *telos* in which God is the order of being itself rather than the being who wills that order. For him 'All things stand together and exist together by one necessity, one reason, one law; and there is one nature of all things, a common to all' (1900, p. 17). His deistic view of providence naturalized Cumberland's 'sentiment of benevolence' implanted by the will of the deity into a 'sense' of order.

Shaftesbury's triple theme of providence, beautiful order and the sense of order is developed in the writings of Hutcheson, Kames and Burke. He and his successors extend Cumberland's reconciliation of individual interest and the public good through a providential morality. All of them share the ideal of a civil society ordered by a moral sense which providentially ensures the harmonious ordering of individual judgements and the general good apart from the direct intervention of the state. This philosophy provides an account of virtue appropriate to the Whig Hellas, one in which virtue is not the creature of law and the state, but the outcome of the providential orchestration of individual interests through the pleasures of the sense of order.

The relation of teleology and civil society intimated in Cumberland's *De Legibus Naturae* is brought out in Shaftesbury's first work 'An Inquiry Concerning Virtue and Merit'.[7] This early essay diagnoses the problems of the post-revolutionary social order which the later teleological metaphysics is prescribed to solve. The author of the 'Inquiry' elevates the dichotomy of private and public interest into a law of nature: 'We know that every creature has a private good and interest of his own, which Nature has compelled him to seek, by all the advantages afforded him within the compass of his make' (1711; vol. I, p. 243). He argues from this axiom that the 'natural' pursuit of self-interest promotes the common good, redefining virtue as the identity of private and public interest: 'That to be well effected towards the public interest and one's own is not only consistent but inseparable; and that moral rectitude or virtue must accordingly be the advantage, and vice the injury and disadvantage of every creature'

(p. 282). Having established that the private and public interest of a creature 'must' coincide, Shaftesbury found the ground of this necessity in the providential *telos*. The *telos* is then interpreted to be a 'substantial form' which ensures the harmony of private and public interest.

Shaftesbury argues against Hobbes that the order of providence, with its expressions in virtue and beauty, is prior to any division of individual interests. He is hostile to any suggestion that order may itself be derived or abstracted from individual things: 'Hence Hobbes, Locke, etc., still the same man, same genius at bottom. – "beauty is nothing" – "virtue is nothing" – So "perspective nothing" – "music nothing." – But these are the greatest realities of things, especially the beauty and order of affections' (1914, p. 178). Instead of beginning with individuals or primary qualities and then deriving general principles of association from their composition, Shaftesbury makes composition prior to individuals. He posits the ultimate reality of beauty and virtue, and claims that individuals embody them. However, this embodiment is equivocal since individuals are not strictly determined to act according to beauty and virtue, but only tend to do so. The difficulties surrounding the determinacy and indeterminacy of individual action collect around the 'capacity' to recognize and act according to the beautiful order, in other words, around taste as a faculty of judgement.

Shaftesbury developed his determination of judgement by a substantial form or 'beautiful order' against Hobbes's view that order was the consequence of the monopolization of judgement by the sovereign. His essay '*Sensus Communis*: An Essay on the Freedom of Wit and Humour' follows Cumberland in maintaining that a ground of obligation already exists in the state of nature:

> Now the promise itself was made in the state of nature; and that which could make a promise obligatory in the state of nature, must make all other acts of humanity as much our real duty and natural part. Thus faith, justice, honesty, and virtue, must have been as early as the state of nature, or they could never have been at all.
>
> (1711; vol. I, p. 73)

The priority of an objective principle of virtue subordinates the contractual legality of the state to the morality of civil society. But the principle of unity remains inchoate; what is the 'that' which founds obligation? how is it recognized? and how may it be acted upon? The problems of judgement which Hobbes tackled in terms of productive legislation return to trouble Shaftesbury's serene Platonism.

The main problem involves the relation between individual interest and the general good or end. Just as in the case of obligation, Shaftesbury points to a necessity for their congruence without explaining it. This is apparent in the following non sequitur: 'There being therefore in every creature a certain interest or good, there must be also a certain end to which everything in his constitution must naturally refer' (p. 243). Neither the *must* nor the unity of interest and end have been demonstrated, and it is hard to avoid the suspicion that their natural unity has been discovered after the fact of their difference. This suspicion is reinforced by Shaftesbury's admission that the relation between the interest of the individual and the end to which it tends is unknowable. The individual interest and end *must* be united, but how this may be accomplished is unknowable: it is the work of a *je ne sais quoi* which directs the judgement of taste. Like Hobbes, though with different results, Shaftesbury represents the problem of relating individual and universal in terms of the different positions which artist and audience have to a work of art.

Historians of criticism have taken Shaftesbury's philosophy of art as an important stage in the development away from neo-classical formalism toward a theory of 'aesthetic response' (see Stolnitz 1961). However, Shaftesbury does not reject formalism for sensibility, but argues that they are compatible. His argument rests on the distinction between the production and the reception of a work of art. The artist produces the work according to strict rules, remaining in full control of the design and ensuring its agreement with nature and propriety: 'Here the unity of design must with more particular exactness be preserved according to the just rules of poetic art; that in the representation of any event, or remarkable fact, the probability or seeming truth (which is the real truth of art) may with the highest advantage be supported and advanced' (1914, p. 33). When presented with this highly rational product, the response of the spectator is irrational:

> Though [the artist's] intention be to please the world, he must nevertheless be, in a manner, above it, and fix his eye upon that consummate grace, that beauty of Nature, and that perfection of numbers which the rest of mankind, feeling only by the effect whilst ignorant of the cause, term the *je ne scay quoy*, the unintelligible or the I know not what, and suppose

to be a kind of charm or enchantment of which the artist himself can give no account.

(1711; vol. I, p. 214)

The rigorous separation of the production of a work according to strict rules from the irrational enjoyment of the same work by the spectator is axiomatic for Shaftesbury's philosophy of art. The same 'feeling only by the effect whilst ignorant of the cause' also founds Shaftesbury's social philosophy. The beautiful order is the rational design of providence which ensures balance and harmony but can only be known through its pleasurable effect of unifying private and public interest. For, Shaftesbury maintains, 'Virtue has the same fixed standards [as art]. The same numbers, harmony, and proportion will have place in morals, and are discoverable in the characters and affections of mankind; in which are laid the just foundations of an art and science superior to every other of human practice and comprehension' (pp. 227–8). Like art, virtue follows a rational design; and like the response to a work of art, the act of virtue is irrationally determined: it is a 'certain just disposition or proportionable affection of a rational creature towards the moral objects of right and wrong' (p. 258). Ignoring the inconsistency in the most important characteristic of a rational creature being not reason but disposition or affection, the question remains of how a disposition may be just, or an affection proportionable; how, in other words, a rational order can also be a *je ne sais quoi*.

The capacity which mediates between the laws of providence and individual judgement, between individual interest and rational end, is itself irrational. It is a 'proportionable' affection, one with the properties of rationality. Shaftesbury develops this notion in terms of the ability of an affection or 'sense' of discrimination. The rational 'senses' of beauty and virtue, for example, discriminate between beauty and ugliness, or between good and bad actions, without being aware of the grounds for their discrimination. Yet in order to work, the discrimination must be both a sense and an idea. Shaftesbury embraces this equivocation in the person of Theocles in the dialogue 'The Moralists, A Philosophical Rhapsody':

Nothing surely is more strongly imprinted on our minds, or more closely interwoven with our souls, than the idea or sense of order and proportion. Hence all the force of numbers, and those powerful arts founded on their management and use. What a difference there is between harmony and discord! cadency and convulsion! What a difference between composed and orderly motion, and that which is ungoverned and accidental!

Now as this difference is immediately perceived by a plain internal sensation, so there is withal in reason this account of it, that whatever things have order, the same have unity of design, and concur in one; all parts are constituent of one whole or are, in themselves, entire systems.

(1711; vol. II, p. 63)

A sense or idea of proportion is brought to each discrimination, but the relation between the perception of sense and the law of the idea is not spelt out. How is the perception of differences by the senses aligned with the unity and design of reason? Shaftesbury consistently describes their relation in terms of a 'proportion' between the manifold of sense and interests, and the unity of idea and end. But he nowhere considers the difficulty involved in establishing this proportion. He sees that the activity of establishing a proportion between sense and idea is pleasurable, but does not explore what this activity involves.

By regarding the activity of establishing a proportion as a *je ne sais quoi*, Shaftesbury separates production from enjoyment. Pleasure issues from objects which are mysteriously brought forward for discrimination according to unknowable laws. The feeling of pleasure dictates, through an unknowable law, which actions will most contribute to the public good. With such theses Shaftesbury reaches a definition of virtue as the harmony of private and public interests, one appropriate to the transition from an aristocratic dominion based on agriculture to an oligarchic dominion based on agriculture and commerce. His writings describe a virtuous state in which the pursuit of private interest providentially results in the general good. But the vision of a Whig Hellas, the virtuous commercial state, requires that the difficult and perhaps contradictory relations of sense and idea, interest and end, be obscured beneath a fog of equivocation, non sequitur, *petito principii* and I know not what.

One outcome of the equivocation of sense and idea is a passive or consumptive rather than active or productive view of action. The product of an action, its 'end', is separated by a *je ne sais quoi* from immediate activity or 'interest'. Shaftesbury's individuals are not autonomous artists rationally producing a work, but spectators of the beautiful order in which they are fortunate to find themselves. In pursuing their individual interests, they constitute the beautiful order, but disown the product of their activity by contemplating it as a spectacle; at no point do they consider themselves as producers or legislators. Shaftesbury's individuals inhabit the realm Arendt termed the 'social', producing neither material nor political works. Compared with Aristotle, for whom political activity is the prerogative of the free, productive activity the burden of the slaves, Shaftesbury's individuals are neither free nor slaves, but intermediate – merchants subject to the laws of exchange. Smith's observation that in a commercial society 'every man becomes in some measure a merchant' holds for Shaftesbury's synthesis of virtue and commerce.

The discourse of 'interest' which underlies Shaftesbury's redefinition of virtue shows the distance between his and classical accounts of virtue, or between the original and the Whig Hellas. In the latter, citizens are merchants exchanging according to individual interest, and finding these interests disposed toward the end of the public interest. The classical distinction between the productive and political classes is dissolved into the unity of civil society. Mandeville's critique of Shaftesbury restates the classical distinction by emphasizing the problem of producing to satisfy desire, and the necessity of politically ordering the collisions in civil society arising from the obstruction of desire. The *Fable of the Bees: or, Private Vices, Publick Benefits* unmasks Shaftesbury's philosophy as aristocratic domination by demonstrating that idea and sense, or 'interest' and 'end', can only be reconciled through violence and deception.[8]

The moral of Mandeville's fable is well known. The hive thrived when catering for vice and luxury, but when it experienced a 'reformation of manners', when the 'knaves turned honest' the inhabitants were left virtuous but destitute. In an essay added to the fable in 1723, 'A Search into the Nature of Society', Mandeville turned the moral of the *Fable* against Shaftesbury:[9] 'This Noble Writer (for it is the Lord Shaftesbury I mean in his *Characteristicks*) Fancies that as Man is made for Society, so he ought to be born with a kind of Affection to the whole, of which he is a part, and a Propensity to seek the Welfare of it' (p. 324). Mandeville is not persuaded by the equivocal moral sense which harmonizes private and public interest; he suggests instead that 'The Sociableness of Man arises from only these two things, *viz.*, the multiplicity of his Desires and the continual Opposition he meets with his Endeavours to gratify them' (p. 344). Mandeville enlists appetite and desire against the claims of virtue; they are the basis of all human activity – against them not even Shaftesbury's 'greatest realities' are safe:

What I have endeavour'd hitherto, has been to prove, the *pulchrum et honestum*, excellency and real worth of things are most commonly precarious and alterable as Modes and Customs vary; that consequently the Inferences drawn from their

Certainty are insignificant, and that the generous Notions concerning the Natural Goodness of man are hurtful, or they tend to mislead and are merely Chimerical.

(p. 343)

Beauty and virtue are revealed as screens for desire and appetite, masks of domination and not the 'greatest realities' eulogized by the philosophical lord.

Mandeville restates the classical division of the political and the productive classes in his distinction between the interests of civil society and the reason of the state. Civil society consists in the pursuit of desire and production for the satisfaction of desire; but since this pursuit leads inevitably to conflict – there being no pre-established harmony between 'interest' and 'end' – it is necessary for the state to channel and restrain the energies of civil society. Not content with denying Shaftesbury's argument that civil society is intrinsically harmonious, Mandeville insists that such harmony can only be achieved through violence:

All sound Politicks, and the whole Art of governing, Are entirely built upon the Knowledge of Human Nature. The great Business in general of a Politician is to promote and, if he can, reward all good and useful Actions on the one hand: and on the other, to punish or at least discourage, everything that is destructive or hurtful to Society.

(p. 321)

Mandeville replaces the *je ne sais quoi* with a cynical I know only too well; in place of providence he puts the manipulative politician. His exposure of the violence of the *je ne sais quoi* served to put Shaftesbury's successors on the defensive.[10]

Mandeville's critique of the equation of virtue and commerce had a considerable impact on eighteenth-century social and political theory. By pointing to the necessity of satisfying desire through production, and of regulating civil society politically, Mandeville restored the distinction of the productive and political classes to social and political theory. The theorists of civil society sought to incorporate certain elements of his critique into a restatement of Shaftesbury's position. Hutcheson's first work explicitly defends Shaftesbury against Mandeville, but the problem of the productive class's place in civil society manifested itself in his exclusion of labour discipline from the working of the moral sense. The most sophisticated response to the problem of production and civil society transformed moral philosophy into political economy. Smith took over Mandeville's insights into production and the division of labour and unified them with Shaftesbury's reconciliation of commerce and virtue. Smith distributes the equivocation of the moral sense across the realms of circulation and production: the object of individual 'interest' was the work produced in the division of labour, while the 'end' of public interest was achieved through the invisible hand of the market. However, the 'beautiful order' of the market and the division of labour are still proportioned through a *je ne sais quoi*, since it is not possible for either the entrepreneurial or the productive classes to have a proper understanding of the rationality of their beautiful orders.

The Institutionalization of Beauty and Virtue

Hutcheson's principle is unphilosophical because it introduces a new sense as a ground of explanation, and also because it sees objective grounds in the laws of sensibility. Wolff's principle is unphilosophical, because it makes empty propositions into principles.

Kant, *Reflection* 6634

Hutcheson's writings underline the relation of the providential moral sense with the developing institutions of a commercial society perceived in Shaftesbury's work, and may be read as the systematization of the moral sense. Beginning with *An Inquiry into the Original of our Ideas of Beauty and Virtue* of 1725 in which, according to the subtitle of the first edition, 'The principles of the late Earl of Shaftesbury are explained and defended against the author of the *Fable of the Bees*,' Hutcheson arrived in *The System of Moral Philosophy* of 1755 at a derivation of the institutions of Pufendorf's natural jurisprudence from the moral sense.[11] However, the institutional superstructure of his natural jurisprudence rested on the unexamined equivocation of sense and idea, prompting Kant to see it as 'unphilosophical'. But it was not only unphilosophical. The establishment of the civility of a commercial society on the moral sense demanded the violent repression of the difference between sense and idea, and their analogues, private interest and public good.

The equivocation of sense and idea is starkly apparent in the Preface to the *Inquiry*:

These Determinations to be pleas'd with any Forms or Ideas which occur to our Observation, the Author chuses to call *Senses*; distinguishing them from the Powers which commonly go by that Name, by calling our Power of perceiving the *Beauty* of *Regularity*, *Order*, *Harmony*, an *Internal Sense*; and that Determination to be pleas'd with the Contemplation of those *Affections*, *Actions*, or *Characters* of *rational Agents* which we call *virtuous*, he marks by the name of a *Moral Sense*.

(1725; p. vi)

In this preliminary definition sense and idea appear to be distinguished in terms of power and form. The 'internal' or 'moral' sense, like the physical senses, is a 'power' while the idea is a 'form'. Yet by defining the power as a '*determination* to be pleased', Hutcheson dissolves the difference between power and form, since a power which is determined is already formed. In the above passage the sense of beauty is a power which has been preformed to cause pleasure upon the observation of an idea or form. The distinction between sense and idea in terms of power and form is extremely equivocal.

The equivocation surfaces in the separate discussions of the idea/ senses of beauty and virtue and their relation to their objects prosecuted in the two parts of the *Inquiry*. Starting with the sense of beauty, Hutcheson distinguishes between the idea and the sense of beauty: 'Let it be observ'd, that in the following Papers, the word Beauty is taken for the idea rais'd in us, and a Sense of Beauty for our Power of receiving this Idea' (pp. 6–7). This distinction might seem a Lockean derivation of the word/idea from the sense/power, except that the derivation works in the opposite direction. The idea is produced or 'raised in us' while the sense is the power to receive the already produced idea; there is no question of the idea arising from any reflection on the senses. The sense is a passive receptive power determined by the idea; but the idea is not an object, even though the sense of beauty perceives it in the same way as a physical sense perceives a material object.[12] What on an initial reading seemed a straightforward derivation of the idea from the sense appears on closer inspection to rest on a complex inversion of Locke's procedure.

The problem of how the idea is 'raised in us' if it is not derived from a reflection on sense will be considered later – this is the problem of the mediation of providence. We shall persist for the meantime with the relation between the idea and the sense. The idea which gives pleasure to the inner sense is characterized by a *je ne sais quoi*; it 'strikes us' immediately in the way objects 'strike' the external senses because of 'its Affinity to the other Senses in this, that the Pleasure does not arise from any Knowledge of Principles, Proportions, Causes, or of the Usefulness of the Object; but strikes us at first with the Idea of Beauty' (p. 10). The idea is known immediately by the power or sense, which when 'struck' experiences pleasure. This view of the immediacy of the sense of beauty – its disinterestedness – was axiomatic for the theory of taste's separation of the sense of beauty from any hint of utility or interest. However, its immediacy rested upon its being struck or determined by an idea, so there can be no comment on the disinterestedness of the sense of beauty until it is known how the idea is produced or 'raised up'. The sense may indeed be disinterested, but the interest may lie in the idea.

The relation between sense and idea informs Hutcheson's distinction between absolute and relative beauty, inherited by Kant as 'free and dependent beauty'. In general the idea 'is raised up' and then 'strikes' the senses. In absolute beauty the idea does not show any trace of being produced, but strikes the senses apart from any object; in relative beauty, the idea is raised up through imitation and strikes the senses through comparison:

> We therefore by Absolute Beauty understand only that Beauty, which we perceive in Objects without comparison to any thing external, of which the Object is suppos'd an Imitation, or Picture; such as that Beauty perceiv'd from the Works of Nature, artificial Forms, Figures, Theorems. Comparative or Relative Beauty is that which we perceive in Objects commonly considered as Imitations or Resemblances of something else.
>
> (p. 14)

At issue is not the object itself, but the object as medium of the idea. Absolute beauty is experienced immediately, while relative beauty arises from representation. The distinction permits a partial clarification of the relation of sense and idea, since it tells us that the idea can be given either absolutely in itself, or comparatively in objects. The difficulty persists, though, of how an idea, in its absolute or relative incarnations, can possibly be given to sense without the sense being in some way preformed to receive it.

The problem of how the idea is raised up in us slides constantly into one of how it strikes the senses, whether absolutely, or relatively through objects. At this point Hutcheson reveals that the idea of beauty is a 'rational principle' which, crucially, is not perceived rationally. He identified this principle as proportionality or 'uniformity amid variety': 'The Figures that excite in us the Ideas of Beauty, seem to be those in which there is *Uniformity amidst Variety*' (p. 15). The senses perceive the principle unreflectively, this perception then produces an idea which strikes the inner sense with a determination to be pleased. Absolute beauty is the immediate perception of the principle of unity amid variety, while relative beauty perceives it in representation: 'As to the Works of *Art*, were we to run thro the various artificial Contrivances or Structures, we should find the Foundation of the *Beauty* which appears in them, to be constantly some kind of *Uniformity* or *Unity* of proportion among the Parts, and of each Part to the whole' (p. 33). The principle of uniformity amid variety, or proportionality, is the foundation of beauty in works of art, and determines the senses and ideas which perceive that beauty. The proportionality embodied in the beautiful object is abstracted into an idea, and then re-perceived as if an object of the sense.

Shaftesbury's claim for the irrational perception of a rationally produced object underlies Hutcheson's proliferation of distinctions between 'rational principle', 'beautiful object', the outer and inner 'senses', and the 'idea'. The pleasure in the beautiful issues from the complicated negotiations between the 'rational principle', 'sense', and 'idea' undertaken behind the back of the individual confronted by a beautiful object:

> in all these Instances of *Beauty* let it be observ'd, That the Pleasure is communicated to those who never reflected on this general Foundation; and that all here alleg'd is this, That the pleasant Sensation arises only from Objects in which there is *Uniformity amidst Variety*; we may have the sensation without knowing what is the Occasion of it.
>
> (p. 26)

It was such claims for the immediacy of the sensation of beauty that led Kant to the conclusion that the theory of taste lacked concepts of universality and necessity, and was thus 'unphilosophical'. However, this was not strictly true. The universality and necessity of the sensation of the beautiful had an objective ground in proportionality – the 'rational principle' of uniformity amid variety – which Kant also found to be the principle of judgement in the third *Critique*. However, Kant thematizes the difficulty of relating proportion to intuition and the understanding, and the place of pleasure in this relation, while Hutcheson accepts pleasure as a *je ne sais quoi*. Providence realizes its rational designs through the pleasure arising in the individual at the sight of the divinely established proportionalities. The pleasure of irrationally perceiving 'uniformity amid variety' or 'design' is the basis of both the sense of beauty and of virtue: 'We generally suppose the Good of the *greatest Whole*, and of *all Beings*, to have been the *Intention* of the *Author* of *Nature*; and cannot avoid being pleas'd when we see any part of this *Design* executed in the *Systems* we are acquainted with' (p. 40). Hutcheson accepts that the proportionality between whole and part is the same as that of uniformity amid variety. Kant, however, later challenges this view by regarding proportion as designating a more fundamental relation. However, the elision of proportion as a relation of unity/manifold and whole/part allows Hutcheson to identify the proportionality which founds the beautiful with that which founds virtue. Virtue is defined as the tailoring, or making uniform, of an individual act to the good of the whole; it is promoted by the same feeling of pleasure evoked by the perception of uniformity amid variety.

Hutcheson makes the transition from the first to the second treatise of the *Inquiry*, from beauty to virtue, by way of pleasure. Pleasure in both the good and the beautiful issues from the contemplation of an unknowable teleological principle. The principle and the capacity of sense for perceiving it are prior to self-interest and legality: 'Our *Sense* of Pleasure is antecedent to *Advantage* and *Interest* and is the foundation of them' (p. 103). This sense of pleasure is ultimately founded in the principle of 'uniformity amid variety', or the providential proportionality. The proportionality is perceptible only through the pleasure of the senses; even moral action is determined by a *je ne sais quoi*:

> We mean by [the moral sense] only *a Determination of our Minds to receive amiable or disagreeable Ideas of Actions, when they shall* occur to our Observation, antecedently of any Opinions of Advantage or Loss to redound to ourselves from *them*; even as we are pleas'd with a regular Form or a harmonious Composition, without having any Knowledge of Mathematicks, or seeing any Advantage in that Form, or Composition, different from the immediate Pleasure.
>
> (p. 124)

Both the sense of beauty and the moral sense are perceived immediately, yet are rational determinations of a unity unknown to the individual. But there is an important difference between the two senses. The moral sense is not only contemplative, but practical; it configures discrete individuals into a harmonious social whole through the individual pursuit of pleasure.

As with Shaftesbury, Hutcheson's account of the pleasures of beauty and virtue emphasizes the virtues of passive contemplation. The pleasures of contemplating objective proportion are not the active desires for material objects which Mandeville saw underlying industry and order. We shall see later Smith's ingenious solution of the problem which united the pleasures of beauty and virtue with the spur to industry and the production of commodities. Meanwhile, remaining with Hutcheson, the passive pleasures of beauty and virtue are severed from materiality and industry. In the early pages of the *Inquiry* it seemed as if the pleasures of proportion would alone suffice to produce order; but in the course of the text, pleasure is subordinated to the promotion of industry:

> That we may see the Foundation of some of the more *important Rights* of *Mankind*, let us observe, That probably nine Tenths, at least, of the things which are useful to Mankind, are owing to their *Labour* and *Industry*; and consequently all men are oblig'd to observe such a Tenour of Action as shall most effectually promote *Industry*; and to abstain from all Actions which would have a contrary effect.
>
> (pp. 262–3)

Hutcheson follows Pufendorf in calling these important basic rights of strict obligation 'perfect rights'. They are pre-eminently the respect for property and the honouring of contracts. Having secured the perfect right of property through labour, Hutcheson proceeds to derive the perfect rights of exchange or contract from the division of labour: 'The *Labour* of each Man cannot furnish him with all Necessarys, tho it may furnish him with a needless Plenty of one sort: Hence the *Right* of *Commerce* and *alienating* our Goods; and also the *Rights* from *Contracts and Promises*, either to the *Goods* acquired of others, or to their *Labours*' (p. 265). Here Hutcheson characteristically slips the concrete institution of the labour market into his abstract deduction of right. It becomes apparent that the origin of relative virtue and perfect right lies in the necessity of forcing labour. The benevolent moral sense may ensure a harmonious circulation of goods, but it will not maintain production: 'It is well known, that *general Benevolence* alone is not a Motive strong enough to *Industry*, to bear *Labour* and *Toil*, and many other difficultys which we are averse to from *Self-love*' (p. 263). The general good requires labour, but labour is not secured by the pleasures of the moral sense; therefore it must be compelled through perfect rights and physical force. Aid for 'persons in distress' provided 'they are not made unworthy of the liberality of good men by their sloth or vices' is an imperfect right which no-one is strictly obliged to honour.

The reluctance of individuals to volunteer their labour for the good of the whole is not seen as a contradiction between pleasure and labour, but is attributed to the baneful influence of the 'passions'. Yet even this admission concedes victory to Mandeville, who argued that the selfish passions were stronger than any sense for the whole. The inconsistency which arose in the *Inquiry* between defending Shaftesbury's providential unity of commerce and virtue through a quasi-rational pleasure and promoting industry is left unresolved. In his subsequent work, *An Essay in the Nature and Conduct of the Passions* (1728), Hutcheson responds to the problem with a proliferation of 'senses' – there are now external senses: the sense of beauty (called, following Addison, the senses of the pleasures of the imagination); a public sense; a sense of virtue and vice; and a sense of honour. But what is most significant is Hutcheson's acknowledgement of a difference between sense and reason in terms of 'passion' and 'wisdom', attributes he ascribes to the unproductive and the productive classes. The productive classes are gripped by passion and will not freely work for the common good; therefore they must be made to work by the benevolent wisdom of the political classes, who establish rights and duties to this end. Wisdom channels the passions and private interests according to the public good: 'We have wisdom sufficient to form ideas of *Rights, Laws, Constitutions*; so as to preserve large Societies in Peace and Prosperity, and promote a *general Good* amidst all the *private Interests*' (1728; p. 181). In order to valorize the political judgement of the nonproductive classes it is necessary to jettison the immediacy of the moral sense. The good of the whole, formerly achieved through the pursuit of pleasure, is now attained through the guidance of the wise. The productive classes are compelled to labour by the superior judgement of the unproductive classes, a conclusion which Smith found totally unconvincing, and which he refuted in the *Wealth of Nations*.

Hutcheson's equivocal fusion of the doctrine of the moral sense with the system of rights is apparent in the architectonic of his *System of Moral Philosophy*. Both the *System* and its epitome, the *Short Introduction to Moral Philosophy* (1747) follow the paradigm of Aristotelean practical philosophy, with a section on 'Ethics' followed by one on the 'Law of Nature'. The latter is divided according to the 'doctrine of private rights' or the law pertaining to natural liberty, 'oeconomicks' or the law of the household, and 'politicks', the various forms of civil government and the relation of states with each other. The section on 'Ethics' establishes a foundation for the superstructure of rights by claiming that the system of moral philosophy is the institutionalization of the moral sense implanted by providence. The discussion of the moral sense maintains the providential justification of social order while differing in some important respects from the earlier version in the *Inquiry*. The idea is now emphasized over the sense, so justifying the superiority of wisdom over pleasure:

> We shall thence conclude that all these practical truths discovered from reflection on our own constitution and that of Nature, have the nature and force of divine Laws pointing out what God requires of us ... And when one is persuaded of their Truths, then both our social and our selfish affections will harmoniously recommend to us one and the same course of life and conduct.
>
> (1747; pp. 37–8)

The golden mean of selfish interest and the general good consists in the uniformity amid variety of society. Civil society is regarded as a Palladian building for which the 'great architect' has given both the materials and the plan over for human judgement to complete:

> We see space for further buildings, and indications of the design in the desires and hopes of all ages and nations, in our natural sense of justice, and in our most notable and extensive affections about the state of others, and of the universe; and shall we not confide and hope in the art, the goodness, the inexhaustible wealth of the *great Architect*?
>
> (1755; p. 204)

The *System of Moral Philosophy* does not so much derive the institutions of civil society from providence, than appeal to it for their justification. Ultimately the appeal rests on faith, since we cannot know the ways of the great architect. We must confide and hope in the *je ne sais quoi* behind the obscure 'senses' and the institutions which the wise derive from them.

In spite of the combined efforts of providence and human judgement, commerce and virtue may remain imperfectly aligned, free exchange and the common good may not be so quickly reconciled. The main difficulty is again the promotion of industry: 'The most wealthy must need the goods and labours of the poor, nor ought they to expect them gratuitously. There must be conferences and bargains about them, that the parties may agree on their mutual performances' (1755; p. 174). But what if, despite the conferences and bargains, the poor are still refractory about yielding their labour? Such a violation of divinely instituted exchange is a threat to industry which provokes the just wrath of the wise and most wealthy:

And yet perhaps no law could be more effectual to promote a general industry, and restrain sloth and idleness in the lower conditions, than making perpetual slavery of this sort the ordinary punishment of such idle vagrants as, after proper admonitions and trials of temporary servitude, cannot be engaged to support themselves and their families by any useful labours.

(p. 202)

Slavery may also be justified by providence, and not only as a punishment for 'sloth', but also to encourage others to necessary industry. The contradiction between the pleasures of the imagination and forced labour evokes the *je ne sais quoi*. Providence encourages orderly circulation, a uniformity amid variety; yet the means by which this is achieved is excluded from the process. The material of circulation is either spiritualized into absolute beauty or virtue, or made the object of physical compulsion. The rationality of civil society in the realm of circulation is achieved by the pursuit of pleasure founded on the providential proportionalities; however, the industry which sustains this circulation is the subject of rational direction and violence. Pleasure and violence are inseparable, although this inseparability can only be acknowledged in the *je ne sais quoi* or equivocal sense/idea. The collusion of pleasure and violence emerges when 'The most wealthy must need the goods and labours of the poor.' This labour is secured in two ways: in terms of the market it is secured through a proportioned contract which gives pleasure to all parties; but in terms of production it is secured violently through forced labour. The equivocation of the idea and sense in the realm of circulation masks a violence at the level of production which cannot be known.

Hutcheson rejected Hobbes's identification of state and civil society, and presented an argument for an harmonious civil society based on the providential unity of commerce and virtue. By excluding labour from the working of the moral sense he continued Shaftesbury's limited extension of traditional political theory to the commercial class. This extension was possible only in so far as commerce did not threaten the axiomatic distinction of the political and productive classes. However, production could no longer be annexed to the *oikos* or patriarchal productive unit. A commercial society had a different relation to production, both recognizing and suppressing it. Mandeville's *Fable* challenged this equivocation and the settlement of the old aristocratic theory with a commercial theory of the market as civil society. He showed how the settlement of beauty and virtue with commerce was based on desire and production. Hutcheson's attempt to regain the balance which Mandeville had upset only intensified the difference between a philosophy of circulation – of the relation of individual and universal – and one of production and circulation which thematized the necessity involved in the individual's conforming to the universal.

The means by which he achieved this balance, the sense of beauty and the moral sense, was, like the faculty of taste, both material and ideal, mediated and immediate. The sense of beauty captures this state precisely. As in Shaftesbury, the work of art is the model of an enjoyment which was both material and immaterial, produced but not produced. The work of art did not involve desire or labour in its production; nor was it enjoyed physically. It was formal without being cognitive, material without being a utility; in other words, its production and consumption was disinterested. The work of art was the model for a theory of civil society which wished to escape the legal rationalism of Hobbes and the materialism of Mandeville. In this sense Hutcheson followed Shaftesbury in identifying art and civil society; both rested on the paradox of a disinterested taste. However, this entailed a *je ne sais quoi* attitude toward the source of the 'uniformity amid variety,' as when Hutcheson disavowes the inconsistency between the pleasurable moral sense of the market and the violent compulsion of production. In slavery we find a new synthesis of reason and desire, of legality and production; one in which production is legislated through a law which is not produced.

Critic on the Bench

> When the point to be explained is taken for a cause. vis plastica. instinct, horror vacui, the sense of truth (idiosyncrasy). Home's diverse senses: the sense of justice, the sense of honour, participatory.
>
> Kant, *Reflection* 3160

Henry Home, Lord Kames, combined the careers of judge and critic. The 'search for principles underlying particular rules as they were to be applied to particular cases in practice' which characterized his early writings on law and equity (W.C. Lehmann 1971, p. 27) was extended to the philosophy of art in his influential *Elements of Criticism* of 1762.[13] The reform of Scottish law through principles of equity and the establishment of the elements of criticism were closely related. The principles of law and the elements of criticism were derived from providence, and were identified with the rational senses of 'beauty', 'property', and 'contract' discovered by Shaftesbury and Hutcheson. As with these authors, Kames's search for 'principles' of legal and moral judgement appropriate to the new civil society is mirrored by his search for teleologically guaranteed 'elements' of criticism which would channel the 'luxurious appetites' stimulated by commercial society into a virtuous 'ordering of the ranks'.

Kames crudely fuses natural law, providence and the institutions of civil society. The coarseness of his exposition is evident in the *Essays in the Principles of Morality and Natural Religion* published in 1751. The *Essays* are divided into two groups: the first contains essays on 'Our Attachment to Objects of Distress', 'The Foundations and Principles of the Law of Nature', and 'Of Liberty and Necessity' which defend Hutcheson's moral sense theory against Hume's critique; while the second extends the critique into natural religion and other areas. Kames's main line of defence, as Kant observed, consists in multiplying the inner senses and linking them with an extremely crude teleological naturalism:

> A lion is said to purchase the means of life by his claws. Why? because such is his nature and constitution. A Man is made to purchase the means of life by help of others in society. Why? because from the constitution both of his body and mind he cannot live comfortably but in society. It is thus we discover for what end we were designed by nature, or the author of nature.
>
> (1751; p. 41)

Adam Smith must have groaned at this indiscretion. That the author of nature designed us for an 'end' was a commonplace of eighteenth-century moral philosophy; but it was hardly polite of Kames to express it quite so bluntly. For put that way, it exposes more than just the banality of the providential argument.

Kames compounds the indiscretion by deriving the ensemble of 'senses' from the 'ends' which we are providentially determined to follow. These are suddenly identified with the institutions of civil society; just as providence gives the lion his claws, so it bestows on us the 'senses' or 'feelings' of property and contract: 'We have a feeling of property; we have a feeling of obligation to perform our engagements; and we have a feeling of wrong on encroaching upon property, and in being untrue to our engagements' (p. 119). God commends the institutions of property and contract through the implantation of property and contract feelings. From these feelings

Kames develops a robust theory of justice in which 'Justice is the moral virtue which guards property, and gives authority to covenant' (p. 103).

The pleasure of beauty is an important cog in the divine clock of Kames's universe. After the performance of the primary virtues of property and contract come the nobler sentiments of beauty. Virtue is beautiful, but the pleasures of beauty are insufficient to ensure virtue. Virtue must be founded in obligation, and obligation in pain. However, the pleasures of beauty are not irrelevant to virtue and obligation. Beauty rewards the 'fine points' of virtue; but, more interestingly – as will be seen in the discussion of the *Elements* – a certain amount of pleasure in the beautiful softens up the moral sense, making it more susceptible to pain. But too much softening can weaken the moral sense itself, which is the threat posed by luxury. As in Hutcheson's thought, pleasure and pain are inseparable for Kames. The sense of beauty, then, aids obligation but threatens to degenerate into luxury, tragically ceasing to be virtue's ornament and becoming its adversary:

> We find him [humanity] sensible of beauty, in different ranks and orders; and eminently sensible of it, in its highest order, that of sentiment, action and character. But the sense of moral beauty is not alone sufficient. The importance of morality requires some stronger principle to guard it; some checks and restraints from vice, more severe than mere disapprobation. These are not wanting. To the sense of beauty is superadded a sense of obligation; a feeling of right and wrong, which constitute a law within us. The law enjoins the primary virtues, those which are essential to society, under the strictest sanctions. Pain, the strongest monitor we have is employed to check transgression: while in the sublimer, more heroic points of virtue, where strict obligation ends, pleasure is employed to reward the performance.
>
> (pp. 380–1)

Kames, like Hutcheson, supplements the pleasures of the senses of beauty and morality with the pains of right and obligation. The contemplative pleasures of the imagination cannot secure order – they must be supplemented by the pain of morality. The existence of the sense of beauty shows that humans are not Hobbist beasts, like the aforesaid lion, but must still be tamed by a sense of obligation. This is a discriminative 'sense', being at once (in one sentence) a *'sense* of obligation', a *'feeling* of right and wrong' and a *'law* within us' (pp. 380–1). The law is said to be constituted by the feeling of right and wrong, but the relationship between the principle of law and discrimination is left completely unexplored, being the work of a mysterious providence. But just as Hutcheson's moral sense was supplemented by violence, so is Kames's inner law attended by the 'strictest sanctions'. Only after the stern maxims of justice are fulfilled ('guard property', 'observe contracts') may the pleasures of the senses be indulged.

The teleology of property and contract developed in the *Essays* is carried over into the *Elements of Criticism*. The 'dedication' of the work to George III offers some Machiavellian advice concerning beauty's contribution to order:

> The Fine Arts have ever been encouraged by wise Princes, not simply for private amusement, but for their beneficial influence in society. By uniting different ranks in the same elegant pleasures, they promote benevolence: by cherishing love of order, they enforce submission to government: and by inspiring a delicacy of feeling, they make regular government a double blessing.
>
> (1762; vol. I, p. v)

The Fine Arts encourage a unity of sentiment which unites the 'different ranks' in a benevolent love of order; but the pain implied by the pleasure is never far away since the Fine Arts '*enforce submission to government*'. The unity of ranks in the elegant pleasures soften manners, and makes the ranks more sensitive and easy to order, and more desirous of order. By establishing the 'elements' of universal and necessary judgements of taste, and promoting a sensitively mannered unity of sentiment, Lord Kames makes his contribution to the love of order.

Kames is not blind to the dangers of an excessive delicacy of feeling and, using the *topos* of the corruption of virtue by commerce, warns the King that unregulated commerce may lead to over-refinement and luxury. All is not lost though, for the proper development of the sense of beauty offers a new basis for virtue which does not threaten the progress of commerce (property and contract):

> To promote the Fine Arts in Britain, has become of greater importance than is generally imagined. A flourishing commerce begets opulence; and opulence, inflaming our appetite for pleasure, is commonly vented on luxury, and on every sensual

gratification: selfishness rears its head; becomes fashionable; and infecting all ranks, extinguishes the *amor patriae*, and every spark of public spirit. To prevent or retard such fatal corruption, the genius of an Alfred cannot devise any means more efficacious, than the venting opulence upon the Fine Arts; riches employ'd, instead of encouraging vice, will excite both public and private virtue. Of this happy effect Ancient Greece furnishes one shining instance; and why should we despair of another in Britain?

> (vol. I, p. vii)

This return to the fantasy of the Whig Hellas relieves the agonizing problem Shaftesbury had of how to regulate luxury without law. The excess of wealth threatening virtue may be vented on art. But for this to work, Kames has to show that beauty has the qualities of an inner law which is universal and necessary. He achieves this through a demonstration of the teleological foundation of taste and criticism.

Kames insists that the sense of beauty is grounded in a rational principle, and describes his *Elements* as 'attempts to form a standard, by unfolding those principles that ought to govern the taste of every individual' (vol. I, p. vi). The standard has a prescriptive force derived from the moral sense, to which it is related in being a discriminative feeling governed by a mysterious principle:

> A taste in the fine arts goes hand in hand with the moral sense, to which indeed it is nearly allied; both of them discover what is right and what is wrong: fashion, temper, and education have an influence to vitiate both, or to preserve them pure and untainted; neither of them are arbitrary nor local; being rooted in human nature, and governed by principles common to all men.
>
> (vol. I, p. 6)

The alliance of taste and the moral sense is based on three common characteristics. The first is their shared origin in a 'human nature' characterized by universally shared 'principles'. They are, additionally, both discriminative faculties prone to corruption and open to improvement. The third is less a common characteristic than a mutual support agreement: the moral sense gives taste its prescriptive power while taste enhances the susceptibility of the moral sense.

The first chapter of the *Elements* expands Kames's earlier model of 'human nature', locating the various senses and passions within a providential order. What was previously discussed in terms of lions and clocks is now elaborated into a moralistic theory of art wherein God, human nature, and the elements of criticism are brought face to face. Their meeting is described in chapter 10 on 'Congruity and Propriety':

> The God of nature, in all things essential to our happiness, hath observed one uniform method to keep us steady: in our conduct, he hath fortified us with natural laws and principles, preventive of many aberrations, which would daily happen were we totally surrendered to so fallible a guide as is human reason. Propriety cannot rightly be considered in another light, than as the natural law that regulates our conduct with respect to ourselves; as justice is the natural law that regulates our conduct with respect to others.
>
> (vol. I, p. 348)

The *Elements* continue in this way for hundreds of pages, discussing God's providential arrangement of the senses, of society, and of the artistic representation of them. Volume I discusses such principles as 'Dignity and Grace', 'Ridicule', 'Custom and Habit' in the light of their relation to providence; volume II relates these principles to a neo-classical rhetorical poetic. It is in the conclusion, 'On the Standard of Taste', that Kames returns specifically to the question of the relation of beauty and virtue, moral sense and sense of beauty, introduced in the 'Dedication' of the *Elements*.

The excursus on the 'Standard of Taste' is undoubtedly the most original and interesting part of the *Elements*. In it Kames reconsiders the three common elements of the moral sense and the sense of beauty: origin in human nature, their discriminative character, and mutual support. Beneath the shared characteristics is the providential teleology, unknowable except through its effects. The 'principle' of taste follows from human nature, but can only be known intuitively: 'the conviction of a common standard is universal and a branch of our nature, we intuitively conceive a taste to be right or good if conformable to the common standard, and wrong or bad if disconformable' (vol. II, p. 492). However, we cannot know the common standard except where we 'intuitively conceive' a taste to be right or good. The intuitive conception is a discrimination of the conformity or disconformity of a particular taste, and it is only because we make such discriminations that we are convinced that there is a standard underlying them. The nature of the principle which enables the discrimination to take place remains hidden.

The principles of morality and taste must be at once subjective and objective: subjective as a feeling of discrimination but objective as law. This leads to some patent difficulties, as in this passage: 'every man, generally speaking, taking it for granted that his opinions agree with the common sense of mankind, is therefore disgusted with those who think differently, not as differing from him, but as differing from the common standard' (vol. II, p. 493). The common standard begins to wobble, for if one individual can take it for granted that their taste represents common sense, what prevents another individual with a different taste from doing so? The possibility of a discursive search for consensus conducted by individuals lodging different claims to represent the universal is ignored in favour of a providentially established common conviction of human nature. Human nature is not a common ground of consensus from which individuals may judge the merits of different claims to represent the universal, but is the providential law which legislates the universal:

> upon a conviction common to the species, is erected a standard of taste, which without hesitation is applied to the taste of every individual. That standard, ascertaining what actions are right what wrong, what proper what improper, hath enabled moralists to establish rules for our conduct, from which no one person is permitted to swerve. We have the same standard for ascertaining in all the fine arts, what is beautiful or ugly, high or low, proper or improper, proportioned or disproportioned; and here, as in morals, we justly condemn every taste that deviates from what is thus ascertained by the common standard.
>
> (vol. II, pp. 496–7)

The elision of conviction and rule is characteristic; the universal cannot be known, but must be seen to rule. The individual judgement must be subsumed 'without hesitation' under a general standard. This governs the long series of discriminative oppositions (beautiful/ ugly, high/low, etc.) which reduce to the opposition of pleasure and displeasure. The conviction behind the discriminations is described as the 'standard' of taste or virtue, and no more can be said of it than that it is ordained by the same providence which gave the lion his claws. The standard is not open to negotiation, only application through discrimination. Unfortunately, establishing such discriminations upon a conviction or sentiment gives them an extremely weak basis, making them vulnerable to the corruption of sentiment. The vulnerability of sentiment to corruption requires that it be underwritten by the violence of the firmest sanctions.

Kames's work ventures a settlement between the traditional fear of the luxurious corruption of virtue and the aspiration to justify the virtues of a commercial society through the moral sense. Here beauty and virtue complement one another: virtue provides the prescriptive force for the discriminations of taste, while the pleasures of beauty hone the discriminations of virtue. These complementary activities rest on a providential teleology that raises a standard which is felt but not known in the act of judgement. While beauty vents the tendencies to luxury and sensitizes manners, the order of the commercial society is ensured by the feelings of property, contract, etc., which are unthinkable without the strictest sanctions. The equivocation of 'sense' and 'reason' identified by Kant as the main philosophical inadequacy in Shaftesbury, Hutcheson, and Kames, dissolves reason into the unknowable yet unnegotiable conviction behind the discriminations of sense, which can only be maintained through force.

Form and Discrimination

> Whether Hume is right: that great beauties are exceptional because exceptional beauty (or beauty in itself) is alone called great, that is, tautologously. Whether beauty is only called great comparatively, or whether it has its ideal in itself.
>
> Kant, *Reflection* 986

The difficulty of legitimating a discriminative sentiment with a law or standard is uppermost in the theory of taste. All the theorists point to a 'conformity' or 'proportion' between sentiment and reason which is a *je ne sais quoi*, or gift of providence. Hume's writings on criticism address this problem, but attempt to solve it without recourse to divinity. In the *Treatise of Human Nature* (1739) he considers the 'conformity' between the discrimination of sense and the law of reason to lie in an artificially produced form. He justifies the relation between the legislation of form and the production of objects with reference to production in general, but ends by privileging the production of fine art. In his later texts the insight into the source of the conformity between sentiment and reason is abandoned. In *An Inquiry Concerning the Principles of Morals* (1751) Hume figures the distinction of reason and sentiment in terms of God's being and His will, while in *Of the Standard of Taste* (1757) he sees the conformity between them as unknowable, yet leaving a trace or 'mark' in history.

Hume envisaged the *Treatise of Human Nature* as five books, billed in the 'Advertisement' to the *Treatise* as: (i) 'Of the Understanding' (ii) 'Of the Passions' (iii) 'Of Morals' (iv) 'Of Politics' and (v) 'Of Criticism'. The complete performance depended on 'the approbation of the public', which was, alas, not forthcoming. Following the lack of acclaim for the first three books, those on politics and criticism remained unpublished, probably unwritten. As a consequence, the existing *Treatise* gives only a partial picture of Hume's projected 'science of man'. Hume makes the following division of the science in the 'Introduction' to the work:

> The sole end of logic is to explain the principles and operations of our reasoning faculty, and the nature of our ideas: morals and criticism regard our tastes and sentiments: and politics consider men as united in society, and dependent on each other. In these four sciences of *Logic, Morals, Criticism, and Politics*, is comprehended almost every thing, which it can any way import us to be acquainted with, or which can tend either to the improvement or ornament of the human mind.
>
> (1739; pp. xv–xvi)

Although the criticism and politics[14] were not completed, it is possible to conjecture their contents from scattered passages in the *Treatise* and from those essays in *Essays, Literary, Moral, and Political* intended to correct and supplement it.

The place of criticism within the science of human nature can be established by plotting its relation to other parts of the science. In the *Treatise* Hume emphasizes the similarities between criticism and morals over the differences between criticism and logic. In the later writings he is concerned more to distinguish logic from taste than to point to similarities between morals and criticism. In the *Treatise*, both criticism and morals are founded upon the discrimination of pleasure and pain. Both sciences have to show that this discrimination is regular and law-like, but they also have to establish whether pleasure and pain are the origin or the consequence of the ideals of beauty and virtue.

Book II, Part I, section viii of the *Treatise* considers the distinction of beauty and deformity. The difficulties of this chapter are important for drawing out the relation of Hume's theory of taste to morals. It begins by ascribing beauty to whatever 'gives us a peculiar delight and satisfaction' (p. 298) and deformity to whatever causes pain. The distinction of beauty and deformity is immediately allied to pleasure and pain, these 'are not only necessary attendants of beauty and deformity, but constitute their very essence' (p. 299). Pleasure and pain are not predicated in a judgement of taste but define its terms. They also constitute the distinction of virtue and vice; but what is vital to both discriminations is that they are regular, and indicate the presence of a hidden law.

Hume establishes the regularity of the discriminations of pleasure and pain by aligning them with a 'principle'. He follows Hutcheson in relating pleasure to the principle of utility, but refrains from deriving utility from providence. He favours a form of teleological argument which maintains the *effect* of providence in utility while overlooking what the tradition saw as the *source* of utility in the providential being (Shaftesbury) or will (Hutcheson) of God. For Hume pleasure is a subjective response to utility; he ignores the theological question of the ultimate source of this utility. This discretion leads to difficulty, since – by separating utility from the being of God – Hume raises the problem of the relative priority of pleasure and utility: it is equally plausible that a thing is useful because it gives pleasure, as that it gives pleasure because it is useful. Adam Smith later oscillated between the two positions, eventually opting for the former. Hume, however, embraced both relations of pleasure and utility, and presented them in two distinct accounts of pleasure and its objects.

The problems of the precedence of pleasure or utility and the source of the regularity of the discriminations of pleasure and pain are highlighted in Hume's illegitimate deductions of the rules of art from utility. For example: 'the rules of architecture require, that the top of a pillar shou'd be more slender than its base, and that because such a figure conveys to us the idea of security, which is pleasant; whereas the contrary form gives us the apprehension of danger, which is uneasy' (p. 299). Here the rules of architecture are derived from utilitarian considerations of security and danger (a distinction Burke later used to found the distinction of the beautiful and the sublime). Yet earlier on the same page Hume stated that pleasure and pain constitute the essence of beauty and deformity; now they seem to follow from utilitarian considerations of security and apprehension of danger. The subordination of pleasure and beauty to utility is underlined in the comment that although beauty may only be discerned and not defined, it is 'nothing but a form, which produces pleasure' just as 'deformity is a structure of parts, which conveys pain' (p. 299). Pleasure and pain no longer 'constitute' beauty and deformity, but are 'produced' and 'conveyed' by form and deformity; but then these follow in their turn from the 'power of producing pain and pleasure'. Hume's description of these intellectual contortions as an 'argument I esteem just and decisive' (p. 300) is unconvincing. The restless movement between pleasure as constitutive and constituted betrays difficulty in conceiving how a discrimination can be regular, and where the source of its regularity lies. The problem of the precedence of pleasure or utility has not been addressed, nor have the theoretical transitions from utility to a form of utility, and from the form of utility to beauty and pleasure.

The main difficulty lies in the spurious validity given utility by renaming it the 'form' of utility. To speak of a form of utility gives to individual utility an objective universality and necessity. However, the transition from individual to formal utility requires a principle, a theoretical substitute for providence which would articulate each individual utility within an harmonious whole. Once the providential guarantee for the form of utility has been abandoned, beauty is prone to be dispersed among the particularities of the useful. As Burke was to point out, the equation of beauty and utility overextends the category of beauty: ploughs and saddles are useful and give pleasure, but this does not make them beautiful.

At some points in the *Treatise* Hume recklessly endorses the wide equation of utility and beauty and, forgetting his earlier definition of beauty as a *form*, identifies it with useful *objects*: 'This observation extends to tables, chairs, scritoires, chimneys, coaches, saddles, ploughs, and indeed to every work of art; it being a universal rule, that their beauty is chiefly deriv'd from their utility, and from their fitness for that purpose, to which they are destin'd' (p. 364). This 'universal rule' prefers the beauty of useful objects over the form of beauty; all works of art, all produced objects, which are appropriate to the end for which they were produced, are beautiful. This argument falters when it specifies the beauty and utility of those peculiar objects which form the fine arts. Hume's philosphy of fine art is usually read as the crude Horatian argument that works of art are beautiful because they promote morality. He does indeed approach such a position in his essays 'Of Refinement in the Arts' and 'Of Tragedy' but these by no means exhaust the resources of his theory of taste. Beyond the 'saddle and plough' account of the beauty of all useful objects, it is possible to discern another more interesting argument in the *Treatise*. In this Hume confronts the problem of the origin of *form* in pleasure and utility, and revises his understanding of the utility of fine art. This argument, recognized by Adam Smith as Hume's real achievement in the philosophy of art, derives the formal principle of utility from a theory of society.

Before excavating this argument it is necessary to consider briefly Hume's moral philosophy. The relationship between the critical and the moral departments of Hume's 'science of man' is more subtle than is usually acknowledged. Virtue gives a sensation of pleasure and is in accord with utility; the specific utility determining virtue is the good of the whole:

> Now justice is a moral virtue, merely because it has that tendency to the good of mankind; and, indeed, is nothing but an artificial invention to that purpose. The same may be said of allegiance, of the laws of nations, of modesty, and of good manners. All these are mere human contrivances for the interest of society.
>
> (p. 577)

Such an account of utility holds only if there be a principle or prior determinant of the public interest – the role played by providence in Shaftesbury, Hutcheson and Kames. In rejecting providentialist argument Hume is left with the problem of the form of utility, of how to relate individual with social utility or the 'good of mankind'. Hume discovered such a principle in sympathy: 'as the means to an end can only be agreeable, where the end is agreeable; and as the good of society, where our own interest is not concern'd, or that of our friends, pleases only by sympathy: It follows that sympathy is the source of the esteem, which we pay to all the artificial virtues' (p. 577). As the basis for the esteem paid to the artificial virtues which ensure the equivalence of individual and social utility, Hume's theory of sympathy seems an intermediate stage between the unification by providence employed by his predecessors and Smith's 'invisible hand'. Indeed, the synthesis of universal and individual in sympathy is figured, as is the moral sentiment of Smith's early *The Theory of Moral Sentiments* (1759), in terms of the catoptric trope of mutually reflecting mirrors.

The development of Hume's account of the form of beauty in the *Treatise* is inseparable from his philosophy of sympathy: 'Thus it appears, *that* sympathy is a very powerful principle in human nature, *that* it has a great influence on our taste of beauty, and *that* it produces our sentiment of morals in all the artificial virtues' (pp. 577–8). Sympathy has a 'great influence' on the taste of beauty and 'produces' our sentiments of morals. Hume uses a metaphor of catoptric illusion to explain how sympathy moves between individual and general utility. The sum of individual reflections on each others' actions produces a reflected utility or 'form of utility' which is re-experienced by the individual as sympathy, a feeling for the whole:

In general we may remark, that the minds of men are mirrors to one another, not only because they reflect each others emotions, but also because those rays of passions, sentiments and opinions may often be reverberated, and may decay away by insensible degrees. Thus the pleasure which a rich man receives from his possessions, being thrown upon the beholder, causes a pleasure and esteem; which sentiments again, being perceiv'd and sympathis'd with, encrease the pleasure of the possessor; and being once more reflected, become a new foundation for pleasure and esteem in the beholder.

(p. 365)

In this passage, later criticized by Smith, the infinity of past and present reflections assumes independence from the individual mirrors, becoming a form whose effect is felt through the sentiment of sympathy. The field of mutual reflection is held to be the sublimated utility which forms the ground of pleasure in the fine arts. The utility of works of art differs from that of useful objects in being a highly mediated expression of the form of utility.

The utility lying at the source of the pleasure in the fine arts is not immediate and personal, like that of enjoying a saddle, but issues from a form produced by reflection and experienced as sympathy. This argument is analogous to the providentialist ascription of pleasure to the affective experience of the *telos* or unifying principle of society. One of its consequences is that an individual may, through sympathy, find something beautiful and pleasant which for them has no immediate utility, and carries with it the apprehension of danger: 'as when the fortifications of a city belonging to an enemy are esteem'd beautiful on account of their strength, tho' we could wish that they were entirely destroy'd' (pp. 586–7). On this occasion, immediate and reflected utility may be said to conflict. This position marks another stage in the development of the argument for 'disinterested perception' as a source for beauty: in Shaftesbury such disinterest resulted from a contemplation of the *je ne sais quoi*, while in Hume the 'unknowable' has been specified as the artificial, historically produced, formal utility of society.

Hume now bases the rules of art on the refinement of sympathy; we do not use the fine arts as we would a scritoire or a saddle since their utility is formal, end-directed without an immediate end:

There is no rule in painting more reasonable than that of balancing the figures, and placing them with the greatest exactness on their proper centres of gravity. A figure, which is not justly ballanc'd, is disagreeable; and that because it conveys the idea of its fall, of harm, and of pain: Which ideas are painful, when by sympathy they acquire any degree of force and vivacity.

(pp. 364–5)

This explains how Hume was able to maintain a theory of beauty resting on saddles and scritoires alongside one demanding the strictest rules of decorum: the former is based on immediate, the latter on reflected utility. Hume's dual theory of art seems to contain both Shaftesbury's enjoyment of the *je ne sais quoi* abstracted from desire and immediate utility, and Mandeville's identification of beauty and desire for objects. But he is careful to keep the two philosophies apart: the enjoyment of a useful object is rigorously distinguished from the formal and contemplative pleasures of 'fine art'. The 'ordering of the ranks' advocated by Kames is maintained in Hume's two-tiered philosophy of art. We shall see below how Smith, in his critique of Hume, sought to synthesize the two arts of immediate and reflected utility.

The separation of the two arguments is the result of Hume's not fully exploring the source and character of the regularity between sentiment and reason. He attributes such regularity to utility, and relates utility to desire for an end, seeing the origin of pleasure to lie in the realization of ends. But his distinction between material utility – the pleasures of a good saddle – and formal utility – the pleasure of fine art – remains tied to the dichotomy of sentiment and reason. The nature and the source of their conformity remains unexplained. The impasse reached in relating the discriminations of sense and the laws of reason is renegotiated in the first appendix to *An Inquiry Concerning the Principles of Morals*, 'Concerning Moral Sentiment'. Now, when discussing the relation of logic, morals, and criticism, Hume emphasizes the differences between criticism and logic over the former's similarity with morals.

Hume offers five distinctions between logic (the science of reason) and criticism (the science of taste). These are stated in terms of (i) the knowledge claims of each faculty (ii) their modes of representation (iii) the connection of each with moral action (iv) their procedures and (v) their 'standards' or sources of validity. In terms of knowledge claims, reason 'conveys the knowledge of truth and falsehood' while taste 'gives the sentiment of beauty and deformity, vice and virtue' (p. 484). Although both faculties are discriminative, reason distinguishes between truth and falsehood in terms of knowledge, while taste distinguishes between beauty/deformity and vice/virtue according to sentiment. The distinction is then developed in terms of the modes of representation pertaining to reason and sentiment: reason 'discovers objects, as they really stand in nature, without addition or diminution' while taste 'has a productive faculty; and gilding and staining all natural objects with the colours, borrowed from internal sentiment, raises in a manner, a new creation' (p. 484). The perceptions of reason neither add nor subtract from its objects; it is in some sense objective and mimetic, while those of taste are productive, re-producing its objects by adapting them to its desire.

Hume's third distinction contrasts the influence of reason and taste on the passions. Reason can only determine the means for attaining the ends given by the passions, but taste can establish ends, and constitute desire, 'as it gives pleasure and pain, and thereby constitutes happiness or misery, becomes a motive to action, and is the first spring or impulse to desire and volition' (p. 484). Reason is disinterested, and neither alters its object of perception nor offers any motive for action; taste, on the other hand, changes its object and motivates actions. This leads Hume to his fourth distinction of reason and taste. The disinterestedness of reason allows it to be used as an investigative instrument: 'From circumstances and relations, known or supposed . . . [reason] leads us to the discovery of the concealed and unknown.' Taste however, does not follow the train of demonstrative argument, but judges subjectively, and 'makes us feel from the whole a new sentiment of blame or approbation' (p. 484). Reason is an analytical faculty following objective judgements, while taste is synthetic, adding to the perception a subjective sentiment of praise or blame. Yet the nature of the synthetic judgement of taste is even more complicated than it seems here.

The exposition of the differences between taste and reason takes an astonishing turn in the discussion of their sources of validity. Here the sceptical Hume is found distinguishing critical and logical validity in terms of the difference between the ontological and voluntarist views of God. Reason and the validity of logic are founded on the *being* of God while taste and the standard of criticism depend on His *will*. Hume is a Thomist or Spinozist in matters of reason, and a Scotist or Cartesian in matters of taste. The validity of reason is eternal and unchangeable, issuing from the divine being whose laws are independent of even God's will: 'The standard [of reason] . . . being founded on the nature of things, is eternal and inflexible, even by the will of the Supreme Being.' The standard of taste, by contrast, is subjective, not fixed in being but ordained by the divine will: 'the standard [of taste] . . . is ultimately derived from that Supreme will, which bestowed on each being the peculiar nature, and arranged the several classes and orders of existence' (p. 484). But not only does the singularity of each being issue from God's will, but also the classification and ordering of beings. These are the province of reason and should be independent of even God's will; but here they are found to share an origin with the pleasures of taste. The validity of reason, it is suggested, is in some way subordinate to that of taste.

There is one God for reason, another for taste. This equivocal divinity has implications for criticism. Taste is subjective and capricious, but evinces a regularity which suggests it possesses a validity similar to logic. The addition of a subjective sentiment to a perception occurs with regularity and possesses the properties of universality and necessity. But then again it seems as if God's will, the source of the regularities of taste, the law of the distinction of pleasure and pain, also founds the classificatory system and validity of reason. The regularities of the discriminations of taste in a sense underly those of reason. How might this be thought?

In the essay 'Of the Standard of Taste' (1757) Hume transforms the two utilities of the *Treatise* and the divided God of *Concerning Moral Sentiment* into a play of sceptical paradoxes. The standard of taste is recognized to be indeterminate: it has neither the understanding's concern with the universal nor sentiment's dispersal in particulars, yet possesses characteristics of both. Hume hopes to 'mingle some light of the understanding with the feelings of sentiment' (1757, p. 139) by establishing a rational standard or rule of taste, but says he would be content with a convincing sensible discrimination: 'It is natural for us to seek a *Standard of Taste*; a rule, by which the various sentiments of men may be reconciled; at least, a decision afforded, confirming one sentiment, and condemning another' (pp. 135–6). The difficult relation of rule and discrimination is separated into a desire for a rule and a voluntaristic decision confirming a particular discrimination. The rule is only perceptible through the conviction of the discrimination.

In his exploration of the relation of rule and discrimination, Hume finds that although the judgements of reason and the responses of sentiment differ, there is nevertheless a 'conformity' between objects and sentiment. And this conformity, which regularizes the discriminations of sentiment, is analogous to the rule of reason:

> The difference, it is said, is very wide between judgement and sentiment. All sentiment is right; because sentiment has a reference to nothing beyond itself, and is always real, wherever a man is conscious of it. But all determinations of the understanding are not right; because they have a reference to

something beyond themselves, to wit, real matter of fact; and
are not always conformable to that standard. Among a thousand
different opinions which different men may entertain of the
same subject, there is one, and but one, that is just and true;
and the only difficulty is to fix and ascertain it. On the contrary,
a thousand different sentiments, excited by the same object,
are all right: because no sentiment represents what is really in
the object. It only marks a certain conformity or relation
between the object and the organs or faculties of the mind;
and if that conformity did not really exist, the sentiments could
never possibly have being.

(p. 136)

The judgements of reason must be conformable to 'real matter of
fact' and this conformity must be 'fixed and ascertained'. But
sentiment is first denied any such conformity with objects, since it
does not represent what is really there. Its pleasure is produced in
the encounter with an object. But then this encounter, in its myriad
forms, nevertheless marks a 'certain conformity or relation' without
which, indeed, sentiment could not exist. The existence of sentiment
depends on a prior regularity between the object and the mind; the
discriminations of sentiment are as conformable as those of reason.
And while Hume does not identify the source of this regularity as
'providence', his argument is formally similar to that of the
providentialists who argued that proportion preceded both sentiment
and its object. The 'certain conformity or relation' registers the return
of the *je ne sais quoi*. By letting sentiment 'mark' an unknown order
or design – a pre-established harmony – Hume allows it to mediate
between univeral rule and individual discrimination; it is neither
universal nor individual but marks a 'relation' which includes both.

The sentiment of the beautiful is not self-referential, nor does it
bow to an external rule; it marks a 'certain conformity' which exceeds
both reason and sentiment. The 'certain conformity or relation' leaves
marks which may be traced over time. The regularity or 'form' of
discrimination which is felt only as conviction at the moment of
decision, becomes manifest in history:

The relation, which nature has placed between the form and
the sentiment, will at least be more obscure; and it will require
greater accuracy to trace and discern it. We shall be able to
ascertain its influence, not so much from the operation of each
particular beauty, as from the durable admiration, which attends

those works, that have survived all the caprices of mode and fashion, all the mistakes of ignorance and envy.

(p. 138)

Hume attributes the obscurity of relation between form and sentiment – the law of discrimination – to prejudice and the capricious distraction of fashion. This attribution enables him to translate the problem of 'marking' the relation into that of marking the critic: 'But where are such critics to be found? By what marks are they to be known? How to distinguish them from pretenders? These questions are embarrassing; and seem to throw us back into the same uncertainty, from which during the course of this essay we have endeavoured to extricate ourselves' (p. 144). The question of judging judges cannot be answered if the difficulty of judgement has itself not been tackled. For by what criteria do we distinguish between judges? For both judgement in general and the judging of judges Hume appeals to history; time not only manifests the conformity of sentiment and form, but also vindicates the righteous judge.

The source of the obscurity of the relation of form and sentiment, of rule and discrimination, may lie elsewhere. In the distinction of the validities of reason and taste, Hume sees God as both subject to the laws of the universe and creating them by His will. The conformity of reason to its objects rests on universal law, but then both the objects and the laws of reason are creatures of God's will. A similar structure of argument, without the divinity, underlies the distinctions of form/sentiment and rule/discrimination. The conformity of reason is univocal, but that of taste and the sentiments is plural. Taste produces its objects, and the laws under which they are enjoyed; reason on the other hand is given its objects and its law. It is possible to be more specific and say that reason is given its objects and laws by taste, by the sentiments. Objects are produced according to the pleasure which they will give, but pleasure is determined by the attainment of an end. But the end is also legislated by pleasure, so there is a relation or conformity between legislation of ends and the production of objects. It is this relation which is marked in the regularities between the form of law and the discriminations of sentiment.

For Hume the relation of law and production was unknowable, and the source of the obscurity of the relation between law and discrimination. The obscure relation was not immediately dissolved into the workings of providence, but left open. As with Shaftesbury and Hutcheson, the relation was marked by pleasure, but Hume also intimated that it was formed by pleasure. There was the pleasure of attaining an end, but the ends themselves were constituted by pleasure. Hume divided the pleasures according to those in an object which satisfied an end, and those of contemplating ends apart from any object. The relation between the two was not openly acknowledged, although it was conceded to be 'obscure'. Hume's scepticism regarding the knowledge of this conformity met with two responses. The first, represented by Burke, was a forceful restatement of the providential character of this relation. The second, worked through by Smith, pointed to a notion of productive legislation underlying the obscure conforming and relating of law and sentiment.

Materials for a Good System

> To make psychological observations, as Burke did in his treatise on the beautiful and sublime, thus to assemble material for the systematic connection of empirical rules in the future without aiming to understand them, is probably the sole duty of empirical psychology, which can hardly even aspire to rank as a philosophical science.
>
> Kant, *First Introduction to the Critique of Judgement*

Kant's estimation of Burke's *A Philosophical Enquiry into the Origin of our Ideas of the Sublime and Beautiful* (1757) echoes Lessing's earlier judgement of it as 'uncommonly useful as a collection of all the occurrences and perceptions which philosophers must assume as indisputable in enquiries of this kind. He has collected all the materials for a good system.'[15] It confirmed his general view of British enlightenment thought as 'unphilosophical'. However, this judgement underestimates the systematic character of the providential argument in which Burke sets his empirical observations. The *Philosophical Enquiry* is a restoration of the providential argument following Hume's sceptical revolution.

The system informing the *Philosophical Enquiry* is betrayed in the Preface to the first edition. Here Burke deplores the confusion of the sublime and the beautiful, and states three conditions necessary to distinguish between them. The conditions are: the passions in the subject; the properties of the object; and their unification in 'laws of nature':

> Could this [confusion] admit of any remedy, I imagined it could only be from a diligent examination of our passions in our own breasts; from a careful survey of the properties of

things which we find by experience to influence those passions; and from a sober and attentive investigation of the laws of nature, by which those properties are capable of affecting the body, and thus exciting our passions.

(1757; p. 1)

At the outset of his 'empirical investigation' Burke defines the sublime in terms of the *topoi* of the theory of taste, and prosecutes his enquiry according to the passions of the subject, the properties of the object, and the laws of nature which unite them.

The primary subjective passions underlying the distinctions of the beautiful and the sublime in Part I of the *Philosophical Enquiry* are the familiar terms of the distinction of pleasure and pain. Here they are derived from sociability and self-preservation:

> Most of the ideas which are capable of making a powerful impression on the mind, whether simply of Pain or Pleasure, or of the modifications of those, may be reduced very nearly to these two heads, *self-preservation* and *society*; to the ends of one or the other of which all our passions are calculated to answer.
>
> (p. 38)

The passions are 'calculated' to contribute to society and self-preservation: the pleasure in the beautiful excites the sociable passions of sympathy, imitation and ambition, while the pain of the sublime raises the self-preservative passions of pain and danger. The identity of the calculator is revealed when the principles of self-preservation and society along with their associated passions are aligned with a providential natural law; they are no less than the instruments of God's design for human society:

> Wherever we are formed by nature to any active purpose, the passion which animates us to it, is attended with delight, or a pleasure of some kind, let the subject matter be what it will; and as our Creator has designed we should be united by the bond of sympathy, he has strengthened that bond by a proportionable delight; and there most where our sympathy is most wanted, in the distresses of others.
>
> (p. 46)

Pleasure expresses the 'bond of sympathy' by which God binds society, and this bond is ensured by a 'proportionate delight'. The passions of self-preservation, the individual or asocial passions are, the argument continues, harmonized with the sociable passions by a natural law.

The natural law cannot be known through reason, it can only be felt. Like Shaftesbury, Burke hurries to place the distinction of private and public goods in a cosmic setting, one described in the *Reflections on the Revolution in France* (1790) as a 'primaeval contract' or Chain of Being whose designs exceed the purview of reason:

> Each contract of each particular state is but a clause in the great primaeval contract of eternal society, linking the lower with the higher natures, connecting the visible and the invisible world, according to a fixed compact sanctioned by the inviolable oath which holds all physical and all moral natures, each in their appointed place.
>
> (1790; pp. 93–4)

Society is bound by an oath exacted by supreme necessity, 'a necessity that is not chosen, but chooses, a necessity paramount to deliberation, that admits no discussion, and demands no evidence' (p. 94). Both the learned and the 'less inquiring' recognize providence in this necessity, as they do in its institutions of law and the state: 'They conceive that He who gave our nature to be perfected by our virtue, willed also the necessary means of its perfection – He willed therefore the state – He willed its connexion with the source and original archetype of all perfection' (p. 95). Burke hastens to assure us that he 'does not aim at singularity' in what he says, admitting himself 'unable to distinguish what I have learned from others from the results of my own meditations' (p. 96). The main object of his meditation was clearly the tradition of British providential social theory.

The same providence that presides over the *Reflections* also guides the passions in the *Philosophical Enquiry*. A pre-rational moral unity disposes the selfish and the social passions toward the greatest good. Burke identifies the sublime passions in Part II of the *Philosophical Enquiry* with the principle of self-preservation. The feeling of the sublime is aroused when the individual is faced with the unknown, infinite in extent and power, which threatens its existence. Burke confirms the source of this passion in individual self-preservation by considering the susceptibility of the senses to the sublime: 'Having thus run through the causes of the sublime with reference to all the senses, my first observation ... will be found very nearly true; that the sublime is an idea belonging to self-preservation. That it is therefore one of the most affecting we have' (1757, p. 86). The various empirical observations on the sublime follow the systematic aim of establishing the relation of the sublime to the principle of self-preservation.

The same conclusion holds for Burke's discussion of the beautiful these observations are not unsystematic. In Part III of the *Philosophical Enquiry*, the heart of the book, Burke discusses the sociable passions and beauty. His exposition of the beautiful eliminates such candidates for the principle of beauty as proportion, utility, and perfection on the grounds that they are rational and abstract, applying a concept to what should be an immediate, affective response. Like the other philosophers of taste he does not rest the response to beauty on the perception of a rational principle, but neither does he see it as a mere accident of sentiment; beauty always has its reasons, but they belong to providence.

Burke's critique of rational principles of beauty anticipates his elevation in the *Reflections* of the affections of providential natural law over the exercise of 'artificial reason'. The intellectual principles of beauty privilege artificial reason over immediate sensation: the principle of proportion, for example, 'must therefore be considered as a creature of the understanding, rather than a primary cause acting on the senses and imagination. It is not by the force of long attention and enquiry that we find any object to be beautiful; beauty demands no assistance from our reasoning; even the will is unconcerned' (p. 92). The principles of utility and perfection are rejected in a similar manner: they are creatures of the understanding, abstract concepts applied by the understanding after a response to a beautiful object. The response itself is like the necessity which chooses but is not chosen, immediate and beyond deliberation.

Although the response to the beautiful object is irrational, it does not lack necessity. This is not imposed artificially by the understanding but issues from the divine institution of the social passions:

> Whenever the wisdom of our Creator intended that we should be affected with anything, he did not confide the execution of his design to the languid and precarious operation of our reason; but he endowed it with powers and properties that prevent the understanding, and even the will, which seizing upon the senses and imagination, captivate the soul before the understanding is ready either to join with them or to oppose them.
>
> (p. 107)

Such 'powers and properties' which bypass reason are unknowable;

they seize the senses and imagination but will not be seized by the reason. They nevertheless legitimate the individual passions by appeal to the authority of the 'primaeval oath', whose conditions cannot be known. The attractions of beautiful sociability and the terrors of sublime self-preservation are the means by which providence ensures social order. The two passions unite the individual and the social, laying down the unknowable law of a providence which chooses but is not chosen.

In the final paragraph of the *Philosophical Enquiry* Burke locates his book within the debate over the standard of taste:

> It was not my design to enter into the criticism of the sublime and beautiful in any art, but to attempt to lay down such principles as may tend to ascertain, to distinguish, and to form a sort of standard for them; which purposes might be best effected by an inquiry into the properties of such things in nature as raise love and astonishment in us; and in showing in what manner they operated to produce these passions.
>
> (p. 176)

The problem of establishing a standard of taste was especially difficult for Burke since he rejected all rational principles of taste. His work faced the problem of relating discrimination and legislation, of making the passage from principles which 'tend to ascertain' and 'distinguish' to 'forming a standard for them'. Just as in the philosophy of taste in general, a principle was assumed to underlie discriminative judgement which formed a standard for discrimination. Burke's principle consisted in a providential unity experienced through the discriminations of the senses. This argument was challenged by Hume's 'Of the Standard of Taste' which was published soon after the *Philosophical Enquiry* in the *Four Dissertations*. Burke felt sufficiently threatened by Hume's essay to include in the second edition of the *Philosophical Enquiry* a supplementary 'Introduction On Taste' which, amid much bluster, proposes that the faculty of 'taste' take its place alongside reason: 'On a superficial view, we may seem to differ very widely from each other in our reasonings, and no less in our pleasures: but notwithstanding this difference, which I think to be rather apparent than real, it is probable that the standard both of Reason and Taste is the same in all human creatures' (p. 11). Only probable? Burke supports his argument for the standard of taste by postulating taste as a divinely ordained faculty with the properties of both reason and sentiment: 'I mean by the word Taste no more than that faculty, or those faculties of the mind which are affected with, or which form a judgement of the works of imagination and the elegant arts' (p. 13). Burke's faculty of taste comes to assume the properties of Hutcheson's sense of the beautiful – it is a judgement of the senses with the properties of reason – being a faculty of the mind which is both 'affected by' and 'forms a judgement of' the work of imagination. Burke leave us with this ambiguous faculty, resting on the validity of the standard of taste, which in its turn rests upon the ambiguous faculty, the circular argument being closed by appeal to the inscrutable designs of providence.

Burke's philosophy of art is not simply a collection of empirical observations awaiting arrangement into a system. His observations assume that the passions are aspects of a providential design for human society. The distinction of the sublime and the beautiful follows the distinction of the asocial and sociable passions, the two forces of sublime individuality and beautiful sociability being harmonized by providence. Burke's work defends the theory of taste's intimations of providence in the universal and necessary validity of the response to a beautiful object. His defensive response to Hume's sceptical critique of this tradition is in utter contrast to Smith's transformation of the philosophy of taste and civil society into political economy.

Taste and the Wealth of Nations

What is the rule of application (practically the application of judgement) on an object of judgement (the sympathy of others and an impartial spectator).

Kant, *Reflection* 6628

Adam Smith considered the sense of beauty or taste to be 'often the secret motive of the most serious and important pursuits of both private and public life' (1759, p. 181) and, what is more, one of the main causes contributing to the development of a commercial civilization. These claims followed from his definition of beauty as the pleasure of perceiving the fitness or proportion of a means to an end apart from any consideration of the end – a phenomenon Kant later described as *Zweckmässigkeit ohne Zweck*. The pleasure in a means apart from its end transforms itself into the drive towards the endless accumulation of means characteristic of an expanding commercial civilization. This drive was guided by the invisible hand of providence or the *je ne sais quoi* which ensured the realization of the *end* of a prosperous and well-mannered society.

By fusing commerce and virtue through the *je ne sais quoi* Smith, like his predecessors, sought to remove virtue from the orbit of the direct legislation or 'policy' of the state. He transformed the continental tradition of *Polizeiwissenschaft* – the legislation of manners (see below, chapter 3) – into *An Inquiry into the Nature and Causes of the Wealth of Nations*. He promoted the creation of wealth over the 'policy' of legislating the common welfare: the improvement of manners would not be achieved through the 'policy' of the state but through increasing opulence and eroding relations of dependency. The emergence of a well-mannered civil society is the unintended consequence of the pursuit of wealth and not the intended consequence of legislation.

The confrontation of the theory of taste and civil society with *Polizeiwissenschaft* issued in the *Wealth of Nations*. The course of this conflict may be traced through Smith's lectures on moral philosophy, delivered at Glasgow University between 1752 and 1764, and regarded as the matrix of his subsequent publications. According to a student of Smith's, John Millar, the lectures were divided into four parts: natural theology, ethics, jurisprudence, and police. Little is known of the lectures on natural theology except what may be conjectured from the traces of them left in the other writings. The lectures on ethics were the basis of the *Theory of Moral Sentiments* first published in 1759 and revised in 1761 and 1790. In the early 1760s Smith expanded the lectures on jurisprudence at the expense of ethics, and of this part of his course two lecture transcripts have survived as the *Lectures on Jurisprudence*. By 1776 in the *Wealth of Nations* the treatment of justice was in its turn firmly subordinated to that of police, revenue, and arms, with the emphasis firmly placed on police.

Barring the discovery in a Scottish attic of a previously unknown transcript of Smith's lectures on natural theology, we are unlikely to know more about the contents of these lectures than we do from Millar's description and the scattered theological episodes in other writings. The *Theory of Moral Sentiments* for example, while containing no proofs of the 'being and attributes of God' clearly assumes a specific relationship between religion and the 'principles of the human mind'. The similarity between Smith's view of these 'principles' and those of the other thinkers discussed in this chapter is striking. Smith's principles are characterized by the familiar disposition of sentiment and reason: principles are rational sentiments, rational in respect of their end but sentiments with regard to their means. The rationality of a particular sentiment was established by providence.

Smith's account of the relation of providence and the sentiments in the *Theory of Moral Sentiments* takes account of Hume's utilitarian critique of the providential argument. His case rests on the distinction between means and ends, and the propensity for human means to become ends in themselves. Behind this propensity was a division of the realms of efficient and final causes: humanity concerns itself with efficient causes while final causes are God's responsibility:

> though, in accounting for the operations of bodies, we never fail to distinguish in this manner the efficient from the final cause, in accounting for those of the mind we are very apt to confound these two different things with one another. When by natural principles we are led to advance those ends, which a refined and enlightened reason would recommend to us, we are very apt to impute to that reason, as to their efficient cause, the sentiments and actions by which we advance those ends, and to imagine that to be the wisdom of man, which in reality is the wisdom of God.
>
> (1759; p. 87)

What are the ends or 'final causes' which God has in mind for humanity, and how does he realize them? God wishes to maximize human happiness and achieves this through his 'viceregents', the sentiments: 'Since these, therefore, were plainly intended to be the governing principles of human nature, the rules which they prescribe are to be regarded as the commands and laws of the Deity, promulgated by those viceregents which he has thus set up within us' (p. 165). As mediators the 'viceregents' have both divine and human characteristics; Smith even describes their action as 'the slow, gradual, and progressive work of the great demigod within the breast' (p. 247). The demigod suffers a Manichean struggle between its divine and human elements, a conflict Smith had earlier represented in terms of the viewpoints of the partial and the impartial spectators:

> The supposed impartial spectator of our conduct seems to give his opinion in our favour with fear and hesitation; when that of all the real spectators, when that of all those with whose eyes and from whose station he endeavours to consider it, is unanimously and violently against us. In such cases, this demigod within the breast appears, like the demigods of the poets, though partly of immortal, yet partly too of mortal extraction. When his judgements are steadily and firmly directed by the sense of praiseworthiness and blame-worthiness, he

seems to act suitably to his divine extraction: But when he
suffers himself to be astonished and confounded by the
judgements of ignorant and weak man, he discovers his
connexion with mortality, and appears to act suitably, rather
to the human, than to the divine, part of his origin.

(p. 131)

The fluctuation between the human and divine aspects of sentiment
leads to a disproportion between empirical and transcendental
standards, here between the judgements of the actual and the impartial
spectator, and later between market and real price in the *Wealth of
Nations*.

In the long run God's will prevails over human obstruction in
realizing his end of maximizing happiness:

all the inhabitants of the universe, the meanest as well as the
greatest, are under the immediate care and protection of that
great, benevolent, and all-wise Being, who directs all the
movements of nature; and who is determined, by his own
unalterable perfections, to maintain in it, at all times, the
greatest possible quantity of happiness.

(p. 235)

The universe itself is nothing but an 'immense machine' for the
production 'of the greatest possible quantity of happiness' (p. 236).
The relationship between a machine and happiness in Smith's thought
is not accidental. It is not simply that a machine produces happiness
or 'enjoyment', but enjoyment itself consists in the contemplation of
machines, or stated less provocatively, of means abstracted from their
proper ends. The desire to maximize the enjoyment of contemplating
means apart from their ends is not only the 'secret principle' of the
development of civilization, but also the origin of the sentiment of
beauty.

Smith discusses the sentiment of beauty in Part IV of the *Theory
of Moral Sentiments*, 'On the Effect of Utility upon the Sentiment of
Approbation'. He directs his account against Hume, dismissing his
explanation of the beautiful by immediate utility as 'so very obvious
that nobody has overlooked it' (p. 179). He proceeds more positively
to generalize Hume's second derivation of beauty from 'reflected
utility', using it to explain both immediate and reflected beauty. The
sentiment of beauty for both the 'owner' and 'spectator' cannot be
distinguished in terms of immediate or reflected utility since both
pleasures arise from abstracting means from ends: 'the exact

adjustment of the means for attaining any conveniency or pleasure, should frequently be more regarded, than that very conveniency or pleasure, in the attainment of which their whole merit would seem to consist' (pp. 179–80). Action is not motivated by the desire to attain any particular end, but by the pleasure arising from the employment of the means to that end. More effort is spent in pursuit of the pleasure of the means than would have been spent in the rational attainment of the desired end. Smith illustrates this proposition with a parable:

When a person comes into his chamber, and finds the chairs all standing in the middle of the room, he is angry with his servant, and rather than see them continue in that disorder, perhaps takes the trouble himself to set them all in their places with their backs to the wall. The whole propriety of this new situation arises from its superior conveniency in leaving the floor free and disengaged. To attain this conveniency he voluntarily puts himself to more trouble than all he could have suffered from the want of it; since nothing was more easy, than to have set himself down upon one of them, which is probably what he does when his labour is over. What he wanted therefore, it seems, was not so much this conveniency, as that arrangement of things which promotes it.

(p. 180)

The parable of the chairs involves no less than the origin of civilization, or the transition from 'natural indolence' to 'civilized industry'. This transition raises the question of why so much more effort should be spent in disposing the means to a particular end than are necessary for the immediate enjoyment of that end. In the parable a person wishes to sit in their chamber; the chairs are there, but they cannot take their ease before *voluntarily* spending a great deal of effort in properly arranging them. Against Hume's notion of an immediate utility, Smith suggests that the desired end of pleasure and happiness is 'naturally confound[ed] in our imagination with the order, the regular and harmonious movement of the system, the machine or oeconomy by means of which it is produced' (p. 183) and it is this 'confounding' which encourages the expenditure of more effort and the production of more goods than is necessary for the satisfaction of immediate desires.

The amateur furniture removals exemplify the happy deception which has encouraged the development of civilized society:

It is this deception which rouses and keeps in continual motion the industry of mankind. It is this which first prompted them to cultivate the ground, to build houses, to found cities and commonwealths, and to invent and improve all the sciences and arts, which ennoble and embellish human life; which have entirely changed the whole face of the globe, have turned the rude forests of nature into agreeable and fertile plains, and made the trackless and barren ocean a new fund of subsistence, and the great high road of communication to the different nations of the earth.

(pp. 183–4)

The pleasure in contemplating a means apart from its end contributes to civilization in two ways: it replaces the 'natural' alliance of desire and need with one which aligns desire and imagination, wherein 'the eye is larger than the belly' and the 'capacity of his stomach bears no proportion to the immensity of his desires' (p. 184), so transforming 'natural indolence' into 'unrelenting industry' (p. 181). The accumulation of means through an industry driven to satisfy insatiable desire leads to the general benefit of society: the owners of private property not only make themselves rich in the pursuit of their imaginary desires, but also contribute to the wealth of the nation, for

They are led by an invisible hand to make nearly the same distribution of the necessaries of life, which would have been made, had the earth been divided into equal portions among all its inhabitants, and thus without intending it, without knowing it, advance the interest of the society, and afford means to the multiplication of the species. When Providence divided the earth among a few lordly masters, it neither forgot nor abandoned those who seemed to have been left out in the partition.

(pp. 184–5)

Providence's noble lie induces us to accumulate means beyond any particular end which they may serve, and thus not only drives the machine of the economy, but also stimulates the civic energies invested in the polity:

All constitutions of government, however, are valued only in proportion as they tend to promote the happiness of those who live under them. This is their sole use and end. From a certain spirit of system, however, from a certain love of art and contrivance, we sometimes seem to value the means more than the end, and to be eager to promote the happiness of our fellow-creatures, rather from a view to perfect and improve a certain beautiful and orderly system, than from any immediate sense or feeling of what they either suffer or enjoy.

(p. 185)

The accumulation of the means to produce wealth and the establishment of the political means to order society together lead to the 'orderly and flourishing state of society' (p. 88) which in its turn is 'agreeable' to contemplate and improve further.

The two contributions of the sense of beauty to civilization are complementary but still separate in the *Theory of Moral Sentiments*, which in many ways follows Mandeville's call for civil society to be regulated by the state. The insatiable desire to accumulate means apart from ends contributes to the common welfare through increasing wealth, but is supplemented by the 'perfection of police' (p. 185) or the political direction of wealth in the interest of the common welfare. As is well known, by the time he wrote the *Wealth of Nations*, Smith was convinced that a flourishing society was automatically an orderly one requiring the minimum of political intervention. The transition from the position on the relation between wealth and order in the *Theory of Moral Sentiments* to that in the *Wealth of Nations* is clearly apparent in the *Lectures on Jurisprudence*. In the lectures on police, Smith develops a critique of continental *Polizeiwissenschaft* which replaces the legislation of manners with the equation of increasing opulence and the improvement of manners. In the introduction to his lectures (Report dated 1766), Smith defines jurisprudence as 'the theory of the general principles of law and government' and defines its scope as the 'four great objects of law . . . Justice, Police, Revenue, and Arms' (1978, p. 398). The object of justice – 'security from injury' – is private and public law, while the objects of police are 'the cheapness of commodities, public security, and cleanliness', more broadly speaking 'the opulence of a state' (p. 398). Revenue and arms, while formally distinguished from police, are presented in the lectures as branches of it. The emphasis in Smith's police theory on public cleanliness, security, and the regulation of markets or 'cheapness' follows the continental pattern, even though he was in the process of transforming *Polizeiwissenschaft* into the new science of political economy.

Smith's reworking of the continental concept of police is apparent at the beginning of his section 'Of Police'. He observes that

in cities where there is most police and the greatest number
of regulations concerning it, there is not always the greatest
security. In Paris the regulations concerning police are so
numerous as not to be comprehended in several volumes. In
London there are only two or three simple regulations. Yet in
Paris scarce a night passes without somebody being killed,
while in London which is a larger city, there are scarce three
or four in a year.

(p. 486)

Smith conjectures that the difference between an orderly and a
disorderly community is due less to the degree of regulation than to
the structure of manners. The main cause of the nocturnal bloodletting
in Paris is the 'remain of feudal manners, still preserved in France'
wherein the nobility keep on a large body of retainers who are
responsible to their lords but not to themselves. With such a structure
of manners not even a library of police regulations would suffice to
maintain order. Instead of using police measures to suppress the
symptoms of corrupt manners, Smith advocates a policy which would
reform manners through encouraging independence and opulence.
With this he overturns the traditional concepts of police and arrives
at the conclusion that the least policey is the best policy:

Nothing tends so much to corrupt mankind as dependencey,
while independencey still encreases the honesty of the people.
The establishment of commerce and manufactures, which
brings about this independencey, is the best police for
preventing crimes. The common people have better wages in
this way than in any other, and in consequence of this a general
probity of manners takes place thro' the whole country.

(pp. 486–7, see also p. 539)

With this conclusion Smith gives the definitive answer to the problem
of the relation between wealth and virtue which had exercised the
theory of civil society. A reformation of manners directed by the state
through legal regulation dealt only with symptoms; the proper way
to reform manners was to encourage the development of a commercial
civilization whose citizens would be free, and responsible only to
themselves.

On the continent police theory remained preoccupied with the
legislation of the common welfare, but in Smith's hands it became
concerned almost exclusively with 'the consideration of cheapness or

plenty, or, which is the same thing, the most proper way of procuring wealth and abundance' (p. 487). In other words, the legislation of manners is succeeded by the encouragement of industry. In the *Theory of Moral Sentiments*, industry is encouraged by the taste for beauty which spurs 'natural indolence' to efforts beyond what is necessary for survival. It is similarly argued in the *Lectures on Jurisprudence* that:

> As the delicacey of a man's body requires much greater provision than that of any other animal, the same or rather the much greater delicacey of his mind requires a still greater provision, to which all the different arts [are] subservient. Man is the only animal who is possessed of such a nicety that the very colour of an object hurts him. Among different objects a different division or arrangement of them pleases. The taste of beauty, which consists chiefly in the three following particulars, proper variety, easy connection, and simple order, is the cause of all this niceness.
>
> (p. 488)

It is paradoxically this very sensitivity founded on the taste of beauty which leads to the voluntary expenditure of industry; indeed 'The whole industry of human life is employed not in procuring the supply of our three humble necessities, food, cloaths, and lodging, but in procuring the conveniences of it according to the nicety and delicacey of our taste' (p. 488). The limited needs or 'natural wants of mankind' give way in a commercial civilization to the limitless demands of taste and imagination. The satisfaction of imagination's desire requires a limitless expansion of industry and trade, made possible by the 'disposition to barter and exchange' (p. 493) or 'trucking disposition', and the social and technical division of labour which it generates. Opulence, or the 'multiplication of the product', ensures that the demands of the imagination continue to be both met and stimulated.

The continual expansion of industry and imagination was by no means an accidental or an unregulated process; yet the necessity and the regulation of this expansion are not the outcome of human foresight. In fact, given that the demands of imagination are limitless, and that the number of transactions and subdivisions of labour are infinite, there is no possibility of their limits or extent being perceived let alone regulated by a human legislator. But behind the infinities of desire and its transactions, and the infinite subdivision of labour lie divinely established proportions. For example, commerce and the division of labour are proportioned in the 'necessary connection' of natural and market price. Disproportions arise from 'errors of police' which arise from regulating without proper knowledge of what is to be regulated. The *je ne sais quoi*, unknowable because infinite, may only be regulated by the divine and not the human hand.

Although 'proportion' is one of the most frequently used words in the first book of the *Wealth of Nations*, Smith nowhere explicitly acknowledges its relation to providence.[16] Yet proportion was the central concept of Hutcheson's providential theory, and operates analogously in Smith's political economy. Only providence can discern the order implicated in the infinity of human actions, and only it can regulate these actions according to the maximization of happiness. The order behind the infinite number of human actions and subdivisions of social and technical divisions of labour is scarcely discernible by human perception. At the beginning of the *Wealth of Nations* Smith maintains that the division of labour is so extended that no 'impartial spectator' could possibly take it all in; the number of invisible hands at work is infinite:

> every different branch of the work employs so great a number of workmen, that it is impossible to collect them all into the same workhouse. We can seldom see more, at one time, than those employed in one single branch.
>
> (p. 14)

Unlike the earlier theorists of taste, who relegated production by removing labour from view, Smith transfigures it into a demiurgic power visible only through its products. This is apparent in his almost Whitmanesque epic of the labourer's woollen coat – 'coarse and rough as it may appear' – in which the 'number of people of whose industry a part, though but a small part, has been employed in procuring him this accommodation, exceeds all computation':

> The shepherd, the sorter of the wool, the wool comber
> Or carder, the dyer, the scribbler, the spinner,
> The weaver, the fuller, the dresser,
> With many others,
> Must all join their different arts in order
> To complete
> Even this homely production.
>
> (p. 22, orthography adapted)

The wealth of the nation is dictated by the proportion of production and consumption, which is established by the extent of the division of labour (production) and the proportion of productive and unproductive labour (consumption): the two factors are mediated through exchange. A developed division of labour is not possible without developed exchange relations; but exchange raises the problem of a measure for the equivalence or proportionality of the goods to be exchanged. Once again the infinity of transactions means that no measure can realistically be contrived to regulate exchange relations, nor can an empirical average be used to determine relations. Smith requires an analogue of the standard of taste, a standard for judgement which is both transcendent and immanent; he found this in the quantity of goods commanded by a given quantity of labour. Like the standard of taste, quantity of labour is 'the real measure of the exchangeable value of all commodities' (p. 47); however, the idea of a *real* measure is not readily comprehensible: how is its reality to be distinguished from empirical reality? The question whether labour was a 'real measure' because it constituted the reality of commodities remained central to political economy up to and beyond Marx's *Capital*.

Having established an 'absolute' standard, Smith relates it to the fluctuations in market price. The distinction between real and nominal value employed in the *Wealth of Nations* is an analogue of the distinction between the judgement of the impartial spectator and the sum of empirical spectators proposed in the *Theory of Moral Sentiments*. There arises from the incalculable sum of empirical judgements and transactions in the market a 'nominal standard' which will tend always toward the 'real standard' if it is not obstructed by 'errors of police':

> But though the market price of every particular commodity is in this manner continually gravitating, if one may say so, towards the natural price, yet sometimes particular accidents, sometimes natural causes, and sometimes particular regulations of police, may, in many commodities, keep up the market price, for a long time together, a good deal above the natural price.
>
> (p. 77)

Market prices deviate from their orbit around natural prices because of the imperfect judgements made by participants in the market; however, they always tend to the level of natural prices due to the latter's 'gravity'. It is the latter, the equivalent of Hume's 'mark' of a certain conformity, which maintains the proper proportion between labour and price, between production and consumption.

The maintenance of the proportion between production and

consumption ensures both the maximization of happiness/pleasure and its optimal distribution. This result does not follow from the conscious judgement of either society or the state. Not one of the three fundamental orders of society – landowners, labourers, and employers – are in a position to judge accurately what action would best contribute to the common welfare. The landowners' position is closely tied up with the *general* prosperity of society because any improvement in productive power in general leads to a rise in rents. However, this result comes to the landowners as a gift of fortune; so while their interest is objectively one with the general interest, they cannot subjectively perceive the connection between their personal and the general prosperity:

> When the publick deliberates concerning any regulation of commerce or police, the proprietors of land never can mislead it, with a view to promote the interest of their own particular order; at least, if they have any tolerable knowledge of that interest. They are, indeed, too often defective in this tolerable knowledge. They are the only one of the three orders whose revenue costs them neither labour nor care, but comes to them, as it were, of its own accord, and independent of any plan or project of their own.
>
> (1776; p. 265)

The interests of the second order of society, the labourers, are equally related to the general interest. The increase in productive power, while not increasing the proportion of society's wealth paid in wages, as with rent, nevertheless increases the absolute amount involved. But while the landowners were too indolent to inquire into the relation of their partial interest to the general interest, the labourers are too hard-worked to judge:

> though the interest of the labourer is strictly connected with that of the society, he is incapable either of comprehending that interest, or of understanding its connection with his own. His condition leaves him no time to receive the necessary information, and his education and habits are commonly such as to render him unfit to judge even though he was fully informed.
>
> (p. 266)

The third order, the employers, do not enjoy an automatic connection of their particular interest to the general interest. Smith showed that the rate of profit declined with the prosperity and rose with the declension of society. It follows that the political judgement of this order can only be relied on if its members work against their own interests; and Smith does not trust them to do so. Yet it is the 'merchants and master-manufacturers' from this class who 'by their wealth draw to themselves the greatest share of the public consideration' (p. 266); as Smith wryly observes,

> As their thoughts, however, are commonly exercised rather about the interest of their own particular branch of business, than about that of society, their judgement, even when given with the greatest candour (which it has not been upon every occasion), is much more to be depended upon with regard to the former of those two objects, than with regard to the latter.
>
> (p. 266)

He concludes his consideration of the political judgement of the employers with a frank warning about the partiality of those 'who generally have an interest to deceive and even to oppress the public'.

Not one of the three orders of society is able to exercise political judgement concerning the common welfare. Neither the landowners, nor labourers, nor employers are in a position to legislate from the standpoint of the 'impartial spectator'. However, this is not as disastrous a conclusion as it might appear if one remembers that Smith considered fully rational political judgement to be impossible in any case. The proportionality between production and consumption is best served by each order pursuing its own interest in civil society and forswearing political regulation. This is because the pursuit of self-interest has been providentially ordained to secure the common welfare; human interference would only distort the providential proportionalities. For Smith, not only is it evident that 'every individual . . . can, in his local situation, judge much better than any statesman or lawgiver can do for him' (p. 456), but furthermore, individual judgement automatically contributes to the common welfare. This result is of course the work of the celebrated invisible hand; in the pursuit of self-interest through empirical judgements the individual is 'led by an invisible hand to promote an end which was no part of his intention. Nor is it always the worse for the society that it was no part of it. By pursuing his own interest he frequently promotes that of society more effectively than when he really intends to promote it' (p. 456).

Smith does not use the image of the invisible hand very often; but it is an apt one for the providence characteristic of eighteenth-century theories of taste and civil society. God orchestrates individual judgements through sentiments and so maximizes happiness; this follows from the increase in wealth and personal autonomy. Production is promoted by the pleasures of taste, of contemplating and enjoying means apart from ends, which encourages the exorbitant expenditure of effort. This emphasis on production is carried through to the notion of the proportions which ensure the common welfare; proportionality is produced, as acknowledged in the use of labour as a measure of value. These proportions, attributed to God, are rational principles which ensure that the sum of individual interests tends toward the common welfare or maximization of happiness. They serve to conform wealth and virtue; virtue would be ill served by the legislation of manners advocated earlier in the century by Dennis and which remained the principle of continental *Polizeiwissenschaft*. Smith transformed police into the wealth of nations on the basis of the providential theory of civil society current in Britain; but he also transformed that theory. The *je ne sais quoi* remained the principle which bought private and public interest into harmony, but it was no longer based on the suppression of production. Political judgement was directly related to place in the production process; neither the labourers, the merchants, nor the landowners were in an objective position to legislate for society, but if they collectively pursued their own interests then the responsibility for good manners and the common welfare might safely be left to providence.

Taste and Civil Society

> Every political commonwealth may indeed wish to be possessed of a sovereignty, according to laws of virtue, over the spirits [of its citizens]; for then, when its methods of compulsion do not avail (for the human judge cannot penetrate into the depths of other men) their dispositions to virtue would bring about what was required.
>
> Kant, *Religion Within the Limits of Reason Alone*

Kant denied the title of philosophy to the British theory of taste because it did not properly account for the universality and necessity of its judgements. It neglected the subsumptive moment of judgement, and was precipitate in attributing law-like properties to its discriminations. Furthermore, it tended to confuse the sensible and the intellectual capacities, committing in Kant's eyes the amphiboly of sensualizing the concepts of the understanding. The two objections are related in so far as discrimination is the prerogative of sensibility, while subsumption under a law is the work of intellect. In published texts and unpublished reflections Kant consistently criticized the theorists of taste for giving the discriminations of sensibility the properties of rational law. He did not deem this to be philosophy.

It is noteworthy that Kant states his criticisms in comparative terms: if Hutcheson is unphilosophical, then so is Wolff; if Locke is amphibolous, then so is Leibniz. We shall see in chapter 4 that this is a deliberate strategy on Kant's part, a means of displaying the 'bias of reason' through the comparison of traditions of argument. In the present case he compares the traditions of judgement developed by the British and German enlightenments. The neglect of subsumption in favour of discrimination distinguishes the British theory from German tradition's neglect of discrimination in favour of subsumption. The former's tendency to give sensibility the properties of reason contrasts with the latter's granting of the properties of sensibility to reason. For Kant, neither tradition observes the 'transcendental distinction' of sensibility and intellect, and their cognates of discrimination and subsumption. Speaking specifically of Locke and Leibniz, but with the traditions which they represent in mind, he distinguishes his approach from theirs in the following terms:

> Instead of seeking in understanding and sensibility two completely distinct sources of representations which can only validly judge of things in conjunction [*Verknüpfung*], each of these great men holds on to one of the two, which in their opinion relates itself immediately to the thing in itself, the other doing nothing but to confuse or order the representations of the first.
>
> (1781; A271/B327)

In several other places Kant insists that the transcendental distinction must first be made through 'reflection', and then the two sources brought together in a controlled manner. While the place from which this distinction might be made is in question, its necessity is ineluctable. The two sources cannot be elided at the outset of any philosophical enquiry.

By first establishing the transcendental distinction and then dissolving it, the conformity of concept and intuition expressed in their universal and necessary conjunction is allowed to come forward. In the case of the British and German traditions, this conformity is forced back. The consequence of this repression is that judgement is reduced to violation; it is the forced conformity of concept and intuition. Both the British and the German traditions realize this consequence; both are founded on repressions of the transcendental distinction; both are methodologies of compulsion. However, the character of repression differs between the two traditions, as becomes clear when they are compared. Behind the two accounts of judgement is a repressed art of judgement, one which surfaces in the confrontation of their biases toward excessive discrimination and subsumption.

The consequences of the repression of the art of judgement by methodologies of compulsion become apparent in theoretical, practical and aesthetic philosophy. The repressions articulate different formations of modernity, different negotiations of the relation of production and legislation. The problems surface most insistently in the difficult relation of judgement and pleasure. In the *Critique of Judgement-Power* Kant strives to characterize a 'technic' or 'art' of judgement which would unite autonomy and autopoiesis, legislation and production. He proceeds by comparing the aporias of the British and German accounts of judgement. The basic problem consists in showing how the conformity of concept and intuition may be produced. This conformity was intimated in Smith's perception of a relation between judgement and production, but was unacknowledged by the majority of the theorists of taste and civil society. For them the providential laws of taste legitimated the pleasurable discriminations of the various senses, while the laws of production were applied with pain and compulsion.

The particular form which the theory of taste took in Britain stemmed from the realignment of state and civil society prepared in the revolutions of the seventeenth century. The new theory of civil society hammered out of the Revolution Principles not only reworked the relation between wealth and virtue, but did so on the basis of the faculty of taste. The outcome was a philosophy of taste which differed considerably from the German philosophy of aesthetics. While British philosophers elaborated a justification of a moral civil society, their German contemporaries concentrated on justifying the welfare absolutism of the 'police-state'. The providentially regulated, sensible discriminations of the British theory of taste were appropriate to its efforts to legitimate the harmonious working of civil society apart from the state and law. The German tradition, on the other hand, saw the common welfare as promoted by the legislative discipline of the state.

The British theory of taste is inseparable from the justification of civil society. It refuses Hobbes's and Mandeville's claims that civil society is marked by an irreconcilable clash of individual wills and desires which could only be brought into harmony by the action of the state. The theorists of civil society argue that sensible discriminations are legitimated by a providential logic, which ensures the good of the whole. They neither accepted the premiss that individual desires and interests were divergent, nor the conclusion that the state was required to legislate the common good. But the invocation of the logic of sensible discrimination involves taste in the equivocations of sense and idea, precisely the amphiboly Kant identifies in the first *Critique*.

The equivocation results from the source of the conformity of law and discrimination, or intellect and sensibility, being made into a *je ne sais quoi*. Any notion that this conformity might be produced remained unconsidered until Hume and Smith. The theorists of taste surrender production, part of the original formative activity of taste, to compulsion. This abstraction from production, the I know not how, has its counterpart in the obsession of the moral philosophers with sloth. In the realm of circulation the moral sense is king; but its writ does not run to production – here rules compulsion and the threat of slavery. Yet the goods on which the virtuous circulation of civil society depend cost effort to produce, and were the source of conflict, but this conflict is relegated from civil society. The producers are not recognized as part of civil society, their productive activity does not fall within the orbit of wealth and virtue. And yet the whole of the harmonious circulation of civil society depends on the *je ne sais quoi* of their effort.

It should be remembered that the theoretical alliance of wealth and virtue expresses an extension of aristocratic political domination to include commerce. Aristocratic theories of virtue did not recognize the productive classes as citizens. In Aristotle, productive and mercantile activity were not worthy activities for free citizens but work for slaves. In the eighteenth century mercantile activity was brought into the pale as a respectable activity for virtuous citizens, but productive activity remained excluded. The physical origins of the goods consumed or circulated was not a fit subject for discussion. The labour theory of property is an especially ironic example of this exclusion. The labour involved was either placed in an ahistorical limbo, or was done by one's servants; and as they were not citizens, their labour was of no political significance.

The theory of taste and civil society saw the source of the conformity to law of its discriminations to consist in a *je ne sais quoi*, a divinely established proportionality. It was providence which gave to its discriminations their necessary and universal validity. Such a position was for Kant an exaggeratedly one-sided account of a proper art of judgement, and its bias or disproportion had violent consequences. Instead of thinking of proportion as constituted through free self-legislation and production – the two elements of the activity of taste – the theory of taste surrendered both autonomy and production. Autonomy was surrendered to the tutelage of an unknown providence which directed individual interests to the general good through the leading strings of sensible pleasure, while production was relegated to pain and compulsion.

The theory of taste's conformity of law and discrimination, sense and reason, was a forced one. It lacked what Kant called 'transcendental reflection', remaining a symptomatic rehearsal of the violent conforming of reason and sensibility. Its symptoms, moreover, were dangerous, with implications beyond the sphere of theoretical and aesthetic philosophies. This was because judgement was an art applied in all areas of human culture, including its reflection on itself in critical philosophy. The question arises of how it is possible to achieve a transcendental reflection on judgement through judgement; how it is possible, as beings of sensibility and reason, to achieve 'in the first place a reflection, that is, a determination of the location to which the representations of things that are being compared belong, namely whether they are thought by the pure understanding or given in appearance by sensibility' (A269/B325).

Kant tackled the problem of the place from which to judge of judgement by appealing to the evidence of the 'bias of reason' evinced by the history of philosophy. By comparing the lack of reflection of the British tradition of taste with the German philosophy of aesthetics, he was able to achieve a point of vantage from which to judge of judgement. This was his procedure in the *Critique of Judgement-Power*; but for this to be appreciated it is necessary first of all to turn to the formation of aesthetic theory in Germany and its place within the ideology of the police-state.

3

Aesthetic and the Police-State

Polizei and Philosophy

No one can force me to be happy in the way in which he conceives of the welfare of others ... Under such a *paternal government* the subjects, as immature children who cannot distinguish what is truly useful or harmful to themselves, would be obliged to behave purely passively and to rely upon the judgement of the head of state as to how they *ought* to be happy, and upon his kindness in willing the happiness of all. Such a government is the greatest possible *despotism*.

Kant, *Religion Within the Limits of Reasons Alone*

Both Frederick the Great (1712–86) and Adam Smith saw the maximization of happiness as the purpose of government, and both described the four main functions of government as justice, revenue, arms, and police.[1] But they would have disagreed irreconcilably over how to employ these functions in maximizing happiness. Frederick justified his policy according to the tenets of the *Polizeiwissenschaft* which Smith was reformulating in terms of the theory of civil society. Smith's conclusion that happiness was maximized in a minimally regulated commercial society contrasted starkly with Frederick's conviction that the state should legislate the happiness of its citizens. For Frederick there was no civil society in which individuals could legislate for themselves and make their own judgements; this was the function of the state and its enlightened bureaucracy.

Frederick's position had a theoretical pedigree in Christian Wolff's (1679–1754) systematic philosophical justification of the ideology of the police-state.[2] Wolff's system intellectually and institutionally dominated German philosophy in the second third of the eighteenth century. It was the intellectual face of the Fredrickian state, determining the content and character of Frederick's law code, the *Allgemeines Landrecht des preussischen Staats* (ALR) promulgated in 1794. Yet the ALR proved to be the swansong for both the police-state and the Wolffian philosophy: the reforms of 1806 confirmed the transition from *Polizei* to *Rechtstaat* – the police to the legal-state – and precipitated the total eclipse of Wolffianism.

The Stein/Hardenberg reforms were the culmination of a movement which had been gathering momentum in the Prussian bureaucracy and army since the 1780s.[3] This movement took ideological inspiration from two sources: Smith's *Wealth of Nations* and Kant's critical philosophy.[4] Both sources were understood as fundamental critiques of the intellectual foundations of the police-state: Smith's work transformed police into political economy; while Kant's critical philosophy demolished the philosophical credentials of Wolffianism. His critique exposed the incoherence of the metaphysical principle of rational perfection which underlay the entire Wolffian system, and which was used to justify legislating the common welfare.

Kant's critique of Wolffianism cast it as the antipode of the British theory of taste. Where the latter privileged discriminative over subsumptive judgement, and sensibility over intellect, Wolffianism emphasized subsumption over discrimination and privileged intellect over sensibility. Neither thematized the relation between discrimination/sensibility and subsumption/intellect, and both repressed the difficulty in which Kant discerned the aporia of judgement and the amphiboly of the concepts of reflection. The Wolffians even appealed to the difficulties of judgement to legitimate their justification of the disciplinary laws of the police-state. Kant's critique of the Wolffians' rationalistic account of judgement was an encoded criticism of the political consequences which they drew from it.

The terms of Kant's critique were anticipated by Wolffians such as Gottsched, Bodmer and Breitinger, and Baumgarten, who recognized the problem of relating discriminative and subsumptive judgement and sensibility and intellect from within the philosophy of art. Baumgarten's invention of the science of aesthetic, and Herder's development of it into a philosophy of history, represent the most imaginative attempts to escape the philosophical and political consequences of Wolffianism before Kant. The character and implications of these critiques are best understood in the context of the philosophical articulation of *Polizei*, and the problems of judgement and sensibility associated with it.

Polizei as a practice long preceded its philosophical articulation in *Polizeiwissenschaft* and Wolffianism. The term *Polizei* is thought to originate in the translation of Aristotle's *Politics*, and was used to describe the administrative innovations of Burgundy and France in the fifteenth century, innovations which were transplanted to the Habsburg court and entered Germany as imperial police-ordinances. The ordinances were issued to meet immediate and specific social problems which were not covered by existing law or custom. The administrative technique of the police-ordinance, developed in the imperial chancellery and city councils in the early sixteenth century, was taken up by the territorial princes in the seventeenth, and applied to a wide variety of social problems.

The history of the territorial police-state may be divided into two phases separated by the Thirty Years War. The first phase is characterized by *ad hoc* reactive measures to pressing social problems, while the second, the era of the police-state proper, employed the police-ordinance as a means for achieving the consciously formulated ends of security and welfare. In the first phase, *Polizei* was reactive, maintaining the structure of manners which was threatened by the decay of the *Standestaat* (or estates-society) and the institutional crisis provoked by the Reformation. In the second phase the character of *Polizei* changed from being an improvised administrative technique into the structural principle of the absolutist order. *Polizei* became an active interventionist form of social regulation with a new ordering principle for social relations based on bureaucratic administration, militarization of social relations, and the unity of politics and economics. At the root of the new policy was a non-traditional legitimating principle: its reordering of social relations discarded the traditional legitimations of the 'good old law' and appealed instead to the equitable principle of the *gemeinen Nutz* or common welfare.[5]

The experience of Prussia exemplifies how *Polizei* was used to centralize the state at the expense of aristocratic and municipal civil society. The process of reordering the institutions of the *Standestaat* commenced in the middle of the seventeenth century with a series of fiscal manoeuvres by the Great Elector (1640–88) which divided the urban and rural classes and ensured undisputed supply for the standing army. This was then used, in Königsberg, to crush further resistance to the centralizing measures of the state. Frederick William I (1713–40) intensified this policy and constructed the 'Prussian Welfare State' – a military bureaucracy ruled by the monarch through an attenuated ministerial system.[6] The challenge to the privileges of the aristocracy and the cities issued in the establishment of a new social order based on bureaucratic administration according to *Polizeiwissenschaft*'s principle of the common welfare. This policy of disciplining the civilian population for their own welfare was continued by Frederick the Great, who took care to absorb aristocratic opposition into the Officer Corps and the bureaucracy (see Rosenberg 1958). An important part of the legitimacy of the police-state was the ideological justification represented by *Polizeiwissenschaft* and its philosophical analogues.

The transition from a reactive *ad hoc* to an active and systematic *Polizei* involved systematizing the administrative technique into a political philosophy. The systematization of *Polizei* was indebted to interpretative techniques developed in jurisprudence and philosophy. The centralized disciplining of society accomplished by the police-state in the eighteenth century would not have been possible without its theoretical articulation in *Polizeiwissenschaft* and bureaucratic cadres trained in this discipline; but the organization of the discipline itself was indebted to philosophy. However, the relation of *Polizei* and philosophy went far deeper than this picture of philosophy simply supplying the means of systematizing the diverse materials of *Polizeiwissenschaft* might suggest.

The basic principle of *Polizei* – the legal ordering of social relations according to the common welfare – was adopted by Leibniz (1646–1716) and Christian Wolff as the axiom of their 'rational jurisprudence'. Yet although *Polizeiwissenschaft* and the philosophically based rational jurisprudences of Leibniz and Wolff both sought to promote the common welfare through legislation, they differed in their expositions. *Polizeiwissenschaft* was a pragmatic discipline which organized its materials according to the administrative structure of the state, while rational jurisprudence organized its materials according to the tradition of practical philosophy. Nevertheless, Wolff's metaphysical justification of the axioms of *Polizei* played a significant role in legitimating the pragmatic efforts of the police ideologists.

The title given to the first university chairs of *Polizeiwissenschaft*, endowed in 1728 by Frederick William II at the 'new' Prussian universities of Halle and Frankfurt-an-der-Oder, reflects the pragmatic stamp of the discipline. The chairs in '*Cameralia, Oeconomica, and Polizeisachen*', were intended to train bureaucratic cadres in running the police-state. So much is apparent from an introduction to the subject written by one of the new professors, Justus Christoph Dithmar's (1677–1735) *Introduction to the Economic, Police and Cameral Sciences*. For Dithmar, 'cameralia' teaches the administration of the prince's personal domain; 'oeconomica', the general administration of production in town and country; and '*Polizeisachen*' how to preserve the *Wesen* of the state, being a commentary on a selection of Prussian police-ordinances. All three elements are understood as subdivisions of a general *Polizei*, which 'may rightly be called the life and soul of a state' (Small 1909, p. 228). *Polizei* unites the three administrative departments of the state in the end (*Zweck*) of promoting the common welfare.[7] For Dithmar, the purpose of cameralia is to show 'how the princely revenues may be raised, improved and applied for the maintenance of the community [*gemeines Wesen*]' (p. 227); oeconomia pursues the 'promotion of temporal happiness'; while *Polizei* teaches how to maintain the state 'with a view to general happiness, in good condition and order'. The task of *Polizeiwissenschaft* is to instruct bureaucrats in the administrative techniques required to maximize the 'common welfare'.[8]

The principle of the common welfare pragmatically developed in *Polizeiwissenschaft* was sublimated in the philosophical systems of Leibniz and Wolff. They allied the principle with one of metaphysical perfection, seeking to establish a 'rational jurisprudence' based on the notion of the perfection of being, which would unite logic, metaphysics, and law in a comprehensive philosophical system. Leibniz's conception of 'rational jurisprudence' changed considerably through his career; in many respects the later fragments mark a great departure from the perspective that determined his early political activity at the court of Mainz in the late 1660s. While there are traces of *Polizei* in his work (see Haase 1966, *passim*), they do not have the structural importance which they have in Wolff's system, which identifies *Polizei*'s principle of the common welfare with metaphysical perfection. Wolff grounded his entire system upon the principle of perfection, first establishing it logically and metaphysically, and then working it through as the *Grundnorm* of his political philosophy. His vision of the perfect society was that of a well-ordered police-state dedicated to maximizing the common welfare.

While Leibniz's philosophy provided a framework for the philosophy of the police-state – contemporaries invariably spoke of the 'Leibniz-Wolff Philosophy' – it also posed an immense challenge to it. Wolff appealed to Leibniz's thought to justify his system, but others appealed to it to justify their critiques of that system. Even Kant distinguished the first *Critique* from the 'Leibniz-Wolff Philosophy' by designating it an apologia for Leibniz. The reason for these differences lay in the development of Leibniz's thought, especially his understanding of perfection. His early view of perfection as the rational unity of a manifold changed in his later philosophy into the maximization of self-proportioning activity. His alignment of proportion and activity in the later theory of justice anticipates Kant's attempt to show that proportion was produced. However, it was Wolff's enormously influential system which cemented the alliance between the early enlightenment and *Polizei*. He maintains that clear perception is rational and sensible perception confused, insisting that the unity in manifold of perfection can only be perceived by reason. He transfers the distinction of clear and obscure perception from epistemology to political philosophy, mapping the distinction onto state and society. The citizens or matter of the state are formed for their common welfare according to the rational judgement of the monarch and his bureaucrats.

In spite of its iron-clad appearance – cross-referenced numbered paragraphs – Wolff's system was extremely fragile. Indeed, the dense interconnections between the parts of the system ensured that if one part fell into question, the whole structure was liable to collapse. The identification of rational perception and judgement with perfection was soon questioned, even within the Wolffian camp. The weak link was the judgement of art. The perception of perfection through a work of art was not rational, nor was its judgement subsumptive. In trying to develop an account of the judgement of art, the first generation of Wolffians undermined the entire system. Johann Christoph Gottsched (1700–66) sought a compromise in which the faculty of taste applied the laws laid down by reason; but his residual rationalism was abandoned by the Swiss critics, Bodmer and Breitinger, who insisted that the lower faculties had an immediate perception of perfection and could legislate for themselves.

The most far-reaching vindication of the autonomy of the lower faculty was made by Alexander Gottlieb Baumgarten (1714–62). His reconciliation of system and art postulated a form of knowledge which was perfect, but not rational. Given the brittleness of the Wolffian system, this concession threatened to break the equation of rationality and perfection. The implications of such a concession were far-reaching, and were embraced by Baumgarten in his theoretical philosophy. There was no objection to perfection being mediated irrationally; nor should judgement be confined to the subsumption of a sensible manifold under a rational unity. This development implied a critique of Wolff's political philosophy which identified rationality with the police-state. A mode of judgement was possible which, while neither rational nor the prerogative of the state, was nevertheless perfect. It followed that civil society would be able to order its own welfare, and not be subsumed beneath the rational legislation of the state and its bureaucracy. This implication was not developed by Baumgarten in his practical philosophy, where he remained an orthodox Wolffian. However, there are indications in the unfinished *Aesthetica* that he was extending his theoretical insights to practical philosophy. It was not fortuitous that Herder (1744–1803) presented his extremely radical claim for human autonomy and self-production or 'culture' in terms of a development of Baumgarten's aesthetic.

By the end of Frederick's reign Prussia had entered a severe economic, political, and cultural crisis which led, in the wake of military defeat, to the dismantling of the police-state in 1806. The responsibility for the failure of the police-state did not only lie with external, conjunctural difficulties, but within *Polizeiwissenschaft* itself. The modernizing principle of the 'common welfare' was given an archaic institutional embodiment in a grotesque inflation of the domestic relations within a household. The well-ordered police-state was conceived as a giant *oikos* with an omniscient *Landesvater* at its head, supervising in detail the activities of his servants and keeping his subjects in tutelage, treating them as the children of the house. This patriarchal model of social organization was axiomatic to *Polizeiwissenschaft* and the practice of the police-state. It contrasts sharply with the British attempt to elaborate a new model of social relations based on market instead of household, and on the separation rather than unification of state and civil society.

The later German enlightenment rebelled against what Kant cryptically described as the 'self-imposed tutelage' of the police-state. Following the increasingly apparent ossification of the Prussian police-state, the ideology of the common welfare and the paternalism of the state were rejected. The theoretical deconstruction of this ideology mounted by Wolff's early critics was extended to political philosophy by Herder and Kant. They refused the Wolffian notion of perfection, seeing the unity in a manifold as a product of autonomous activity. Their insistence on the free political judgement of the citizen replaced Wolff's view that judgement is the responsibility of the sovereign or *Landesvater*. The thoroughness of this critique is reflected in Kant's attack upon Wolff's notion of perfection in each of the three *Critiques*: the first criticizes the use of the principle of perfection in metaphysics; the second undoes the principle of practical perfection; while the third severs the vital conjunction of perfection and pleasure. The critique of Wolff's notion of perfection was also the critique of the police-state, against which Kant proposed the self-legislation of freedom in a theory of culture anticipating the reform of the police-state in 1806.

Rational Jurisprudence

> The Critique of Pure Reason can thus be seen as the genuine
> apology for Leibniz.
>
> Kant, *On A Discovery*

'Rational Jurisprudence' was Leibniz's title for his lifelong ambition
to establish a metaphysically grounded theory of justice. The
project consisted in the *reconcinnation* of law and the *emendation* of
metaphysics.[9] The first was the modernization and codification of
Roman law according to the rational method, while the second was
directed toward resolving the differences between the traditional
Aristotelean metaphysics of the natural law tradition and the
voluntaristic nominalism of modern rights theory. The change in
Leibniz's conception of the metaphysical foundation of justice between
his early and late writings was consequential for the development of
German philosophy in the following century. His early formal account
of justice as a proportion between such contraries as part/whole,
individual/universal, and manifold/unity was systematized by Christian
Wolff, while his later dynamic account, which saw justice as a
proportion between activity and passivity, was adopted by Herder and
Kant in their critiques of Wolffianism.

The aim of Rational Jurisprudence is the fusion of metaphysical
perfection, justice, and pleasure. In its first version dating from the
end of the 1660s, perfection is seen as unity in a manifold, and
justice as a proportion between part and whole, or individual and
universal. The relation of proportion and pleasure is extremely
problematic at this stage because pleasure rests on proportion, yet
also exceeds it. The excess of pleasure over proportion led Leibniz
to inquire, in later versions of the Rational Jurisprudence, into the
production of proportion through culture, the proportion being no
longer that of part and whole, but of activity and passivity.
This development changed the entire character of the Rational
Jurisprudence, and undermined Leibniz's persistent attempts to align
it with the ethos of the police-state.

The term 'Rational Jurisprudence' first appears in Leibniz's
correspondence during his stay at the court of Mainz in the late
1660s.[10] As part of his diplomatic work in the strategically important
Ecclesiastical Principality, Leibniz drafted memoranda on the severe
economic and institutional crisis of the Empire and the deterioration
in international relations. His *Securitas Publica* (1670) diagnosed the
illness of the ailing body politic of the Empire, and recommended a

strict regimen of police-state measures for its cure.[11] These included the reassertion of imperial authority through the establishment of a standing army, a central treasury, and the reform of the representative institutions of the Estates – precisely the treatment being administered by the Great Elector in the Prussian territories.

The modernization of imperial legal institutions was the most important factor in the consolidation of central authority. In a letter to the Emperor of August 1671, Leibniz proposed to reform the administration of justice by producing a short, rationally organized code of the contemporary Roman law used in the imperial courts. He described his code as

> a quintessence of clear and brief laws, and their *Iustificatio*. This quintessence of Roman laws, or *Elementa Iuris Romani hodieque attendi brevis et certi*, may consist in one sole Table the size of a large Dutch land-chart, wherein also all chief rules are comprised, so that from their *Combination* all possible questions can be decided, and the *fundamenta* of all *actiones, exceptiones, replicae* etc., can be directly pointed out as *imitamine Edicti perpetui novi*; nor have such plans ever been attempted before, let alone accomplished.
>
> (cited in Meyer 1952, p. 174)

The specific political reforms proposed by Leibniz were inseparable from his broader intellectual concerns. The law reform project formed the reconcinnation part of the Rational Jurisprudence, complementing the section on the metaphysical foundations of justice. In letters to Prince Johann Friedrich von Braunschweig-Luneberg and to Antoine Arnauld in 1671, Leibniz describes his Rational Jurisprudence as comprising two works, a 'chart' containing the essence of law, and a '*kleines Werk*' on the 'Elements of Natural Law'. He completed neither, and only a few studies for the law reform project and a few drafts of the '*kleines Werk*' have survived. The former, including the programmatic *Ratio Corporis Juris Reconcinnandi* of 1668, do not add much to what is known of the project from the correspondence. But enough has survived of the '*kleines Werk*' to permit a reconstruction of Leibniz's early account of justice. This not only enables us to understand the relation of his metaphysics of justice to his work in law reform, but also to recognize how far he reworked his theory of justice following the radical change in his metaphysics during the crucial stay in Paris of the early 1670s.

The *Akademie Ausgabe* (vol. VI/2, section 12) contains six surviving fragments from the projected '*kleines Werk*' on the elements of natural law. The first is a series of annotations on Grotius, and the second and third fragments are a series of definitions of justice and equity. The fourth and most finished fragment is an incomplete draft of the projected Part I, while the fifth and sixth fragments are sizable drafts of Part II of the book. It is the last three fragments, but especially the fourth, which are most significant for Leibniz's early theory of justice. The editors of the *Akademie Ausgabe* have pointed out references to other of Leibniz's writings in these fragments: one to his *Preface to an Edition of Nizolius* of 1670 in the fourth, and another to the *New Physical Hypothesis* of 1671 in the sixth fragment. The fifth fragment also deploys modalities of combination taken from the 1666 *Art of Combination*. These references couch Leibniz's early theory of justice in the intellectual matrix of his early metaphysics.

Leibniz claimed in his letter to Johann Friedrich that his '*kleines Werk*' would explain the important questions of the '*Juris Gentium und publicii*' to any rational person who followed its method. From fragments five and six this method appears to be the art of combination, although it is apparent that Leibniz's ambitions for his method exceed the reconcinnation of Roman law. Through definitions, theorems and various modalities of combination he would derive a model of a just society. The basis of this society is a notion of justice as objective harmony, administered by a law code with the flexibility of a logarithmic table. The theory of justice informing these fragments was established in the fourth of the surviving fragments – *The Elements of Natural Law* – which represents Leibniz's attempt to ground justice in terms of his early metaphysics.

The core of the *Elements* is a definition of happiness:

> It is obvious that the happiness of mankind consists in two things – to have the power, as far as it is permitted, to do what it wills and to know what, from the nature of things, ought to be willed. Of these, mankind has almost achieved the former; as to the latter, it has failed in that it is particularly impotent with respect to itself.
>
> (1670–1; p. 131)

Or, to say the same in the 'tragic style': 'Now that we are conquerors of the world, there assuredly remains an enemy within us; everything is clear to man but man, the body to the mind, and the mind to itself' (p. 132). Happiness eludes us because political self-control has not matched the progress of control over nature, a pre-enlightenment statement of the 'dialectic of enlightenment'. In other words, the development of the productive relation to nature has not been matched by one in law and politics:

> the blame for the imperfection of natural science must fall
> back upon the public, since they could improve it if everyone
> wished it, and if individuals wished that all should wish it in
> general? All will not do together, however, what individuals
> can and will do, unless the matter is attacked in the right way
> and on the basis of the secrets of true politics [*ex verae politicae
> arcanis*], by those to whom it is given to make themselves happy
> through this part.
>
> (p. 132)

Human happiness is to be promoted through a 'true politics', the
key to which is the 'Rational Jurisprudence' or 'that science which
shows how individuals should give way to the good of all if they wish
happiness to revert to themselves, increased as by a rebound'
(pp. 132–3).

The foundation of the Rational Jurisprudence or 'science of
happiness' – the 'basis of the secrets of true politics' which will unite
and augment private and public welfare – is an objective definition
of justice. This runs as follows:

> For since justice consists in a kind of congruity and proportional-
> ity, we can understand that something is just even if there is
> no one who practices it or upon whom it is practiced. Just so
> the relations of numbers are true even if there were no one
> to count and nothing to be counted, and we can predict that a
> house will be beautiful, a machine efficient, or a commonwealth
> happy, if it comes into being, even if it should never do so.
>
> (p. 133)

Here Leibniz introduces the metaphysical basis of his jurisprudence:
the objectivity of justice is a 'kind of congruity and proportionality',
but what kind? The answer to this question is to be found in Leibniz's
account of the objective congruity and proportionality of the individual
and the universal developed in the early metaphysical writings. Since
the *Elements* presuppose this account, a digression from the theory
of justice to Leibniz's early metaphysics of proportionality is
unavoidable.

One of the main motivations of Leibniz's early metaphysical
thinking was the critique of the nominalistic foundation of modern
philosophy and its voluntaristic implications for the theory of justice.
This is clearly expressed in the *Preface to an Edition of Nizolius* where

Leibniz distinguishes his position from those of Hobbes and other contemporary philosophers. He points to Hobbes's drawing of voluntaristic conclusions from nominalist premises as an example of the dangers of the nominalism:

> Occam himself was not more nominalistic than is Thomas Hobbes now, though I confess that Hobbes seems to me to be a super-nominalist. For not content like the nominalists, to reduce universals to names, he says that the truth of things itself consists in names and what is more, that it depends on human will, because truth allegedly depends on the definitions of terms, and definitions depend on the human will.
>
> (1670; p. 128)

Hobbes is not alone in adopting a nominalist position, 'The same thing is true of all the reformers of philosophy today; if they are not super-nominalists, they are almost all nominalists' (p. 128). The difference between Hobbes's nominalism and the nominalism of the 'reformers of philosophy' – a term for the Cartesians – lies in the agent of the will: for Hobbes human will is fundamental; for the Cartesians, the will of God.

Leibniz argues against the nominalist premiss of both human and divine forms of voluntarist argument; his argument for a real definition rests on the existence of an objective order of relations, testified by arithmetic: 'In arithmetic, and in other disciplines as well, truths remain the same even if notations are changed, and it does not matter whether a decimal or duodecimal number system is used' (p. 128). Nizolius's argument for the nominal status of universals is criticized with reference to the objective relations of part and whole expressed in a number system: 'He tries to convince us that a universal is nothing more than all singulars taken simultaneously and collectively and that when I say, "Every man is an animal", the meaning is that all men are animals. This is indeed true, but it does not follow that universals are collective wholes' (p. 128). Leibniz refuses to accept Nizolius's nominalist claim that a universal is simply a collection of singulars:

> you are mistaken, Nizolius. The discrete whole contains another genus besides the collective, namely, the distributive ... The error of Nizolius is, in truth, no small one, for it conceals an important consequence. If universals were nothing but collections of individuals, it would follow that we could attain no knowledge through demonstration – a conclusion which

Nizolius actually draws – but only through collecting individuals or by induction. But on this basis knowledge would straightway be made impossible, and the skeptics would be victorious. For perfectly universal propositions can never be established on this basis because you are never certain in induction that all individuals have been considered. You must always stop at the proposition that all the cases which I have experienced are so. But since, then, no true universality is possible, it will always remain possible that countless other cases which you have examined are different.

(p. 129)

If a collection of singulars remains incomplete, there can be no orderly judgement or demonstrative knowledge. But Leibniz evades these 'Humean' objections by recasting the relation of universal and individual in terms of part and whole united by an objective distributive principle. Demonstrative knowledge is possible through the generalization of the 'distributive principle'. The question how part and whole are related through the 'distributive principle' now becomes central to Leibniz's metaphysics.

In the *Art of Combination* the 'distributive principle' is called 'union': 'In union the things between which there is this relation are called parts, and taken together with their union, a whole' (1666; p. 76). Leibniz's critique of nominalism requires that 'union' be not simply a subjective rule for the composition of part and whole, but a designation of their objective relation. The definition of union as an objective relation of part and whole, their proportionality, tempts Leibniz to identify metaphysics and mathematics. In the *Art of Combination* the number system denotes a relation which is prior to the distinction of part and whole; number is an 'incorporeal figure' which 'arises from union' and denotes a relation prior to the existence of individual beings: 'For number is a kind of incorporeal figure as it were [*quasi figura quaedem incorporea*], which arises from the union of any being whatever; for example, God, an angel, a man, and motion taken together are four' (p. 77). Leibniz gives the *relation* of beings, whether corporeal or incorporeal, priority over their existence. Number figures the relation of beings, expressed in their union, and is accordingly an index of metaphysical relation: 'Since number is therefore something of greatest universality [*quiddam universalissimum*], it rightly belongs to metaphysics, if you take metaphysics to be the science of those properties which are common to all classes of beings' (p. 77). Parts are brought into a whole through the disclosure of their relation, the rule of their composition, or 'union', being figured in terms of mathematical relation.

Metaphysics and mathematics form a unified science in which metaphysics considers configured being, the part and the whole, while mathematics considers the possibilities of configuration (variation) according to a particular union. This unification of metaphysics and mathematics was Leibniz's 'mother of invention'. The premiss that wholes are composed of parts *and* their relation, along with the conclusion that it was possible to determine the number of possible variations of a whole had important implications for many branches of knowledge. It enabled Leibniz to show not only that an existing body of knowledge was imperfect, but also how to perfect it through exhibiting relations of parts and wholes potential but unacknowledged in any given body of knowledge.

Leibniz applied the method of the *Art of Combination* to outlining a rational legal system. This step marked a revolution in jurisprudence which, prior to Leibniz, had no conception of a system of law which might be restructured and supplemented according to rational principles. Applying the method to jurisprudence permitted Leibniz to demonstrate the existence of 'gaps' in a legal system. Accordingly, the first application of the method in the *Art of Combination* concerns a topic in Roman law. Analysing the parties to a contract of mandate yields the mandator, the mandatory, and a third party, and the art of combination tells us that there are seven complexions of three things (in Leibniz's terms three '1nions', three 'com2nations', one 'con3nation'). Yet the *Corpus iuris* offers only five of the seven possible combinations, leaving gaps in the law. While one combination can be disqualified, 'There remain thus six classes. Why they kept only five, omitting the con3nation, I do not know' (1666; p. 81). By approaching the law of mandate as a system of possible combinations, Leibniz was able to show that the law was incomplete.

In the eighth application of the *Art of Combination* Leibniz extends the reform of a discrete area of law to that of an entire legal system. Here he proposes to use the *art* to establish a gapless legal system which would foresee all possible cases and remove any possibility of sovereign or judicial arbitrariness:

For one cannot always wait for the lawmaker when a case arises, and it is more prudent to set up the best possible laws without defects, from the first, than to intrust their restriction and correction to fortune; not to mention the fact that in any

state whatsoever, a judicial matter is the better treated, the less
it is left to the decision of the judge.

(p. 82)

The law as a whole may be reduced to its elements and recombined
into a comprehensive and rational system. The execution of judgement
according to this system is a matter of rational administration. The
judge will apply the law to the case before him by establishing which
of the variations of the complexions is represented by the case. When
the union or distribution of possible cases is known it will be possible
to locate the particular case on the 'dutch land-chart' of all possible
cases. The legal system as a whole will be able to anticipate all
possible cases or combinations that may come before it.

The method of judgement and invention represented by the *Art
of Combination* underlies both parts of the Rational Jurisprudence.
The reduction of a complex whole to its elements and complexions
informs the reconcinnation of Roman law, while the metaphysics of
relation underlying the method is used to found the theory of justice
in the 'Elements of Natural Law'. Returning to where we left that
text, at the definition of justice as 'a kind of congruity and
proportionality' (1670–1; p. 133), it is now possible to specify what
kind of congruity or proportionality is intended. The definition of
justice may be rephrased in the language of Leibniz's early metaphysics
as: justice is the relation of congruity or proportionality between
whole and part, as configured by a 'distributive principle' or 'union'
between individual utility and the good of the whole. With this, the
focus of enquiry shifts from the *kind* of congruity and proportionality
between part and whole to the *nature* of their 'union'. In the letter
to Arnauld, Leibniz explains the 'distributive principle' or 'union'
through a crude analogy with the operation of multiplication; but he
was not satisfied with subsuming human action under simple
mathematical operations. He sought a 'union' which would deliver
the congruity and proportion of individual free will with the collective
good, and this he found in the concept of pleasure.

Leibniz opens his definition of justice by stating the condition that
individual and collective goods are inextricable: 'From the beginning,
however, both our own good and that of others are involved in the
question of right' (1670–1; p. 133). Unfortunately, it is difficult to
see how the two goods can be related except through an instrumental
means/end relation: 'But, you ask, how is it possible that the good
of others should be the same as our own and yet sought for its own
sake? For otherwise the good of others can be our own good only
as means, not as end' (p. 136). It is necessary to find a third term

or 'distributive principle' which will unite part and whole, individual good and the good of all, without preferring one over the other. Leibniz's response to the above question subordinates both individual good and the good of the whole to the pleasant: 'I reply on the contrary that it [the good of others] is also an end, something sought for its own sake, when it is pleasant' (p. 136).

Pleasure is the 'union' which ensures the 'congruity and proportion' of individual utility and the good of the whole. Leibniz figures the union through pleasure by the catoptrical analogies of 'double refraction' and 'double reflection':

> But as a double refraction can occur in vision, once in the lens of the eye and once in the lens of a tube, the latter increasing the vision of the former, so there is a double reflection in thinking. For every mind is something like a mirror, and one mirror is in our mind, another in the mind of someone else. So if there are many mirrors, that is, many minds recognizing our goods, there will be a greater light, the mirrors blending the light not only in the eye but also among each other.
>
> (p. 137)

The individual mirror receives an image transmitted through the order of mirrors, to which it contributes by reflecting it again, until eventually the distinction of individual and universal is overcome in a blaze of mutually reflecting glory.[12] Pleasure is both the condition for the reflection, the order of mirrors, and its outcome, the individual experience of pleasure. The difficult union of these two aspects is expressed in Leibniz's chiastic definition of pleasure: 'For everything pleasant is sought for its own sake, and whatever is sought for its own sake is pleasant; all other things are sought because of the pleasure they give or conserve or whose contrary they destroy' (p. 136). Since pleasure is the union which manifests an objective relation between the individual and the universal, it may be understood from either standpoint. From the individual standpoint 'whatever is sought for its own sake is pleasant' while from the universal standpoint 'everything pleasant is sought for its own sake'. But the object sought 'for its own sake' is already constituted as pleasant; for what is sought is pleasant, but the pleasant is constituted by everything which is sought for its own sake. Yet the totality of 'everything pleasant' is not a nominalist universal abstracted from things which have been found to be pleasant. The constitution of the pleasant somewhere between individual and universal pleasures is thought in terms of a system of mirrors which augment pleasure in transmitting it. Although Leibniz's metaphor anticipates Hume's, and shares its difficulty of relating individual and reflected pleasure, he refuses to separate individual and universal goods or 'utilities', but insists on their relation.[13]

The difficulties with Leibniz's pleasure principle follow from his early metaphysic of relation which united part and whole through a distributive principle. Leibniz sought to establish pleasure as a distributive principle which would simultaneously order individuals into a whole and yet be constituted by those individuals: individual pleasures are qualitatively defined by the pleasure of the whole which in its turn is constituted by the sum of individual pleasures. Leibniz illustrated this phenomena, which he later described as simultaneous 'production and being produced', through the analogy of the 'double reflection' of an individual mirror within a system of mirrors. He later discarded this metaphor of relation and rethought the excess or augmentation involved in the double reflection of parts and whole – constituting and being constituted into an order – in terms of action and passion. This revision was possible only in the wake of his spectacular progress in mathematics during his stay in Paris (1672–6), which fundamentally altered his view of the relation of quantity and quality. One of the consequences of his confrontation with avant-garde mathematics in Paris was the rejection of his early number theory which considered the relation of number and the number system in terms of part and *whole*. His new understanding of infinity and the infinitesimal led to a revision of the extensive metaphysic of part and whole in the direction of an intensive metaphysic of action and passion.

The extent of this revision is apparent in the difference between Leibniz's early and late philosophy. The difference is underlined in the 1695 *Specimen Dynamicum*'s self-criticism of the metaphysics underlying the theory of motion and body proposed earlier in the *New Physical Hypothesis* (1670). Leibniz concluded that

besides purely mathematical principles subject to the imagination, there must be admitted certain metaphysical principles perceptible only by the mind and that a certain higher and so to speak, formal principle must be added to that of material mass, since all the truths about corporeal things cannot be derived from logical and geometrical axioms alone, namely, those of great and small, whole and part, figure and situation, but that there must be added those of cause and effect, action

and passion, in order to give a reasonable account of the order
of things.

(1695a; p. 441)

The geometrical axioms must be supplemented by dynamic principles,
a supplement which entails adding dynamic principles of demonstration to analytical demonstrations which rest on the inclusion of
the predicate in the subject. This distinction, recognized by Kant as
an anticipation of his distinction of analytic and synthetic judgements,
underlies Leibniz's further distinction of contingent and necessary
truths, along with their principles of contradiction and sufficient
reason. It rests on a metaphysics of culture which thematizes the
production and being produced of both subject and substance in
terms of the negotiation of its active and passive powers.

Leibniz's account of culture extends his view of knowledge as the
subsumption of parts under a whole or the unification of a manifold,
into the production by a subject of the objects of knowledge and the
recognition of this productive activity. The distinction between
perception and apperception central to both the *New Essays on Human
Understanding* (1703–5) and the *Monadology* (1714) is reformulated in
terms of active and passive knowledge. There is a continuum between
the passive perception of the dispersed variety of things and their
apperceptive unification; between the perceived *petit perceptiones* and
the apperceived clear thoughts. The manifold of perception is a
passive disposition of a subject's power, while its unification through
apperception is active; 'Substances have metaphysical matter or
passive power insofar as they express something confusedly; active
insofar as they express it distinctly' (c. 1690a; p. 365). The relation
between unity and manifold is no longer thought in terms of part
and whole, but in terms of activity and passivity. This change shifts
the metaphor of unification from the inclusion of parts in a whole
through reflection to an active/passive production. Consciousness is
the *activity* of consciousness on the materials of perception, and
given that the materials of perception are already conformed to
consciousness, already present in the subject, consciousness is the
process of self-formation. Leibniz compares this process to the work
of a sculptor, describing it as the perfection of culture.

The implications for Rational Jurisprudence of translating the
discourse of whole and part, or unity and manifold, into one of
activity and passivity are worked through in the metaphysical and
juristic writings of the 1690s. The new metaphysical definition of
perfection appears in the fragment *On Wisdom* (mid to late 1690s),
where it consists in 'any elevation of being . . . which shows itself in

a great freedom of power and action, since all being consists in a kind of power; and the greater the power, the higher and freer the being' (c. 1690b; p. 426). Perfection is no longer a 'kind of proportionality' between part and whole but a negotiation of activity and passivity. The relation between such contraries as manifold and unity, individual and universal, is thought in terms of active and passive dispositions of power. The proportion or harmony of one and many, the core of Leibniz's identification of justice and love, consists in the power to reveal unity in and through plurality:

> The greater any power is, moreover, the more there is found in it the many revealed through the one and in the one, in that the one rules many outside of itself and represents them in itself. Now unity in plurality is nothing but harmony, and since any particular being agrees with one rather than another being, there flows from this harmony the order from which beauty arises, and beauty awakens love.
>
> (c. 1690b; p. 426)

The 'in and through' of unity in plurality denotes the active and passive dispositions of power. It consists in the negotiation of perception – the representation of the many – with apperception – the revelation of their unity; in this negotiation the subject produces plurality *in* its objects, and comes to recognize its unity *through* them. The negotiation of activity and passivity – the monad – is located on a continuum stretching from pure passivity to pure activity. Such continuity makes it possible for Leibniz to claim that 'happiness, pleasure, love, perfection, being, power, freedom, harmony, order, and beauty are all tied to each other, a truth which is rightly perceived by few' (p. 426). They are all aspects of a dynamic perfection, or ascent of the continuum through activity culturing its passivity and clarifying its representations. Perfection is not a state, but a work or elevation of being. Beauty, love and happiness are stages of the work of recognizing the order or harmony between activity and passivity. The work of recognition is Leibniz's answer to the difficulty of aligning knowledge and will stated at the outset of his early Rational Jurisprudence. Then his definition of right as 'the power to do what is just' – harmonizing will and knowledge – leaves the difficulty unresolved, since nothing prevents the 'just' from being defined voluntaristically as the 'power to do'. In the later metaphysics of perfection, will and knowledge are related in a reciprocal culturing wherein *conatus* and representation are inseparable phenomena of the negotiation of activity and passivity which constitutes the universal process of self-cultivation or perfection.

The process of cultivation replaces the 'unions' and 'distributive principles' of the early Rational Jurisprudence as the metaphysical foundation of justice. The essay *On the Radical Origination of Things* (1697) departs from the same disequilibrium of control over nature and self-control diagnosed in the *Elements of Natural Law* as the chief impediment to happiness. But this disequilibrium is now placed in the context of culture as a negotiation of activity and passivity. The 'radical origination' of things refers to the activity which perpetually produces things, but which misrecognizes itself when it sees its products as 'having been' produced: 'It is evident, however, that existing things are continuously issuing from this source and are being produced and have been produced by it, since no reason appears why one state of the world should issue from it rather than another, that of yesterday's rather than today's' (1697; p. 489). The activity of bringing forth things is accompanied by a passive experience of them as things which are given. There is a pre-established harmony between the active and the passive dispositions of consciousness, but not the extensive, structural proportion imagined by Wolff and criticized by Kant. The disposition of power provides a new foundation for Rational Jurisprudence's equation of social and technical progress. Where Leibniz previously saw a contradiction between the advance in human control over nature and stagnation of human self-legislation, he now regards the imbalance as part of culture's negotiation. The emphasis on reciprocal activity and passivity leads to a change in the conception of justice: it is no longer seen as an objective proportion, but is the maximization of activity, in other words – perfection.

The 'secret of a true politics' explored in the *Elements of Natural Law* is revisited in the later work. Justice is no longer a congruity or proportion of whole and part, but a maximization of a dynamic perfection. But the 'true politics' of this maximization is still expressed in the vocabulary of the police-state ('best-ordered', 'common good'):

> For we must recognize that just as care is taken in the best-ordered republic that individuals shall fare as well as possible, so the universe would not be perfect enough unless as much care is shown for individuals as is consistent with the universal harmony. No better measure for this matter can be set up than the law of justice itself, which dictates that each one shall take part in the perfection of the universe and his own happiness according to the measure of his own virtue and the degree to which his will is moved toward the common good.
>
> (p. 490)

Perfection consists in technical and social cultivation, but although

Leibniz sees no limit to technical cultivation – 'a great part of our earth has now received cultivation and will receive it more and more' (p. 491) – he arrests social cultivation at the level of the police-state. His mature Rational Jurisprudence still comprises the codification of Roman law and the statement of an equitable definition of justice which will regulate society. But the content of the definition of justice and its constituent elements of pleasure, the good, beauty, and love has changed considerably with the revision of the metaphysics underlying them.

Here, as in the *Elements of Natural Law*, Leibniz's definition of justice still rests on pleasure, but pleasure is now understood as a 'knowledge' or 'feeling' of perfection: 'Pleasure is a knowledge or feeling of perfection, not only in ourselves, but also in others, for in this way some further perfection is aroused in us' (c. 1694–8; p. 83). Since perfection consists in the enhancement of activity, pleasure must be the experience of this enhancement. It is stimulated by relating to degrees of perfection in objects and in others; indeed the two relations cannot properly be distinguished:

> We do not always observe wherein the perfection of pleasing things consists, or what kind of perfection within ourselves they serve, yet our feelings [*Gemüth*] perceive it, even though our understanding does not. We commonly say, 'There is something I know not what, that pleases me in the matter.' This we call 'sympathy'. But those who seek the causes of things will usually find a ground for this and understand that there is something at the bottom of the matter which, though unnoticed, really appeals to us.
>
> (c. 1690b; p. 425)

The *je ne sais quoi* in the perfection of pleasing things, and in ourselves, was figured in the *Elements of Natural Law* by the 'double reflection' in a system of mirrors. The difficult relation of pleasure in an object and the pleasure of reflection is now seen to have a 'ground' which is unnoticed, but nevertheless appeals to us through pleasure. This is the negotiation of activity and passivity: the pleasure in an object arises from an acknowledgement that it has been brought before us by our activity. A work of art 'creates a sympathetic echo in us, to which our animal spirits respond' (p. 426); the sympathetic acknowledgement promotes our activity, and so increases our perfection.

The enhancement of our activity through the acknowledgement that an object has been brought forward by our activity is a special case of the mutual enhancement of activity in love. Here increase in activity is reciprocal and incremental, for if pleasure in the perfection of others enhances our own, and if 'To love is to find pleasure in the perfection of another' (1694–8; p. 83), then finding pleasure in the perfection of another enhances our activity and gives pleasure to the other by enhancing their own. The reciprocal augmentation of individual and universal pleasures achieved through reflection in the early chiasmus is now described in terms of the increase in power and activity following the enjoyment of perfection.

The reciprocity of pleasure in the mutual recognition of love is felicity, and the science of achieving felicity is wisdom. From these elements, Leibniz proposes a definition of justice which, while formally similar to the earlier definition, has a different metaphysical grounding: 'Justice is charity or a habit of loving conformed to wisdom' (p. 83). Justice is equated with love in the enhancement of activity through the recognition of others, either in themselves or in the products of their activity. However, Leibniz does not use this definition of justice to expand the notion of the general welfare or happiness of human societies. Instead, when he classifies societies in the fragments *On Natural Law* and *Divisio Societatum*, the principle of maximizing activity is articulated in terms of the police-state notions of the common welfare.

In the first fragment Leibniz defines a society as 'a union of different men for a common purpose' (1693–1700b; p. 428), and ranks societies according to their purpose. At the peak of the hierarchy is 'The most *perfect society* . . . that whose purpose is the general and supreme happiness' (p. 428). The most perfect spiritual society is the society of the holy, while the most perfect temporal society is civil society, whose 'purpose is temporal welfare'. In the *Divisio Societatum* Leibniz employs a different method of division, but arrives at the same conclusion that civil society is based on the common welfare. He classifies societies as equal or unequal according to the relation between ruler and subjects, and limited or unlimited according to their purpose: 'An unlimited society concerns the whole life and the common good [*gemeine Beste*]. A limited society concerns certain subjects, for example trade and commerce, navigation, warfare and travel' (1693–1700c; p. 429). The highest form of society is unlimited and equal, combining the equal relation of love with the common welfare. This is the society of love in which justice and the maximization of activity are the same. Such a society would only be possible 'If everything in the world were arranged in the most perfect way' (p. 430) and in this case ours is not the best of all possible worlds. The next best society is the unlimited, unequal society, which closely resembles the patriarchal police-state:

An unlimited unequal society exists between rulers and subjects. Such rule occurs for the sake either of improvement or conservation. If it is for the sake of improvement, it really takes place between parents and children, or whom we so rear that they receive their welfare from us, and are under our rule alone ... But if such rule [*Regierung*] is for the sake of conservation, it exists between master and servant and consists in the master assuring the servant's welfare, while the servant submits to the master's rule.

(p. 429)

The enhancement of activity in mutual recognition is impractical, and in its place Leibniz proposes the police-state's care for the welfare of its subjects at the price of their obedience.

Leibniz's account of the degrees of right also arrives at the princely, absolutist, unlimited, unequal society in which the *Landesvater* promotes the welfare of his childlike subjects. Leibniz derives the validity of Ulpian's three degrees of right – strict right, equity, and piety – from metaphysical perfection as translated into the principle of the common welfare. In the preface to the *Codex Iuris Gentium* (1693) he identifies strict right with Aristotelean commutative justice and the Grotian *facultas* (Pufendorf's perfect right), and equity with distributive justice and the *aptitudo* (imperfect right). Unlike Hutcheson, who defended Pufendorf's claim that imperfect rights were supported by moral obligation, Leibniz attributes to them the character of legal obligation. His model for such rights is the system of police or 'political' laws[14] promoting the common welfare: 'it is here that the political laws of a state belong, which assure the happiness of its subjects and make it possible that those who had a merely moral claim acquire a legal claim; that is, that they become able to demand what it is equitable for others to perform' (p. 172). The moral claim is insufficient to ensure happiness and must be backed by the force of legal obligation. This conclusion differs considerably from the British theorists of civil society who maintained that happiness would be maximized through the moral sense. For Leibniz, the 'unlimited and equal' civil society governed purely by moral sense was a utopia; the best possible state attainable in this world is the 'unlimited and unequal' one, where the maximization of happiness is achieved through the police legislation of an enlightened monarch.

The maximization of happiness remained the object of both the early and the later versions of the Rational Jurisprudence. Both versions agreed that the best means for achieving happiness was through the codification of law according to an objective concept of justice by an absolute monarch. The object of codification was not simply to provide a legal framework for dispute settlement, but to maximize happiness or the common welfare. In Leibniz's version of rights theory the basic natural right was not a right to property or security but to happiness. This right was based on objective justice, and was not the nominalist consequence of superior power maintained by Hobbes, nor the consequence of some innate appetite for society. Both these positions led to a distinction between law and morality, between strict justice and equity which Leibniz refused to accept, insisting instead on the legislative promotion of the right to happiness.

The credibility of Leibniz's revision of rights theory depended on the plausibility of his metaphysical account of justice. The weakness of the early version of the Rational Jurisprudence lay in its definition of justice as a 'kind of proportionality' on the analogy of the relation of part and whole. However, his subsequent development in mathematics and his recognition of inexhaustible proportions led him to seek a more fundamental metaphysical foundation for justice in perfection. Perfection subsequently became the most important concept of German philosophy in the eighteenth century and remained fundamental to the German Enlightenment until challenged by Kant in the *Critique of Pure Reason*. However, the notion of perfection promoted by Wolff and his followers was little more than a caricature of Leibniz's position.

The underestimation of Leibniz's metaphysics is starkly apparent in the fate of the *Meditations on Knowledge, Truth and Ideas* (1684) in which Leibniz presented the various grades of consciousness. The influence of this text on German philosophy cannot be overestimated; it provided the vocabulary and framework for all epistemological speculation prior to Kant's *Critique of Pure Reason*. Its distinction of clear and obscure ideas, and their further subdivision was read through Wolff, who understood it as classification of discrete and closed classes of knowledge rather than a provisional figuration of a continuum. Wolff transformed Leibniz's dynamic relation of unity and manifold back into a spatial relation of part and whole, an interpretation which was widely disseminated through innumerable philosophical textbooks and dictionaries. Yet it grievously misrepresented Leibniz's position: the main point of the *Meditations* is not the distribution of discrete classes of knowledge but the principle which divides its continuum. The classes of knowledge represent degrees of recognition: they are not, as Wolff thought, generically distinct. Recognition as the principle of division is clearly stated in the first distinction of obscure and clear knowledge: 'A concept is

obscure which does not suffice for recognizing the thing represented
... Knowledge is clear, therefore, when it makes it possible for me
to recognize the thing represented' (1684; p. 291). Knowledge involves
the recognition of things represented, it consists in discriminating
between them. This work of discrimination and recognition is
prosecuted through all the grades of knowledge up to the highest
grade of intuitive knowledge where the work of recognition contem-
plates itself in and through its efforts. The *Meditations* offer another
version of Leibniz's notion of culture as the production 'through and
in' of subjects and their objects.

Wolff's idea of perfection returns to Leibniz's early metaphysic of
part and whole, understanding it in terms of the proportion between
the one and the many rather than the negotiation between activity
and passivity. For him perfection consists in the subsumption of
individuals under an extensive universal rather than in the mutual
culturing of action and passion. The development of culture for Wolff
is conceived through a subsumptive model of judgement, in contrast
to Leibniz's discriminative model of recognition. But this abstract
subsumption raised problems for judgement in general, and especially
with regard to pleasure. By seeing pleasure as consisting in the
mutual recognition of subject and its other, Leibniz was able to avoid
thinking of it as a predicate. The pleasant was not a predicate applied
to an object, but marked the negotiation of activity and passivity
which allowed objects to come forth. But Wolff's view of pleasure
as a predicate applied subsumptively to objects led to the difficulties
which eventually brought about the ruin of his system.

The collapse of the Wolffian system began with the problem of
the pleasure taken in the beautiful. The difficulties with the
subsumptive model of judgement were most exposed in the necessity
of bringing the judgement of a work of art under abstract rules.
Although Gottsched tried to apply Wolff's subsumptive model of
judgement to art, it was Baumgarten who realized that a Wolffian
philosophy of art entailed the thorough reform of the Wolffian
philosophy. But this reform had implications for other parts of the
system, such as political philosophy, which required the subsumptive
model of judgement to legitimate its view of the police-state legislating
the common welfare. The apparently minor problem of pleasure in
the beautiful brought down the whole Wolffian edifice or 'Dream
Castle of Reason' as Kant described it. The development of philosophy
after the Wolffian hegemony was cast as a return to Leibniz. Leibniz's
role in the foundation of Wolffianism led Kant to accuse him along
with Wolff in the 'Amphiboly' of intellectualizing sensibility, but also
to claim his inspiration for the destruction of Wolffianism in the
Critique of Pure Reason.

The Dream Castle of Reason

Those who throw out Wolff's system and the procedure of the *Critique of Pure Reason* can have nothing else in mind than throwing off the fetters of science altogether and changing work into play, certainty into opinion, and philosophy into philodoxy.

Kant, *Critique of Pure Reason*

Wolff intended his system to forge the 'fetters of science' and to shape institutions, and it was successful in both respects. It determined the shape and language of philosophy in Germany for almost a century, and legitimated the world-view of the administrative stratum who managed the police-state. It exists in two versions: an extremely influential German version published between 1713 and 1721, and a less influential Latin version begun after Wolff's expulsion from the Prussian University of Halle in 1723, and continued after his triumphant return on the accession of Frederick II in 1740. Both versions begin with a Logic, which establishes the demonstrative procedure of the system, followed by an exposition of the four parts of Metaphysics: Ontology, Psychology, Cosmology, and Theology. The Metaphysics provides the foundation for the volumes on Ethics and Politics in which the welfare and security policies of the *Polizeistaat* receive their philosophical apotheosis.

Wolff's system is similar to Leibniz's Rational Jurisprudence and was described by contemporaries as the 'Leibniz-Wolff Philosophy'.[15] Like Leibniz, Wolff sought a metaphysical foundation for justice in a reconciliation of philosophical modernism and scholastic metaphysics. The young philosopher introduced himself to Leibniz by forwarding him his *Philosophia practica universalis, mathematica methodo conscripto* (1703) in which he derives a theory of justice from metaphysical principles. But this work, the matrix of Wolff's later system, was conceived independently of the Leibnizian Rational Jurisprudence which it closely resembled. In spite of initial similarities, there are great differences in both the form and content of the two philosophers' work. Most of Leibniz's writings are short pieces, or correspondence; his ideal of the scientific community was the academy of specialists. Wolff, on the contrary, was a teacher, and his system emerged from his lectures written not for a community of experts, but for students and a wider public. So, while Leibniz wrote mainly in Latin and

French – the languages of international scholarship and diplomacy – Wolff wrote in German.[16]

In the course of translating concepts such as perfection, the principles of contradiction and sufficient reason, and the notion of pre-established harmony from Leibniz's Latin and French, Wolff adapted them to an already formed philosophical intuition. The distance of this intuition from the dynamism of Leibniz's mature metaphysics is apparent in Wolff's definition of the central concept of perfection as 'unity in a manifold'. This return to the position of the young Leibniz re-invoked many of the difficulties of his early Rational Jurisprudence, especially those of how to relate part and whole in an objective proportion. However, in Wolff these are raised to the dignity of a system in which part and whole, individual and universal, are forced to conform.

The forced conformity of the system is disguised by its appeal to metaphysical first principles. In the preface to the 1721 edition of the German Metaphysics Wolff wrote:

> All the other parts of philosophy are grounded in the doctrines of this book. If one looks at the Ethics, or the Politics, or even at those essays where I try to pave the way to a more precise knowledge of nature and art, one will find that I refer everywhere to the *Metaphysics*, and cite those §§ where the reasons for what is to be proven are to be found.
>
> (1719; Preface)

All Wolff's readers will testify to the remorseless trail of cross-references (§§) which must be followed to establish even the most trivial point, and will sympathize with Hegel's description of this philosophy as 'barbarism of pedantry or pedantry of barbarism'. Yet the chains of Wolff's remorseless demonstrations – his fetters of science – are anchored in the shifting sands of an equivocation regarding the logical and ontological aspects of possibility. The equivocation becomes manifest when the *Metaphysics* appeals to the *Logic* to prove its grounds, leaving open the question of the systematic priority of logic or ontology. It was this equivocation which made Kant describe Wolff in the *Dreams of a Visionary* as a 'dream castle builder' with 'contradictory visions' which in the *Critique of Pure Reason* he traces to the inability of the logical principle of contradiction to determine 'the possibility of such an object, as may be conceived through the concept' (A220/B268). For Kant, Wolff is too hasty to conform logical possibility and existence, and although the 'greatest of all dogmatic philosophers', his system is fundamentally flawed.

His haste is apparent in the founding definition of the subject matter of philosophy at the beginning of the Logic: 'Philosophy is a science of all possible things, how [*wie*] and why [*warum*] they are possible' (1713; § 1). Wolff claimed to have 'discovered' this definition in 1703, and to have 'always directed all my thoughts on philosophy according to [it]' (1728; § 29). The elision of '*wie und warum*' – 'how and why' – follows from not distinguishing logical from real grounds. This is manifest in the definition of the logical principle of contradiction in the *Metaphysics*: 'Something cannot simultaneously be and not be. We call this proposition the principle [*Grund*] of contradiction' (1719; § 6). It is unclear in this definition whether it is the *fact* that something cannot both be and not be that constitutes the principle of contradiction, or whether it is the principle of contradiction which *dictates* that something cannot both be and not be. The real *Grund* or 'how' of a thing is not distinguished from its 'why' or logical *Grund*.[17] But this failure to make the distinction is not merely an oversight, for the entire system rests on the identification of the orders of being and logical relation without which the 'systematic' exposition of being was not thought to be possible.

The conflation of logical and real possibility structures Wolff's ontology which, as 'general metaphysics', is the foundation for the 'special metaphysics' of psychology, cosmology and theology. The title of the ontological chapter of the *Metaphysics* – 'On the first Principles/Causes of our Knowledge and of Things in General' – shows that the *Gründe* of knowledge and of things in general are assumed to be the same. Kant follows the structure of Wolff's *Metaphysics* in the first *Critique*, replacing the ontology chapter with a 'Transcendental Analytic' which distinguishes between the two senses of *Grund*, and then unfolding the consequences of the critical distinction for the three departments of special metaphysics in the 'Transcendental Dialectic'. Here he attributes Wolff's elision of logical and real ground to his failure to make the transcendental distinction between understanding and sensibility:

> the understanding cannot be permitted to transgress the limits of sensibility within which objects can alone be given to us. Its principles [*Grundsätze*] are merely principles [*Prinzipien*] of the exposition of appearances, and the proud name of Ontology, which takes on itself to provide a systematic doctrine of the synthetic a priori knowledge of things in general [*von Dingen überhaupt*] (as in the principle of causality), must without doubt stand aside for a humble Analytic of pure understanding.
>
> (A247/B303)

For Kant the conformity of understanding and its objects cannot simply be assumed; it is not enough to identify real and logical grounds, their relation must be specified. He focuses his attention on Wolff's account of causality, where the unjustified identification of the two grounds is most exposed.

One of the peculiarities of Wolff's treatment of causality is that he does not regard it as a relation but as a thing: 'the principle/cause [*Grund*] is that through which one is able to understand why something is; the cause [*Ursache*] is a thing [*Ding*] which contains in itself the *Grund* of something else' (§ 29). Here, in spite of the apparent distinction of *Grund* and *Ursache*, Wolff elides the two: the *Grund* is that through which one can understand why something *is*, and the cause is a *thing* which contains the *reason* for something else. Cause stands to effect as a more extensive to a less extensive logical class; it *contains* its effect. Wolff entitles the containment of the effect in the cause 'the principle/cause [*Grund*] of sufficient reason', retaining the equivocation of *Grund*.

The principle of sufficient reason is mapped onto physical causation through an analogy between causation and logical implication. Just as the more extensive class can be shown through the principle of contradiction to include the members of less extensive classes, so through the principle of sufficient reason, greater causes contain lesser, and the lesser are their effects. Wolff is seeking a logical *order* of causation:

> Because everything has a sufficient reason [*zureichenden Grund*] for being, so there must always be a sufficient reason why in simple things alterations follow each other in this and not in any other way, why in composite things the parts are composed in this and not any other way . . . Truth is accordingly nothing else than the order in the alterations of things.
>
> (§ 142)

The order of sufficient reason is both ontological and epistemological: it objectively structures composites and offers rules for their recognition: 'one knows the truth when one understands the *Grund* why this or that can be, that is, the rules of order which are to be found in things and their alterations' (§ 145). Wolff moves from recognizing regularities in the perdurance and alterations of things to postulating an objective order underlying them. He assumes that thought and its objects are conformable, entitling this conformity 'perfection', but without ever justifying his assumption. He does not conceive of order, as does Kant – in terms of a system of principles which 'anticipate' their objects by producing their conformity to its

laws – but assumes that the same order underlies both the bringing
forth of objects and their ordering.

The order recognizable in the regularities of existence and alteration
is the visible aspect of metaphysical perfection. In an order the parts
form a whole, while in perfection they do so according to a 'common
ground' or *Zweck*: 'Perfection consists in pure order. For wherever a
perfection is present, everything relates itself to a common ground,
from out of which one can explain why something exists besides
another, or why it follows it' (§ 156). Perfection is the distributive
principle which relates parts to whole, and is thought by Wolff in
terms of the 'harmony of the manifold' (§ 152). Wolff sees perfection
as the extensive maximization of possibilities, or the harmony of the
greatest number of parts in a whole. Just how far this definition of
perfection is from Leibniz's is apparent from Wolff's illustration of
a perfect unity of parts and whole – the mechanics of a watch.
However, the watch example is more complicated than it might
appear, for Wolff also suggests that the mechanical perfection of a
watch is subordinate to its reason (*Grund* or *Zweck*), which is to tell
the time. Whatever its subtleties, this perfection is not the same as
Leibniz's maximization of activity, although it approaches his early
position in maintaining that the 'collective-principle' (in Wolff the
Grund or *Zweck*) of a whole must both proportion and be proportioned
to its parts.

Wolff does not allow the proportioning and proportioned character
of perfection to be thought dynamically. He does not follow Leibniz
in conforming objects to the laws of thought through a negotiation
of the active and passive dispositions of power. He instead hypostatizes
the distinction of active and passive dispositions, projecting them
onto psychological faculties and even social institutions. This only
raises anew the problem of how these distinct faculties can be made
to conform to each other. Wolff postulates a power (*Kraft*) which
underlies both active and passive dispositions, providing a ground for
their conformity, but distributes the power hierarchically between the
higher and lower faculties of the soul according to their degree of
representative power. The 'lower faculties'[18] of sensibility and
imagination are low grades of representative power and, following
Leibniz's schema in *Meditations on Knowledge, Truth, and Ideas*, are
usually obscure but may occasionally be clear. Understanding
(*Verstand*) is a higher grade of representative power and is always
clear and distinct: 'The understanding is the capacity of clearly
representing the possible. This distinguishes the understanding
from the senses and the imagination, for which, by themselves,
representations can at most be clear, but not distinct; but when the

understanding is involved, they become distinct' (§ 277). The higher and lower faculties are modifications of a single power of representation, but how is this modification achieved? How does a unified power come to distribute itself?

The distribution of the power of representation into higher and lower faculties is the work of the higher faculty. The 'self-culture' or 'enlightenment' of the power is accomplished through the clear and distinct concepts of the higher faculty which form 'the grounds for the rules, according to which the soul is directed as much in knowledge as in willing and not-willing, which are consequently those of logic, ethics and politics' (§ 191).

The rules governing the relations of the higher and the lower faculties are made by the higher faculty, the consequence of the distribution of the faculties is also its cause. Faced with this difficulty, Wolff postulates a unity which precedes even the unity of the representative power underlying the distribution of the faculties. Unlike Leibniz, Wolff does not understand this unity intensively as a power, but extensively as an order. The distribution of the single power among the faculties is ordered by a perfection which guarantees the conformity of the objects of sensibility with the laws of the understanding.

The derivation of the will from reason is an important feature of the transition from the *Metaphysics* to the ethical and political parts of the system. Wolff makes this transition by identifying perfection qua truth with perfection qua good, and, through this, equating reason and will. When the soul represents perfection as the true, its representative power is distributed between the higher and lower faculties; similarly, when representing perfection as the good, the same power is distributed among the lower and the higher faculties of sensible desire and will. As with the faculties of knowledge, Wolff maintains that the practical faculties conform to each other because they are different grades of the same power, yet insists that the rational will legislates for sensible desire:

> the sensible desires and the will do not require a different power from the representative powers of the soul ... because the sensible desires as much as the will arise from representations of the good. As we take pleasure in that which we represent to ourselves as good, so the soul determines itself to try and produce this sensation, or (which is just the same) to determine itself so that such sensations are produced.
>
> (§ 878)

The faculties of the soul dispose themselves, in both cognition and volition, to maximize the representation of a perfection, whether as true or as good. But such perfections are rational, and so the rational faculty is considered to have a more distinct knowledge of the true and the good than the sensible.

The hierarchy implied in the distinction between the lower and the higher faculties becomes increasingly apparent as Wolff unfolds the system. The difficulties it involves are allowed to surface in his account of pleasure and art, but are rigorously suppressed in the ethics and politics. In the discussion of art in §§ 404–11 of the *Metaphysics*, Wolff defines pleasure (*Lust*) as 'an intuition [*Anschauung*] of perfection' so admitting the possibility of a perfection being perceived by sensibility. He quickly retracts this admission by questioning the judgement of the lower faculty; it is prone to deception since it does not judge a perfection according to clearly perceived rules (the prerogative of the higher faculty): 'It is not necessary that pleasure be grounded in a true perfection, it suffices if an illusion of it is at hand. For we see everyday, that people take pleasure from something which is imperfect because they take it for perfect' (§ 405). In order properly to perceive a perfection and so avoid deception it is necessary to know its rational grounds, but the capacity for such knowledge is not granted to the lower faculty. Nevertheless the admission of even the possibility of judging a perfection without rational knowledge threatens the hierarchy of the faculties.

The question of the pleasures of art presents Wolff with an aporia of judgement. These pleasures consist in intuiting a work's perfection, yet such intuitive perception of a perfection is fallible. In order to avoid deception it is necessary to know the rules of a perfection, yet once this knowledge is gained the perception is no longer intuitive. If the pleasures proper to the lower faculty are at best the appearance, at worst the illusion of perfection, what use are they except as propaedeutics to the rational appreciation of a perfection according to rules? And once they are appreciated by the higher faculty what distinguishes them from the rational knowledge of philosophy? Wolff did not solve this problem but sat on the fence, claiming that the sensible perception of a perfection by the lower faculty *and* the rational perception of that perfection were *both* proper to art. We shall see that this irresolution led to differences within Wolffianism, with one party defending the claims of the higher, and another defending those of the lower faculty.

Wolff was not so irresolute when it came to the relation of the lower and higher faculties in his ethical and political philosophy. He describes a will which acts according to the directions of the lower faculties of sensibility and imagination as being in slavery: 'Because the affects originate in the senses and imagination, the domination of the senses, imagination and affects result in human slavery' (§ 491). The freedom of the higher faculty is opposed to the slavery of the affections, for here since the rational 'insight into the order of things shows what is good and bad, better or worse, the reason is the *Grund* of freedom' (§ 520).

Wolff grounds the unity of thinking and willing in perfection, converting the good into the best, and claiming that the perfect will wills the best: 'a will is perfect then, when each and every act of will agree with each other, when none opposes another. Opposition cannot happen when the motivation of a will is the representation of the best. And consequently the most perfect will has for its motivation a complete representation of the best' (§ 907). The definition of a perfect will excludes the lower faculty from determining action, since only the higher faculty is capable of a complete representation. Only the higher faculty is free to judge what is best, for the harmony of wills, or the perfection of social life, follows from an exclusively rational representation of the best.

The systematic exposition of being rests on the identification of logic and ontology; any discrepancies between being and thinking arise from the distorting effect of the obscure representations of the lower faculty. The hegemony of the higher faculty is essential for Wolff's account of the most perfect social order. Here Wolff's chains of syllogistic inference cannot be properly understood apart from their polemical context. His political philosophy develops the critique of Hobbes begun by Cumberland and Pufendorf which maintained that a right always presupposes a duty or obligation.[19] Wolff was dissatisfied with Pufendorf's founding of obligation and the various offices of human society in the principle of sociability, and replaced it with that of rational perfection. However, his understanding of perfection differs greatly from Cumberland's. For Cumberland and his successors, perfection manifests itself in the affections of the moral sense and taste; but for Wolff, such affective action is slavery. The maximization of perfection in the best society demands a conscious perception of that perfection; the responsibility for this lies with the higher faculty alone. There is no theoretical space in this political theory for a civil society with canons of judgement independent of the rational legislation of the state.

The differences between Wolff and the theorists of civil society become apparent in the diverse ways in which they apply the metaphor of the hand of God. For Wolff it is not 'invisible', inscribing its law in the sentiments of humanity, but obscurely perceived and requiring clarification by human reason. The engraving (plate 2) which forms the frontispiece to his shorter writings promises to make 'that which is obscure clear'. Following his earlier statement of the platonic unity of the good and the true comes the idea of the rule of the higher faculty embodied in the philosopher king. This points to the transformation of the higher and lower faculties into a social distinction, one which becomes increasingly apparent as the system develops, and which dominated German philosophy up to and including Kant. On the one hand are the enlightened servants of the philosopher king, and on the other the confused *Pöbel* or rabble. And just as the task of the higher psychological faculty is to raise the lower faculty from its confusion so it is for the enlightened to raise the unenlightened from their confused condition. But the relation of the two faculties is extremely problematic, for in the same way that the nature of art is contradicted by being made rational, the aim of enlightenment (rational freedom and autonomy) is contradicted by being legislated from above.

Wolff's political philosophy suffers this contradiction. Most commentators are outraged by its mix of rights theory and authoritarianism, and usually attempt to defend its liberal while deploring its illiberal aspects. However, it is important to recognize the sources of this ambiguity in the aporias raised by his account of judgement. Wolff finds it difficult, both in the philosophy of art and politics, to account for how individual and universal are related in judgement. The difficulty arises from his uncompromisingly subsumptive model of judgement in which the manifold of the lower is unified by the higher faculty. The lower faculty is violated by the higher; it is represented as unconscious and passive against the consciousness and activity of the higher. In the philosophy of art the giving of rules to sensibility annuls the definition of beauty as the confused perception of a perfection. The lower faculty is even more repressed in the political philosophy where there is no possibility that the 'rabble' of the lower faculty could order themselves; they must be ordered from on high.

Wolff would have found the British argument for the mediation of individual action and the social welfare through the affective 'moral sense' completely unacceptable. Indeed, he went further than Pufendorf in developing the authoritarian implications of the revisions of rights theory in the direction of *Polizeiwissenschaft*. He achieves this through a verbal elision of the metaphysical perfect good with the *gemeine Beste* of *Polizeiwissenschaft*, and erects on this basis a model of a rational society in which social welfare is administered by a bureaucracy representing the 'higher faculty'. The culmination of the system, Wolff's vision of a rational society, is none other than the police-state.

The suppression of the lower faculty by the higher in the interest of perfection, has its precise analogue in the suppression of civil society by the rational state in the interest of the *gemeine Beste*. The details of the analogy are worked out in the ethical and political parts of the system. Ethics considers the duties of humans in the state of nature where, for Wolff, rights are firmly subordinated to duties. The first of its three sections – 'On the Acts and Omissions of Humanity in General' – grounds the duties of humanity in the law of nature, which turns out to be none other than the 'maximization of perfection' (1720; § 45). The second and third sections – on the duties of humanity to itself and to God – systematize duties according to the categorial imperative to maximize perfection. Wolff insists that the law of nature and the duties derived from it are rational, and can only be recognized by the higher faculty, since 'The senses prevent human beings from living in accord with the law of nature. This takes place in two ways: either they are deceived by them in their judgements, or they distract the attention necessary for an orderly course of life' (§ 180). It is not possible to live in accord with the laws of nature without consciously recognizing them; however, this recognition requires that the imperfect freedom of the state of nature be surrendered for the more perfect freedom of life in society.

The transition from the natural to the civil state reveals two sides to Wolff's idea of freedom. Freedom is defined negatively as the 'dominion over the senses, imagination and the affections' (§ 184) and positively as the maximization of perfection. The negative aspect of freedom is expressed at § 863 in terms of the limitation of aristocratic privilege: the limitation suppresses the 'natural freedom' of the aristocracy in the name of reason and the community. But what is the positive content of this freedom? Wolff answers this question in his *Politics*, the culmination of his system. The only constitution capable both of limiting the *Willkür* or arbitrariness of the aristocracy and of realizing the perfection of the common welfare is the police-state.

The derivation of the institutions of the police-state from the positive and negative concepts of freedom is fully realized in the *Politics*. The book is divided into two parts: the first 'On Human Societies' discusses marriage, parenthood and the household economy; while the second 'On the Community [*gemeinen Wesen*]' surveys the various forms of community, along with the civil law, the forms of administration and the conduct of war. For Wolff, the basic law of the community is the imperative to maximize welfare and ensure security: 'The common welfare and security is thus the highest and final law of the community; and the rule by which everything in the community is to be decided is: do that which furthers the common welfare and preserves security' (1721; § 215). This imperative, indistinguishable from the equitable principle of *Polizeiwissenschaft*, disregards estate privileges: all political judgements are governed by the imperative to maximize the common welfare and security. But, in contrast to the professors of police, Wolff did not openly derive his imperative from the practice of absolutist administration, but gave it a metaphysical foundation in perfection: 'Perfection consists in a harmony of a manifold; so everything to do with the institution and administration of the community ... must harmonize with the common welfare and security; from this it is clear how one can judge the perfection of a community' (§ 224). The perfection of a community consists in the harmony of the institutions of administration with its end, which is to maximize the common welfare and security. Although his exposition is more noble, his conclusions agree completely with the police theorists on both the purpose of the state and means by which to realize it.

The realization of the common welfare and security is the responsibility of the enlightened authorities to which the people are bound in obedience. In the original social contract, the authorities assume the duty of promoting welfare and security while the people adopt the duty of obedience: 'The authority undertakes to apply all its power and care toward ensuring that it considers all serviceable means for the furtherance of the common welfare and security and makes all the arrangements necessary for its accomplishment; conversely the subjects are obliged to do willingly whatever is considered to be good for them' (§ 433). The authorities' responsibility is discharged through legislation and administration. In the latter case authority is delegated to officials who ensure the maximization of welfare and security within their designated areas. The authority to make judgements regarding which actions will promote welfare and security is reserved for the enlightened sovereign and his delegated administration. The earlier statement of the principle 'Do whatever will promote the common welfare and security' undergoes an administrative metamorphosis into 'Permit whatever will promote the common welfare and security.' The officials alone have sufficient insight into the common welfare to make such a judgement.

The main means of promoting welfare and security is through legislation; the legislator and his officials have the responsibility for determining the common welfare through law: 'The authorities by means of their power can command what the subjects should do and not do; but the actions of the subjects are to be governed by the civil law; they have above all to give sufficient laws, and where they find laws are lacking, to fill the gap with new laws' (§ 468). The contradiction involved in enlightening from above has already been noted in the legislation of freedom and autonomy. Wolff never tackles this contradiction, for while championing negative freedom from the senses or from aristocratic caprice, he fails to question the restriction of positive freedom to the higher faculty or state. The contradiction in the imposed tutelage of the lower to the higher faculty, civil society to the enlightened ruler, manifests itself in the case of legislation. What is required from the people is the willing obedience which follows from their confidence in the wisdom of their rulers in matters concerning the common welfare. This may be achieved through public discussion or through deception. The first method acknowledges the role citizens have in deciding their laws, while the second assumes that they have to be deceived for their own good. As with the relation of the higher and lower faculties in the philosophy of art, Wolff accepts both positions: at one point he argues that the authority of the laws should be clearly and distinctly recognized by all citizens:

> It is for this reason – that it is impossible that one could live according to an unknown law – that new laws must be made publically known, which happens when they are posted in public places where everyone can read them, or are read out in public assemblies, or are distributed by the official press. And for this reason no order of the authorities receives the power of law before it is published, that is, made public in one of the above-mentioned ways.
>
> (§ 416)

However, this view of the publication of laws is contradicted by Wolff's justification of spectacle in the following terms: 'The common man, who depends on his senses and can barely use his reason, is unable to grasp what royal majesty is; but through the things which he takes in through his eyes and which affect his other senses, he knows majesty, power and force with an indistinct but clear concept' (§ 466). The authority of the state is presented to the lower faculty or the 'common people' in a way that will ensure their obedience, but which cannot possibly contribute to their enlightenment or enable them to assume the responsibilities of autonomy. They are not allowed to judge for themselves.

Wolff's entire system rested on his intuition in 1703 into the unity of logic and ontology, of thinking and being. Without this intuition the systematic exposition of metaphysics, ethics and politics would have been impossible: questioning this unity would have threatened the whole enterprise. Retrospectively, it is clear that the dream castle was built on sand, but for a time its foundations seemed to be sound. Although the public enthusiasm for Wolff waned after 1740, his institutional influence among the intellectuals and bureaucrats of Fredrickian Prussia remained strong.[20] This is not too surprising, since his philosophy offered a metaphysical justification of their existence. His students were prominent in all the institutions of the state, and played a prominent role in the drafting of the Prussian law code.

The growing strength of institutional Wolffianism contrasted considerably with the growing doubts about its intellectual foundations. The dream castle was already under external attack before 1740 and, more worryingly, suffered from internal dissension. With the accession of Frederick the Great, Wolff's old adversaries, the Pietists, were shorn of their influence at court and were forced to substitute argument for intrigue as the means of settling their differences with him. Crusius's demolition of the principle of sufficient reason was important not only because of its influence on Kant, but also because it exposed Wolff's equivocal use of *Grund* to be an illegitimate fusion of logical principle and physical cause. Within Wolffianism, dissatisfaction focused on the problem of the philosophy of art. Since Wolff could not admit access to perfection except through the higher faculty, he refused the lower faculty any legitimate claim to knowledge. The hierarchy was questioned in Baumgarten's aesthetic, which gave the lower faculty its own voice and logic. But if two qualitatively different logics are admitted, one of the higher and one of the lower faculty, the identification of being and a single logic which is necessary to found the system is threatened, along with the political conclusions drawn from it.

The heat raised in the debates about the proper relation of the higher and lower faculties was generated by the open secret that they also referred to the enlightened rulers and the unenlightened subjects. Postulating a distinct logic of the lower faculty struck at the political result of the Wolffian philosophy, the enlightened police-state. The logic of the lower faculty had its correlate in a civil society ordering itself from below. It was from out of the problem of sensibility that Kant developed a root-and-branch critique of the Wolffian philosophy which exposed its original metaphysical equivocation and replaced its justification of the police-state with a theory of culture. Awakening from his dogmatic slumbers, he was able to bring the despotic tutelage of the dream castle before the harsh light of the critical tribunal. But his indictment of Wolffianism would not have been achieved without the internal subversion and external attacks of his predecessors.

Art and the Lower Faculty

The splendour of the rainbow of the setting sun.
Cato's death. Sacrifice
Our current constitution allows women to live
Without men which spoils everything.

Kant, *Marginalia to the Observations on the Feelings of the Beautiful and Sublime*

In Wolff's system the realization of freedom and perfection was achieved through the higher faculty of reason cultivating the lower sensible faculty. But unlike Leibniz's universal process of culture, which was based on the continuum of representations, Wolff restricted the scope of culture to the cultivation of the lower, sensible faculty by the higher, rational one. Consequently, the attainment of a political culture, the realization of perfection and freedom, was not the responsibility of individual citizens making judgements in civil society, but that of philosopher bureaucrats who judged what was best for the common welfare. However, when the Wolffians of the 1730s realigned the rational and the sensible faculties in the context of the philosophy of art they removed the epistemological prop to this political position. Their grounding of the continuity of sensibility and reason in the productive autonomy of the imagination opened the gates to a less hierarchical notion of political culture.

The fragility of the Wolffian model of subsumptive judgement first became apparent on the margins of the system in the philosophy of art, and it was there that Wolffianism began to unravel. The system simply could not accommodate beauty. For if art is an adequate representation of a perfection, then it must be rational, but then it ceases to be art, since the most beautiful poetic form would be the syllogism. But if it is conceded that art is a non-rational representation of perfection, then a perfection has been mediated without the intervention of the rational faculty. This apparently innocent concession spelt the end of Wolffianism, since it calls into question not only Wolff's synthesis of logic and ontology and the bifurcation of the faculties which followed from it, but also the hierarchical notion of political culture. The philosophy of art became the locus of the internal crisis of Wolffianism.[21]

The dream castle collapsed in two stages. The first stage was dominated by the debates in the philosophy of art of the 1730s and 1740s which recast the Wolffian division of the faculties in terms of the productive autonomy of imagination, while the second developed the consequences of this revision for theoretical and practical philosophy. In the first stage there were basically three positions, represented by the Leipzig philosopher Johann Christoph Gottsched (1700–66), the Swiss critics Johann Jacob Bodmer (1698–1783) and Johann Jacob Breitinger (1701–76), and the Halle and later Frankfurt a.d. Oder philosopher Alexander Gottlieb Baumgarten (1714–62). Although the violence of the polemic between Gottsched and the Swiss has since become legendary, the real victor was Baumgarten. His position was the most inclusive, and the philosophical language which he evolved to defend it came to dominate the philosophy of art.[22]

Although Bodmer was the first to propose a comprehensive philosophical treatment of art according to Wolffian principles in 1727,[23] the palm for executing the first Wolffian philosophy of art must go to Gottsched's *Versuch einer critischen Dichtkunst* (1730). Gottsched was a committed Wolffian: he presented theses on Wolffian topics at Königsberg and Leipzig in the early 1720s, and was appointed Professor of Logic and Metaphysics at Leipzig in 1731 (Cruger 1884, p. xxiii). This curriculum vitae distinguishes him from the Swiss critics in one important respect: he was not a critic turning to the Wolffian philosophy for a theoretical framework, but a fully trained and committed Wolffian. The ambition of his *Dichtkunst* was not simply to ground traditional German poetic and French theory of taste in the Wolffian philosophy, but to complete the Wolffian system by incorporating poetics. The two ambitions are reflected in the division of the *Dichtkunst* into general and special parts which situate the schema of genres developed by traditional poetic within a philosophical analysis of the elements of poetry.

It is in chapter 3 of the first part of the *Dichtkunst* – '*Vom guten Geschmacke eines Poeten*' – that Gottsched works hardest to bring together German poetic, French theory of taste, and the Wolffian philosophy.[24] Gottsched suggests that the French controversies over whether taste was dictated by reason or sentiment had been fruitless because the French thinkers lacked one, if not two of the three qualifications necessary to answer the question. These qualifications were: (i) a knowledge of (Wolffian) psychology; (ii) a knowledge of (Wolffian) logic; and (iii) a knowledge of formal poetics. In Gottsched's own words, whoever wishes to understand taste

> must first of all philosophically understand the powers of the human soul, especially the workings of the sensitive and judging understanding. He must be adept in logic so that he can make a good explanation according to logical rules of the things and

expressions which present themselves. Finally, he must be well practised in poetry and whatever other arts are being discussed. A description of good taste cannot be made properly without these three items.

(1730; pp. 169–70)

Since the French disputants lacked the Wolffian qualifications in psychology and logic, 'it is no wonder that they could never agree among themselves nor enlighten us Germans better. Our countrymen have tackled the matter with much greater skill, and have been able to proceed with far greater thoroughness' (p. 170). Unfortunately the German Wolffians' superior grasp of fundamentals did not prevent their disputing taste, and the book which was supposed to end controversy only fanned its flames.

Gottsched's version of the Wolffian system presented in his *Erste Gründe der Gesammten Weltweisheit* (1733) offers some interesting variations on Wolff's system, and clarifies the disputed discussion of taste offered in the *Dichtkunst*. The work follows the Wolffian practice of dividing subject matter into theoretical and practical parts: the former includes Metaphysics according to the familiar division of Ontology, Psychology, Cosmology, and Theology; while the latter includes disquisitions on General Ethics, Natural Right, Virtue, and Prudence. Within this structure there are some striking innovations, such as a preface on the history of philosophy and the inclusion of far more material from the natural sciences than was customary in works produced on the Wolffian treadmill. But when it came to essentials, Gottsched remained an orthodox Wolffian. Philosophy (*Weltweisheit*) is 'a science of happiness, as Leibniz was the first to describe it' (1733; § 1), and the key to happiness is perfection, defined in the Ontology as 'the harmony of a manifold' (§ 256). In his identification of perfection and beauty Gottsched accepts a rationalist account of beauty:

> Whatever is according to this rule serves the perfection and beauty of the whole; whatever deviates from it is an error. Beauty and perfection arise from observing the rules of composition which are only conceded by very few, for it often happens, that one, particularly in matters of sense governed by indistinct or completely obscure rules, makes uneven and often false judgements of what is beautiful or perfect.
>
> (§ 258)

While Gottsched echoes Wolff's denigration of sensibility, his view that the senses obscure the grounds of *judgement* and not perception in general is an original development. He develops the notion of judgement further in the section on Psychology, where he discusses the grounds for judging (or misjudging) a perfection, and derives the following definition of taste:

> If one perceives a consensual unity in a composed concept, one which is not clearly apparent and whose rules of perfection cannot be explained, then one judges this thing to be beautiful, just as we would find the same in the opposite case ugly. The soul's power of judging between perfection and imperfection is called taste. This is called good when it is correct – that is, in accord with the rules of art – bad when it judges incorrectly.
>
> (§ 929)

The most interesting aspect of this definition is the way taste and judgement are placed between the rules and the object or work of art: taste does not subsume an object under rules, yet judges according to them. This marks a subtle advance on Wolff's position since here taste discriminates whether the rules of perfection are present in a particular instance; it does not apply those rules to an object, nor need it have clear and distinct knowledge of those rules. In this way Gottsched maintains a normative poetic while acknowledging a continuity between subsumption and discrimination.

This account of taste is fundamental to the *Dichtkunst*, where taste is seen to discriminate between perfections according to clear but not distinct concepts: it 'is only concerned with clear but not completely distinct concepts of things, and only distinguishes between those things that are judged by mere perception' (1730; p. 172). Nevertheless, the rational rules of beauty still apply even though they are not consciously recognized at the moment of judgement: 'The rules which have been introduced into the fine arts do not follow from mere subjective obstinacy, but are grounded in the unalterable nature of things themselves, in the agreement of the manifold, in order and harmony' (p. 174). Gottsched draws out of this discussion the general principle applicable to all the fine arts that: 'Such taste is good which agrees [*übereinkommt*] with the rules established by reason' (p. 176). The word which Gottsched uses to describe the relation between the rules and the discriminative faculty is *übereinkommen* – to agree or come to a compromise. This is far from the rigid subsumptive judgement employed in Wolff's account. Good taste agrees with the rules, but does not apply them directly in its judgements. Taste then, assumes a position between the higher and the lower faculties; but it does not overcome the distinction since it depends on the rules of the higher faculty for its judgements, and is allotted only the limited office of discrimination. Taste does not legislate for itself, is not autonomous, but only applies the laws of the higher faculty.

This refinement of Wolff's psychology has been seen by some commentators as the establishment of a 'critical competence' appropriate to the new 'public sphere' (*Öffentlichkeit*) opened by the Enlightenment in Germany.[25] But far from modifying Wolff's police-state model of the faculties, Gottsched inserts taste as an administrative layer between the legislative higher and the legislated lower faculty. The restriction of critical competence to adjudication corresponded to the intermediate nature of the administrative classes such as lawyers, priests and academics who were the main *Öffentlichkeit* addressed by the Enlightenment. While Gottsched's account of taste freed it from the aristocratic particularism of the French theories, it remained with its legislator and administrators firmly within the paradigm of the police-state; it did not anticipate the autonomous public sphere of a nascent civil society.

This is disclosed in the practical part of the system where Gottsched follows the Wolffian practice of deriving the existing police-state from rational principles:

> The basic law of all societies is this – do everything that furthers the welfare of the whole society or common welfare, and do not do anything which in any way checks or hinders it . . . It can happen that occasionally the welfare of the whole society contradicts that of an individual member, but the former must be given precedence, for the whole is more important than a part; for we know that when various rules of perfection collide, one must make the exception of the lesser rule.
>
> (1733; § 315)

The responsibility for ensuring the common welfare rests with the monarch, who 'must in all these matters show his care for the common welfare in producing new regulations and laws' (§ 402). The citizen is not entitled to political judgement according to self-legislated laws since judgement is the prerogative of an administrative stratum, which judges according to laws instituted by the sovereign for the common welfare.

Gottsched's philosophy ingeniously revised Wolff's system while leaving its structure intact – which was of course the point. He succeeded in giving taste a Wolffian foundation – transforming the rules of formal poetics into the rules of perfection – without threatening the foundations of the system. His compromise was subtle but brittle, and the equivocation of taste's politic mediation between the lower and higher faculties was dangerously exposed. This was apparent to Bodmer and Breitinger, who entered into a long and often bitter dispute with Gottsched on that for which there is no more disputing: taste.

Bodmer and Breitinger had no interest in defending the Wolffian system; they were critics before they were Wolffians. Wolff offered them a philosophical basis for their criticism and they were indifferent to the impact their innovations in the philosophy of art might have upon the system as a whole. Their irresponsibility roused Gottsched's ire, and provoked fierce disagreements upon the topics of taste and imitation. At stake in the interminable debate was the relation of the rational and the sensible faculties. In his book of 1740 with the same title as Gottsched's, Breitinger flatly denies that taste obeys, or even agrees with a canon of rules established by reason: 'it is impossible to teach and present good taste through the rules that make up a comprehensive system of art, because its judgements are tied to particular occasions that would have to be judged according to a particular viewpoint and according to the composition of particular things' (1740; p. 430). Instead, he and Bodmer consider imagination to work according to its own rules which only become apparent in works of art. The task of criticism is to draw out the rules of imagination as they manifest themselves in the work, and not to discriminate between works according to a body of rules already established by reason. For them taste involves recognition and not ascription, a view of the immanent laws of imagination that had consequences for the doctrine of imitation. In Gottsched's *Dichtkunst* imitation unified perfection and beauty, since the rational perfection of the world was imitated in the sensible medium of the fine arts. In contrast to this Wolffian position, Breitinger's *Dichtkunst* rejects this doctrine in favour of a Leibnizian position in which the subjects of imitation are the possible worlds actualized in imagination: 'For I may take it as given that poetry, insofar as it is distinguished from history, borrows its originals and the substance of its imitations less from this world than from the world of possible things' (p. 57). This form of imitation Breitinger called 'poetic'; the other sort, Gottsched's, he called 'dogmatic'. In his poetic the imagination was autonomous, producing works according to its own laws against which they were to be judged.

The implications of this position are developed in Bodmer's *Critische Abhandlung* (1740), one of the first manifestations of the growing influence of Baumgarten's aesthetics on the language of criticism. In the first chapter, Bodmer draws a Baumgartian analogy between the logic of reason and that of the imagination, saying 'It has sometimes occurred to me that the imagination, as well as the understanding, is in need of its own logic' (p. 6). The logic of the higher faculty connects concepts in propositions and syllogisms, while the logic of the imagination connects sensible images in tropes and poems: 'The metaphorical-image of the logic of phantasy arises from the binding together of things that can be imagined together, just as in logic proper the propositions arise from the conceivable connection of concepts' (p. 6). Breitinger follows Baumgarten's substitution of the poetic 'sensible-image' of poetics for the 'concept' of traditional logic, and his adaptation of the logical architectonic of concept–proposition–syllogism, to the content of sensible-image–trope–poetic discourse. He also develops the view that the logic of the imagination differs from logic proper, but was probably more extensive than it. Such a sophisticated articulation of the Swiss position was only conceivable in the wake of Baumgarten's *Reflections on Poetry* (1735) which presented these and other more radical positions.

Bodmer and Breitinger were unable to recognize the implications of their critical innovations for the Wolffian philosophy. They lacked the thorough knowledge of the system necessary to work through the consequences of ascribing an autonomous logic to the imagination, of conceding legislative authority to the lower faculty. The ascription by the Swiss thinkers – who were steeped in British culture – of autonomy to sensibility anticipated the public sphere as civil society far more than did Gottsched's 'critical competence'. Perhaps the incomprehensible rancour between Leipzig and Zürich followed from a political difference expressed in the language of imagination, imitation, and taste? The ascription of legislative authority to the imagination by the Swiss critics, and their view that taste involved the recognition of autonomously developed rules of judgement, presupposed a public sphere based on mutual recognition of the criteria of judgement. This was quite distinct from Gottsched's restriction of legislative authority to the rational faculty, and his view of taste as the administration of discrimination according to given laws.

While the polemic raged between Leipzig and Zürich, the position elaborated by Baumgarten quietly gained ground. His projected science of aesthetic combined the systematic virtues of Gottsched with the critical flexibility of the Swiss. Baumgarten was recognized in the mid-1730s as the leading expositor of Wolff's philosophy, and his first loyalties were always to the system. What made his aesthetics so influential was his recognition that the system had to be extended in order to accommodate art. Unlike Gottsched who contrived a fragile settlement of the conflict of the faculties, Baumgarten proceeded to rethink the grounds of their antagonism; but unlike the Swiss, he was fully aware of the systematic implications of his revision. His aesthetics pointed beyond Wolff, and if he was unable fully to unfold the revolutionary implications of his thought for himself, he gave inspiration and a philosophical vocabulary to thinkers like Herder and Kant who were only too willing to do so for him.

Art in the System

A metaphysical cyclops who lacked the critical eye.
Kant, *Reflection* 5081

The difficult task of locating art in the philosophical system was tackled in various ways. Wolff seemed unaware that his 'rational thoughts' on art were inconsistent, and while Gottsched struggled to accommodate art within the system, Bodmer and Breitinger threw off its fetters entirely. Baumgarten chose the most difficult option, which was to extend the system in order to accommodate the experience of art: the new philosophical discipline of aesthetic announced the system's thorough reform. Nevertheless, the new discipline was awkwardly placed within and without the system, being both a discrete part of it – the philosophical treatment of art – and, as the science of sensibility, its foundation. The problems arising from aesthetic being both part and foundation of the system were never resolved by Baumgarten. They were noted by Kant, one of his closest readers, who in the *Critique of Pure Reason* deemed the first project to have failed, but who employed the results of the second project in the division of Transcendental Logic into aesthetic and logic. He subsequently made the relation of art and the system the central theme of the *Critique of Judgement-Power*.

The importance of Baumgarten's invention of aesthetic for the history of philosophy is not disputed, although its significance is not fully appreciated.[26] His philosophy resists interpretation, not only because it is presented in the Wolffian idiom of cross-referenced tomes written in Latin, but also because it is incomprehensible apart from its systematic and institutional setting. It is necessary to understand why aesthetics suffered the contradiction of being both at the basis and at the margin of the system. This question may be approached through the breakdown of a systematic treatment of art in the aesthetic of the early *Reflections on Poetry* (1735), and then according to the foundational aesthetic worked out in the *Philosophia Generalis* (1742), the *Metaphysica* (1739) and other systematic works. The *Aesthetica* (1750–8) may then be placed as a fragmentary attempt to unify the two aspects of aesthetic within a philosophy of education or culture. But first it is necessary to glance at the institutional setting of these works.

The three main sources for establishing the institutional framework of the development of Baumgarten's thought are the autobiographical introduction to his first work *Reflections on Poetry*, and the biographical memoirs by Meier and Abbt. Meier reports that Baumgarten read Wolff at Halle during the early 1730s when it was still illegal to profess the Wolffian philosophy in Prussia.[27] According to Meier, he began with Wolff's conspectus of the German system, the *Anweisung* of 1726, and went on to the mathematical and the logical writings. In spite of this industry Baumgarten could still claim that 'scarcely a day has passed for me without poetry' (1735; p. 15). His researches in the Wolffian philosophy and his passion for poetry came together in 1734 when he began teaching 'young men preparing for the university, in poetics along with the so-called rational philosophy' (p. 15). His first work, the *Reflections*, developed out of this teaching activity, and was published in 1735.

In the following year Baumgarten lectured at Halle University on Wolff's Logic (from which the ban had been lifted), and subsequently gave lectures on Wolff's Metaphysics, which, since it was still illegal, he adapted and reworked into his own *Metaphysica* published in 1739. He was appointed Professor *extra-ordinarius* at Halle in 1737 and lectured on logic, metaphysics, natural law and philosophical ethics. Abbt's observation on this teaching profile gives an interesting perspective on the institutional locus of Baumgarten's thinking: 'He had already in 1737 given the then fashionable encylopaedic lectures on everything which did not belong to the three higher faculties' (1763; p. 225). This was a very important development in the history of German philosophy, and marked a significant contribution to the dispute over the role of philosophy (*Weltweisheit*) in the university, one which began with Thomasius and Wolff at the beginning of the century and was still alive when Kant published *The Conflict of the Faculties* in 1798.

The background to this development is given by McClelland in his study of the German university from 1700 to 1914. The creation of a system of philosophy was a self-conscious claim for the precedence of philosophy over the three traditional higher faculties of theology, law and medicine. At this time philosophy still had its medieval status as a subordinate faculty: 'The philosophical faculty remained largely an ante-chamber to the higher faculties, for teachers as well as students. And it did not lose its preparatory function until later in the eighteenth century, even at Göttingen. Yet the struggle for equality with the other faculties had already begun' (1980, p. 42). An important strategy in this struggle was the transformation of philosophy into an encyclopaedic discipline. This was expressed in the curricular arrangements at the new University of Göttingen:

> in addition to the traditional introductory course of logic, metaphysics, and ethics, Göttingen offered lectures in empirical psychology, the law of nature, politics, physics, natural history, pure and applied mathematics (including surveying, military and civilian architecture), history and its auxiliary sciences such as geography, diplomatics, science, art, and ancient and modern languages.
>
> (p. 43)

In order to maintain intellectual credibility and to distinguish itself from the traditional faculties, philosophy had to claim a distinctive method and a universal systematic viewpoint. This lay behind the near obsession of eighteenth-century German philosophers, from Wolff to Kant, with the methodology of philosophy and the necessity of its systematic presentation.

Wolff had been an early casualty in the curricular wars between systematic philosophy and the traditional faculties. His expulsion from Prussia in 1721 was instigated by members of the theological faculty whose prerogatives were threatened by his new, systematic 'rational theology'. Baumgarten's encyclopaedic lectures of 1737 appear in this light as a renewed campaign in favour of philosophy's claim for superiority over the other faculties. He continued the struggle after his translation in 1740 to the University of Frankfurt a.d. Oder where, according to Meier, 'He taught all the parts of philosophy as in Halle, and lectured for the first time on aesthetics itself, and an introduction to philosophy as a whole. He lectured on physics, and the science of the rights and duties of social life' (1763; p. 20). Baumgarten's published works emerged from these lectures: the *Aesthetica* from the aesthetics lectures; the *Philosophia Generalis* out of the introduction to philosophy as a whole; the *Ethica Philosophica* and the *Jus Naturae* out of the lectures on the rights and duties of social life. He was also associated with a work on *Polizeiwissenschaft*,

De Disciplinus Oeconomico politico-Cameralibus.

Before surveying the position of aesthetic in the architectonic of systematic philosophy, it is vital to examine its own architectonic as a philosophy of art. Not being aware of the similarity between the organization of the *Aesthetica* and the *Reflections on Poetry* can lead to confusion over the relationship between the two works. The architectonic of the *Aesthetica* is clearly set out in § 13 of the Prolegomena to the work, where the subject matter of aesthetics is divided into theoretical and practical parts: the former gives the general rules of poetics, the latter gives their application in a particular work. The theoretical part is itself divided into three sections: Heuristic, Methodology and Semiotic. This division corresponds to the classical division of rhetoric into *inventio*, the rules for the 'discovery' of the subject matter of a discourse; *dispositio*, the rules for the arrangement of the subject matter into a clear order; and *elocutio*, the rules for a convincing presentation of the discourse. Correspondingly, Heuristic treats of the material of a poem; Methodology of the ordering of the materials in a poem; and Semiotic of their presentation in appropriately beautiful language. What has come down as the *Aesthetica* represents only a fragment of this project.

A surviving transcript of Baumgarten's Frankfurt lectures on aesthetic ends at § 613 (corresponding to the end of volume I of the *Aesthetica*), suggesting that neither in print nor in his lectures was Baumgarten able to complete even the first part of his philosophy of art. It seems that his was indeed the 'abortive attempt' described by Kant in the *Critique of Pure Reason*. Some commentators have turned to Meier's *Anfangsgründe aller schönen Wissenschaften* (1748–9) for a clue to the shape of the complete work; but Meier is an unreliable witness to Baumgarten's intentions, and a better idea of the plan of the *Aesthetica* is available from the earlier *Reflections on Poetry*. If we take one of Meier's comments on that work literally – 'He here achieved for the first time the outline of his aesthetica' (1763, p. 46), it is reasonable to read the early work as a groundplan of the later *Aesthetica*.

Baumgarten's conspectus in the Preface to the *Reflections on Poetry* implicitly follows the rhetorical schema laid out in the introduction of the later work:

through § 11 I shall be occupied in developing the notion of a poem and the appropriate terminology. From § 13 to § 65 I shall try to work out some view of poetic cognition. From § 65 to § 77 I shall set forth that lucid method of a poem which is common to all poems. Finally from § 77 to § 107 I shall subject poetic language to a rather careful investigation.

(1735; p. 36)

Excepting the introductory paragraphs §§ 1–11, it is apparent that §§ 13–65 on poetic cognition correspond to *inventio* and Heuristic; §§ 65–77 to *dispositio* and Methodology ('lucid *method*'); and §§ 77–107 to *elocutio* and Semiotic. In the *Reflections on Poetry*, therefore, we have a complete sketch of the entire theoretical aesthetic which Baumgarten left incomplete on his death. This places both the *Reflections on Poetry* and the question of Baumgarten's subsequent development in a new light. Given the consistency between the fundamental structure of the two texts, the earlier work represents the nearest Baumgarten came to developing a complete philosophical treatment of art, and the development represented by the *Aesthetica* appears less as an 'abortive attempt' than as a nuanced reconsideration of a previous achievement.

Baumgarten's claim in the preface to the *Reflections on Poetry* 'that philosophy and the knowledge of how to construct a poem, which are often held to be entirely antithetical, are linked together in the most amiable union' led to a major reform of the Wolffian philosophy. His attempt to unite philosophy and poetics culminated in his announcement in the last pages of the book of a new philosophy in which logic as an art of judgement would be complemented by aesthetic as an art of invention, the former arranging and disposing the materials produced by the latter. Implied in this extension of philosophy was the claim, later made explicit in the *Metaphysica* and *Aesthetica*, that aesthetic and rational knowledge differ in degree but not in kind. The bringing forth of objects in sensibility is related to their disposition by reason, but not in the restricted sense suggested by Wolff.

In the introduction to his lecture course on aesthetics Baumgarten gives a historical justification of his extension of philosophy to include a doctrine of sensibility, suggesting that early Greek philosophy emerged from poetry: 'Their insight was not purely distinct. Their first philosophy was indistinct and mythical' (1742; p. 67). The ambition of the *Reflections on Poetry* was to reconcile the rules for rational thinking with a set of rules for aesthetic thinking, thereby reconciling *aestheta* and *noeta* and settling the old dispute between the poets and the philosophers. In other words, the reform of philosophy lay in its recollection of its origins in poetry. It was axiomatic for Baumgarten that poetry was sensible knowledge, so it followed that an important step in the recollection of philosophy's origins lay in the philosophical consideration of poetry. The return to the origins of rational thinking in sensibility and poetry was intended to result in the reunion of thought and sensibility in an expanded system of philosophy.

The historical continuity of poetry and logic has analogues in the relation between aesthetics and logic, and that of the higher and the lower faculties (both psychological and institutional!). It is testimony to the transitional and experimental character of Baumgarten's thought that he habitually identified the historical, the doctrinal and the psychological aspects of continuity. This is also reflected in his insistence upon both continuity and rupture within the three continuities/oppositions of poetry/philosophy, aesthetics/logic, and higher/lower faculties, which followed from his use of both formal and dynamic notions of perfection. When he considers the oppositions in terms of continuity he follows a Leibnizian form of argument in which opposition simply expresses a difference in degree of recognition; but when he considers them taxonomically, he follows the Wolffian argument for a specific difference between the classes of perception. He does not rigorously pursue the implications of univocal continuity which Leibniz established on the identification of perfection and activity, but resorts to Wolff's formal notion of perfection as extensive unity within multiplicity. As a result poetry/philosophy, aesthetics/logic and higher/lower faculties are both continuous and discrete. The flexibility which this gave him enabled Baumgarten to dissolve some of the rigid demarcations of Wolff's system without abandoning its structure. It was in this sense that he was acknowledged by Herder as a transitional thinker, one with the role of opening new horizons without being able to follow through all the implications of his innovations.

The *Reflections on Poetry* perfectly expresses the equivocation of Baumgarten's thought. The book is based on the assumption that poetry and sensibility are identical and that the philosophical treatment of poetry is one with that of sensibility. Furthermore, the project of a *philosophical* treatment of poetry assumes the continuity of aesthetic and rational thinking: for if, as Wolff thought, indistinct thinking was repellent to philosophy, then there could be no philosophical treatment of indistinct thinking. Here Baumgarten's insight into the continuity of perception permits him to extend the scope of the system, while maintaining the systematic distinction between higher and lower faculties. The philosophical treatment of sensibility/poetry is the work of the higher faculty which would account for its own operations in logic, and for those of the lower faculty in aesthetic. But such a philosophical account of sensibility requires that sensibility and reason are both continuous and discontinuous. The fruits of the equivocation were reaped by some of Baumgarten's less reputable epigones who reversed the order of poetry and philosophy, producing those poetic accounts of philosophy, and aesthetic accounts of logic, which littered the Berlin bookstores in the 1750s.

The philosophical account of sensibility developed by Baumgarten in the *Reflections on Poetry* begins with a Wolffian definition of sensible experience, which is then elaborated in the guise of a rhetorical poetic. The object of inquiry is the 'sensate discourse' expounded according to the rhetorical schema of *inventio, dispositio,* and *elocutio*: 'The various parts of sensate discourse are: (1) sensate representations, (2) their interrelationships, (3) the words or articulate sounds which are represented by the letters and which symbolise the words' (1735, § 6, repeated at § 10). Aesthetic, or the doctrine of sensibility, is the exposition of sensate discourse according to the production of its sensate representations, their interrelationship, and their semiotic. The paradigmatic sensate discourse is the poem, and so the analysis of sensate discourse will focus on the poem. In fact, the focus of the *Reflections on Poetry* is even more specific, it being a loose commentary on Horace's *Ars Poetica*. This adds another confusing dimension to the work, for in spite of its philosophical innovation, the *Reflections on Poetry* follows a venerable tradition of German poetics (including Gottsched's *Dichtkunst*) which styled themselves as commentaries on Horace.

The first part of the book, *inventio* (§§ 13–65) considers the perfect sensate representations which form the materials of a poem. At this stage Baumgarten follows the Wolffian division of representations according to clarity, while later, in the *Aesthetica*'s 'Special Theory of Beautiful Cognition', 'clarity' is only one of six categories determining a 'beautiful thought'. Nevertheless, clarity in the early text does not designate a Wolffian description of a class of representations, but is a principle for dividing a continuum:

> In obscure representations there are not contained as many representations of characteristic traits as would suffice for recognizing them and for distinguishing them from others, and as, in fact, are contained in clear representations (by definition). Therefore, more elements will contribute to the communication of sensate representations if these are clear than if they are obscure. A poem, therefore, whose representations are clear is more perfect than one whose representations are obscure, and clear representations are more poetic than obscure ones.
>
> (§ 13)

Following the division between clear and obscure degrees of

recognition, Baumgarten divides representations into distinct and indistinct degrees of recognition. Perception is an act of discrimination, an act of judgement, not as in Wolff's subsumption of individuals under universals, but as in Leibniz's discrimination of differences. The insistence on the distinction between classes of distinct and indistinct representations keeps sensibility and reason, poetry and philosophy firmly apart:

> Distinct representations, complete, adequate, profound through every degree, are not sensate, and, therefore, not poetic . . . This is the principal reason why philosophy and poetry are scarcely ever thought able to perform the same office, since philosophy pursues conceptual distinctness above everything else, while poetry does not strive to attain this, as falling outside its province.
>
> (§ 14)

Baumgarten admits the Wolffian distinction between distinct and indistinct representations, while undoing it by pointing in § 16 to *degrees* of confusion ranging between intensive and extensive clarity. The admission both of a rigid distinction between confused and clear representations in §§ 14–15 and the possibility of a continuum of degrees of clarity in § 16 underlines Baumgarten's attempt to recover Leibnizian insights while preserving Wolffian structures.

The paradigm of a clear but indistinct representation is the image. The image is accordingly the most suitable material for a poem. Baumgarten arrives at this conclusion by showing that the representation of an individual has more extensive clarity than the representation of a species, which in its turn is more extensively clear than the representation of a genus (§§ 18–20). Images are the aesthetic equivalent of concepts in logic; they are representations which form the materials arranged in the discourse. The remainder of the discussion of invention discusses the use of images in poetry, and is especially concerned to justify two venerable propositions in the philosophy of art: (i) art is mimetic, and (ii) *ut pictura poesis* – poetry is like painting.

Both propositions are justified in terms of the new philosophy, and both justifications are related. In the case of imitation the effect of images is similar to that of sensation: 'The more clearly images are represented, the more they will be similar to sense impressions, so that they are often equivalent to rather weak sensations. Now to represent images as clearly as possible is poetic. Therefore it is poetic to make them very similar to sensations' (§ 38). Here Baumgarten interprets mimesis as the imitation of the *effect* of an object upon sensibility and not simply as the imitation of an object. His justification is couched in terms of the degree of intensity of a representation, and contrasts with those of both Gottsched and the Swiss. Baumgarten employs it in his reading of the *ut pictura poesis* proposition, where he anticipates Lessing's celebrated rejection of the proposition in *Laocoon*. Baumgarten agrees that poetry and painting seek the same end – of maximizing indistinct clarity – but distinguishes between the mode of presentation proper to each art: 'the grouping of poetry, meaning by this the poem, with painting, is to be understood in terms not of the art involved but of the effect achieved' (§ 39). Once again Baumgarten retains the traditional *topoi* while changing their meaning. In spite of using traditional terminology and working in the traditional format, Baumgarten's conclusions are not only opposed to Gottsched's, but also more radical than Bodmer and Breitinger's. His reformulation of the doctrine of mimesis permits him to include among valid poems 'heterocosmic fictions', which include 'things which are not sense impressions or images or fictions or true fictions' (§ 56) and 'utopian fictions' 'in which there is much that is mutually inconsistent' (§ 57).

Before leaving Baumgarten's discussion of *inventio* for *dispositio* we should consider another of Baumgarten's reformulations of a traditional *topos*. This is the maxim that poetry should encourage morality through 'delight and instruction'. Baumgarten avoids the traditional restriction of art to edifying subject matter by drawing the implication from Wolff's identification of the faculties of representation and volition that whatever pleases instructs by definition:

> Since desire, so far as it derives from a confused representation of the good, is called sensate, and since, on the other hand, a confused representation, along with an obscure one, is received through the lower part of the cognitive faculty, we can apply the same name to confused representations, in order that they may be distinguished from concepts distinct at all possible levels.
>
> (§ 3)

Since both desire and pleasure are effects of the representation of the same perfection, and the sensation of pleasure marks an indistinct recognition of the good, instruction may legitimately be subordinated to delight.

With § 64 of the *Reflections on Poetry* Baumgarten completes the first of the three sections of his rhetorical schema; in the *Aesthetica* this section remains incomplete after 904 paragraphs. The discussion of *dispositio* over §§ 65–77 in the *Reflections on Poetry* was not even drafted for the *Aesthetica*, and so remains the only evidence we have of how Baumgarten envisaged the second part of the science of aesthetics. The analogy of aesthetics to logic still holds, for while the first part considered the invention of the elements of cognition – the image or concept – the second considers their ordering into discourse. The logical discourse of the syllogism has its analogue in the aesthetic discourse of the poem. *Dispositio* or 'Methodology' is concerned with the order of a discourse, defined by Baumgarten as its theme: 'By theme we mean that whose representation contains the sufficient reason of other representations supplied in the discourse, but which does not have its own sufficient reason in them' (§ 66). The theme determines a concatenation of representations, ordering their relation, but is not itself exhausted by those relations; it contains the sufficient reason of a discourse but exceeds the narration of the discourse. The use of the term 'sufficient reason' is an important clue not only to Baumgarten's account of poetic method but also to the relationship of philosophy and poetry. He follows Wolff in maintaining that every event must have a sufficient reason for its occurrence, and this rule must be followed in the poetic as in the real world. However, where Gottsched interpreted this rule as meaning that poetry must be bound to the chain of sufficient reason as manifest in the actual world, Baumgarten distinguishes between two notions of the world: the world as the product of God and the world as the outcome of human artifice.

Baumgarten compares human with divine artifice. Just as the real world follows the laws of sufficient reason, so must the artificial world of the poem: 'We observed a little while ago that the poet is like a maker or a creator. So the poem ought to be like a world. Hence by analogy whatever is evident to the philosophers concerning the real world, the same ought to be thought of a poem' (§ 68). Following Leibniz's *Theodicy* (described as an 'excellent book' at § 22), Baumgarten likens the poetic theme which supplies a sufficient reason to a discourse, with the 'Great Theme' 'given in the rule of order by which things in the world follow one another for disclosing the glory of the Creator, the ultimate and highest theme of some immense poem, if one may so speak' (§ 71). The creative power of invention and the ordering activity of disposition complement one another in the creation of an artificial world (heterocosmos). The creation and ordering of the poet is compared with God's creation and ordering of the cosmos. The desideratum of productive activity is the ordering of fantasy and desire, or in Baumgarten's words: 'We have now set limits and put a curb to the fantasy and unbridled licence of the wit, which might shamefully abuse the preceding propositions [on unlimited mimesis], where we not only admitted images and fictions into a poem but assumed their perfection' (§ 68). Baumgarten then recognizes the potential autonomy of human productive energy while seeking to bring it under the laws of perfection.

Once again Baumgarten positions himself between Leibniz and Wolff. Where Leibniz united production and ordering in the self-sculpting of the human subject and Wolff repressed production in favour of heteronomous ordering, Baumgarten adopts a position which recognizes productive activity but seeks to order it rationally. When he discusses the poem Baumgarten is speaking by proxy of sensibility in general. Indeed, without conceding that the poesis involved in creating a heterocosmic poem is analogous to that of creating a heterocosmic world it is impossible to understand the later systematic articulation of aesthetic in the *Philosophia Generalis*. It is this broad notion of production that permitted Herder to develop a philosophy of history on the basis of Baumgarten's aesthetic.

Before proceeding to a discussion of the systematic articulation of aesthetic it remains to consider the third and final part of the *Reflections on Poetry*, §§ 71–101 corresponding to the rhetorical division of *elocutio* concerned with the presentation of a discourse. Baumgarten derives the poetic figures and meters from their effect on the listener. Where in the first two sections the emphasis lay on the production of a poem, here it lies in the reception or the spectator's 'judgement of sense'. Baumgarten defines the judgement of sense as 'A confused judgement about the perfection of sensations' (§ 92) and he identifies it with taste. A judgement of sense estimates the presence of a perfection according to the degree of pleasure, and not according to clarity of cognition: 'Their variety [length of syllables] is not of course felt distinctly if they are not scanned, but it is observed confusedly by the mind and to this extent furnishes sufficient matter for the judgement of the ear' (§ 101). From the pleasure accompanying the judgement of sense, an unapperceived ordering of experience, Baumgarten derives metre and rhythm: 'The kind of measure that, through the ordering of all the syllables in the discourse, promotes pleasure in the ear is called metre. If measure determines pleasure through many syllables following one another without any definite order, it is called rhythm' (§ 103).

The relationship between the three sections of the *Reflections on Poetry* is now apparent. There is an objective order of perfection which human artifice raises through its productive activity. The materials are given through *inventio*, ordered according to *dispositio*, and the production and ordering related through the pleasures of the *elocutio.* This is not done consciously but through an indistinct perception of perfection, experienced as pleasure. Both production and reception contain a moment of transcendence which orders activity (measure, sufficient reason) and which is experienced as pleasure.

The three parts of the *Reflections on Poetry* – invention, disposition, and presentation – progress from the production of poetic representations, through their ordering, to their presentation. It is noteworthy that so far in the text the word 'aesthetic' has not been mentioned: it first appears in the final paragraphs of the book (§§ 107–17) where Baumgarten adds 'at the end a few words on poetics in general'. In these closing words Baumgarten effects a palace coup within the Wolffian system and proclaims a new science. The claim that philosophical knowledge must concern itself with the lower cognitive faculty challenges the rationalism of the Wolffian system:

> Philosophical poetics is the science guiding sensate discourses to perfection; and since in speaking we have those representations which we communicate, philosophical poetics presupposes in the poet a lower cognitive faculty. It would now be the task of logic in its broader sense to guide this faculty in the sensate cognition of things, but he who knows the state of our logic will not be unaware how uncultivated this field is. What then? If logic by its very definition should be restricted to the rather narrow limits to which it is as a matter of fact confined, would it not count as the science of knowing things philosophically, that is, as the science for the direction of the higher cognitive faculty in apprehending the truth? Well then, Philosophers might still find occasion, not without ample reward, to inquire also into those devices by which they might improve the lower faculties of knowing, and sharpen them, and apply them more happily for the benefit of the whole world.
>
> (§ 115)

There are several things to note in this important passage. The first is the identification of the lower cognitive faculty as the productive or inventive faculty. Philosophical poetics is concerned with the perfection of discourse, but the representations communicated in a discourse must originate somewhere; they do not originate in the higher cognitive faculties, which merely order representations, so there must be another, inventive faculty which produces them. The second important point is the extension of logic to include the representations produced by the lower faculty. The ordering of these representations forms an important field for philosophical reflection, as was shown in the doctrines of *dispositio* and *elocutio*. A third point to note is the educational project of 'improving' and 'perfecting' the lower faculty 'for the benefit of the whole world'. This theme became central in the later *Aesthetica*, and marked the transition from a static psychology to an historical account of the emergence of the higher faculty through the self-cultivation of the lower. Although using Wolffian terminology, Baumgarten revolutionized the form and content of the system, so preparing the way for Herder's philosophy of history and Kant's transcendental logic.

On the basis of these arguments Baumgarten lodged his claim for the foundation of a new science of perception, a claim which he supported with an appeal to tradition:

> The Greek philosophers and the Church fathers have already carefully distinguished between *things perceived* [ά] and *things known* [ά]. It is entirely evident that they did not equate *things known* with things of sense, since they honoured with this name things also removed from sense (therefore images). Therefore *things known* are to be known by the superior faculty as the object of logic; *things perceived* [are to be known by the inferior faculty, as the object] of the science of perception, or *aesthetic*.
>
> (§ 116)

The distinction between the modes of perception requires a distinction between the sciences: things known form the province of logic, while things perceived form the province of aesthetic; however, both are necessary to philosophical knowledge. This claim in the *Reflections on Poetry* formed the basis of Baumgarten's reformation of the Wolffian philosophy.

One of the most remarkable features of Baumgarten's new science was its scope. This was the result of its polemical origin: the contents of aesthetic were developed against certain features of the Wolffian philosophy. Aesthetic was a palimpsest science which superimposed a response to the problem of including art in the Wolffian system, a recognition of the claims of sensibility to philosophical knowledge, and an attempt to broaden Wolffian logic to include the reflection on sensibility. The complexities of the *Reflections on Poetry* indicate the difficulty Baumgarten faced in achieving a sharp definition of his new science, and this already complex picture became even more involved when he sought to marshal aesthetics into the struggle of philosophy with the higher faculties of theology, law and medicine.

In this struggle aesthetic played an important role in defining philosophy as a universal, encyclopaedic science (*Weltweisheit*) against the particularistic claims of the higher faculties.

The already complex picture of aesthetics that emerges from the *Reflections on Poetry* becomes even more complicated in the *Philosophia Generalis* and the *Metaphysica*, where it is seen as fundamental to the system. In the *Philosophia Generalis,* published posthumously in 1770 but probably based on his introductory lectures to 'philosophy as a whole' (see above, p. 151), Baumgarten puts the case for philosophy against the faculties 'which are called superior'. Since the higher faculties depend on the logic and metaphysics developed by philosophy to order their materials, they are inferior to philosophy. Furthermore, the subject matter of theology was covered by theoretical philosophy (1770; § 223), and the subject matter of law and medicine by practical philosophy: 'Therefore [philosophy] naturally holds the first place among the disciplines' (§ 96). Underlying this extravagant claim was the extended notion of logic Baumgarten had developed in the closing pages of the *Reflections on Poetry*. Logic has two parts: aesthetic and logic *stricte dicta*; but aesthetic is now cast as an interpretative discipline or organon which complements the subsumptive activity of logic. To claim that logic *stricte dicta*, whose subject matter was largely syllogistic reasoning, was central to the activities of the higher faculties would have been absurd; but not the claim for a logic incorporating aesthetic as an interpretative discipline. For the business of the higher faculties in the German universities was to a great extent still the interpretation of canonic theological, legal and medical texts. The extension of logic to include aesthetic as an interpretative discipline gave substance to Baumgarten's claim that the higher faculties were methodologically dependent upon philosophy. Their activity in interpreting texts relied upon the 'method' or doctrine of interpretation established in the aesthetic section of the expanded logic.

Baumgarten defines philosophy as the 'knowledge of the qualities of things' and divides it into the philosophical organon, theoretical philosophy and practical philosophy (§ 146, see also the introduction to the *Acroasis Logica*). The first part or organon presents the rules of interpretative and subsumptive judgement, namely aesthetics and logic. Theoretical philosophy considers the four branches of metaphysical knowledge according to Wolff – ontology, cosmology, psychology and theology – and additionally physics. Finally practical philosophy follows the Aristotelean division of ethics and politics. It may be noted in passing that there are some striking resemblances between Baumgarten's and Kant's organization of philosophy. The latter's Transcendental Analytic is the only other example in the eighteenth century of the division of logic into aesthetic and logic *stricte dicta*, while the *Critique of Pure Reason* was intended as an organon for the legitimate pursuit of theoretical and practical philosophy.

With Baumgarten's rigorous division of the 'Organon' into aesthetic and logic, the already strained bounds of aesthetic in the *Reflections on Poetry* are stretched to breaking point: the list of contents of aesthetic covers over ten pages, and includes the arts of imagination, ingenuity, memory, prevision, chrestomantia through oracles, the reading of augurs, cryptography and many more (§ 147). He divides aesthetic as the science of sensitive knowledge into two parts: aesthetic *ipsam* and aesthetic as *ars signandi*. The former subdivision includes the poetic and psychological aspects of aesthetic (for example, *ars imaginandi* and *ars mnemonica*), aesthetic as a discipline of judgement (*ars diiudicandi seu critica aesthetica*) and also as the art of divination (*ars praevidendi et praesagiendi*). The second subdivision of aesthetic is an *Ars signandi et ex signis cognoscendi* and is composed largely of a '*Philologia Universalis*'. Aesthetic is now extended into a general theory of interpretation in which the logical rules of syllogistic reasoning are complemented by an art of judgement or *ars diiudicandi* for the interpretation of all forms of signification. Baumgarten's 'Organon' examines two basic forms of judgement: the application of a general rule to a particular case in logic and the extraction of significance from a particular case in aesthetic. What unites the two forms of judgement is their relation to perfection: logic subsumes the particular case under the rational order of perfection while aesthetic discerns the perfection implied in the particular case. This distinction will become clearer if we consider the relation of aesthetic and logic in the theoretical section of Baumgarten's philosophy, as it was expounded in his *Metaphysica*.

Baumgarten agrees with Wolff that representations are produced by the representative power of the soul: 'Thoughts are representations. Therefore the soul is a representative power' (§ 506), but emphasizes the continuity of the power of representation. For him distinct and confused thoughts are stages on a continuum of recognition and not generically distinct classes of representation. This emphasis changes the character of the representative force, for instead of being divided into a lower faculty of perception which presents representations for judgement by the higher estimative faculty, the two operations take place simultaneously in every perception as dispositions of representative power. Confused perception registers the bringing forth of things, their production, while distinct perception is conscious of the laws through which things are given, and by which they may be discriminated:

I perceive some things clearly, some things confusedly. Whoever thinks something confusedly, does not discriminate between its characteristics, but merely brings it forth, represents it. For if the characteristics of a confused representation are distinguished from each other, the confused representation is thought distinctly; and if it were not possible to recognize the confusion of characteristics, we would not be in a position to distinguish confused from other representations. Therefore whoever thinks confusedly, represents something as obscure.

(§ 510)

The obscurity of a confused thought is caused by self-consciousness not recognizing the laws by which it has brought things forth, but encountering these things as present. Since the power of representation simultaneously produces and orders its representations, it is vital to regard these dispositions as modalities, and not as distinct faculties. So while designating the modalities of the representative power in terms of distinct and obscure representations, Baumgarten re-introduces Leibniz's *petit perceptiones* in the 'pregnant thoughts' of § 517 to maintain the continuity of grades of representative power. Indeed, Baumgarten develops criteria of discrimination far more precise than Wolff's single criterion of visual clarity (clear/obscure, distinct/indistinct). He distinguishes between grades of consciousness in terms of quantity, extension, content, and breadth of consciousness, nobility, gravity, majesty, and poverty and levity. These apparently random criteria of discrimination are fully articulated in the *Aesthetica*'s six categories of aesthetic invention.

Baumgarten maintains Wolff's vocabulary of higher and lower faculties even though he rejects the separation of the active and passive dispositions of the representative power which it presupposes. This leads to the problem of restricting the content of the two faculties, given the potentially infinite number of gradations of consciousness they contain. This is apparent in Baumgarten's subdivision of the lower cognitive faculty – 'the representative power brings forth sensible perceptions by means of its lower faculty' (§ 521) – into subfaculties such as sense, fantasy, perspicuity, memory, creative facility, prevision, judgement, *et al*. The science of all these faculties is, of course, aesthetic: 'Aesthetic is the science and disposition of sensible consciousness (it is the logic of the lower faculties, the philosophy of the graces and the muses, lower epistemology [*gnoseologica inferior*] the art of thinking beautifully, and the art analogous to reason [*ars analogi rationis*] (§ 533). Yet more meanings of aesthetic are revealed in this passage, notably '*gnoseologia inferior*' and the '*ars analogia rationis*'. Their inclusion indicates a new emphasis in aesthetic: the science is concerned not only with describing the contribution of the lower faculties to generating the content of representations, but also with their estimative function.

For Baumgarten the estimative function of the faculty of representation consists in discriminating between perfections and imperfections: 'My recognition of the perfection and imperfection of things is judgement. Therefore I have a power of judgement' (§ 606). The estimation of perfections consists in judging the degree of unity in diversity manifest in a particular representation: so when a judgement is distinct, it is 'intellectual', when indistinct it is 'sensible' or a 'judgement of taste': 'The law of the faculty of judgement is: the perfection or imperfection of a thing may be recognized through whether its manifold are in harmony or disharmony. The faculty of judgement may do this distinctly or indistinctly, its judgements being sensible or intellectual. Sensible judgement is taste in the broad sense' (§ 607).

In one of the earliest uses of the word *critique* in German metaphysics, Baumgarten identifies critique with the art of judgement: 'Critique in the broad sense is the art of judgement. Thus critical aesthetic is the art of forming a taste, or the art of sensible judgement. Critique in the narrow sense, as it is generally seen, consists in intellectual judgement and is the science of the rules of judging distinctly between perfections and imperfections' (§ 607).

The extension of the activity of judgement to the lower faculty challenges Wolff's reservation of the prerogatives of judgement to the higher faculty. The generalization of critical activity to all levels of perception also changes the character of judgement: it is no longer, as it was for Wolff, the subsumption of individual representations under a rationally perfect universal, but the discovery or estimation of the presence of perfection in even the most indistinct perception. Critique trains the higher and the lower faculties to discriminate between perfections. Yet the political implications of the extension of critical competence to the lower faculty are not drawn out by Baumgarten. He did not carry judgement as critique over from theoretical into practical philosophy; in the latter, the Wolffian division of the faculties and the privileges of subsumptive judgement continued to rule.

Baumgarten's practical philosophy follows the Aristotelean division of ethics and politics, adding a doctrine of natural right. The appetitive faculties direct action according to the representation of the good, identified with perfection. At this point Baumgarten's recognition of the claims of the lower faculty to the exercise of judgement blurs; in practical philosophy only the higher faculty has the capacity to act according to a considered decision of the will. Certain representations determine the perceiver to action: the lower appetitive faculty determines action through 'blind' instincts and affects, while the higher faculty deliberates and acts according to a rational determination of the will. In contrast to the theoretical philosophy, where the two faculties were understood as degrees on a continuum, they are now conceived as antagonists. Harmony between the higher faculty of will and the lower appetitive faculties is only possible after the lower have been brought to order by the higher.

Baumgarten's practical philosophy remains closely tied to Wolff's. Perfection is the abstract good which can only be rationally willed; and the rational decision of the will requires the suppression of the affects. Unlike indistinct thoughts, the affects do not partake in any significant degree of perfection; they are not the practical equivalent of 'pregnant thoughts' but obstacles to a rational judgement of the good. One of the reasons for this asymmetry between Baumgarten's theoretical and practical philosophies is the latter's emphasis on external obligation. Baumgarten was unable to rework the legacy of Pufendorf and Wolff in the same way that he reworked Wolff's theoretical philosophy.

Baumgarten also follows Wolff in restricting ethics to the study of obligation in the state of nature in the *Ethica Philosphica* (1740) and *Initia philosophiae practicae*, and politics to the study of civil obligation in the *Jus Naturae* (1763). The *Ethica Philosophica* defines ethics as the 'knowledge of internal human obligation in the state of nature' (1740, § i) and distinguishes between general and special obligations. Both rest on natural law, identified with divine law: 'For all natural law, all ethics, all practical philosophy embrace the divine laws' (§ lxxxxi). The source of obligation is the perfection of the divine laws, but this can only be recognized through the higher faculty of reason. But because the rational discrimination of perfection is unsatisfactory in the state of nature, certain canons or laws of judgement have to be established in positive law.

In the *Philosophia Generalis* Baumgarten organizes his discussion of politics according to the various forms of associations and their corresponding obligations, a schema recalling Leibniz's earlier division of societies. The primary division is between simple and composite associations, simple associations being structured according to paternal, matrimonial, and filial obligations. Composite associations are divided according to family, economic (household), and civil obligations, the latter subdivided according to private and public; public obligation is further subdivided further according to personal obligations of the ruler and public obligations such as justice, security and the common welfare. Baumgarten's surviving texts in practical philosophy discuss various aspects of this schema. They are all characterized by the relegation of personal obligation and judgement to the rational judgement of the state.

This asymmetry between theoretical and practical philosophy is a striking feature of Baumgarten's philosophy. His theoretical philosophy exceeds the limits of Wolff's system, while his practical philosophy stays within its bounds. Consequently, Baumgarten favours distinct paradigms of judgement in the two branches of his system. The theoretical branch extends judgement into a discriminative activity common to all grades of perception, while the practical branch restricts it to the subsumptions of the higher faculty. Additionally, in theoretical philosophy the two faculties cooperate in judgement, while in the practical philosophy the higher faculty stands aloof from the lower. The theoretical philosophy's discriminative model of judgement rests on a continuum of recognition, while practical philosophy insists on the subsumptive model of judgement which follows the opposition of the higher and the lower faculties.

One of the consequences of Baumgarten's inability to pursue his reform of theoretical philosophy into the realm of practical philosophy is the restriction of aesthetic to theoretical philosophy. The extension of judgement to all levels of perception, and the understanding that judgement produces both its objects and the laws by which it discriminates between them, allows him to unite sensible perception and production in general with critical judgement and poesis in particular. Yet this insight into the unity of the productive and discriminative aspects of judgement is not carried through into practical philosophy. There is no trace in Baumgarten's practical philosophy of the self-ordering of society: the lower 'faculties' are at best passive material waiting to be ordered from above, but are usually pictured as threats to the deliberations of the higher faculty.

This restriction of aesthetic to theoretical philosophy was not only inconsistent with Baumgarten's view of the identity of perfection and the good, but also threatened his attempt to found the philosophical system on the basis of aesthetic as the science of interpretation and discrimination. He gave no reason why the validity of judgement as discrimination should not be extended from the perception of theoretical to practical perfection, nor did he explain why human *perception* proceeded according to a discriminative model of judgement, and human *action* according to a subsumptive one. These problems were tackled in the *Aesthetica*, where aesthetic judgement is extended to practical philosophy through a theory of aesthetic education. This view of the culture of the power of representation through education would have completed his revision of the Wolffian philosophy, but illness prevented him from realizing the synthesis, and left only the suggestive fragment of the *Aesthetica*.

The recognition of the need to extend the scope of aesthetic is evident in the differences between the *inventio* of the *Reflections on Poetry* and the '*Heuristica*' of the *Aesthetica*. The first section of the earlier work defined the sensate representation according to the single criterion of clarity. In the later work, '*Heuristica*' is divided into beautiful cognition 'in general' and beautiful cognition 'in particular', the latter comprising seven sections, of which only the first five were completed. Six of these sections concern the several criteria of discriminating between aesthetic representations: *ubertas*, *magnitudo*, *veritas*, *lux*, *certitudo*, and *vita*. This is a significant advance on the single criterion of clarity employed in the *Reflections on Poetry*; but even more important is the first of the seven sections on the 'aesthetic character'. The discussion of the formation of the 'aesthetic character' follows Quintilian's *Education of the Citizen Orator* and registers a radical change of ethos from the *Reflections on Poetry*. In place of the earlier, Wolffian discussion of the power of representation, Baumgarten emphasizes the formation of an 'aesthetic character'. The first of the seven sections adds to the six characteristics of a beautiful representation which have to be covered in an aesthetic education the qualities of character necessary to begin such an education – *natura*, *exercitas*, *disciplina*, *impetus*, *correctis*. The emphasis on education represents Baumgarten's attempt to develop the practical implications of aesthetic ignored in his previous practical philosophy.

In the 'Prolegomena' to the *Aesthetica*, Baumgarten establishes the metaphysical conditions for the programme of education advocated in the rest of the book. The first sign of his departure from his earlier position is the subtle shift in his definition of aesthetic. The definition of aesthetic in the *Metaphysica* was:

Scientia sensitive cognoscendi et propendi est Aesthetica (logica facultatis cognoscitivae inferioris, philosophia gratiarum et musarum, gnoseologia inferior, ars pulcre cogitandi, ars analogi rationis).

(§ 533)

The definition in *Aesthetica* is similar, but with one important difference:

Aesthetica (theoria liberalium artium, gnoseologia inferior, ars pulcre cogitandi, ars analogi rationis,) est scientia cognitionis sensitivae.

(§ 1)

In both definitions aesthetic is the science of sensible knowledge that includes the *ars pulcre cogitandi* and an *ars analogi rationis*. The change from *philosophia gratiarum et musarum* to *theoria liberalium artium* is insignificant, but the deletion of any reference to the *logica facultatis cognoscitivae inferioris* points to a radical change in Baumgarten's view of aesthetic. The erasure of the psychological distinction of higher and lower faculties reflects the commitment to the continuity of distinct and indistinct knowledge. In the lecture transcript he went so far as to describe the truth claims of both logic and aesthetic as 'truths of aesthetico-logic' (§ 424). The truths of logic and of aesthetic differ only in degree and not in kind. It was on this basis of the continuity of knowledge that Baumgarten established his programme of aesthetic education.

The notion of a 'natural aesthetic', or a sensibility to be cultured through education, is central to the *Aesthetica*. The work of educating this sensibility is not delegated to reason but is undertaken by the entire economy of human powers. The challenge which this notion of education poses to traditional views, enlightened and unenlightened, is reflected in the embattled tone of the Prolegomena. It is largely a defence of aesthetic against objections on two fronts. Against the (Wolffian) objection that the realms of aesthetic and imagination are unworthy of philosophy Baumgarten answers: 'the philosopher is a man among other men, and it cannot be well if he considers such a large part of human knowledge beneath his dignity' (§ 6). This reply shows how the continuum of representations is extended into a comprehensive anthropology in which all forms of human activity and knowledge are worthy of philosophical attention. A similar insistence on the continuity of human knowledge is evident in his reply to the objection that 'confused thoughts are the mother of error':

a) But confusion is the indispensible condition for the discovery of truth, for nature makes no leaps between darkness and light. Twilight lies between night and day. b) For this reason one must be concerned with confused knowledge, in order to avoid the errors which beset those who ignore it. This is not to praise confused knowledge, but to improve it, remembering that an element of confusion is unavoidable.

(§ 7)

The extension of the principle of continuity into an anthropology is complemented by an emphasis on the development of knowledge: distinct representations can only be understood through their origins in indistinct representations. The defence of these anthropological and genealogical insights marks a decisive break with the Wolffian enlightenment – which countered darkness with light rather than showing, in Baumgarten's words, that twilight stands between night and day.

In his reply to the final objection Baumgarten defends himself against both Wolffian and Pietist complaints that the lower faculties should be resisted and not encouraged. In the *Aesthetica* he defends himself against the recognizably Wolffian position that 'It is better to combat the lower faculties than to excite and confirm them' (1750; § 12). The same objection is encountered in the lecture transcript, but expressed in a Pietist idiom: 'They say that the Bible tells us to crusade against the flesh, the corrupted lower faculty of the soul, and not to improve it' (1742; § 11). His replies to the objections are addressed in their respective idioms. In the *Aesthetica*, apart from a glancing reference to the parable of the talents, he defends the lower faculties in secular terms:

a) It is not necessary to tyrannize the lower faculties, but to guide them.
b) In so far as it can, aesthetic will undertake this guidance.
c) The aesthetician does not want to excite and confirm the corruption of the lower faculties, but to order them properly so that they do not become more corrupted through abuse, for one must avoid their misuse without suppressing a divinely bestowed talent.

(1750; § 12)

The Wolffian tyranny of the higher over the lower faculty forgets the lower faculty's potential for self-education. Aesthetic will help realize this potential or divinely bestowed talent. The revaluation of sensibility is even more apparent in the lecture transcript. Baumgarten employs an unmistakably Pietist idiom to evoke the potential for earthly perfectibility, for a cultivation of immanent but unrecognized traces of divine perfection in the world. He claims that the Pietist objection to aesthetic:

confuses the suppression of the sinful with its total destruction. The latter ignores human nature, which is not the way of the Christian religion; this seeks only to govern this confused knowledge. Aesthetics does not strengthen fleshy desires, but convinces them of the advantages of fearing God . . . If one says that they can only be brought to fear God through supernatural means, and not through art, then one underestimates that some degree of improvement can be achieved through human arts without divine aid. Since there is a trace of God's likeness in this knowledge, we can make it clearer through aesthetic and understand it better.

(1742; § 11)

In both idioms aesthetic is defended as providing an education in discrimination between perfection and imperfection in the world and the soul, so contributing to the development of sensibility toward perfection. This would be accomplished through neither the religious ascesis of Pietism, nor the secular ascesis of Wolffianism, but through the realization of divine talents and the development of innate perfections. The pleasures of the senses are formative and vivifying, and are not the opponents of reason.

Baumgarten's view of education as the realization of innate perfections differs considerably from Wolff's view of culture as the submission of sensibility to rational perfection. The potential to perfect or realize innate perfections characterized human perfection and is the source of beauty: 'The goal of aesthetics is the perfecting of sensible knowledge as such, by which is meant beauty' (§ 14). The *Aesthetica* represents the transition from Wolff's static rational notion of perfection, with its accompanying subsumptive model of judgement, to a dynamic view of perfection as the activity of perfecting through education. In this view judgement is both productive and discriminative, both aspects united in realization. Baumgarten then succeeds in finding a place for art within systematic philosophy, but at the expense of the system.

The text of the *Aesthetica* begins with the natural aesthetic and proceeds to an account of its perfecting. Both reason and sensibility are involved in this activity, but in an harmonious manner: 'The lower faculties must harmonize with the higher' (1750; § 38). This harmony presupposes the unity of the two faculties in a single power of representation. Education was the discovery of the rules implicated in sensibility; this rationality is more extensive than the reason of the higher faculty, for 'It is necessary to distinguish between using reason and making syllogisms' (§ 38). Reason consists in the self-realization of the representative power through the discovery of innate perfections. Beneath its luxuriance of detail and numbing distinctions the fragmentary *Aesthetica* describes nothing less than the process by which reason gives itself both objects and law.

The inability to complete the *Aesthetica* can be seen as symptomatic of Baumgarten's intellectual predicament. His attempt to introduce art into the system meant that the system had to be fundamentally transformed. Instead of Wolff's emphasis on subsumption without discrimination, Baumgarten tried to re-establish the system on the unity of production and estimation, while preserving as much of it as possible. The failure of this attempt, described by Kant as 'abortive', meant that there could be no return to the Wolffian system. Although it was never his intention, Baumgarten's aesthetic released a host of second-rate thinkers from the fetters of systematic thinking. It was against their efforts that Herder and Kant took on Baumgarten's task of re-establishing the foundations of systematic thinking: Herder in a philosophy of history, and Kant in a critical survey of the foundations of systematic philosophy. In order to situate these recoveries of the system it is necessary first to examine the unsystematic philosophies released by Baumgarten against which both philosophers defined their positions.

Aesthetic to Philosophy of History

Herder is very much against the abuse of reason through abstract thinking in which one neglects the concrete. But the universal is not always abstracted, for a great deal is self-sufficiently universal. Such are all judgements which do not depend *in concreto* on experience, but where the judgement of experience itself required a priori principles.

Kant, *Reflection* 911

Writing from Berlin on 13 November 1765, Lambert complained to Kant, 'Hereabouts one philosophizes exclusively about the so-called beautiful science'. The author of the *Observations on the Feelings of the Beautiful and the Sublime* (1764) replied sympathetically, complaining of the 'wearying chatter' of those 'with whom the only evidence of taste is that they talk about taste' (1968, p. 49). The exchange is indirect testimony to the explosion of writings stimulated by Baumgarten's *Aesthetica* during the 1750s and 1760s, a phenomenon which prompted Herder to complain 'We live, alas, in the epoch of beauty' (1769a,

p. 59). Both he and Kant condemned the mediocrity of this literature, but their judgement of it, and their own thinking about aesthetics, differed on one crucial issue. Kant did not distinguish between Baumgarten and his epigones; they were all involved in the same 'abortive attempt' to produce a science of taste. For Herder, Baumgarten's writings inaugurated a revolution in philosophy which his epigones threatened to reduce to a psychology of taste. So while Kant fused the arguments of Baumgarten and his followers into the single argument for 'aesthetic judgement' analysed in the *Critique of Judgement-Power*, Herder undertook to defend Baumgarten from his disciples. The difference in interpretative strategy contributed to the differences which later emerged between the two on the issue of aesthetics.

The defence of Baumgarten's aesthetics against the disciples and detractors who threatened to reduce it to a dispute about taste is the key to Herder's early polemics. This is first apparent in Herder's critique of Baumgarten's self-professed disciple, Georg Friedrich Meier, who used a discourse of aesthetic against Gottsched in the Leipzig/Zürich controversy. Meier's early writings *Untersuchung einiger Ursachen der verdorbenen Geschmacks der Deutschen* (1746–8) and *Beurtheilung der Gottschedischen Dichtkunst* (1747, dedicated to Bodmer and Breitinger), are tedious polemics against Gottsched which curiously arrive at the same conclusions as the latter's *Dichtkunst*. For Meier the task of aesthetics is the promotion of taste, which he defines, like Gottsched, as the 'competence' (*Fertigkeit*) of the 'lower power of judgement' (*untere Beurtheilungskraft*) (1747; p. 74) to discriminate between perfections. This position is argued at length in the ostensibly Baumgartian *Anfangsgründe aller schönen Wissenschaften* (1748–50). Although the apologia for the new science of aesthetics paraphrases Baumgarten's lectures, and while the architectonic of the *Anfangsgründe* is similar to the *Aesthetica*, it differs from its model in important respects. The most important difference involves the object of aesthetics; for Meier, this is not the scientific understanding of sensibility, but the promotion of 'beautiful thinking': to use Kant's later terminology, Meier restricts aesthetics to the 'cultivation of taste'.

This was not Herder's understanding of aesthetic; he considered it a strict science 'if science is considered correctly and not according to Meier's conception of it' (1769a; p. 26). He rebukes Meier in the fourth *Kritische Wälder* (1769) for the confusion of aesthetic and the theory of taste, and insists that the two projects be rigorously distinguished: 'The one is an *ars pulcre cogitandi*, the other *scientia de pulcro et pulcris philosophice cogitans*; the one can only make connoisseurs of taste, while the other should make philosophers of it. The mixture of the two concepts leads to a monstrous aesthetic, and when Meier adds to his explanation that it "improves" sensible perception, one knows even less' (1769a; p. 23). Herder mercilessly exposes the close connection between Meier's version of aesthetic and the narrow early enlightenment notions of perfection, and insists that the value of Baumgarten's thought lay in its critique of these notions. It was evident to Herder that Meier's championing of Baumgarten's aesthetic not only failed to do it justice, but probably did it harm.

Herder's treatment of Meier was mild in comparison with his attack on Baumgarten's critic Friedrich Justus Riedel in the same fourth *Kritische Wälder*. His targets were Riedel's *Theorie der schönen Künste und Wissenschaften* (1767) and his *Ueber das Publicum* (1768). Riedel's *Theorie* was an eclectic mixture of French, British and German ideas organized according to three psychological *Grundkräfte* or 'basic powers': 'Philosophy, insofar as it is concerned with the vocation of humanity, has three objects, just as humanity has three objects of its thinking, acting and its feeling – the True, the Good, and the Beautiful' (1767; p. 7). One of the puzzling features of this definition is its unconscious allusion to three of the four medieval transcendentals: the Good, the True and the Beautiful. The One appears as their common principle – the unity in manifold. This is one of the many reincarnations of the transcendentals in German enlightenment thought, and ironically may derive from Baumgarten's discussion of them in his *Metaphysica*. In Riedel's case they are translated into the psychological faculties of the *sensus communis* (the true), the moral sense (the good, borrowed directly from Hutcheson), and taste (the beautiful). Aesthetics in Riedel's *Theorie* is demoted from being the master science of obscure perceptions to the rank of 'The philosophy of taste' (p. 8). Herder concentrated his attack on Riedel's faculty philosophy, complaining that the proliferation of *Grundkräfte* was enough to drive him back to the Wolffian philosophy. For him the precision of the Wolffian school compared favourably with the 'Crusian–Riedel labyrinth – where more and more *Grundkräfte* are wildly entangled, where the most composed and contrived capacities of the soul become basic perceptions out of which everything one wants, or does not want, follows, where the human soul becomes a chaotic abyss of inner, immediate feelings, and philosophy becomes sentimental and obscure gossip' (1769a; p. 12). Herder objected to the transformation of what he judged to be the outcome of a long history of culture into immediate 'senses'. Taste for example 'is not a basic power, not a general power of the soul, but an habitual application of our judgement to an object of beauty' (p. 36). He considered the faculties as achievements of the culturing of confused ideas, and not immediate givens: to take them for such misunderstands both the origins and the development of the human psyche. The faculty for judging between true and false, good and beautiful, beautiful and ugly, was a product of human self-cultivation and not a *Grundkraft*. For Herder the study of this self-cultivation was the proper object of the science of aesthetic intimated by Baumgarten.

Herder employed his discovery of a philosophy of history in Baumgarten's aesthetic against the Berlin philosphers Mendelssohn and Sulzer. Their understanding of Baumgarten's psychology did not stretch beyond the acknowledgement of the unity of the soul and the plurality of its obscure perceptions; they did not see it as an account of self-cultivation. Where Herder set himself to trace the historic development of the 'unity in a manifold of representations', Mendelssohn and Sulzer were content to state it formally in terms of perfection. For them the mediation of the unity and the manifold was not achieved through self-cultivation, but through the abstract principles of 'beauty' and 'harmony'.

This is apparent in Mendelssohn's essay *Über die Hauptgrundsätze der schönen Künste und Wissenschaften* (1757), where the unity of the soul and the plurality of its representations were harmonized through 'the beautiful': 'Beauty is the autocratic mistress of all our perceptions, the ground of all our natural drives, and the vivifying spirit that transforms speculative knowledge of truth into perception and that kindles active resolution. She enchants us in nature where she may be found originally but dispersed; and the human spirit knows how to imitate and reproduce her' (1757; p. 174). Mendelssohn self-consciously fuses Shaftesbury's 'beautiful order' and Baumgarten's philosophy in the notion of the mediation of perfection through the beautiful. He finds the source of the beauties of art and nature in the harmony between subjective and objective perfection. The harmony may be either conscious or unconscious: in the former case it belongs to the clear knowledge of the speculative sciences; in the latter, to the confused knowledge of the 'beautiful sciences'.

The notion of a harmony between objective and subjective perfection proved very influential, it also formed the basis of Sulzer's *Untersuchung über den Ursprung der angenehmen und unangenehmen Empfindungen* (1751) and Eberhard's *Theorie der schönen Wissenschaft*, (1783, dedicated to Mendelssohn). Sulzer, however, determines the relation of subjective and objective perfection more precisely by developing the notion of the power of judgement. He accepted Wolff's definition of the soul as a single power of representation, and derived the feeling of pleasure from its free play. He illustrates

his thought with an analogy between the power of the soul and a
flow of a river: anything which conduces to the free flow of
representations is agreeable; anything obstructing it, disagreeable:
'The soul resembles a river which peacefully flows as long as its path
is not disturbed. It will rise and rage as soon as a dam is set against
its course. This is the origin of unpleasant sensations or displeasure'
(1757; p. 12). A condition for the free flow of the power of
representation is perfection, or unity in plurality, for 'no object is
beautiful for the senses if it doesn't contain a manifold in unity'
(p. 28). Unlike Mendelssohn, Sulzer is not content simply to name
this proportion 'the beautiful' but sees the unification of a manifold
as a work whose achievement causes pleasure. With this active view
of perfection as a work, Sulzer points beyond the formal notion of
perfection, but does not fully unfold the implications of his thought.

Sulzer takes two positions on the unification of a manifold. Both
suppose that the unification is the work of consciousness, that
perfection is realized, but one returns to a formal notion of perfection,
while the other hesitantly points beyond it. In the first case, Sulzer
maintains that there is an objective proportion underlying the
distinction of unity and manifold, which is realized in perception
(p. 54). In the second Sulzer tries to think of the unification as an
activity, relying on the same analogy of the catoptric anamorph as
was earlier used by Hobbes. The anamorph discovers/produces unity
in a manifold:

> every beauty contains a mass of particular ideas, and it proceeds
> to represent to us a confused idea of the whole, until we have
> found the unity through which we can develop the manifold,
> and the idea of the whole, which was previously indistinct,
> becomes clear. It is like the optical images which one puts
> under a cylindrical mirror. They appear to be grotesque figures
> in which one cannot discern the slightest order, until the
> mirror is placed in the middle of them, and the scattered parts
> are drawn and unified, and what initially appeared a shadowy
> caricature becomes a beautiful column [*Bildsäule*]. Unity does
> for the beautiful what the mirror does in this case.
>
> (pp. 39–40)

The cylindrical mirror effects the unification of a manifold, yet
transcends the dichotomy of unity and manifold. It is transcendental,
not in the medieval sense of an objective proportion, but as a
technology for the configuration of activity. The cylindrical mirror of
the anamorph belongs neither to the object nor to perception, yet

serves to unify them. It serves here, as it did for Hobbes and the Mersenne circle, as an analogy for the simultaneous invention and disposition of the objects of perception. Sulzer then takes a further step toward specifying the transcendental production of unity in a manifold which anticipates Herder and Kant's solutions. The sensations in the soul are awakened or produced by the 'impressions of the tools of sensibility' which, like the catoptric anamorph, work the manifold of perception into a new product or unity. The tool becomes the transcendental, and the unification of a manifold in consciousness is understood to be produced.

Although Sulzer experiments with the production of unity in a manifold, he quickly falls back to Mendelssohn's formal position. He does not unify the argument for an objective proportion of unity and manifold with that of their production. However, by setting out the two arguments he offered, in Herder's words, 'the metaphysical basis for a future aesthetics' (1769a; p. 174). His eventual preference for the objective definition of perfection led him to follow Meier, Riedel, and Mendelssohn in reducing aesthetic to a theory of taste. So much is apparent in his encyclopaedia of the fine arts – the *Allgemeine Theorie der schönen Künste* – which aimed to promote taste and human happiness through the fine arts. The '*sittliche Bildung der Gemüthes*' (ethical cultivation of the spirit) (1771–4; p. v) was to be promoted by over 1300 pages of alphabetically organized definitions and concepts from the fine arts. And as Herder pointed out in his review, the *Allgemeine Theorie* was a *summa* of enlightenment aesthetic theory as well as a monument to its formal, paternalistic didacticism.

Herder's esteem for Baumgarten is in sharp contrast with the near contempt he showed for his followers. Even as late as the *Kalligone*, published ten years after the *Critique of Judgement-Power*, he laments: 'if only [Baumgarten] had completed his aesthetic' (1800; p. 261). Earlier, in a letter to Nicolai in February 1767, he describes Baumgarten, along with Abbt and Heilmann, as 'writers who have given me the greatest pleasure, and whom unfortunately Germany has lost far too early' (1767a; p. 175). He proposes to write memorial essays on the three writers, and in the essay '*Von Baumgartens Denkart in seinen Schriften*', presented what is still one of the finest appreciations of the philosopher's achievement. There he situates the inventor of aesthetics as

A Wolffian philosopher and a Christgauer poet in one person; admittedly at that time a rare and stimulating event; a time when nothing was thought to be more antithetical than taste and philosophical reflection; when one philosophized over everything one knew and did not know, if not beauty and the philosophy of art. Then emerged the philosopher who first took it in his head to unite the two, which were already joined in the formation of his thinking, and who tried to see whether the Wolffian philosophy could be extended to include poetry.

(1767; p. 184)

Herder sees Baumgarten's 'metapoetics' or synthesis of poetry and philosophy as resting on a general theory of reflexive knowledge. This theory understands experience as the reflection upon sensibility, and sees poetry and philosophy as different modes of reflection. It is this anthropological and historical foundation to the unification of philosophy and poetry which Herder defends against the understanding of aesthetic as a philosophy of taste.

Herder's transformation of Baumgarten's aesthetic into a philosophy of culture follows three main paths of development. The first, marked by the two Berlin Academy prize essays on the *Origin of Language* (1771) and on the *Knowledge and Sensation of the Human Soul* (published in 1775), expands Baumgarten's psychology into an account of the 'entire economy' of human perception and action. The second is the philosophy of art anticipated in the *Reisejournal* and developed in the book *Plastik* (1778) and the third is the philosophy of history developed in *Yet Another Philosophy of History* (1774) and later in the *Ideas for a Philosophy of the History of Humanity* (1784–91). The three paths converge on a vision of proportion as a dynamic 'economy' produced by the free exercise of human judgement.

Herder's notion of proportion differs considerably from other eighteenth-century accounts: it is not a providentially established form mediated through sensible or intellectual judgement, but the realization of human productive and communicative capacities through reflective judgement. His first systematic discussion of this dynamic view of proportion appears in the *Essay on the Origins of Language*. Deviating unrepentantly from the Academy's brief on the origin of language, Herder concentrates on the problem of the emergence of consciousness from human sensibility. In place of discrete faculties or capacities for thinking, willing, and language, he proposes a totality of human powers which structures itself through 'reflection':

in order to avoid confusions of [knowing and willing] with separate faculties of reason, we shall call the complete disposition of human nature reflection [*Besonnenheit*].[28] It follows through those binding rules by which the words sensibility and instinct, phantasy and reason are but determinations of a single power in which opposites sublate each other [*wo Entgegensetzungen einander aufheben*] that – unless human beings were to be purely instinctual animals, they would have to be reflective beings by means of a free-acting power of the soul.

(1771, p. 31; p. 132)

Free reflection is an act of judgement, which Herder understands as an apperceptive discrimination:

The human being shows reflection when the power of its soul acts so spontaneously that in the vast ocean of sensations rushing in on it, it may pick out, so to speak, one wave on which to fix its attention and be conscious of doing so. It shows reflection when from the fleeting dreams of images which flit past its senses, it can arouse itself to a moment of alertness, concentrate deliberately on one image, observe it quietly and clearly, isolate some characteristics of it, and identify it as this object and no other. It shows reflection not only in recognising clearly or distinctly the properties of the objects before it, but also by recognising the properties which distinguish objects from each other. This first act of apperception renders a clear concept: it is the first judgement of the soul.

(pp. 34–5; p. 135)

Apperception takes place through the establishment of signs, which do not signify objects but acts of reflection. These signs are words, specifically verbs denoting the act of reflection, which are then recognized in reflection. The first act of consciousness is a separation – as Hegel later put it, an *ur-theilen* or originary separation – both of objects from each other and of the human subject from objects. However, this activity of judgement is always reflective; the separation is unified by the very act of reflection:

It is remarkable how this self-created inner sense of the spirit constitutes in its very origin also a means of creating unity [*Verbindung*]. I cannot conceive my first human thought, cannot form my first reflective judgement, without having or desiring a dialogue in my soul; the first human thought encloses the ability to converse with others. The first sign which I grasp is both a distinguishing word for me and communicative word for others.

(p. 47; p. 141)

The original exercise of freedom in reflection and judgement is both a separation and a unification; it is an activity which establishes a proportion between the two modes of judgement.

Herder's philosophy of language transforms Baumgarten's nascent theory of aesthetic education into a theory of culture. It renders explicit the relation between consciousness, sensibility and freedom implied in Baumgarten's psychology. The self-cultivation of sensibility is achieved through the free action of reflection and judgement, with language serving as the means by which this activity becomes the history of the self-cultivation of humanity. In other words, Herder's philosophy of language follows from his philosophy of culture and is an aspect of his generalization of the Baumgartian problematic of the cultivation of the sensibility into a philosophy of history.

Another aspect of Herder's development of aesthetic is the philosophy of art, represented by his pivotal work on sculpture, *Plastik*, written in the late 1760s and published in 1778. This work revolutionized Baumgarten's aesthetic in both form and content, and stands beside the *Critique of Judgement-Power* as a sublation of eighteenth-century debates in the philosophy of art. It is based on an entirely different notion of sensibility from other enlightenment aesthetics, as is indicated by Herder's choice of sculpture as his canonical art form, in contrast with Baumgarten and his followers for whom the canonical art was poetry. This assumption had already been challenged by Lessing's distinction between poetry and painting in the *Laocoon* in terms of their different modes of perception and representation: the representation of bodies in space is the prerogative of painting, while that of actions in time is the prerogative of poetry. Yet Herder's appeal to sculpture in *Plastik* differs fundamentally from Lessing's reading of the Laocoon group in his celebrated treatise.

One of the many paradoxes of Lessing's extraordinary book is that the work of art which he compares with Virgil's representation of the death of Laocoon in the *Aeneid* is not a painting but a sculpture. Yet whenever Lessing discusses the sculpture of the death of Laocoon it is as if he were describing a painting. This reduction of sculpture to painting did not simply follow from Lessing being acquainted with the Laocoon only through reproductions, but was the direct outcome of his account of perception and representation. His division of the arts according to temporal or spatial representation rested upon a visual paradigm of perception; bodies in space and actions in time are both given to vision. He considers even the most celebrated depiction of productive activity in world literature – the forging of Achilles' shield – from the standpoint of the spectator:

> We see not the Shield, but the divine artificer at work upon it. He steps up with hammer and tongs to his anvil, and after he has forged the plates from the rough ore, the pictures which he has selected for its adornment stand out one after another before our eyes under his artistic chiseling. Nor do we lose sight of him again until all is finished. When it is complete we are amazed at the work, but it is with the believing amazement of an eye-witness who has seen it in the making.
>
> (1766; p. 68)

Lessing distinguishes between poetry and painting in terms of two forms of spectatorship; Herder, however, shows in *Plastik* that sculpture depends on a notion of experience that exceeds vision, the experience of the maker rather than the viewer.

On the title page of *Plastik* Herder slaps the 'epoch of beauty' in the face with a sentence from Diogenes Laertes – 'What is beauty – that's a blindman's question.' In the text he overturns the German Enlightenment's visual paradigm of the clear and distinct perception of a perfection in favour of a notion of perfection as 'form' or proportion which is produced and experienced through the entire economy of the senses. The distortion of this economy in favour of visual perception contributes to the creation of an '*ophthalmit*' culture which 'with thousands of eyes, without feeling, without probing [*tastende*] hand, remains all the time in Plato's cave with no concept of any physical characteristics' (1778; p. 7). Here the original meaning of taste comes through in the verb *tasten*, to test or to try, which is here quite distinct from the metaphorical *Geschmack*. As in the *Essay on the Origin of Language*, judgement is not a visual discrimination which sorts perceptions according to spatial criteria but an act of the entire economy of human power. For Herder this was manifest in the experience of the child, who:

> grasps, grips, takes, risks, probes, measuring with feet and hands, creating around itself with certainty and security the first, most difficult but necessary concepts of body, form, magnitude, space, distance and suchlike . . . Here, where vision

and feeling are ceaselessly bound, and each through the other is investigated, extended, raised, strengthened, is formed here the first judgement.

(pp. 7–8)

Visual discrimination rests on a foundation of a tactile experience, and it is on this experience that Herder intends to establish his philosophy of art: the visual sense 'borrows from and builds on other senses, its auxiliary concepts must be its foundation, which it only illuminates. If I don't penetrate into these concepts of other senses, if I don't seek shape and form, and instead of looking – grasp fundamentally, I will float eternally in the air, swimming among the soap bubbles with my theories of beauty and truth' (1778; p. 11). Through a 'fundamental grasp' of experience as sensibility Herder seeks to achieve the unification of the theory of perception and theory of art intimated by Baumgarten's *Aesthetica*.

Fundamental to this enterprise is an understanding of perfection and form which follows from the view of judgement as a process of tactile investigation rather than optical discrimination. Perfection is not a static proportion between part and whole, but a dynamic economy of forces; form consists in the embodiment of these forces: 'Beauty is only transparency, form, sensible experience of purposive perfection, vivacity, human health. The more a part signifies what it should signify, the more beautiful it is. And only inner sympathy, that is feeling and the transposition of our ego into the thoroughly probed shape [*durchtastete Gestalt*] is the guide and familiar of beauty' (p. 56).

The production of form and proportion out of the reflective employment of the economy of forces is the origin of beauty. It is not realized through a visual representation of a perfection which separates representation and represented, but through the work of embodiment which reveals and embodies (*durchschein*) the perfection. For Herder this embodiment is best realized in the 'complete presentation' of sculpture and not in the 'narrative magic' (p. 17) of painting. Furthermore, the activity of judging is itself plastic and reflective; it is not determined by the discrimination of clarity or distinctness, but by the tactile 'bringing forth' or production of objects.

With this unification of the philosophies of art and sensibility, Herder brings out what was latent in Baumgarten's aesthetic and arrives at a position similar to that of the late Leibniz. Both see perfection as a potential for activity, and its realization as a formative activity; the embodiment of perfection is understood as a reflective process of self-sculpting. This was a break with the predominantly visual paradigm of perception endemic to the German enlightenment, with its corollary of a passive, policed subject. The relation of a visual paradigm of perception and the politics of the police-state was manifest in Wolff and the early Wolffians and not entirely escaped by Baumgarten. Although the latter maintained the visual discourse of clear and distinct ideas, he extended the categories of a beautiful perception and emphasized the work of recognition. Judgement was not simply a discriminative faculty which administered the laws of reason, but an autonomous and productive power of the subject which both gave itself laws and discriminated according to those laws. Herder realizes the aesthetic and political implications of this position far more rigorously than Baumgarten, developing the former in *Plastik* and the latter in his philosophy of history. The understanding of beauty as sensibility bringing itself into the light contrasts with the enlightenment's desire to bring light to the sensibility; in the former, the senses are active and productive, in the latter they are passive and policed.

The Wolffian enlightenment narrowed freedom and judgement to the welfare activities of the all-seeing police-state. The split between the passive lower and the active higher psychological faculties, figured in terms of darkness and light, was projected onto the division of state and society. Herder's critique of the politics of this position culminates in *Yet Another Philosophy of History* where he again criticizes the visual model of perfection from the standpoint of the economy of human powers, asking rhetorically 'Is the whole body just one big eye?' (1774; p. 199). Herder's notion of perfection is dynamic, a proportion which is historically produced and, having its being in time, unavailable to the vision of the 'one big eye'. In history the relation between part and whole remains open, with proportion at any one time manifesting itself in incongruity:

A nation may have the most sublime virtues in some respects and blemishes in others, show irregularities and reveal the most astonishing contradictions and incongruities. These will be all the more startling to anyone carrying within himself an idealized shadow-image of virtue according to the manual of his century ... But for him who wants to understand the human heart within the living elements of its circumstances, such irregularities and contradictions are perfectly human. Powers and tendencies proportionally related to given purposes do not constitute exceptions but are the rule, for these purposes could scarcely be attained without them.

(1774; p. 184)

Proportion and perfection are not considered as ideals to be imposed by enlightened bureaucrats, but are the products of the exercise of free judgement.

The imposition of an ideal perfection upon the exercise of freedom is the ambition of a state abstracted from society. Such was, of course, the contemporary state of the 'epoch of beauty' in which

> Each cog is kept in place by fear or habit or affluence or philosophy, and what are so many great philosophically governed herds but crowds held together by force like fenced-in cattle. They are supposed to be able to think, but perhaps thought is only spread among them up to a certain point.
>
> (p. 200)

Herder unmasks the 'philosophically ruled' state as the denial of freedom and judgement: 'In its totality and in its minutest parts, it is entirely controlled by the thought of its master' (p. 200). It arrests history and imposes a pattern upon society as if upon a blank canvas in which 'each man is to wear the uniform of his station in life, to be a perfect cog in a perfect machine' (p. 200). Against the ideology of the police-state with its inscription of an ideal notion of perfection upon society through the administrators' monopoly of judgement, Herder argued for the reflective judgement of free citizens.

Herder accomplishes the transition from aesthetic to culture through an exposure of the relation of perception, beauty, and freedom. At the bottom of this lay his dissent from the enlightenment notion of perfection. The proportion of unity and a manifold did not of itself constitute perfection; what was more important was the *production* of unity in a manifold. Perfection is embodied by and in activity, and is not simply a set of relations which might be represented on a surface. Instead of reducing aesthetic to taste (*Geschmack*) by legislating judgement, Herder emphasizes the productive discrimination of *tasten*. He points to an alignment of beauty, production, and autonomy in the production of proportion which synthesized a view of beauty as embodiment with a notion of culture as the self-cultivation of freedom through reflective judgement. With this position, the epoch of beauty and the police-state is theoretically superseded.

Aesthetic and the Police-State

> But woe to the legislator who wishes to establish through force
> a polity directed to ethical ends. For in so doing he would not
> merely achieve the very opposite of an ethical polity but also
> undermine his political state and make it insecure.
>
> Kant, *Religion within the Limits of Reason Alone*

The traditions of taste and aesthetic culminate in Smith and Herder's
attempts to uncover the sources of the conformity of judgement and
its objects. Both try to sublate the difficulties raised by the repression
of the conformity between production and legislation in their
traditions; one in a political economy, the other in a philosophy of
history. Neither tradition acknowledged the constitution and being
constituted of judgement, or the instituting of the institutions of
judgement in a community, as the work of productive legislation.
The art or technic of judgement which produced the proportionality
of production and legislation was disowned, but in different ways.
Both traditions separated the elements of judgement, only to force
them back together again. In the theory of taste, the law of the
discriminations is given by providence, while production becomes a
je ne sais quoi. In aesthetic, the law is administered upon its subjects
and objects, denying them any autonomy. In both cases the
proportionality produced by judgement can only be recognized
through the pleasure in beauty. Beauty holds the promise of a freedom
which legislates and produces for itself, and becomes not only the
necessary supplement of the theories of civil society and the police-
state, but also their point of crisis and disruption.

The locus of the difficulties with judgement in the German
tradition was perfection. Leibniz's accounts of freedom and judgement
in his Rational Jurisprudence were inseparable from his understanding
of perfection. The move from a structural to a dynamic perfection
changed his view of the relation of individual and universal
in judgement. Instead of subsuming part by whole, judgement
discriminated between the levels of activity or perfection present in
individuals. This dynamic perfection was expressed as love, the
pleasure of mutual recognition and enhancement of power. However,
this philosophical emendation of the Christian vision of the community
of love – the harmony of freedom and justice – was not politically
feasible. Instead Leibniz offered a sublimated version of the
compromise of the Lutheran church with the temporal ruler, in which
morality was given the force of legal obligation. The moral obligations

of Canon law previously administered by ecclesiastical courts were assumed by the temporal ruler and administered through police-ordinances.

In Wolff's philosophy, perfection was structural, an extensive rather than a dynamic order: the famous pre-established harmony which for Leibniz was a harmony of forces, became with him the unity of parts under a whole. The order of perfection was only perceptible through reason, whose insight was obscured by sensibility. Judgement ordered the medley of perceptions from above, unifying them under the tutelage of reason. In his jurisprudence, social perfection, identified with the common welfare, could only be achieved by the rational legislative activity of the enlightened sovereign. This account of judgement was threatened by the difficulties posed by art and by human freedom. The judgement of art implies the mediation of a perfection not involving reason; while the legislation of freedom places society in tutelage to the state. The obsessive attempts to establish a Wolffian philosophy of art strove to articulate a form of judgement which was rational but not subsumptive. This was accomplished within the Wolffian system by Gottsched's separation of the adjudicative and legislative powers, but already Bodmer and Breitinger had renounced their early Wolffian position for a view of judgement as the discrimination of the laws of the imagination.

Baumgarten's aesthetic represented a thorough reform of the Wolffian theoretical philosophy. It vindicated the lower faculty's ability to perceive perfection and to judge for itself according to its own laws. The theoretical innovation destabilized Wolff's system, and threatened the foundations of its practical philosophy. This was not immediately apparent to Baumgarten, whose practical philosophy remained relatively untouched by the advances in his theoretical aesthetic. This neglected aspect of Baumgarten's thought was developed by Herder, who extended the notion of judgement as discrimination to practical philosophy. He transformed the latter into a philosophy of history whose object was the productive and legislative activity of humanity. Herder replaced the predominant visual model of perception with a sculptural one which emphasized the formation of a discrimination through the bringing forth of an object. The same notion of formation also characterized his view of the constitution of society, as citizens autonomously forming themselves into an object. They were not ordered as if on a visual surface by a superior eye, but were themselves both the material and the producers of their society.

Herder's term for the process of productive discrimination was *tasten*. The roots of this word are the same as those for the activity of taste. Herder returns to the original meaning of the word as an activity, as distinguished from the French faculty of *goût* carried over into German as *Geschmack*. For him perfection is neither rational nor affective, but a disposition or *habitus* realized in activity. Consequently, his view of the mediation of providence differs from both the British and the German traditions. It is not mediated through a sense, nor through reason, but is realized in activity. The hand of God is neither invisible nor personified in the philosopher ruler, but embodied in the hands of the child which, through testing and moulding its surroundings, cultivates itself.

Both Smith and Herder try to transcend their respective traditions, but their accounts remain implicated in the ways we have seen. They both recognize that production and legislation are bound together in some way, but neither achieve a satisfactory account of this binding or proportion. Both react against the excesses of their traditions, and propose alternative relations of production and legislation to the violent scissions and unifications of their predecessors. But neither directly addresses the difficulty with judgement-power which gave rise to the forced unifications in the first place. It is Kant's achievement to bring both traditions to judgement, to show not only the necessity of the aporia of judgement, but also the sources of this necessity. In doing so, he raises the question of how the proportions of judgement are instituted, and leaves it open.

Part II

Das kleine wird hier groß, das dunckle hell
gemacht, doch unverändert Bild und
Farbe beybehalten.

4

Judgement before the Critique

Orientation in Tradition

I have had to deviate from the opinions of famous men, some
of whom I even mention by name.
Kant, *New Exposition of the First Principles of Metaphysical
Knowledge*

The textual topology of the *Critique of Judgement-Power* has been set
at issue in recent deconstructions of the text. Derrida's reading in
'Parergon' thematizes the inscription – or is it a bootlace? – which
determines the 'frame' of the text. For Derrida the determination of
what is within and without the text, is an indispensable condition of
'deconstructive labour', but has he properly framed this text? His
underestimation of tradition as 'an old liaison difficult to break off',
a 'second-hand frame one is having trouble selling and that one wants
to unload at any price' (1978; p. 72) suggests not.[1] Kant's view of
tradition is rather more involved, and requires a different 'frame'.
Within this frame, named here 'orientation in tradition', we can
appreciate how Kant's recognition of the aporia of judgement points
beyond the frame of judgement to a legislative production which
aligns pleasure with proportion.

What then is Kant's position on philosophical tradition? Or would
it be more proper to inquire after his position in it, or over it, under
it, even beside it? None of these spatial torsions are appropriate, for
he does not have a position vis-à-vis tradition, but is disposed toward
it. The question then is not one of the ins and outs of tradition, but
of the thinker's stance toward it. Kant champions an active
appropriation of tradition against a passive one, distinguishing his
stance from those who work the Wolffian or some other 'philosophical
treadmill'. Yet, although he is at times tempted to cut the 'Gordian
knot' of tradition, he distinguishes himself from those 'innovators'

who would scale its wall. How then does he take his stand against tradition?

In the Preface and Introduction to the *Critique of Pure Reason*, Kant distinguishes 'the faculty of reason in general' from the philosophical tradition of 'books and systems'. However, the presence of a library of books and systems in the pages of the *Critique* suggests that reason and tradition are more closely implicated than its author is prepared to admit. For although the object of critique is named as the 'faculty' of reason, this 'faculty' only becomes manifest in philosophical tradition. While Kant claims to find 'complete knowledge' of the workings of pure reason in his 'own self' he is only able to explore this self through a dialogue with tradition. In fact, Kant's disavowals of tradition in the parerga of the *Critique* are given the lie not only by the dense intertextuality of the pre-critical writings, but also by the procedure of the critical philosophy itself. The mutual implication of reason and tradition is finally acknowledged by him in the post-critical works.

In the pre-critical philosophy Kant set out to 'reform' the internally divided tradition of metaphysics by bringing the opposed parties to arbitration. Here, as throughout his work, tradition is a divided heritage, one in conflict with itself. At this stage, however, Kant is quick to transform the divisions within tradition into the symptoms of a reason divided against itself. The abstraction of a divided faculty from a divided tradition corresponds to the emergence of judgement as the central issue in Kant's thought during the 1760s. Kant infers an underlying 'bias of reason' from the recognition that the metaphysical tradition is composed of a collection of contradictory judgements. Consequently, the project of reforming the tradition of such judgements is succeeded by the reform of the bias of the faculty of judgement from which they sprang.

The reform of the bias of reason consists in establishing a sound method. But unlike Descartes, Kant did not base his method on the immediate certainties of reason, but on the evidence of its duplicity attested by tradition. The Cartesian spirit of the Introduction to the first *Critique* – there where Kant seeks a 'reliable touchstone' for estimating tradition from within the faculty of reason alone – is belied by his practice. The 'touchstone' is in some sense within and without tradition. In his notion of judgement as orientation Kant thematizes this paradox of a biased reason deriving an accurate standard of judgement from the history of its misjudgements.

The notion of orientational judgement had considerable implications for Kant's understanding of method. In his early writings, method is a hermeneutical procedure through which judgement orients itself with regard to the inconsistent judgements embodied in the tradition. Later, after coming to regard tradition as an expression of the bias of judgement, he generalizes method into the means of orienting the working of the faculty of judgement itself. The orientation of judgement among judgements is transformed into the orientation of judgement in general. This elision persists into the critical philosophy, and is first thematized in the *Critique of Judgement-Power*.

Notwithstanding this development, Kant's method remains in many ways immanent to philosophical tradition. Perhaps its most persistent characteristic is the view that method does not judge according to given criteria, but is the discovery of criteria through acts of judgement. Method 'surveys' the terrain of reason and establishes an 'inventory' of its possessions; it is an act of self-orientation within tradition. The terrain of reason is already cultivated – its possessions are not 'original acquisitions' to which method could presume to have immediate access – and so it is restricted to surveying and testing the titles of previous occupants. It may be objected that method could not begin to orient itself in this way if it did not stand in some privileged position outside of tradition. However, once more in contrast to Descartes, Kant did not establish this position at the outset of his enquiry, but made his object the search for it.

It might seem as if the peculiar status of judgement in Kant's writings stems from its indeterminate *position* with respect to tradition, and so yields to a deconstruction. The letter to Lambert dated New Year's Eve 1765 gives an unassailable alibi against such a frame-up. In one of the earliest avatars of the *Critique of Pure Reason*, Kant claims to be writing a book on the 'proper method of metaphysics (and thereby also the proper method for the whole of philosophy)' (1967, p. 48). While claiming to have employed this method in exposing the incorrect judgements bequeathed by the philosophers, Kant admits to finding it difficult to state what it consists of: 'though I had plenty of examples of erroneous judgements to illustrate my theses concerning mistaken procedures, I did not have examples to show *in concreto* what the proper procedure should be' (pp. 48–9). The method is a procedure for criticizing tradition, one which cannot be stated apart from its work in assessing the claims brought before it. This method does not stand in an instrumental relation to tradition, but adjudicates within it.[2]

Kant remained uncertain as to the place of method in tradition, even when this problem was transformed into the determination of the critical work of the faculty of judgement with respect to judgements. On some occasions, method and judgement are viewed as immanent critique and performative discrimination within tradition;

on others they are seen to be without tradition and constituted apart from it. This awkward relation to tradition persists in the critical philosophy, except there it is subordinated to the wider problem of establishing criteria by which judgement can judge its judgements. It also surfaces in the distinction between discriminative and subsumptive modes of judgement elaborated in the 'Appendix' to the 'Transcendental Dialectic' of the first *Critique*. However, just as traces of method's difficulty with tradition persist in the first *Critique*, so may intimations of the later general problematic of judgement be discerned in the pre-critical writings.

As said, Kant was unable to state the method directly in the pre-critical writings; he invariably resorted to analogy. It is a touchstone (*Probierstein*), an optical parallax, the act of inverting biased scales. In his first published work, *Thoughts on the True Estimation of Living Forces* (1747), he even compares it to the sword which cut the Gordian knot: 'Our method is ultimately a sword against all the knots of subtleties and distinctions' (§ 91). In the introduction to this work Kant laments 'That no proportion and similarity can be found in the perfection of the human understanding, as there is in the structure of the human body.' This legitimates his open attack on the authority of a misshapen tradition; not even the work of such revered masters as Newton, Leibniz and Wolff are safe from the inquisition of method.

In spite of the tenor of the attack on the fathers which is echoed in several of the early works, Kant by no means rejects tradition in favour of a Cartesian pure enquiry. Although he will deviate from the opinion of famous men in the *New Exposition of the First Principles of Metaphysical Knowledge* (1755), he nevertheless describes his procedure as 'testing' judgements. A case in point concerns those made about the principle of contradiction: 'I will attempt first by a more careful investigation to test statements – usually put forward with more confidence than accuracy – about the supreme and indubitable primacy to all truths of the principle of contradiction' (1755; p. 58). Kant offers a more picturesque version of this 'method' three years later in the *New Theory of Motion and Rest* (1758). He appeals to sound reason to legitimate his dispute with tradition, and observes:

If, in a philosophical question the unanimous judgements of philosophers was a wall, to climb over which was considered a crime as reprehensible as that of Remus, I might not be permitted the cheek of pitting my opinions, which are justified by nothing but sound reason, against the venerable heap of decisive precedents. I might, if it occurred to me to dispute a law which according to the law of succession had already been for centuries the indisputed property of the philosophical textbooks, decide that I was already too late and should hold back.

(1758; p. 15)

What is the character of the investigation of such venerable propositions as the principle of contradiction or the distinction between motion and rest? What is the procedure or method which Kant employs in his judgements of tradition, and how does he justify the liberty to employ it?

Already in the *New Exposition* Kant is clear what method is not. The passive reproduction of philosophical tradition is obviously unattractive to him, he is uneager 'to imitate the practice of those who, slavishly tied to I know not what rule of method, appear in their own eyes not to have proceeded properly and rationally unless they have reviewed from A to Z whatever they have discovered in the writings of the philosophers' (1755; p. 59). He will later distinguish such 'imitation' of tradition, from 'following' it. This distinction, pivotal for the third *Critique*, is complemented by Kant's equally vehement rejection of philosophical innovation. He continues the earlier passage from the *New Theory*:

But seeing around me a vast crowd of enterprising heads, who do not want to have anything to do with the law of respect, and who are sufficiently regarded that their opinions are tested and reflected upon, I resolved to join in for the same happy fate with an investigation of motion and rest.

(1758; p. 15)

While Kant is prepared to take advantage of the liberty of innovation, he wishes to separate himself from a school of innovators who automatically dismiss tradition; he is no Wolffian:

I well know that those gentlemen who are accustomed to throw away as chaff all those thoughts that have not been thrown up from the Wolffian treadmill or some other edifice of learning, will at first sight hold the effort of testing unnecessary, and make clear that the whole discourse is incorrect.

(p. 15)

Kant refuses to be either a traditionalist or an innovator in philosophy; where then, if anywhere, does he stand?

The spectacle of a divided tradition suggests to Kant that something is amiss not simply with the empirical judgements possessed by individuals but with the faculty of judgement itself. Already in the *True Estimation* he maintains that error is less the fault of men than of mankind, but in the early 1760s he extends this cliché to the fundamental predicament of human judgement. This realization surfaces in the critique of the tradition of Aristotelean syllogistic published as *The False Subtlety of the Four Syllogistic Figures* (1762). The intricate art of syllogistic reflected the 'lot of human understanding: either it is too preoccupied and tends toward caricature, or else it tears after grand objects and builds castles in the air' (1762; p. 57). Human judgement is congenitally disoriented: it distorts its object by either regarding it too closely, or from too great a distance; it lacks internal measure. The disorientation of reason and understanding is traced back to judgement's lack of proportion, its veering between oversubtlety and extravagance. Proper method comes to be seen less as a mode of arguing between opposed positions within philosophical tradition than a reform of the disorderly judgement which manifested itself in those positions.

The problem arises of the neutrality of method with regard to the exorbitance of judgement. Are the estimates of method immune to the congenital defect of judgement? Does method escape what is described in the *Dreams of a Visionary elucidated through the Dreams of Metaphysics* (1766) as the 'bias of reason'? Kant's treatment of the problem is subtle: method consists of procedures by which judgement may exhibit its own bias. The exhibition of bias permits judgement to orient itself with regard to tradition. Kant hints at this understanding of method amid the delirium of the *Dreams*. The book unsettled Kant's contemporaries, and is still kept under the table today – and for good reason. Kant admitted to Mendelssohn that he wrote the book 'in a most disorderly manner' with his mind 'in a state of paradox'. In the satires on mystics and metaphysicians – dreamers of visions such as Swedenborg and dreamers of reason such as Wolff – Kant's usual restraint breaks down. His admission that the scale of reason is 'not quite as impartial as we may think' (1766; p. 349; p. 688) anticipated the later crisis and collapse of the enlightenment.

In replying to Mendelssohn's criticism, Kant carefully distinguishes his 'repugnance and even some hatred' of contemporary metaphysics from his respect for metaphysics as such. It is because he considers the 'supreme good of mankind' to depend upon a sound metaphysics that he is incensed at its abuse. Contemporary metaphysicians such as Wolff and Crusius presume to judge God, Being, the World, and the Soul without first examining the bias of their judgements. Kant invites Mendelssohn to join him in this examination, one which occupied him up to and beyond the critical philosophy. The revelation of the bias of reason is the task of method, which in the *Dreams of a Visionary* is identified as the judgement of judgement.

The notion of method being the judgement of the judgements of tradition is laid out in the fourth chapter of the work entitled 'A Theoretical Conclusion From all the Remarks Contained in the First Part'. The first part of the text insists on the ineluctable illusion arising from the bias of reason, while the conclusion attempts to establish procedures for disclosing the bias. Kant offers two analogies, both involving the exhibition of bias. The first involves a pair of scales, the traditional figure of judgement:

> The loading of the scales which are set according to commercial law as a measure for trade can be detected when one exchanges the trays holding the goods and the weights. The same trick can be used to make the bias of reason expose itself in philosophy, without which it would not be possible to come to an agreement simply through the comparative weighing of judgements.
>
> (pp. 348–9; p. 67)

In order properly to judge between two philosophical arguments it does not suffice to weigh them comparatively – as Kant did in the *True Estimation* – since the scale itself is suspect. The assessment of discrete judgements must be accompanied by an assessment of the scale, an exhibition of its bias. If they are not aligned to compensate for bias, then their judgement cannot be trusted.

Kant's description of the re-orientation of the scales of judgement merges into the second analogy of the parallax. This trigonometrical technique situates an object according to its angular displacement vis-à-vis an observer; conversely, the mapping of the angular displacement may also be used to situate the observer. Kant's method here involves the imaginary displacement of his own reason by the 'common reason of mankind', examining his own judgement from the standpoint of a reason 'strange and external' (p. 349; p. 67). In this way judgement itself may be judged: 'The comparison of the two observations may produce a strong parallax, but that is also the only means of preserving oneself against optical illusion, and of correctly placing concepts in the place they should stand with regard to the human faculty of knowledge' (p. 349; p. 68).

Kant consistently refuses to state his method directly, and does not develop his analogies. But they do indicate the character of the method which will reform metaphysics. In a sense the method is performative, exposing the asymmetries and disproportions of bias through the re-orientation of judgement.

The bias of reason discerned in the *False Subtlety* and the *Dreams* to veer between excessive subtlety and generality re-appears in the *Critique of Pure Reason* as the 'two-fold, self-conflicting interest' of reason. The bias or 'two-fold interest' disorients the judgements of the philosophers before they even come to utter a judgement. The reason is interested first of all in the heterogeneity and differences between individual things, an interest manifest in the 'faculty of distinction' and which leads to excessive subtlety in discrimination. But it also possesses an interest in the homogeneity and unity of things, manifest in the 'faculty of wit' which drives the reason toward excessive unification. The play of the two interests is manifest in philosophical tradition:

> In this way, one thinker may be partial in the interest of manifoldness (according to the principle of specification), while another is partial to the interest of unity (according to the principle of aggregation). Each believes they have their judgement through insight into the object, but merely ground it on a greater or lesser dependence on one of the two principles, which themselves do not rest on objective grounds, but are derived from an interest of reason.
>
> (A666/B694)

The interminable disputes over the characteristics of men, animals, vegetables, and minerals are due 'to the two-fold interest of reason, one party taking to heart or affecting this interest, another party that one' (A667/B695). The interests of reason manifest the bias of reason which precedes any particular judgement on any particular subject – animal, vegetable, or mineral. Kant describes their expression as maxims of reason which anticipate the discrete judgements of the understanding.

If reason is inevitably interested, how then can it be possible to disclose its bias? Kant sets out a procedure by which the conflicting interests of reason may be exhibited with respect to a third interest in continuity. Continuity forms the horizon within which the bias may be exhibited; it offers a means by which the bias of reason may be re-oriented:

> One can regard every concept as a point, which, as the station of an observer has its own horizon, that is a set of things which may be represented and as it were surveyed from it. It must

be possible to assign an infinite set of points within this
horizon, each of which has its own narrower viewpoint ...
But it is possible to determine for different horizons or genera
a corresponding number of concepts, and it must be possible
to think a common horizon from which they can be surveyed
as if from a central point; and to be led from the higher to
the highest genus which is the universal and true horizon, one
that is determined by the viewpoint of the highest concept and
which contains within it all manifoldness as genera, species,
and subspecies.

(A658/B686)

What is most significant here is the passage between the horizons:
it is the journey which is essential, not the horizons through which
it travels. These are revealed as partial and biased. The continuity
of the trajectory locates the bias, and turns the interests against each
other. The method as procedure or orientation provides 'a way of
adjusting their competing claims', in which 'I am led to this highest
standpoint by the law of homogeneity, and to the lower standpoints
with their enormous variety by the law of specification' (A659/B687).
The journey is only possible because of the continuity between unity
and the manifold which is neither unity nor manifold, and arrives at
an orientation of the interests according to the horizon of continuity.

The faculty of judgement is disposed to bias before it undertakes
any judgements. If it is left uncorrected it will tilt toward excesses
of discrimination or unification. The task of method is to exhibit the
bias, and since bias is inevitably asymmetrical, it may be exposed by
such re-orientation as reversing the scales, or calculating the parallax.
Implied in both of these procedures is the dislocating and relocating
of the horizon of judgement. But in order to accomplish this,
judgement must become an object for itself or else the bias of reason
will remain hidden. In other words, a biased judgement cannot
immediately judge itself, but can do so only through its products –
judgements. The bias is revealed in the medium of tradition as the
distorted body of judgements. With the legacy of earlier disputes
before it in the records of tradition, judgement may re-orient itself
and become aware of its bias.

In the first *Critique* Kant discovers the source of the bias of
judgement in the confusion of sensible and intelligible elements in
human judgement. He recommends that the two sources of knowledge
be distinguished through a 'transcendental distinction'. This distinction has not so far been made within the philosophical tradition,
which is beset by the symptomatic instability of judgement. The task

of critique is to orient judgement with regard to the distinction, which is thus cast as the horizon of self-orientation within tradition. The relationship between critique and tradition intimated here was set out most clearly in the seminal article *What is it to Orient Oneself in Thinking* which Kant contributed to the *Berlin Monatsschrift* in 1786.

The article was his reluctantly submitted contribution to the Mendelssohn/Jacobi dispute over Lessing's alleged 'Spinozism'. Although the text is not now widely known, it may be said to form part of the hidden agenda of twentieth-century philosophy, appearing, often unacknowledged, at crucial junctures in texts such as Heidegger's *Being and Time* and Derrida's 'Restitutions'.[3] In it, Kant laces together the issues of the transcendental distinction and method's relation to tradition. In the latter case his position is consistent with his pre-critical writings: he is neither an innovator nor a traditionalist. The third way, critique, both innovates and conserves by establishing a horizon within which to view the disproportions of tradition.

The basic issue is the possibility of making the transcendental distinction of sensible and intelligible elements of knowledge from within the predicament of their combination. For metaphysics to be preserved from the 'enthusiasm' of both rationalists and mystics, it is essential that this distinction be made. The Wolffian method assumes the distinction but is defenceless against its Pietist critics; Mendelssohn's 'common sense' is equally prone to the attacks of Jacobi and other enthusiasts. The only way to preserve metaphysics is to establish a procedure for determining the proper relation of the sensible and intelligible realms.

Kant offers another analogy, but one which this time he fully develops. He offers the example of spatial orientation, and the nature of directionality. In order to orient ourselves spatially we must make a distinction between left and right; but how can this distinction be made? In Kant's words, is it transcendental or empirical, in Heidegger's is it ontic or ontological? We shall see in the next section that Heidegger's decision in *Being and Time* to assign this distinction to ontic determination does Kant an injustice, making the difference empirical: it isn't, but then neither is it transcendental. Meanwhile, we should linger with the main point of the analogy, which concerns the possibility of making the distinction in the first place.

Spatial orientation rests on a difference which is in a sense outside of and yet underlying spatial orientation. Dropping the spatial metaphors, it assumes a procedure or activity of distinction. With a concrete employment of the horizon metaphor employed in the *Critique* Kant writes:

To orient oneself means, in the proper sense of the word, from a given region (in which we divide the horizon into four) to discover the remainder, namely the ascendent. If I see the sun in the sky and know that it is midday, then I also know how to find south, west, north, and east. To this purpose I require above all the feeling of a difference in my own subject, namely between the left and right hand. I call it a feeling because there is no apparent difference between the two sides in intuition.

(1786; p. 134)

It is because this differentiating activity cannot be represented in intuition that Kant calls it a feeling, or an 'affection' of the subject. This indicates that it does not form part of either the sensible or intelligible realms, but is yet essential for their proper calibration. It is because of this ability to distinguish (*subjektiver Unterscheidungsgrund*) that human perception can orient itself to 'objective givens'. Kant imagines that if through some wonder the heavens were inverted, and west became east, it would not be perceived by human intuition, even though the catastrophe would be felt through the feeling of distinction.

Satisfied for tonight that the heavens are still where they should be, Kant makes his way home. His capacity to distinguish allows him 'to make my way in otherwise well-known streets, in which I cannot distinguish a single house'. And then when he gets home 'In the darkness I can orient myself in my familiar room so long as I lay hold of a single object whose position I can remember.' But what if the person who disturbed Adam Smith's room in chapter 2 had also been at work in Königsberg that night? What if, even worse than simply disordering the chairs, he precisely reversed the position of all the furniture? Kant would then be lost, no longer master in his own house: 'I wouldn't be able to find myself in a room where all the walls were otherwise the same' (p. 135).

Safely home, the furniture restored to its proper place, Kant begins to unfold the analogy. How do we orient ourselves in the 'immeasurable and for us dark night of the dense space of the supersensuous' (p. 137)? How can we ensure proper orientation in metaphyiscal knowledge? Kant postulates a metaphysical subjective capacity for distinction, a metaphysical need (*Bedürfnis*), which, like the elementary distinction in space, allows us to orient ourselves. However, we are not now simply orienting ourselves through the streets and houses of Königsberg, but through the arguments of the metaphysicians. Orientation in thinking becomes orientation in tradition.

The capacity for distinction by which we orient ourselves in the metaphysical tradition is also called a feeling. This rational feeling, which Kant compares with the *moralisches Gefühl* is provoked by asymmetry or disproportion. If the heavens had been reversed, our spatial distinction would make us feel disoriented, even though we could perceive no apparent difference. Similarly, we may feel the insufficiency of a metaphysical judgement without being able to adduce the grounds for our dissatisfaction. In Kant's words, uttered against Mendelssohn's claim to objectify the principle of orientation for metaphysics, 'Reason cannot feel, it has insight into its deficiency, and effects through the knowledge-drive [*Erkenntnistrieb*] and the feeling of need' (p. 139). The '*Vernunftsglaube*' or rational faith is the means by which the philosopher can orient himself among the metaphysical judgements of the tradition; it is the 'guide or compass through which the speculative thinker orients himself in reason's disputes in the field of supersensuous objects' (p. 142). Tradition is neither imitated nor rejected, but followed, compass in hand.

Kant describes the capacity or power of distinction which is not implicated in the 'objective givens' of objects or tradition as a 'subjective ground of distinction [*subjektiven Unterscheidungsgrunde*] for the determination of reason's own faculty of judgement [*Urteilvermögens*]' (p. 135). This ground of distinction is a disposition or stance of the subject which registers its encounter with the 'objective givens' and traditions of judgement. As the power of distinction it does not fall to the bias of judgement; but neither can it be stated in terms of judgement. Kant uses the language of feeling to describe it, although the implications of this move are not fully worked out until the *Critique of Judgement-Power* where the alignment of feeling, judgement, and tradition is traced onto the aporia of judgement.

The procedure of exhibiting the bias of reason through tradition and the feeling of distinction is clarified in Kant's post-critical polemics. In these, his ambiguous relation to tradition is provoked into a crisis by the attack on the critical philosophy mounted in the late 1780s by Eberhard and other Wolffians in the *Philosophisches Magazin*. For Eberhard and his colleagues, Kant reports, the Leibniz-Wolffian philosophy already contained 'all that is true in the new philosophy' as well as 'a well-grounded extension of the sphere of the understanding' (1790c; p. 187; p. 107). The accusation of irrelevance prompted Kant to justify the 'originality' of his philosophy. In the polemic *On a Discovery According to which any New Critique of Pure Reason has been made Superfluous by an Earlier One* (1790), as well as in his response drafted to the Berlin Academy's Prize Essay question *What Real Progress Has Metaphysics Made in Germany since the Time of Leibniz and Wolff?* Kant set out his relation to the Leibniz-Wolffian philosophy in some detail. His self-justifications offer valuable insights into his attitude toward tradition in general, as well as to the Leibniz-Wolff philosophy in particular.

In the two apologies Kant deals explicitly with his complex relation to philosophical tradition. He concludes the polemic of 1790 with the remarkable claim that 'The *Critique of Pure Reason* can thus be seen as the genuine apology for Leibniz' (p. 250; p. 160). This remark is justified by the distinction between the active and passive appropriation of tradition, already developed in the pre-critical writings, but now made in terms of 'imitation' and 'following' developed in the third *Critique*. But the *Critique of Pure Reason* is not only an apology for Leibniz against his 'partisans' or imitators, but also 'for many different past philosophers, to whom many historians of philosophy, with all their intended praise, only attribute mere nonsense' (p. 250; p. 160; see also A13/B27). The imitators are unable to distinguish between the letter and the spirit, between what a philosopher said, and what he meant to say:

> Such historians cannot comprehend the purpose of these philosophers because they neglect the key to the interpretation of all products of pure reason from mere concepts, the critique of reason itself (as the common source of all these concepts). They are thus incapable of recognizing beyond what the philosophers actually said, what they really meant to say.
>
> (p. 251; p. 160)

Here the *Critique* is revealed as the redemption of philosophical tradition, and not its destruction. It would reveal what is immanent in the tradition, but could not be perfectly expressed by it. In this sense it is an active appropriation of tradition, an apology for it which opens the possibility of 'comprehending' and 'recognizing' the bias which afflicts all the 'products of pure reason from mere concepts'.

In the drafts for the *Prize Essay* Kant explores the procedures required for such an act of appropriation. The dark night of metaphysics becomes 'a boundless sea in which progress leaves no trace and on whose horizon there is no visible destination that allows one to perceive how near one has come to it' (1791; p. 51). Yet oblivious to their disorientation, the 'metaphysicians wander confidently on'. They do so because of the nature of metaphysics, which Kant defines as 'the science of advancing through reason from knowledge of the sensible to knowledge of the supersensible' (p. 52). There are no immanent procedures governing the transition from sensible to supersensible, no obvious indications of disorientation. It is, accordingly, 'a transition that – if it is not to be a dangerous leap, inasmuch as it does not involve a continuous development in the same order of principles – requires careful consideration that checks progress at the boundaries of both realms' (p. 79). It is indisputable that Kant is calling for a distinction to be made between the two realms, but how can such a distinction be made? Kant finds it possible to make the distinction by orienting himself among the previous judgements of the metaphysicians, the reports they sent back from their wanderings on the boundless sea.

The problem recurs of establishing a position within tradition from which to undertake the 'careful consideration' which would distinguish between sensible and supersensible. Or rather, the problem of determining a procedure or method for demarcating the realms. For method is neither within nor without tradition, but is its performance, a recapitulation or narration which is also its transformation. Kant describes this orientational procedure in this marvellous synoptic passage:

> In order to have a criterion to assess what has *recently* occurred in metaphysics, one must be aware of what *previously* happened. And both of these must be compared with what should have happened. However, in accordance with |received| maxims of method, we shall go back through and reconsider the progress that has been made in metaphysics, that is, intentionally regard it as negative progress. Even if the errors are deeply rooted and their results widely circulated, something to the good of metaphysics can be achieved, just as he who has lost his way and returns to the point from which he set out and takes compass in hand is at least praised for not continuing to wander along the wrong path; nor has he stood still, but has rather gone back to his point of departure in order to orient himself.
>
> (p. 55)

We must have a criterion in order to be aware of tradition, but we can only gain this if we allow ourselves to wander lost. Then, if we return, we may orient ourselves with our knowledge of tradition and the compass of our discrimination. We do not gain freedom from imitating or rejecting tradition, but only by following it. We do not cast it off, nor do we stand within or without it; we do, however, come to recognize how it has appropriated us, and in so doing appropriate it.

Kant identifies three stages of tradition: the dogmatic, the sceptical, and the critical. They correspond to the imitative, innovative, and appropriative dispositions toward tradition. The play between the dogmatic and sceptical philosophies is repeated symptomatically throughout the history of philosophy. The judgements of the dogmatists – whose ranks include 'those from times even more ancient than Plato's and Aristotle's through to Leibniz's and Wolff's period' (p. 57) – summon a sceptical riposte 'which always endures in good minds everywhere' (p. 59). But this play between dogmatism and scepticism is repudiated by the critical appropriation which differs from both.

The differences between the three dispositions toward tradition are most clearly set out in the political metaphor of the phases of philosophy set out in the 'First Preface' to the first *Critique*. The government of metaphysics under the dogmatists was despotic, and its legislation 'still bore traces of the ancient barbarism'. Its regime collapsed into anarchy, giving rise to the sceptics, a 'species of nomads, despising all settled modes of life'. With the critical philosophy, the despotic conformity to law of the dogmatists and the lawless freedom of the sceptics – the parallel between their relation and that of the understanding and imagination is not fortuitous – is overcome as reason undertakes to legislate its own freedom by instituting 'a tribunal which will assure to reason its lawful claims, and dismiss all groundless pretensions, not by despotic decrees [*Machtsprüche*], but in accordance with its own eternal and unalterable laws. The tribunal is none other than the *Critique of Pure Reason* itself' (Axii). The dogmatist's slavish obedience to tradition and the innovator's anarchy are brought to book in the self-orientation and legislation of the critical tribunal, a court which is also a text. With the institution of the tribunal we return to the problem of the relation of the faculty of pure reason and the tradition of books and systems. Tradition is judged according to the laws of pure reason, which are themselves discovered in the course of judging tradition. For reason orients itself, and is able to institute a critical tribunal, only through a recognition of its own bias as manifest in the records of its history.

Even in his early writings Kant considered the bias of reason to be an inevitable feature of human judgement. In this he followed the Renaissance tradition which places judgement between the intelligible and sensible realms: the realm of sense offers the spectacle of diversity, while the intelligible realm holds the promise of absolute unity. The ability to discriminate between objects of sense is shared by humans and animals, while the ability to unify is proper to human beings and God. Animals, though, cannot be said to judge, since their sensible discriminations are not conceptual; nor can God be said to judge, since the unity of his understanding is not discursive. Only humans judge, only they are able to synthesize discrimination and unification. But this synthesis is unstable, it veers from excessive discrimination to excessive unification.

The inexorable bias of the faculty of judgement arises from its impossible mediation of the sensible and intelligible aspects of human existence. An essential preliminary to ordering this instability is the demarcation of the discriminations of sensibility from the unification of reason. This demarcation – orientation in thinking – is the working through of judgement (*Ausübung*) through the tradition of judgements. This culturing of judgement is expressed in appropriation, the phenomenon of 'realization and restriction' in which the restriction of the bias of judgement realizes the power of judgement. This phenomenon underlies all acts of judgement, whether they be theoretical, practical, or aesthetic.

It is not possible to judge the bias of judgement without assessing the tradition of judgements. Judgement can only orient itself through the evidence of its bias exhibited in tradition, since judgement cannot summon itself to appear before itself. In orienting himself with respect to the theoretical, practical, and aesthetic aspects of judgement, Kant assessed the bias of reason betrayed in the two traditions explored in Part 1 above. He did not imitate either of them, nor did he innovate; he sought to orient himself through them. In terms of Kant's appropriation, the Wolffian account of judgement proposed empty concepts, while the British version did not go beyond blind discriminations. Kant began to orient his judgement in the pre-critical writings, and continued in the *Critiques*. The critical trinity may be read as exercises in the orientation of judgement, using the British and German traditions to indicate the bias of reason.

Derrida has framed Kant with a totally inappropriate position before tradition. His tradition, the beloved metaphysics, was not an old liaison which he was unable to ditch; nor was it four times round philosophy in any uncomplicated sense. He practised it, or worked it through (*Ausübung*), he did not imitate or try to sell it off at any price. Indeed, the relation to tradition is a constitutive part of transcendental philosophy, and not simply an appendix or supplement to it. Kant's early appropriation of the traditions of taste and aesthetic is reviewed in this chapter, while the working through of the crisis of judgement, which is also a crisis of tradition, is analysed in the following one.

Theoretical Judgement

Now the critique of reason has appeared and assigned mankind
a thoroughly active existence in the world. Mankind itself is
the original maker of all its representations and concepts, and
ought to be the sole author of its actions.

Kant, *The Conflict of the Faculties*

In the post-critical polemics of the 1790s Kant claimed that the
superiority of the critical over the Wolffian philosophy lay in its
recognition of a 'transcendental distinction' between the sensible and
intelligible aspects of experience. Wolff and his followers, he argued,
distinguished only formally between sense and understanding in terms
of grades of consciousness. This formal distinction permitted the
elaboration of metaphysical theses and principles such as the identity
of indiscernibles, the principle of sufficient reason, the system of pre-
established harmony and the monadology. Kant set himself to question
the legitimacy of such theses and principles from the standpoint of
the 'transcendental distinction' and found them wanting.

This post-critical version of the origins of critical philosophy –
Kant testing metaphysical theses according to the 'transcendental
distinction' – inverts the historical order of events. For historically
tradition preceded method, with Kant discovering the distinction in
the course of his critique of Wolffian metaphysics.[4] Three broad
stages may be identified in the discovery and implementation of the
'transcendental distinction'. The first begins with the *True Estimation
of Living Forces*, and supplements the Wolffian 'formal' with a 'real'
distinction. The second stage, whose beginnings are identifiable in
the *Enquiry Concerning the Clarity of the Principles of Natural Theology
and Morals* (1764), and which is fully developed in the *Inaugural
Dissertation* of 1770 – *The Form and Principles of the Sensible and
Intelligible Worlds* – distinguishes between sensible and intelligible
sources of experience in order to detect the bias of reason. The third
stage establishes the conditions for a legitimate transgression of the
transcendental distinction, described as the justification of 'synthetic
a priori judgements' which occupied Kant during the 'silent decade'
of the 1770s, and whose results emerged in the critical philosophy
of the 1780s.[5]

Before following the course of the emergence of the transcendental
distinction and its significance for judgement, we should see how
Kant himself understood its significance in the wake of the *Critiques*.
Kant's main difference with the Wolffian tradition involved the proper

object and method of metaphysics. In his drafts for *What Real Progress Has Metaphysics Made in Germany since the Time of Leibniz and Wolff* he defines metaphysics in terms of progressing from knowledge of the sensible to knowledge of the supersensible (1791, p. 52). Wolffians would have found little to argue with in this definition, since they admit only a 'formal distinction' between the sensible and supersensible and see the transition from one to the other as continuous. Kant, in contrast, regards this transition as a dangerous leap into the unknown, a risky enterprise requiring prudent preparation in the self-orientation of reason with respect to its capacities. The task of preparation is assigned to the propaedeutic discipline of ontology which analyses 'experience into concepts that lie a priori in the understanding and that are used in experience' (p. 53). Kant's ontology, re-titled 'Transcendental Analytic' in the first *Critique* and 'Transcendental-Philosophy' in the *Prize Essay* rests on the rigorous distinction of sensible and supersensible knowledge. The distinction rules out any steady transition between the two realms; if we believe there is such a transition, Kant warns 'We climb only to fall deeper.'

Without the transcendental distinction, metaphysics possesses no criterion to assess its judgements apart from the principle of contradiction. But for Kant this principle is 'empty' and unable to legitimate judgements about the supersensible, since metaphysicians have 'only to be careful not to allow [their] judgements to contradict one another – something it is perfectly possible to succeed at – even though these judgements and the concepts they are based on may be utterly empty' (1791; p. 56). The 'emptiness' of such judgements is the consequence of their inadequately determining the relation between concept and object. Kant claims that the principle of sufficient reason, which in the Wolffian philosophy is supposed to achieve the relation of a judgement to an object, collapses into the principle of contradiction:

> Now once again all of metaphysics hangs upon a single hinge, whereas previously there were supposed to have been two. For the mere consequence of a principle, taken in its entire universality and without the addition of at least a new condition of its application, is certainly not a new principle which repairs the defect of the previous one.
>
> (1790c; pp. 195; p. 114)

The view that the Wolffian principle was empty, lacking any condition for its application, was axiomatic for Kant. It was of course already recognized by Wolffians such as Baumgarten; but Kant's solution broke out of the Wolffian confines by making the problem of 'application' the occasion for a new transcendental logic.

Kant's early writings appeared against the backdrop of the widespread critical reaction against the Wolffian philosophy which had been gathering momentum since the 1740s.[6] In this critical movement, which countered Wolffian rationalism with an appeal to the immediacy of affects and the will, the principle of sufficient reason was tested and found wanting; it did not provide an adequate condition for the application of the principle of contradiction. Since Wolff did not admit a fundamental distinction between logic and being, there was no real theoretical problem involved in reconciling them in judgement. Wolff's critics, however, severed their identity and maintained instead that existence was experienced immediately through will or affection and not through the logical rules of the understanding. In the face of the opposed immediacies of the concept and the affections and will, Kant took Baumgarten's path of reconciliation. As we have seen, Baumgarten supplements the logic of subsumptive judgement with the discriminations of aesthetic, so conceding to sensibility and existence a value different from logic, but without fully developing the radical implications of this position. With Kant, even in his earliest writings, we can see the radical ambition to transcend the bias of reason by giving legitimacy to both concept and sensibility.

All of Kant's pre-critical writings sever being and logic by distinguishing existence from the principle of contradiction: it is axiomatic that existence exceeds logic. This is most clearly expressed in the statement in *The Only Possible Proof for the Existence of God* (1763) that 'existence is not a predicate'. For Wolff, existence was a predicate which complemented possibility; for Kant, on the contrary, existence 'possesses' 'characteristics' which escape logical predication. Stated baldly, Kant maintained that for human beings existence involved spatial and temporal relations which were not logically determined. They were not, as the Wolffians claimed, well-founded but confusedly perceived phenomena of the concept, but possessed their own inner principles and differences. This separation of spatial and temporal existence from conceptual determination is evident at an early stage in Kant's critique of the principle of sufficient reason and the identity of indiscernibles, but was first thematized in 1770 as the transcendental distinction between the sensible and the intelligible worlds.

However, once made the distinction had to be transgressed, for it merely formalized the bias of reason by pointing to the 'empty' immediacy of the concept and the 'blind' immediacy of sensibility or will; it did not bring the two together in a legitimate judgement. The nature of such judgement remained deeply problematic, in and even after the critical philosophy. Indeed Kant came, in the *Critique of Judgement-Power*, to recognize it as inevitably aporetic. The original distinction had to be made and unmade, and this was literally unthinkable.

It is in the *New Exposition* (1755) that Kant first establishes an independent or 'new' metaphysical position against the tradition's bias of reason. His 'new exposition' redefines the Wolffian principles of contradiction and sufficient reason in the light of Crusius's objections to them, and introduces the additional (Crusian) principles of succession and co-existence. In a series of influential works published during the 1740s Crusius exposed the Wolffian equivocation of logical and real ground, insisting instead on their rigorous distinction. While accepting this critique, Kant tempered its conclusions by proposing to explore the proper relation between the logical and the real orders divided by Crusius. This approach distinguished Kant from both Wolffians and critics and anticipated his later transcendental logic. Even at this early stage in his thought he is more interested in the process by which the dichotomy is made and overcome than in simply separating its terms.

The *New Exposition* also anticipates Kant's later complaints about the 'empty tautologies' of Wolffianism. He mercilessly exposes its *petitio principii* and tracks them down to their source in Wolff's equivocal definition of *ratio* (*Grund*):

> The illustrious Wolff's definition seems to me to be afflicted by an error which requires correction. For he defines reason as that which shows why [*cur*] something is rather than is not. Here he without doubt insinuates what is to be defined into the definition. For while the little word 'why' [*cur*] appears to common-sense sufficiently clear to be included in the definition, it secretly introduces into it the notion of reason which is to be defined.
>
> (1755; p. 393; p. 67)

However, Wolff's definition of reason is not only tautologous, it is also equivocal since the 'reason why a thing is' refers to reason not only in the sense of a real ground or efficient cause of the 'reason why', but also to the logical ground or final cause of the 'reason that'.[7] Kant's discrimination of the equivocation follows Crusius's distinction of logical and real ground. Kant differentiates the meaning of reason in terms of 'that which determines *antecedenter* and that

which determines *consequenter* (p. 392; p. 66). The two determinations
are distinguished according to the two senses of the 'little word
"why"': *ratio antecedenter* corresponds to 'the reason why or the reason
of being or becoming' and *ratio consequenter* to the 'reason that or
the reason of knowing'. From this distinction of the ontological and
epistemological aspects of reason, Kant proceeds to a fundamental
critique of Wolff, and, surprisingly, to a defence of the principle of
sufficient reason.

Kant recognizes the importance of Crusius's critique of Wolff's
theoretical and practical philosophy, and acknowledges the justice of
Crusius's exposure of

> the ambiguity and variable meaning of the formulation of the
> principle [of sufficient reason]. He correctly remarks, the *ratio
> cognoscenti*, likewise the moral reason and other *rationes ideales*
> are repeatedly taken for real and antecedently determining
> reasons, so that often one can know only with difficulty which
> kind of reason is to be understood.
>
> (p. 398; p. 76)

Kant accepts this criticism, and in his defence of the principle of
sufficient reason 'carefully distinguishes the *ratio veritatis* from the
ratio actualitatis'. So while undoing the Wolffian identity of logical
and real ground he refuses to follow Crusius and other critics in
abandoning all relation between them. He rejects Crusius's denial of
the mediations of logic in favour of the immediacy of existence: 'The
celebrated Crusius supposes that some existents are so determined
through their own actuality, that it is vain to demand anything beyond
it' (p. 397; p. 73). By refusing the opposition between the absolute
identity and the absolute difference of real and logical orders, Kant
finds himself in the predicament of having to rethink how they might
be related.

In the *New Exposition* Kant defends the principle of sufficient
reason by the very point that was meant to demolish it, namely, that
existence cannot be rationally determined. He does this in two ways.
The first is a negative proof for the existence of a determining reason.
Kant explains 'why I reject the proof proposed by the renowned
Wolff and his disciples' in the following way: 'This illustrious man's
proof, as it is clearly expounded by the acute Baumgarten, is briefly
this: If anything had no reason, its reason would be nothing; therefore
nothing would be something, which is absurd' (p. 397; p. 75). Kant
observes that this proof converts the ideal reason of something lacking
a reason into a thing, or rather nothing. However, if this conversion

is resisted it is possible for the proof to hold. It may be shown that although existing things must ideally have a reason, it does not follow that the inability to determine it in full means that something is nothing. Kant sees the inability to attain full rational determination as supporting the view that existence cannot be rationally determined. The concession that existence is beyond full rational determination does not entail that it is 'nothing', but simply that it can not be thought to be a thing.

The second and more positive description of the relation of real and logical reason involves postulating the real principles of succession and co-existence. Kant draws from his principle of determining reason the ostensibly Wolffian conclusion 'that there is nothing in the *rationatum* which is not in the *ratio*'. Yet his version radically reformulates the principle to agree with the distinction *ratio antecendenter* and *ratio consequenter*. Where Wolff distinguished between the *ratio* as possibility and the *rationatum* as actuality, Kant maintains that the distinction is itself a consequence of actuality. In place of the actualization of possibility his metaphysics proposes that actualities be seen to interact. In this interaction the real principles of succession and coexistence are of crucial significance.

The two principles of succession and co-existence arise from mutual relations between distinct substances, and are pertinent in two main areas; firstly the relation between extended substance and other extended substances, and secondly the relation between thinking and extended substance. The first relation raises the problem of motion, the second that of perception. In both cases Kant maintains that the relations between substances can only be understood within the orders of succession and co-existence. Real interaction is prior to the ideal, and not as the Wolffians argued, its consequence.

The view that motion is a real interaction of substances in space and time and not the actualization of a rational possibility is closely connected with Kant's dismissal of the identity of indiscernibles. Kant's rejection of this principle is a constant factor in his philosophical trajectory. Against the Wolffians he argues that a proper determination of a substance requires attention to both internal and external determination: 'Perfect identity of two things requires the identity of all attributes and determinations, internal as well as external. From this thorough determination no-one will except place. Accordingly, those things which are distinguished according to place are not the same, even if all their internal attributes agree' (p. 409; p. 94). Place is as important a determination as possibility – in other words, actual existence in time and space does not simply supplement or complement possibility, but is an integral part of a thing's definition. The nature of a thing is determined as much by its place as by its properties.

Underlying Kant's insistence that place is a determination is the notion that the creative act of God is 'schematized'. God gives things existence and relation; the latter arises from the limitation of the creative act. But the creative act does not exhaust its power through limitation, but rather modulates its activity through a *schema* which both posits the existence of things and relates them to each other: 'The schema of divine intelligence, the origin of all existents, is a constant activity . . . [in which] their continued existence [and] their mutual determinations are always in relation, that is, they act and are acted upon, so that a singular being has an externality which it could not have if it were simply posited as existing' (p. 414; p. 102). The place of things, their externality, is as important to their definition as their internal characteristics. This holds even for the relation of thinking and extended substance. Even at this stage Kant translates divine schematism, or hypostasis – the self-limitation of creative activity – into an account of human activity. Thinking and extended substance are both related and external to each other; the negotiation of their identity and difference is expressed in terms of activity and passivity. The soul is both active and passive, subject of and subject to: 'The soul is subject to internal changes (through the inner sense); and since these cannot arise, from what has been shown, if it is solitary and without relation with others, so something must be present outside the soul, with which it is involved in a mutual relation' (p. 412; p. 98). This mutual relation is experienced as a negotiation of the soul's active and passive dispositions, a negotiation to which Kant, here and later, ascribes the dignity of law: 'the soul is bound by the law that striving (*conatus*) in representations is always conjoined with the striving of substance toward external motion, so much that when one encounters impediments the other is impeded too' (p. 412; p. 100). The specifying of the somatic and intellectual aspects of *conatus* anticipates the view of perception as a negotiation of activity and passivity which Kant develops in his writings of the 1760s.

In spite of such anticipations Kant's exposition of theoretical judgement remains undeveloped in the *New Exposition*. He establishes a position with regard to the bias of reason, but is unable to follow it through. While appreciating both passive and active aspects of experience, Kant does not unite them in a full account of theoretical judgement. He is more precise in his account of practical judgement, and a brief glance at this provides a clue to why theoretical judgement is relatively underdeveloped.

Kant's account of practical judgement in the *New Exposition* rests on a recognition of the role of active and passive elements of experience. Practical judgement mediates spontaneity and receptivity but its activity is diacritical: it distinguishes between possible actions, although the principle of discrimination remains undetermined. However, an exclusively discriminative model of theoretical judgement was not an option for Kant at this time. The difficulty with a discriminative theoretical judgement lies in determining the proper object for theoretical discrimination. Discriminative judgement might be employed to discriminate between rival theoretical hypotheses – that is, in a reading of tradition – but not as the foundation of theoretical judgement. However, three years later in the *New Theory of Motion and Rest* Kant did apply a discriminative model of judgement directly to theoretical experience.

The *New Theory* opens with one of Kant's least restrained invectives against philosophical tradition. It was here we saw him rail against the 'wall' of tradition which it is a crime to scale, and inveigh against those who work the 'Wolffian treadmill'. Instead of choosing between the climb and forced-labour, he decides to follow the example of Descartes and 'forget all received ideas and enter on the path to truth without any other guide than sound reason' (1758, p. 16). But in a familiar inflection this desire is negated on the same page, when Kant sets himself to 'examine and to challenge' the Wolffian notions of motion and rest. The path to truth followed by reason passes through the examination of tradition.

The *New Theory* marks a considerable advance in Kant's notion of theoretical judgement. It examines the problem of how to *distinguish* between motion and rest. Kant observes that judgement is necessarily disoriented by this question since it forgets that the determination of whether an object as in motion or at rest is relative to the spatial horizon in which it is perceived. In the first of many statements that judgement presupposes orientation, Kant writes:

> I can consider a body in relation to other objects which lie immediately around it, and when this relation doesn't change, I can say it rests. But as soon as I regard it in relation to a wider horizon of objects it is possible that the body along with its proximate objects alters its position, so that I may attribute motion to it. Now it is open to me to extend my viewpoint as much as I like, and to regard this body within ever increasing horizons, so realizing that my judgement on the motion and rest of this body is never fixed, but may always change with a new perspective.
>
> (p. 16)

Two points are of interest in this passage: the first is that the distinction of motion and rest is not absolute, but always imputed; and the second, its consequence, is that the theoretical distinction between motion and rest always depends upon a prior spatial and temporal orientation. Consequently, discriminative judgement is never constant, but changes according to its horizon of perception. This is stated unequivocally later in the essay: 'Under what are called "laws of motion" one understands not merely the rules of relation through which colliding bodies are brought before each other, but to a great degree the change of their external state with regard to the space in which they find themselves as well' (pp. 23–4). So apart from the intrinsic interest of this theory of relative motion, the *New Theory* is significant for disclosing an existential orientation prior to the discriminations made by theoretical judgement between motion and rest.

The themes of the *New Exposition* and the *New Theory* are brought together in the 1763 *Attempt to Introduce the Notion of Negative Quantities into Philosophy*. Here Kant extends the distinction of logical and real ground proposed in the *New Exposition*, while continuing to fence off his position from those of Wolff and Crusius. He does so by generalizing the problem of distinguishing between motion and rest into one of distinguishing between positive and negative quantities. The two issues are fused in the critique of the Wolffian view that negation is privation, a consequence of the identification of real and logical grounds. Wolff defined the principle of contradiction as 'something cannot both be and not be', so assuming that logical negation entailed ontological negation. However, Kant finds this notion of negation inadequate and the source of 'a crowd of errors and misprisions in the opinions of other philosophers' (1763a; p. 169).

Against the errors of the Wolffians and the inadequacy of Crusius's critique, Kant extends the distinction of logical and real ground into logical and real negation: 'The former opposition, the logical, is that which until now claimed all the attention. It consists in simultaneously asserting and denying something of the same thing. The consequence of this logical relation is nothing, as it is expressed in the principle of contradiction' (p. 171). In spite of their formal similarities, Kant insists that logical and real negation are distinguished: 'The second opposition, the real, is that in which two predicates of a thing are opposed, but not through the principle of contradiction. Here too the one supersedes [*hebt auf*] what is posited through the other, except that the consequence is something' (p. 171). Logical negation excludes something from a class according to whether it possesses or does not possess a particular attribute. Real negation however, does not simply exclude, but issues in something that can be perceived and represented.

Kant's two initial examples of the distinction between logical and actual negation are taken from the distinction of rest and motion explored in the *New Theory*. Kant first expresses the judgement as to whether an object is in motion or at rest in terms of the principle of contradiction: 'A body in motion is something, a body that is not in motion is also something; but a body which is simultaneously and in the same sense both in and not in motion is absolutely nothing' (p. 171). But for him such a principle is empty, since to distinguish logically between motion and rest in terms of being in motion and not being in motion, ignores the real forces at work. More damningly, it also assumes the definition of motion prior to applying the principle of contradiction; an understanding of the nature of motion is required before one can either affirm or negate it of an object. Using the same example of motion and rest, Kant offers a real distinction: 'The motive power of a body in one direction and an equal effort of the same body in the opposite direction do not contradict each other and are both possible as predicates in the same body at the same time. The consequence is rest, which is something' (p. 171). In the case of actual negation, the distinction between motion and rest does not follow from the privation of motion, but from the balance of opposed forces in an object.

The differences between logical and actual negation are expressed in the differing modes of judgement which follow from them. Judgement according to the principle of contradiction proceeds according to membership or non-membership of a class. According to the principle that a thing cannot both be and not be a member of a particular class, an object in motion cannot both be and not be a member of the class of moving objects. For Wolff all judgements subsumed their objects in this way: either an object belonged to a class or it did not. But as Kant points out there are problems with this model of judgement, since it assumes its 'conditions of application', in other words, the affirmation or denial of membership implies a discrimination that a thing is indeed a member of a class, presupposing a discrimination not covered by the principle of contradiction.

A judgement according to actual negation does not subsume objects under universals but determines their relation to each other, and to the perceptual horizon within which they fall. The determination is illustrated in terms of positive and negative numbers. Kant writes: 'Mathematicians are accustomed to call quantities before which − stands negative quantities, in which it must be remembered, that this does not designate a particular class of things according to their inner constitution, but a counter-relation with certain other things, designated with a +, whose opposition has to be taken together' (p. 174). Position and negation are not concepts beneath which an object may be subsumed, but mark real relations between objects. This generalizes the particular distinction of rest and motion in the *New Theory*, and like that distinction, it follows from the relation of objects to each other and to the perceptual horizon within which they are found.

Kant's favoured examples of actual negation, apart from motion and rest, are taken from accountancy and navigation. His accountancy example runs as follows:

> Say that someone owes somebody A = 100 thalers, then this is a ground for their receiving this amount. But he is also owed B = 100 thalers by them, which is a ground for his receiving this amount. Both debts come to nothing, money is neither given nor received. It is easy to see that this zero is merely a relative nothing . . . and that it is not nothing through the principle of contradiction.
>
> (p. 172)

The classes of debt and credit merely denote the direction of the relation between the two financiers: in respect of each other they can be in the 'contradictory' relation of simultaneously owing and being owed 100 thalers. The relation of position and negation in terms of orientation within an horizon is expressed with equal clarity in the navigation example: 'A ship travels from Portugal to Brazil. + denotes the distances it travels with the morning wind and − those which it loses with the evening wind . . . Those quantities before which − are thus only in so far as they are taken together with those which have + before them' (p. 173). Once more, + and − do not designate classes, but relations between objects and the horizon within which they are perceived.

In a real distinction the most important factor is not the membership or non-membership of a class, but the relation of objects to each other, and to the perceptual horizons of the spectator. Errors of judgement arise from mistaking these relations, such as the Wolffian error of resolving a relation between objects into that of their membership or exclusion from a class. Returning to the distinction of motion and rest: a stationary object is deemed to fall within the class of stationary objects, and it would transgress the principle of contradiction to deem it moving. However, such a judgement admits the given perceptual horizon of the spectator to be absolute, an assumption which cannot be accepted without proper justification.

The distinction of positive and negative quantities holds only for a given horizon. But what is the nature of this horizon? It clearly determines the discriminatory judgements regarding things within it, but not as a law of discrimination. It somehow constitutes the relations of the things it contains, but not as a whole to its parts. It is both objective, being the field within which things are given, and subjective, as the viewpoint from which they are considered. Horizon is best thought in terms of the activity of producing things and placing them in a relation. It is analogous in many ways to the *schema* of God's creative activity proposed in the *New Exposition*, which realizes and restricts itself in bringing objects into existence and maintaining them in particular relations.

In *Negative Quantities* Kant relates horizon, or the configuration of existents, to the imagination. It is through the imagination that the temporal horizon of existents can be established. This undermines the principle of contradiction by showing that its notion of simultaneity – 'a thing cannot both be and not be *at the same time*' – assumes a particular temporal horizon. Kant introduces the question of how it is possible to conceive of something passing out of existence: 'Everyone can understand why something does not exist without a positive ground; but it is not so easy to understand why something that exists ceases to do so' (p. 190). The passing in and out of existence depends on the particular temporal horizon within which a thing is located. Kant focuses upon the transition from one state to another, showing that with a proper temporal horizon it becomes apparent that 'every passing away is a negative coming into existence' (p. 190). It is only within a particular temporal horizon that it is possible to discriminate between existing or not existing.

The terms in which Kant describes the work of the imagination in establishing a temporal horizon anticipates the discussion of schematism in the first *Critique*. The notion of 'abstraction' in the *Negative Quantities*, although couched in Leibniz and Wolff's distinction of clear and distinct representations, has the same function of 'restriction and realization' given to schematism in the *Critique*: 'Every abstraction is nothing else than the suspension [*Aufhebung*] of certain clear representations, which one usually employs, in order that the remainder may thereby be more clearly represented. Everyone knows how much activity is required for this, and so abstraction may be called negative attention' (p. 190). This repression of the work of imagination in abstraction allows a representation to be 'more clearly represented' or realized. The working of imagination itself is described in similar terms to schematism, which Kant described in the *Critique* as 'an art concealed in the depths of the human soul':

> I think at this moment of a tiger. I lose this thought and that
> of a jackal occurs in its place. It may be granted that one
> cannot perceive any particular exertion in the soul which effects
> the supercession of the representations. Yet what a wonderful
> art is concealed in the depths of our spirit that we cannot even
> perceive when it is working, because its actions are numerous,
> and each individual act is obscurely represented.
>
> (p. 190)

In the first case imagination restricts itself in order to raise a universal through abstraction; in the second it runs free in effortlessly producing a host of indistinct representations. A particular disposition of the imagination underlies both the establishment of a temporal horizon for the appearance of discrete representations, and the abstraction of a universal which persists through time. This disposition or work of orientation is perceived in the effort of sustaining an abstraction in which certain discriminations are effaced or 'held in abeyance' and regarded as unknowable in the free play of imagination.

The difficulty of determining the coming into and passing out of existence is related to Kant's refusal to consider existence as a predicate. A thing cannot be subsumed under the class of existing things, since existence is not a genus. This thesis was developed by Kant with increasing confidence through the 1760s. As seen, it emerged from the inadequacies of the Wolffian determination of existence. This was summed up in the statement at the end of *Negative Quantities* that the negation 'because something is, something else is *Aufgehoben*' 'does not happen by the principle of contradiction' (p. 203). If this is conceded, the problem arises of how to determine the coming into existence of a thing apart from the principle of contradiction. In the *New Exposition* Kant stops at the limit of rational determination, and he does so again in the *Negative Quantities*, although here some hints are dropped about possible further determinations of existence.

On the question of the determination of the real as opposed to the logical ground of an existent, Kant refers cryptically to a forthcoming work: 'I have reflected on the nature of our knowledge in regard to our judgements of ground [*Grunde*] and consequence [*Folge*], and I shall soon publish the complete results of these meditations' (1763; p. 204). His hint on the outcome of his meditations is unfortunately just as cryptic: 'From them it will be found that the relation of a real ground to something posited or superseded through it, cannot be expressed in a judgement but only in a concept' (p. 204). The latter proposition is complicated by Kant's distinction between concept and judgement. A year earlier, in the *False Subtlety of the Four Syllogistic Figures*, Kant had clearly stated that a concept was the precipitate of an act of judgement. A concept was defined as the distinct representation which follows the act of discrimination to which 'I clearly recognize something as an attribute of a thing' (1762; p. 58). If the concept is considered the result of an act of judgement, how is it possible for Kant to maintain that the relation of ground and consequent cannot be expressed in a judgement, but only in a concept?

Some idea of why Kant made this distinction can be gathered from looking at his choice of examples. In both the *False Subtlety* and *Negative Quantities* Kant elucidates his point with the same example of the impenetrability of a body. In *Negative Quantities* he introduces a possible explanation for the transmission of motion according to the principle of contradiction: 'If I presuppose the impenetrability which effectively opposes every power that tries to force itself into the space occupied by a body, I can understand the suspension of motion; in this thought I have brought one real opposition to bear on another' (1763a; p. 203). But the concept of impenetrability presupposes an actual opposition, and of this opposition nothing can be said except 'that it does not happen by the principle of contradiction'. From this admission Kant proceeds to make the distinction between concept and judgement. In the *False Subtlety* Kant defines body according to impenetrability, and unequivocally subordinates the concept to the judgement:

> In order to have a distinct concept of body, I clearly represent to myself impenetrability as an attribute. This representation is nothing but the thought 'a body is impenetrable.' It is to be observed here that this judgement is not the distinct concept itself, but the activity through which it is realized; for the representation, which according to this activity springs from the thing itself, is distinct.
>
> (1762; p. 58)

The distinct concept follows the judgement, but the judgement itself employs a concept which is not open to further determination, namely impenetrability. Impenetrability is not a predicate, nor does it refer to a property which defines members of a class; it merely expresses an actual opposition. As such the 'concept' of impenetrability represents the limit of judgement. Judgement presupposes such concepts, but cannot determine them. Unlike Wolff's judgement, which was directed toward analytical transparency, Kant's arrives at 'simple and unanalysable concepts of real grounds [*einfacheren und unauslöslichen Begriffen der Realgrunde*]' (1763a; p. 204). There are then two sorts of concept, those before and those after judgement. The first offer horizons of judgement within which discrimination takes place and are decribed as 'obscure'; the second are the universals under which objects so discriminated may be subsumed and are described as 'distinct'.

In the *False Subtlety* the 'simple and unanalysable concepts' of *Negative Quantities* are not distinguished from the judgements which they make possible: 'Human knowledge is full of such indemonstrable *judgements.*' One important characteristic of such judgements/concepts is that they anticipate the work of recognition which issues in the distinct concept: 'Such [judgements] precede every definition, which is achieved as soon as one represents to oneself what is known immediately of a thing as its attribute' (p. 61). At this stage Kant does not thematize the distinction of simple and unanalysable concepts and judgements, but uses the terms interchangeably to refer to the anticipatory character of recognizing a characteristic of a thing. Later however, in the wake of the transcendental distinction, he codifies the distinction between axioms and *akroamata* as that between things deemed to be 'self-evident' or 'seen', and 'recitals' or 'things heard'. Both are fundamental principles, but the axioms are immediate and 'exhibited in intuition' while *akroamata* are discursive and 'only permit themselves to be expressed in concepts' (1800; § 35). In the first *Critique* the distinction is presented in terms of immediacy and mediation: intuitive axioms are immediate, while *akroamata* require a 'third something' the 'condition of time-determination in an experience' (A733/B761). Here the simple and unanalysable concept/ judgements developed out of the real distinction have been divided into intuition and principles, both of which are required for experience.

The transcendental distinction between the intelligible and sensible elements of experience emerges from Kant's distinction of logical and real ground. Although he first makes this distinction against Wolff in the *New Exposition*, he did not transform it into the transcendental distinction before the *Inaugural Dissertation* of 1770. While the writings of the 1760s distinguish axioms from *akroamata*, this distinction was not mapped on to that of the sensible and intelligible worlds before 1770. Even after this, Kant required a decade to systematize the *akroamata* in the Analytic of the first *Critique*. However, it can safely be said that by the early 1760s Kant had broken the Wolffian identity of logical and real ground, and had reasoned the need for a transcendental logic which would establish the proper determination of existence.

The Only Possible Proof for the Existence of God (1763) puts the seal on Kant's differences with Wolff and his critics by reversing the signs of Wolff's account of the relation of possibility and actuality. The treatise shows no sign of the transcendental distinction since both space and existence are regarded as 'simple concepts'; it nevertheless offers Kant's most rigorous and systematic pre-critical examination of the relation between possibility and actuality. Kant compares the simple concepts or axioms of geometry, such as homogeneous space, with philosophical axioms like the 'concept of existence [*Begriff des Daseins*]'. Both are simple concepts in the sense discussed above, that is, they are the horizons of determination which are not themselves open to further determination. However, this does not deny the possibility of a search for definition through the delineation of what can and cannot legitimately be affirmed and denied of the definand. In the case of simple concepts, judgement may anticipate a definition but can only proceed towards it through discrimination: judgement may distinguish but not subsume. With respect to simple concepts, judgement, to use Kant's later term, is reflective: 'I will proceed as one who seeks a definition and who first of all ensures what may be affirmed or negated with certainty of the object of definition, even if he still cannot establish what the fully determined concept consists of' (1763b; pp. 54–5). Kant calls this procedure of distinguishing between what can be affirmed or denied of a concept his 'method'. Space and existence, for example, may both be determined in terms of what may be affirmed or denied of them without any pretension to exhaustive definition. This position, already stated in the negative proof of the principle of sufficient reason in the *New Exposition*, is only now fully exploited.

The negative discrimination of the notion of existence maintains first and foremost that existence is not a predicate. The denial of the status of predicate to existence directly contradicts Wolff, as does Kant's deduction that existence is prior to possibility. Kant observes that the concept of existence is open to abuse if it is equated with predicates such as extension and whiteness, since it would then be possible 'to deduce being from merely possible concepts'. Instead he maintains that it is not, like a predicate, 'posited with respect to some other thing' but is itself 'absolute position': 'The concept of position [*Position*] or position (*Setzung*] is completely simple and identical with that of being in general' (pp. 58–9). The use of *Setzung* as a synonym for position suggests that it be read actively – from *setzen*, the act of putting or placing.[8] Kant first distinguishes between absolute and relative *Setzung* and then subordinates relative to the absolute. Relative *Setzung* is the ascription of a predicate to a subject, but this ascription is only possible if both subject and predicate are already posited absolutely:

> Something can be posited as relational, or better, be thought merely as the relation of something as a property of a thing. Then being, that is the position of the relation, is only the copulative concept in a judgement. Should not only this relation but the thing in and for itself be viewed as posited, then this being is the same as existence.
>
> (pp. 58–9)

The distinction between relative and absolute position is analogous to that between the existence of things and their relations in the divine *schema* of the *New Exposition*, and to that proposed in the *New Theory* between the relation of things to each other and the horizon within which they are related. The determinate relations of subject and predicate fall within a horizon of absolute position which, as the ground of logical determination, necessarily exceeds it.

Because existence is the ground of the possibility of predication it cannot itself be a predicate. This directly challenges both the Wolffian and Crusian accounts of existence. For Wolff, possibility concerns the ensemble of the predicates of a thing, to which existence must be added as a further predicate; it is the predicate of 'that which is more in existence than possibility' (pp. 60–1). Crusius's position was more specific: 'The famous Crusius counts being somewhere [*Irgendwo*] and being at some time [*Irgendwenn*] as the infallible determinations of existence' (pp. 64–5). Although this position is close to Kant's theory of the actual principles of co-existence and succession developed in the *New Exposition*, he now rejects it as insufficient. Crusius still treats existence as a supplement to possibility, the being somewhere and sometime of a possible being. Instead of Wolff's predication of existence to a possible being and Crusius's predication of '*Irgendwo und Irgendwenn*', Kant tries to prove that existence is the horizon of position which is not itself posited.

In terms of predication: 'in an existent thing nothing more is posited than in a merely possible one (for then it is a question of the predicates of the thing)' (pp. 62–3), Although nothing more is posited *in*, that is, predicated of an existing thing, more is posited *through:*

Something more is posited through [*durch*] an existent thing than through a merely possible one, because this concerns the absolute position of the thing itself. So the thing itself is not posited in mere possibility, but merely the relations of something else according to the law of contradiction, and it remains true that existence can in no way properly be a predicate of anything.

(pp. 62–3)

The existent thing has a relation to existence which cannot be exhausted by a mode of predication which is subsequent to that relation. Predication according to the law of contradiction concerns the relation between already existing things, and it is illegitimate to employ it in understanding the relation of existing things to existence.

This argument reverses the Wolffian project by making existence prior to possibility and its mode of predication. Kant unfolds this consequence by using the logical/real distinction to show that possibility 'is abolished not only if internal contradiction is encountered, but also when no matter or datum for thought exists' (pp. 68–9). This passage implies that existence be a ground of possibility and not merely its complement, and in case this implication is not entirely plain, Kant spells it out: 'All possibility presupposes something actual in which and through which everything conceivable is given. Accordingly there is a certain actuality whose annulment itself would totally annul all internal possibility' (pp. 78–9). The privilege of existence over possibility is the core of Kant's critique of Wolff, and had implications in various fields of philosophy. For the removal of the keystone of the Wolffian system, the equation of the logical and the actual, required either that systematic philosophy be abandoned, or that it be reconstructed on a new basis. Kant reflected on this choice in the Second Preface to the *Critique of Pure Reason*, but in the writings of the 1760s the 'all destroying Kant' was already dedicating his efforts to restoring the metaphysical foundations of systematic philosophy.

In *The Enquiry Concerning the Clarity of the Principles of Natural Theology and Ethics* (1764) Kant took the opportunity offered by the problem set by the Berlin Royal Academy of Sciences on the applicability of mathematical proof to metaphysics to bring together the scattered parts of his Wolff critique. The *Enquiry*'s reflections on method, discriminative and subsumptive judgement, and the nature of existence, take place within the continuing argument with Wolff and Crusius. This is apparent from the contents and organization of the four 'Meditations' which comprise it: the first three distinguish Kant's view of philosophy from Wolff's by means of the distinction of logical and real ground, while the fourth and last employs the distinction in an exposition of the formal and material principles of theoretical and practical judgement.

Kant begins his first 'Meditation' on achieving certainty in mathematics and philosophy by distinguishing between the two ways of establishing a general concept. The first way is synthetic, proceeding through '*Verbindung*' or 'binding' and is followed by mathematics; the second is analytic, proceeding through '*Absonderung*' or separation, and is followed by philosophy. The target of this distinction is, once again, the Wolffian method, which proceeds synthetically from first principles whose axiomatic status was guaranteed by the absence of contradiction. Kant's first criticism of Wolff by name in the *Enquiry* refers to his philosphical proof of the geometrical concept of similarity. This is significant as marking the first step on one of the main paths to the transcendental distinction, which is the realization that topological incongruency is not open to conceptual determination: intuitive identity and difference are rigorously distinguished from conceptual. To recall one of Kant's later examples, the difference between left and right hand may be intuited but cannot be conceptually determined according to internal characteristics. At this stage Kant simply criticizes Wolff's elision of philosophical and geometrical similarity: 'Wolff considered geometrical similarity from the standpoint of a philosopher, seeking to bring it under a general concept of similarity' (1764a; p. 277; p. 7). Kant's understanding of what is at stake in geometrical similarity is extremely complex, and belies his synthetic/analytic distinction. He does not subsume geometrical similarity under a general concept, as in the 'synthetic' procedure of Wolff, nor does he reach a concept of it through analysis. Here, as also in his definition of philosophy in a later 'Meditation', his procedure is rather more involved, and in both cases, the subtlety of his thought belies the analytic/synthetic schema in which he has to present it.

For the purposes of his schematic distinction of analytic and synthetic methods, Kant defines mathematics as the 'arbitrary binding-together of concepts' (p. 277; p. 6). Yet when discussing the construction of a geometrical figure a far more involved procedure emerges. The rule of the relations of intersecting lines within a circle is discovered in the course of construction: 'In geometry, for example, in order to know the properties of all circles, we draw one in which, instead of all the possible intersecting lines, we only inscribe two. From these we can demonstrate the relations, and meditate on the general rule for the relation of intersecting lines for all circles, *in concreto*' (p. 278; pp. 8–9). In the construction properties are discovered, and universal rules disclosed. The universal rule manifests itself in the inscription; the drawing is not an arbitrary subsumption or deduction from an axiom, but is a complex activity of disclosing a rule through production and reflection.

A complex picture of philosophical procedure also emerges in the course of Kant's exposition of the method of philosophy. For the purposes of criticizing Wolff's synthetic procedure, Kant ascribes to philosophy the task of analysing 'confused concepts, to make them complete and determinate' (p. 278; p. 8). Kant exaggerates this aspect of philosophical procedure in order to distinguish his method from the Wolffians':

> Compare this with the philosopher's procedure which has become the fashion in all the schools, and just how upside-down this will be found to be! The most highly derived concepts, which would naturally be the last the understanding would start from, are for them the beginning, because they have in mind the model of the mathematician which they want to imitate completely.
>
> (1764a; p. 289; p. 21)

Instead of proceeding from axioms guaranteed by the principle of contradiction, Kant proposes that philosophy proceed analytically. This critique of the procedure of the Wolffian philosophy is closely allied with the critique of its content in the form of the distinction of logical and real ground. The synthetic method of the Wolffians derives real grounds from the logical – moving from abstract but non-contradictory axioms to the real. Now, just as in the *Only Possible Proof*, Kant reverses the priority of possibility and actuality: he also turns philosophical procedure on its head, beginning with actual concepts and proceeding to determine them. However, in spite of the relative simplicity of the distinction between analytic and synthetic procedures, the actual process of analysis turns out to be rather more complex. On closer inspection it is apparent that the work of philosophical judgement is as complex as the proof of a geometrical proposition by construction.

In the course of philosophical analysis certain basic concepts/ judgements will be reached which cannot be further determined. We have already met these in the *False Subtlety* and *Negative Quantities*. They are characterized as the limits of analysis; they are unanalysable 'either in and for themselves or relating to us'. The examples he offers of such concepts, variously called *Grundbegriffe*, *Elementarbegriffe*, *unerweislichen Sätzen*, and *unerweislichen Grundurteilen*, are extremely significant: 'many concepts are almost unanalysable, for example, the concept of a representation, the being beside or after one another; others are only partially analysable, as the concept of space, time, of the various feelings of the human soul, of the feeling of the sublime, of the beautiful, of the disgusting, etc.' (p. 280; p. 11). The examples of such concepts yields a theoretical constellation which will emerge more precisely in the course of the following chapter; for representation, space, time, and the feelings of the beautiful, sublime, and disgusting are joined by more than the shared characteristic of being difficult to analyse. The difficulty originates in our inadequate knowledge of the 'driving principles [*Triebfedern*] of our nature', which are expressed in the distinctions of desire/aversion (*Lust/Unlust*) and appetite/revulsion (*Begierde/Abscheu*).

The unanalysable concepts share with existence the property of being basic judgements or concepts which as the foundations of judgement cannot be employed as predicates. They form 'judgements' which are prior to judgement, and cannot be further determined by means of it. They are the existential point of departure for philosophical definition, and its analytic terminus; analysis is the process of discovering that which is immanent:

> In philosophy, where the concept of the thing that I must explain is given to me, that which is immediately and first of all perceived in it, must serve as an undemonstrable fundamental-judgement [*Grundurteil*]. Since I do not yet have the complete distinct concept of the thing, but am beginning to look for it, it cannot be demonstrated by means of this concept; it [the fundamental-judgement] serves more as a means of producing [*zu erzeugen*] the distinct knowledge and definition. So before any philosophical exposition of things I must first have fundamental-judgements, and must only take care at this stage that I don't take a derived characteristic to be one which is originary [*ein uranfängliches Merkmal*].
>
> (1764a; p. 282; pp. 12–13)

Analysis begins with unprovable fundamental-judgements and produces the distinct and complete concept by searching for it. The relation of basic judgements or concepts to subsumptive judgement is completely different from that of Wolff and his school. Wolff's axioms, or fundamental concepts, are based on the principle of contradiction, Kant's are themselves fundamental: they are existential orientations which found the possibility of philosophical analysis; they are, in other words, the transcendentals of the transcendental philosophy.

The distinction between fundamental and derived judgement is basic to Kant's transcendental philosophy. It already appeared in the distinction between human and animal modes of discrimination made in the *False Subtlety*. There Kant said that human discrimination differs from that of animals insofar as it presupposes fundamental judgement; he develops this thought in *The Enquiry*:

> We say: a man distinguishes gold from brass when he knows that the density of one metal is not the same as the other. It is also said that a beast distinguishes one feed from another when it eats one and leaves the other. The word 'distinguish' is used in both cases. In the first case it signifies to *know the difference*, which can never happen without *making a judgement*; in the second it only shows that different representations evoke different actions, and here it is not necessary that a judgement precede it ... [the beast] is not in the least able to judge identity and difference.
>
> (p. 285; p. 16)

In human discrimination a judgement precedes the awareness of difference or the performance of a distinction. This yields the paradox, or 'knot' as Kant described it in the *False Subtlety*, that judgement is prior to the very act of distinction which is the necessary presupposition of judgement.

There are then two modes of judgement: the first, fundamental judgement, is expressed in the originary concepts which found the possibility for the second mode of judgement according to discrimination and subsumption. Such primary judgements are described as *augenscheinlichen Urteile* or *unmittelbare Urteile* – immediate judgements. Yet how far can these judgements be properly described as judgements? For Kant tells us in the *False Subtlety* that mediation forms the essence of judgement: 'To compare [*vergleichen*] something as a characteristic with a thing is called judgement' (1762; p. 47). Comparison is not immediate or *augenscheinlich*; yet Kant insists that fundamental judgement is immediate.

An act of consciousness is involved in both modes of judgement: in fundamental judgement this consciousness is immediate, while in derived judgement it is mediated. Fundamental judgements form the starting point of metaphysics, and Kant advises his readers to 'search out those characteristics which definitely lie in the concept of a general constitution [*allgemeinen Beschaffenheit*] through a certain inner experience, that is, an immediately obvious consciousness [*ein unmittelbares augenscheinliches Bewusstsein*]' (p. 1764a; p. 286; p. 18). Kant proposes as an example of this immediate consciousness the Newtonian proposition that bodies attract at a distance. He first examines the notion of 'distance' and finds that distinct bodies do not touch. He then resolves to analyse the notion of touch. Here he adopts a completely different procedure: instead of analysing the concept of contact he provides a phenomenological description of the experience of touching an impenetrable body:

> I now ask myself: what do I mean by touch? I know intuitively (*so werde ich inne*] without bothering with definitions that I judge I touch something from the resistance of its impenetrability. Then I find that this concept arises originally from feeling; for by the judgement of the eye [*das Urteil des Augen*] I can only suppose that one piece of matter will touch another; it can only be known for certain through the observed resistance of impenetrability.

> (p. 288; p. 20)

Kant uses for the first and only time the verb *innewerden* to refer to the intuitive experience of the resistance of thing, or its impenetrability. This word has more of a physical connotation than the intellectualist *wissen*. In this passage the body's reaction to an impenetrable object is a judgement; it is also a feeling, the source of the concepts of impenetrability and touch. Kant then suggests that it is illegitimate for metaphysics to confine itself to anthropocentric notions of contact, impenetrability, and resistance, and that there are other forms of presence: 'Not every immediate presence is a touch' (p. 288; p. 20). However, in the course of the proof it becomes apparent that in the human mode of bringing a thing to presence, feeling, consciousness, and judgement are almost inseparable. This experience is given the untranslatable name *Gemüt* in the *Critique of Judgement-Power*.[9]

The fundamental judgement recalls Herder's notion of *tasten* – Kant's term for this activity is orientation. A prior orientation to the world is presupposed in the discriminative and subsumptive activities of derived judgement. These activities are refinements of original orientation, but cannot take place without it. As such, discrimination and subsumption have a common source, and so are conformable with each other. However, it is precisely this conformity which makes them dangerous, since they can be incorrectly oriented with regard to each other. The object of the transcendental distinction is to separate them artificially in order to bring them together in a proportioned and legitimate accord.

Kant does not establish the transcendental distinction in the *Enquiry*, but he does try to unite the formal and material elements of cognition in a single judgement. His efforts to reconcile the formal principles of Wolff with the material principles of Crusius in theoretical, and the British moral philosophers in practical philosophy reflect this attempt. They are dedicated to producing an account of judgement which is both subsumptive and discriminative. Kant maintains that there are 'indemonstrable propositions' beyond the principle of contradiction, and that insofar as these contain 'the grounds of other knowledge, they are the first material principles of human reason' (p. 295; p. 28). He identifies these elementary concepts or judgements with Crusius's material principles of knowledge, praising the latter's critique of Wolffian 'empty' formal principles of knowledge: 'Crusius is justified when he criticizes other schools of philosophy who would ignore these material principles and attach themselves merely to the formal' (pp. 295; p. 28). However, he draws back from the full implications of Crusius's critique of Wolff, refusing to accept the claim that the truth of a judgement rests on a feeling of conviction:

> For when one maintains that no other ground for truth can be given except that it is impossible to hold it as anything but true, then one is to be understood that no other ground for truth is available, and that knowledge is indemonstrable. Now admittedly there are many indemonstrable knowledges [*Erkenntnisse*], but the feeling of conviction with regard to them is an indication, but not a demonstrable ground, that they are true.
>
> (p. 295; pp. 28–9)

Kant's negotiation of Wolff and Crusius's positions is subtle; he tries to maintain a balance between formal and material elements of knowledge. This is especially clear in his attempt to supplement Wolffian formal morality with the British moral sense theory. Underlying this reconciliation, however, is a broad notion of orientation. Kant's use of the Crusian term 'material principle' as a description of 'immediate judgement' conceals the considerable differences between their positions. Kant's 'material principle' forms a part of a wider, as yet still inchoate account of the orientation of judgement.

Kant made great progress towards stating the transcendental

distinction and developing his theory of judgement in his accounts of the disorientation of judgement in the *Essay on Mental Illness* (1764) and the *Dreams of a Visionary elucidated through the Dreams of Metaphysics* (1766). In these studies of the pathology of judgement, Kant regards judgement in terms of the negotiation of activity and passivity. The *Essay on Mental Illness* establishes a typology of disorders of judgement: Imbecility, for example, is described as a 'weakness of judgement-power,' although the disorder which most interested him was that which allied delusory perceptions with a correct use of logical judgement. In this disorder 'the error consists in the concepts, the judgements themselves, if one were to accept the inverted perception [*verkehrte Empfindung*] as true, can be completely correct, even uncommonly rational' (1764b; p. 267). In the terms of the *Enquiry*, the fundamental judgements are warped, while the derived judgements are sound. In the *Essay on Mental Illness* Kant ascribes this particular delusion to visionaries and prophets; but in the *Dreams of a Visionary* he extends the condition to philosophers.

The *Dreams of a Visionary* is usually remembered – when remembered at all –· as a bizarre episode in Kant's career; how else can one explain this satire on the writings of the mystic Swedenborg? We have already seen that some of Kant's contemporaries held this view, even in the face of his protests that the work was intended as a serious contribution to metaphysics. It is undeniably one of Kant's least controlled texts, but one of the most important for understanding his development. Indeed, among the pre-critical writings it is second in importance only to the *Inaugural Dissertation*.[10] It contains the first attempt to mobilize a version of the transcendental distinction against the fallacies of subreption which inevitably afflict the human judgement in metaphysics.

What most shocked a contemporary such as Mendelssohn about the *Dreams of a Visionary* was Kant's refusal to distinguish between dreamers of visions such as Swedenborg and dreamers of reason such as Wolff and Crusius. Each of them was a '*Luftbaumeister*', all builders of dream castles, elaborate edifices erected upon unexamined and even delusory foundations. Kant equates the mystical world of correspondences evoked by Swedenborg in the reports of his voyages through the universe with 'the dreamland of Wolff built with only a few blocks of experience but with plenty of dodgy concepts, or that of Crusius produced from nothing by the magical power of a few spells about what is thinkable and unthinkable' (1766; p. 342; p. 59). All the dreamers, whether mystics or philosophers, suffer from a disorientation of judgement which takes place before they exercise their logical judgement in the construction of their systems. Given

this, the problem becomes one of how to discriminate between truth
and illusion in fundamental judgement or perception.

The judgement of the dreamers is disoriented before they proceed
to their logical inferences. The senses are deluded before the
understanding sets to work, a fact which makes the delusion difficult
to discern and almost impossible to mend:

> A coherent deception of the senses is a more remarkable
> phenomenon than the deception of reason, the causes of which
> are sufficiently well known and could to a great extent be
> guarded against through the willed direction of the *Gemütskräfte*
> and more effective control over an empty curiosity. But the
> former deception concerns the first foundation of all judge-
> ments, against which, when it is disoriented, the rules of logic
> are of little help.
>
> (pp. 360–1; p. 83)

The work of secondary judgement, however correct, is of no use if
the material of its subsumptions has not been adequately distinguished;
and this occurs when the primary judgement, the combination of
awareness and bodily sensation, is disoriented.

Much of the *Dreams of a Visionary* is concerned with establishing
a criterion for the correct discrimination of the materials of perception
prior to logical judgement. This is difficult because the criterion of
discrimination cannot be a logical rule, since the relations under
consideration are prior to logical determination. Kant identifies the
basic delusion which afflicts Swedenborg, Wolff, and Crusius as the
inability to distinguish properly between inner and outer, between
the imagination and its objects. The 'dreamer of sensations' is
incapable of distinguishing between real and imaginary objects: 'They
read, even when awake, and often with the greatest vivacity of
perception, certain objects as if they were placed among the things
that they really perceive around them' (p. 343; p. 61). The inability
to distinguish is not a logical error, but arises from the disorientation
of the discriminative ability of the sensibility.

The insight that sensibility possesses its own ability to discriminate,
or better, is constituted by the activity of discrimination, develops
into the doctrine of intuition. The earlier horizon of existence, the absolute position of the *Only Possible Proof* is now considered subjectively;
space arises from the discrimination of position. In order to
demonstrate this, Kant returns to his favourite critical hobby-horse
– the identity of indiscernibles. He makes his usual criticism that
position contributes to the determination of an object and yet is not

open to rational determination, and then goes on to state that position is a condition of sensibility: 'We find with the use of the outer senses, that in a perception, beyond the clarity in which objects are represented, we also grasp their place, although perhaps not with the same accuracy on all occasions. For this is a necessary condition of sensibility, without which it would be impossible to represent things as outside us' (p. 344; p. 61). Position for Kant does not only mean spatial position, but also existence, since existence was defined earlier as position. So when we represent existent things, they are first posited as outside us, and then in certain relations to each other.

Fundamental judgement in the *Dreams of a Visionary* consists in the negotiation of human agency and the position of objects as existent. The position of objects resists the projections of the imagination (they are 'impenetrable') and disposes it into active and passive modes. There is in perception a negotiation of activity and passivity which the later critical philosophy distributed across the distinction of intuition and concept. The problem of distinguishing between inner and outer stems from this negotiation of the active and the passive modes of human activity. The shock of activity encountering resistance provokes an act of discrimination which constitutes the distinction of inner and outer, a distinction 'in comparison with which it is possible to distinguish the original image [*Urbild*] from the shadow image [*Schattenbild*], namely the outer from the inner' (p. 343; p. 61). What is crucial is that the distinction between inner and outer is provoked by the resistance of external things. The law of this distinction is not given in a concept, but arises from a capacity to distinguish which is entirely different from that of the understanding.

Kant's main focus in the *Dreams of a Visionary* is disorientation of the distinction of outer and inner. In cases of disorientation the relation between the projected representative field or horizon and the posited objects is distorted, allowing the products of imagination to appear as external objects. Since the establishment of a distinction between inner and outer precedes the subsumptive work of judgement, it is possible for a phantasist to obey the rules of logical reasoning according to the principle of contradiction, and still be rationalizing delusions. Furthermore, there is no logical means by which such delusions can be uncovered since 'the true or apparent perception of the senses always precedes the judgement of the understanding, and has an immediate self-evidence [*Evidenz*] that exceeds all other forms of persuasion' (p. 347; p. 65). It is in order to expose the disorientation of inner and outer perception that Kant develops the various strategies for disclosing the 'bias of reason' analysed above.

The account of the distortions of discriminative judgement applies not only to religious visionaries and lunatics, but also to metaphysicians: not even they are free from the bias of reason. Kant admits toward the end of his increasingly ill-humoured scrutiny of Swedenborg's doctrines that his work had been 'inspired by loftier motives', and that in writing the *Dreams of a Visionary* he had 'a purpose that seemed more important to me than that which I pretended, and this I have considered myself to have achieved' (p. 367; p. 90). The hidden purpose of the satire upon Swedenborg, the subtext of the work, was no less than the re-determination of the subject matter of metaphysics. Instead of regarding it as the search for 'the hidden properties of things through reason' Kant proposes that it restrict itself to enquiring 'what relation the [metaphysical] question has to the concepts of experience on which all our judgements must be founded' (pp. 367–8; p. 91). Kant limits metaphysics to the proper orientation of the understanding; it must survey its founding discrimination of inner and outer, and map its fundamental judgements; in so doing it changes from being knowledge of other worlds to self-knowledge.

This new task for metaphysics involves the self-orientation of the faculty of judgement through a critique of its activities. It intimates the transcendental distinction when it distinguishes the logical subsumption of the understanding from the discriminations of perception, both of which are seen in terms of a balance of activity and passivity. The view of sensibility as a discrimination prior to the judgements of the understanding is developed, along with the earlier arguments concerning the horizon of perception, in *The First Ground for a Differentiation of Regions in Space* (1768).

In the *Dreams of a Visionary* Kant considered the horizon of perception introduced in the *New Theory* and *Negative Quantities* as a subjective projection or 'representative field'. In the *Differentiation* he seems to have returned to a theory of absolute space, presumably derived from Newton, although he is not mentioned by name in the essay. Indeed, the 'Newtonian' space of this essay seems closer to the 'absolute position' proposed in the *Only Possible Proof*, than to the account of space given in the *Mathematical Principles of Natural Philosophy*.[11] But Kant uses it as the starting point for a phenomenology of the body in which various intuitive distinctions are established as prior to rational judgement. In fact, Kant uses the evidence of these distinctions as proof of absolute space at the same time as showing absolute space to be the source of intuitive distinctions.

In the *Differentiation* Kant defends the 'absolute space' of 'the geometers' as a means of attacking the Leibniz-Wolff definition of space as relation. His claim that space is a fundamental judgement is directed against: 'the concept of many recent philosophers, above all the Germans, that space only consists in the external relation of parts of matter which are found beside each other' (1768; p. 383; p. 43). The Wolffians err in failing to distinguish between positional and regional accounts of space, not realizing that a positional account of space according to relations between things presupposes a region within which those relations are posited. The distinction of position and region recalls that between the mutual relation of objects and the horizon within which they are placed proposed in the *New Theory*, and the distinction of absolute and relative position in the *Only Possible Proof*. Consistent with these arguments, Kant maintains that the determination of region (*Gegend*) is not logical, but depends on fundamental, intuitive distinctions which exceed logical determination.

In order to achieve a 'clear proof' of the reality of space apart from relation Kant avoids the 'abstract judgements of metaphysics', relying instead on the 'intuitive judgements of extension [*anschauenden Urteilen der Ausdehnung*]' (p. 378; p. 37). Such 'intuitive judgements' form the non-rational foundation of region as distinguished from the rational determination of position. The latter may be rationally determined since: 'With all extended objects the position of the parts in relation to each other can be known adequately from the object itself' (p. 377; p. 37). Position is determined by the relation of the parts of a whole; region, however, requires an additional determination, one which is not spatial. Region is the ordering of position, but the principle of ordering is not spatial, since this would mean that region was simply the position of positions. As already seen in the *Only Possible Proof*, the position of position is a qualitatively different relation to that between things which have been posited. This is also the case with the distinction between region and position:

> The region, however, with regard to which this order of parts is disposed, relates itself to the space outside it, but not to its places. For this would be no more than the position of just those parts [places] in an external relation; region, however, relates itself to space in general as a unity according to which every extension must be regarded as a part.
>
> (p. 378; p. 37)

Kant apologizes 'if the reader finds these concepts still very incomprehensible' and goes on to explicate this passage in terms of 'intuitive judgements'. These offer a means of explaining how region is not space in general, but a 'unity' which reveals distinct spaces to be related to one another as parts, but not necessarily parts of a whole. Region, in other words, is the transcendental condition of space.

Kant avoids subsuming positions under a universal 'position in general' by conceiving of region as a differentiation of spaces which is not itself spatial. Region is not a universal concept but a heuristic principle of differentiation, perhaps best understood as a form of reflective judgement. Kant discovers the source of the differentiations which constitute region to lie in the comportment of the human body. His approach in the *Differentiation* reveals some fascinating differences with that adopted in the *Dreams of a Visionary*. There Kant derived the differentiation of inner and outer from the active and passive modes of perception, seeing it as the result of an alignment of a projected 'representational field' with external objects. In the *Differentiation* this negotiation of activity and passivity has been replaced by the 'pure relation' of a body to 'original or absolute' space, from which relation arise the differences of above/below, left/ right, and front/back.

Instead of the differentiations arising from the negotiation of projection and resistance, or the active orientation of primary judgement, Kant imagines the 'pure relation' in terms of the violation of the body. The three differentiations arise from the cutting of the body by three intersecting planes:

> Because of the three dimensions of physical space, three planes can be conceived which intersect each other at right angles. Since we know through the senses what is outside us only insofar as it stands in relation to us, it is no wonder that we derive from the relation of these intersecting planes to our body the first ground for producing the concept of regions in space. The plane on which the length of our body stands vertically is called horizontal in relation to us; and this horizontal surface enables us to make the differentiation of regions into above and below. Two further planes may be vertically disposed on this surface, cutting each other at right angles, so that the length of the body can be imagined along the lines of intersection. One of these vertical planes divides the body into two externally similar halves, and delivers the ground for the differentiation of right and left sides; the other perpendicular makes it possible for us to have the concept of front and back sides.

(pp. 378–9; p. 38)

It is evident in this passage that the body comports itself passively to its violation by the intersecting planes which divide and cut it. The differentiations are inscribed on and in the body, and are not produced by its active disposition toward the resistance of external objects. The body is forcibly oriented, and it is only after this orientation that names are given to the resultant 'feelings' of differences.

The basic differences, or 'feelings' of distinction, or 'intuitive judgements' of distinction, determine the recognition of position, but are not themselves positioned. They permit the disposition of positions into regions, but are not themselves positional. They represent non-rational orientations which form a necessary preliminary to any judgement. The materials of a judgement will be unintelligible if they have not been distinguished prior to the act of judgement. Kant offers several examples; the first concerns the orientation of a written text prior to reading it, and spells out the notion of 'misreading' which he earlier used to describe the hallucinations of the visionary. Before interpreting the sense of a page of text it is necessary to position it correctly:

> With a written page, for example, we first differentiate the upper from the lower sides of the text, we observe the difference between the front and the back sides, and then we look at the position of the characters from left to right or inversely. There is always the same position of the parts ordered on its surface, regarding each other and the figure of the whole; one can turn the page as one likes, but with this representation the difference of regions is violated, and being so closely bound with the impression made by the visible object, renders the text read in this way . . . incomprehensible.
>
> (p. 379; p. 38)

Prior to even venturing a judgement, whether on a text or on an object, it is necessary to orient the object according to basic differences; without such an orientation, the object will be unintelligible. Such prior orientations underlie all judgement: 'even our most common knowledge of the position of places would be of no use to us if we could not place the things so ordered, and the entire system of reciprocating positions in a relation to the sides of our bodies through the regions' (pp. 379–80; p. 39). All judgements, whether subsumptive or discriminative, presuppose an orientation according to the intuitive differences which are produced by the positioning of the body in three-dimensional space. They must conform themselves with the intuitive differences.

The *Differentiation* suggests that our experience of space arises from differentiations which are not open to rational determination. Once again, this position is put as a challenge to Wolff's equation of being and logic. Wolff subordinated space and time to relation, so making them into the 'well-founded phenomena' of a rational order; Kant shows that space is an existential relation which resists rational determination. He deploys the basic difference of left and right in a critique of the identity of indiscernibles, showing that the case of incongruent counterparts indicates an existential difference which escapes rational definition. Regarding the differentiation of right and left hand it is clear: 'that the figures of two bodies can be identical, the quantity of their extension the same, and yet an inner difference remains; namely, that the surface that includes the one could not possibly include the other' (p. 382; p. 42). This difference, or *innerer Grund der Verschiedenheit*, distinguishes existence from essence, and repudiates the Wolffian project of total rational definition. Reason and existence are distinguished, and the main source of this distinction lies in the 'intuitive judgement' which orients objects prior to logical judgement. The transcendental distinction has been performed if not recognized. When it was, two years later in the *Inaugural Dissertation*, the problem then arose of bringing together the existential differences of intuitive judgement and the rational identities of conceptual judgement in a new 'transcendental logic'.

Reflecting on his philosophical development, Kant wrote that he suspected the existence of an 'illusion of the understanding' but saw it as if in twilight, before going on to say: 'The year '69 gave me great light' (*Ref.* 5037). The results of this illumination are apparent in the *Inaugural Dissertation* published in the following year. In it Kant formally identifies the transcendental distinction of the material and intelligible aspects of experience which had emerged out of the critique of Wolff, and aligns it with the distinction of real and formal ground. With this distinction he had finally discovered a basis for the reform of metaphysics. Metaphysical axioms and judgements are diagnosed as suffering from a 'contagion of sensible cognition with intellectual'; consequently, a propadeutic to metaphysics was required which would discover the

> criterion for these judgements which may be ready to hand and cognisable with clarity, and as it were a touchstone by which we may distinguish them from genuine judgements and at the same time, should they perchance appear to be firmly attached to the intellect, a certain docimastic art with whose

help a just appreciation could be made of how much pertains to things sensitive and how much to things intellectual.

(1770; § 24)

In 1770 the transcendental distinction served to establish the art of judgement as an *ars docimastica* with which to assay received judgements. Over the next eleven years the project changed considerably, and took on a far more ambitious character. The transcendental distinction as the basis of a metaphysical symptomatology, still reflected in the title of Kant's projected work in 1771 – 'The Bounds of Sense and Reason' – is transformed into the legislation of the legitimacy of metaphysical judgements, a shift reflected in the new title first mentioned in 1772 – 'The Critique of Pure Reason'.

In the first section of the *Inaugural Dissertation* Kant introduces the transcendental distinction in terms of 'the *two-fold genesis* of the concept out of the nature of the mind' and claims that recognizing it 'can help us to secure a deeper insight into method in metaphysics' (§ 1). The epistemological character of the distinction is immediately aligned with the distinction of real and logical ground, which emerged from the critique of Wolff's unproblematic transition from possibility to existence:

> it is one thing, given the parts, to conceive for oneself the *composition* of the whole, by means of an abstract notion of the intellect; and it is another thing to *follow up* [*exsequi*] this general *notion*, as one might do with some problem of reason through the sensitive faculty of knowledge, that is to represent the same notion to oneself in the concrete by a distinct intuition.
>
> (§ 1)

So while it is possible to compose a rational whole from given parts, it is quite another thing to *follow up* this rational whole into existence. The process of realizing a rational whole is as problematic as the exemplification of a concept in intuition. Rational composition is subsumptive since the relation of universal concept and individual existence can only be considered as a subsumption of individuals under a universal: 'The former is done by means of the concept of *composition* in general, in so far as a number of things are contained under it (in mutual relation to each other), and so by means of ideas of the intellect which are universal' (§ 1). Such formal composition, subsuming individual parts *under* universals, is distinguished from real composition. Real composition, which up to now Kant has left unknowable, based on the fundamental concept or judgement, is now specified in terms of the 'law of intuition': 'The second case [of following up into existence] rests upon temporal *conditions*, in so far as it is possible by the successive addition of part to part to arrive genetically, that is by synthesis, at the concept of a composite, and this case falls under the laws of *intuition*' (§ 1). In this case real is distinguished from rational composition in terms of the synthetic activity through which it produces a whole through the addition of parts over time.

Instead of the theoretically undetermined, and undeterminable, fundamental concepts or judgements of his earlier writings, Kant now explicitly relates existence and sensibility, and distinguishes between the sciences of sensibility and logic. He openly accuses Wolff of confusing real and logical grounds in underestimating the significance of the distinction between sensibility and understanding:

> I am afraid it may be that the illustrious Wolff has, by this distinction between things sensitive and things intellectual, which is for him only a logical distinction, completely abolished, to the great detriment of philosophy, that noble institution of antiquity, the discussion of the *character of phenomena and noumena*, and has turned men's minds away from the search into those things to what are very often only logical minutiae.
>
> (§ 7)

For Kant there is, of course, a fundamental distinction between the two sources of knowledge; not simply a *logical* but a transcendental distinction. The meaning of this distinction is disclosed in his definitive dismissal of the existential pretentions of the principle of contradiction.

Kant reverses the signs on the elision of the logical and existential aspects of the principle of contradiction – expressed in the proposition that something cannot both be and not be. His pursuit of the implications of something ceasing to be or coming into being for this proposition is now driven to its radical conclusion. Both the proposition, and the principle of contradiction on which it rests, are overturned by the demonstration that it assumes simultaneity, thus smuggling in an intuitive judgement of time. Kant closes his case for the priority of the existential or real ground over the logical, by showing that not only is the real ground distinct from the logical, but that the logical is dependent on it:

Indeed so far is it from being the case that anyone has ever yet deduced from elsewhere and explained the concept of time with the help of the reason, that rather the principle of contradiction itself has the same concept as a premiss and bases itself on the concept as its condition. For A and not-A are not inconsistent unless they are thought *simultaneously*, (that is at the same time) about the *same thing*. For *after one another* (that is at different times) they *can apply* to the same thing.

(§§ 14–15)

Or, as Kant put the same point again – this time to prove that the experience of time is more fundamental than the principle of contradiction – 'reason itself in using the principle of contradiction cannot dispense with the assistance of this concept [time], to such an extent is the concept primitive and original' (§§ 14–16). In other words, the fundamental principle of the reason cannot be saved without postulating a prior intuitive, existential experience of time, than which there is 'nothing prior and nothing older'.

In place of the underivable basic rational principle of the Wolffians, Kant proposes the 'primitive and original concepts' of space and time. These concepts constitute principles without themselves being principles; they are 'not *rational* at all, nor are they objective *ideas* of any bond [*nexus*], but they are *phenomena*, and while they do indeed bear witness [*testari*] to some common principle constituting a universal bond [*nexus universalis*], they do not expose it to view' (§ 2). Space and time bear witness to a common principle, but are unable to reveal it; they attest to it while keeping it concealed. A clue to their silent testimony is offered by Kant's explanation that space and time are not rational, since they do not subsume things *under* universal concepts, but are 'singular concepts' *in* which sensibles are thought: 'pure (human) intuition is not a universal or a logical concept *under which*, but is a singular concept *in which* sensibles no matter what are thought, and so it contains the concepts of space and time' (§ 12). From this distinction of the properties of concept and intuition, which recalls that made between positing *in* and positing *through* existence in the *Only Possible Proof*, Kant proceeds to distinguish sensible and intellectual knowledge in terms of the discriminative and discursive modes of human understanding:

There is not given [to man] an intuition of things intellectual, but only a *symbolic cognition*, and intellection is only allowable for us through universal concepts in the abstract and not through a singular concept in the concrete. For all our intuition is bound to a certain principle of form [*princio cuidam formae*] under which alone can something be *discerned* by the mind [*a mente cerni*] immediately or as *singular*, and not merely conceived discursively through general concepts.

(§ 10)

In order for individual things to be subsumed under a concept, they have to be distinguished as individual things in intuition; the 'certain principle of form' which achieves this individuation is differential. Human intuition then, is not passive and receptive, but is the act of differentiating between what it brings forth.[12]

This characteristic of human intuition distinguishes it from both animal and divine intuition. The comparison helps us to understand what Kant saw as the 'certain principle of form' at work in human intuition. The *Inaugural Dissertation* is structured around a contrast between human and divine intuition. This marks a change of emphasis from the *False Subtlety*, where Kant contrasted human and animal understanding, seeing in the latter passive acts of discrimination without consciousness. Divine understanding is immediate, and unlike the discursive understanding of human beings it can perceive a manifold 'distinctly at a single glance without the successive application of a measure' (§ 1). Divine intuition is productive; it is not governed by a 'certain principle of form' but forms its own principle: 'divine intuition, which is the principle of objects and not something principled, since it is independent, is an archetype and for that reason perfectly intellectual' (§ 10). The act of divine intellectual intuition is creative; there is no hiatus between the creation and the perception of its objects since there is no passive capacity to interrupt the creative act. Human intuition in complete contrast is not independent, its activity is constantly checked by the impenetrability of things. The interruptions in human intuition constitute a field of differences, founded on a difference between human activity and its objects. These differences can only be overcome in the discursive procedures of the understanding. Between the positing of differences in intuition (the construction of appearance) and their unification by the understanding emerges a notion of experience as orientation.

The main objection to this reading of intuition is Kant's repeated contrast of the passivity of intuition and the activity of the understanding. However, as already noted in connection with the *Dreams of a Visionary*, Kant understood passivity as the passive *disposition* of a projective faculty. This view of passivity as a posture adopted by an active faculty is supported by the account of passivity and affection in the *Inaugural Dissertation*. Here Kant contrasts the activity of divine with the passivity of human intuition: 'Indeed the *intuition* of our mind is always *passive*. And so it is only possible to the extent that something can affect our senses [has the power to affect our sense]' (§ 10). Kant is far from conceiving of affection, a central concept in the post-critical *Opus Postumum*, as mere passivity; in fact he anticipates his later position that affection denotes a negotiation of activity and passivity. The accepted contrast of the utter passivity of intuition and the activity of the understanding is belied by Kant's view of them as specific but complementary dispositions of the same 'faculty of representation'. Regarding this he writes:

> Sensibility is the receptivity of a subject by which it is possible for the subject's own representative state [or condition] to be affected in a definite way by the presence of some object. Intelligence [rationality] is the faculty of a subject by which it has the power to represent things which cannot by their own quality come before the senses of that subject.

(§ 3)

Both are modifications of the subject's representative state: one is the definite affect of the presence of an object; the other a representation apart from immediate affect. Sensibility is the passive disposition of the representative power which merely differentiates between individual objects; intelligence is the active disposition which composes these differences through subsuming them under universals. Although both are dispositions of the same representative power, they must not be confused, and the prevention of such confusion is the task of the *ars docimastica* proposed in the *Inaugural Dissertation*. However, the predicament of human judgement is such that the two modifications must be aligned; the legitimation of this alignment became the legislative programme of the critical tribunal.

The representative power distributes itself between a mode of discrimination and a mode of subsumption. Unlike divine understanding, which is pure activity, and the passive perception of the animals, human understanding is both active and passive. The discriminations of human intuition are neither intellectual nor sensible but attest to a hidden principle of form; they are both principle and principled. As in Aquinas, human understanding both measures and is measured; but for Kant, unlike Aquinas, this activity characterizes not only discursivity but also intuition. Intuition brings objects forth through activity, but represents them as 'outside', as things experienced passively as present. The object only comes to appearance, becomes a phenomenon, through the activity of the representative power; but it is specified as a thing toward which the representative power is passively disposed. The alignment of activity and passivity represented in this movement, the ascription of difference, constitutes the law of intuition.

Kant's doctrine of appearances rests on the active/passive disposition of sensibility. When objects are brought into appearance they have no quality beyond being an excitation or affection of the representative power; they are then specified as appearances according to the 'forms' of intuition:

> For objects do not strike the senses in virtue of their form or specificity. So, for the various things in an object which affect the sense to coalesce into some representational whole there is needed an internal principle in the mind by which these various things may be clothed with a certain specificity in accordance with stable and innate laws.
>
> (§ 4)

Once again Kant prefers the Scotist position that specificity is constituted by difference over the Thomist postulate of the substantial form of objects.[13] The specification of representative affects is an act of discrimination; an active principle specifies representations, distinguishes between their parts, individuates them from others, and all according to stable and innate laws. The basic law of the specification of representative states consists in their ordering according to the principles of time and space. However, this is not the law of the concept, not a universal under which things are legislated, but a *Gesetzmässigkeit ohne Gesetz*, a law through and in which things are brought forth.

Time and space are the fundamental specifications of affective states; they constitute the form of the appearance of an object, since they distinguish the presence of an object within representation. In order for objects to come into appearance they must, in Kant's terms, 'be enfolded' or 'clothed' in the specifications of temporality, but not subsumed under them:

> Time is the *formal principle of the sensible world* which is absolutely first. For all things which are sensible, no matter how, cannot be thought unless either as simultaneous or as placed one after the other, and so are enfolded as it were [*quasi involuta*] by a period of unique time and related to one

another by a determinate position. As a result there necessarily
arises through this concept, which is primary to everything
sensitive, a formal whole which is not a part of something else,
that is the *phenomenal world.*

(§ 14)

Time is now given the properties accorded to existence in the *Only
Possible Proof*: it is the position of positions, a primitive 'concept' prior
to all sensibility – the transcendental involution of things. The notion
of involution is clarified in the discussion of the second 'originary
concept' of space. Space also specifies objects, it too brings them
into appearance according to law:

For things cannot appear to the senses under any species at
all except by the mediation of the power of soul [*vi animi*]
which co-ordinates all sensations according to a law which is
stable and planted in its nature. Since, then, nothing at all can
be given to the sense except in conformity with the primitive
axioms of space and its awareness (so geometry teaches),
whatever can be given to the sense will necessarily accord with
these axioms even though their principle is only subjective.

(§ 15)

This passage offers some more insight into the relation between
activity and passivity in the specification of appearances. Things are
specified, brought into appearance, by a *power* of the mind, which
nevertheless coordinates sensations according to a law. The crucial
relation between law and power is not explored at this stage, but it
constitutes one of the foundations of the constructive critical
philosophy. The relation manifests itself in an abiding disposition, a
rule or 'principle' which specifies the appearance of things. The
specifications realized according to this 'principle' do not exhaust it;
they 'involve' and 'bear witness' to the regularity of the disposition
of power, but do not legislate it.

While it is true that Kant does not directly examine the relation
between power and law in the *Inaugural Dissertation*, he touches on
it indirectly in his notion of 'acquired concepts'. Space and time are
among the acquired concepts which should be distinguished from
both rational 'innate ideas' and empirically abstracted ideas. What
distinguishes Kant's account of the acquisition of concepts from the
empiricist and rationalist versions is the complex set of relations
existing between affection, power, and law. The acquired concepts
emerge when the activity of the soul is stimulated by the presence

of an affection; they are benchmarks for the orientation of the soul's power, or to use Kant's German term *Gemüt*, with respect to objects. They are abstracted from this activity only in the sense that they bear witness to it. Such concepts as 'possibility, existence, necessity, substance, cause, etc., together with their opposites or correlates' are 'concepts abstracted out of the laws planted in the mind by attending to its actions on the occasion of our experience' (§ 7). The acquired concepts are not abstracted from objects, nor from innate ideas of the mind, but from the active/passive disposition of the mind when encountering objects. Experience is not the subsumption of objects under concepts, but a more original disposition which can only be stuttered in the oppositions of philosophical concepts.

Like the acquired concepts mentioned above, time and space are also abstracted from the disposition of the power of representation, but in its discriminative mode. They are distinguished from the other concepts by being the 'original' and 'most primitive' dispositions of the faculty from which the other acquired concepts were derived. Even the traditionally fundamental concept of substance – that which underlies all accidents – is subordinated to time: 'For it is only through the concept of time that we co-ordinate alike substances and accidents whether according to their simultaneity or their succession. And so the notion of time, as being the principle of form, is older than the concepts of substance and accident' (§ 14). Space and time are the original comportments of the representative faculty which specify its immediate affections as appearances. It is only in the wake of this specification that the other acquired concepts can legitimately be employed.

Space and time, although originary among the acquired concepts, are themselves acquired, themselves witnesses to the active/passive disposition of the representative power:

> But truly *each of the concepts* [space and time] without any doubt *has been acquired*, not by abstraction from the sensing of objects indeed (for sensation gives the matter and not the form of human cognition), but from the very action of the mind, an action co-ordinating the mind's *sensa* according to perpetual laws, and each of the concepts is like an immutable diagram, and so is to be cognised intuitively. For sensations excite this act of the mind but do not influence the intuition. Nor is there anything else here born with us except the law of the mind according to which it joins its own sensa together in a fixed manner as a result of the presence of an object.
>
> (§ 15)

Space and time are types or *schemas* produced by the mind when objects are brought into presence; more precisely, they are witnesses to the encounter of human representative power and things. They specify this encounter as the production of appearances.

Space, time and the other *Grundbegriffe* are acquired by 'abstraction' from the activity of the representative power when it encounters things. They are witnesses of this activity, whether in the discriminative procedures of specification in intuition or in the discursive 'recitals' of the understanding's *akroamata*. The presence of objects provokes the active/passive disposition of the representative power, which follows invariable laws of coordination. Unlike divine intuition which creates its objects, human intuition encounters objects. It can only bring things forth according to the laws of specification, or appearance, which express the active/passive disposition of human representative power.

Kant carried this understanding of the active/passive character of human experience through to the *Critique of Pure Reason* and beyond it to the post-critical writings. Staying with the acquisition of concepts, but moving forward to the post-critical polemic against Eberhard, we find Kant making the same points about activity and passivity, but with greater confidence. Concepts are acquired in the act of encountering objects; they do not exist before the act. Human representative power distributes itself into two modes, each of which is essential to experience: on the one hand, the differential specification of things in space and time; and on the other, their unification in concepts:

> There is, however, also an original acquisition [*ursprüngliche Erwerbung*] (as the teachers of natural right put it), consequently also of that which previously did not exist, and therefore did not pertain to anything before the act. Such is, as the *Critique* maintains, *first of all*, the form of things in space and time, secondly, the synthetic unity of the manifold in concepts; for our faculty of knowledge gets neither of these from objects as they are given to it in themselves, but rather produces them out of itself *a priori*.
>
> (1790c; p. 221; p. 135)

While insisting on the transcendental distinction of intuition and the understanding, Kant says not only that both are essential to an experience, but that both have the same origin or 'ground' which allows them to be coordinated: 'But then there must be a ground in the subject which makes it possible that the thought representations originate in this and in no other way, and that enable them to be related to objects not yet given; this ground at least is innate' (p. 221;

p. 135). The consideration of this 'innate ground' will take us to Kant's theories of proportionality and production which he discussed at length in his other text from 1790, the *Critique of Judgement-Power*.

In the *Inaugural Dissertation* Kant was fully aware of the importance of the transcendental distinction, even recognizing that it emerged from an identical ground 'in the subject'. However, the latter aspect was not thematized at this stage, because the focus of interest was the analysis of the subreptic axioms of metaphysics. By separating the two sources of experience, it became possible to perceive how they had been confused in the judgements of the metaphysicians. However, the problem then arises of re-establishing metaphysics after the scrutiny of its judgements in the *ars docimastica* of the *Inaugural Dissertation*. It was important to separate the elements of experience and expose their illegitimate combinations in certain metaphysical judgements; but how was it possible to bring them together to produce legitimate judgements? It is certain from the fact of our experience of things that a *de facto* alignment of sensibility and the understanding takes place, but how may this be legitimated *de jure*; how, in other words, are legitimate, synthetic, a priori judgements possible? After judging the judgements of metaphysics and finding them wanting, the problem arises of how to legislate a relation which itself founds all legislation.

It is apparent from Kant's correspondence of the 1770s that the realization of the importance of this question accounted for the protracted delays in the composition of the first *Critique*. In a letter to Marcus Herz of 21 November 1772, Kant describes how his thinking had moved from a work with the title 'The Limits of Sense and Reason' to one called the 'Critique of Pure Reason'. Kant planned the first project

> to consist of two parts, a theoretical and a practical. The first
> part would have two sections, (1) general phenomenology and
> (2) metaphysics, but this only in regard to its nature and
> method. The second part likewise would have two sections,
> (1) the universal principles of feeling, taste, and sensuous
> desire and (2) the basic principles of morality.
>
> (1967, p. 71)

Yet something fundamental is still missing from this comprehensive scheme, which anticipates the structure of the critical trilogy: 'I noticed that I still lacked something essential, something that in my long metaphysical studies I, as well as others, have failed to pay attention to and that, in fact, constitutes the key to the whole secret of hitherto still obscure metaphysics' (p. 72).

The secret concerns the nature of 'the ground of the relation of that in us which we call "representation" to the object'. Kant criticizes his earlier *Inaugural Dissertation* for remaining content with establishing the transcendental distinction, and not thematizing the problem of the *conformity* between sensible and intellectual aspects of experience:

> In my dissertation I was content to explain the nature of intellectual representations in a merely negative way, namely, to state that they were not modifications of the soul brought about by the object. However, I silently passed over the further question of how a representation that refers to an object without in any way being affected by it can be possible.
>
> (p. 72)

In other words, 'whence comes the agreement' or the 'conformity' of spontaneously produced representations with objects? With this question Kant consciously addresses the difficulty which symptomatically determined the history of the concept of judgement.

Answering this question dictated a transition from the recognition of the transcendental distinction in the 'Bounds of Sense and Reason' to the transcendental deduction of the *Critique of Pure Reason*. The transition represents no less than the attempt to place systematic philosophy on a firmer foundation than Wolff's equivocations. The constructive side of the *Critique* consists in establishing an inventory of the concepts of understanding and finding the principles through which they relate to appearances. At this point in the letter Kant returns to the logical/real distinction with which everything started, first asking

> how my understanding may formulate *real* principles concerning the possibility of such concepts, with which principles experience must be in exact agreement and which nevertheless are independent of experience, [and then admitting] – this question of how the faculty of understanding achieves this conformity with the things themselves, is still left in a state of obscurity.
>
> (p. 72)

But he adopts an optimistic tone; he has classified the categories, and will be in a position to publish the *Critique* 'within three months' – this, remember, is 1772. Over a year later an apology is clearly due, and forthcoming; he writes to Herz at the end of 1773: 'You search industriously but in vain in the book fair catalogue for a certain name beginning with the letter K' (p. 77). Not until the Easter Book Fair of 1781 did that certain name appear before a book entitled *Critique of Pure Reason*; but did this deliver the promised bringing to order of the 'self-alienating understanding under [the] certain and easily applied rules' (p. 77) of the critical tribunal?

If the delay in completing the *Critique* was due to the difficulty of answering the question of how the representative power conformed to objects, it is a wonder the book was finished at all. Or, it might be asked, was the *Critique* ever really completed? If answering the question posed in the letter to Herz constitutes completeness, then no, it remains unfinished. For with this question Kant arrived at the aporia of judgement. How does the representative power dispose itself in well-ordered dispositions according to the alignment of activity and passivity? This does not seem to be a question open to philosophical solution since it concerns the foundation of philosophical concepts; and these, Kant insists, are at best duplicitous witnesses. We know that judgement must both subsume and discriminate, but the alignment of this distinction is twice removed from the original encounter with objects expressed in the distinction.

The first *Critique* establishes the transcendental distinction and then calls for its legitimate suspension in the synthetic, a priori judgement. In the first paragraph of the second (1787) Introduction to the *Critique* Kant points to the alignment of activity and passivity which characterizes human experience:

> That all our knowledge begins with experience cannot be doubted; for how otherwise should our faculty of knowledge be aroused into action if not through objects which stir our senses and partly effect representations, and partly activate our understanding to compare, combine or distinguish them, so manufacturing out of the raw material of sensible imprints the knowledge of objects called experience?
>
> (B1)

It is true that 'we have no knowledge antecedent to experience' but we do have a '*Verstandestätigkeit*' an 'activity of the understanding', which may be activated to produce knowledge through comparison, combination, and distinction. As in the 'original acquisition' the encounter with objects provokes the operation of the synthetic and discriminative aspects of the power of judgement.

Kant now characterizes the transcendental distinction as the separation of the productive activity (the discriminations and subsumptions) from the product ('experience') of the 'self-alienating understanding':

> For it may well be that our knowledge of experience itself is already composed both of that which we receive through imprints, and that which our faculty of knowledge has been induced to produce out of itself by the sensible imprints, such an addition to the basic materials not being distinguishable until practice has made us alert to it, and skilled in separating it off.
>
> (B2)

This image of assaying experience in order to distinguish the raw material of sensation from the labour of the understanding recalls the *ars docimastica* of the *Inaugural Dissertation*. Both here and in the earlier work the issue is how to recognize the transcendental distinction of sensible and intelligible sources of experience. Unlike the earlier text, Kant now insists on going beyond the transcendental distinction, and reconstituting experience philosophically. This enterprise consists in the legitimate suspension of the transcendental distinction in synthetic, a priori judgements, which follow from the recognition that an object is produced according to a given proportion.

In the first edition of the Introduction Kant says of the synthetic, a priori judgement that 'a certain mystery lies here concealed' and observes in a footnote to this passage that the 'vain attempts' of the metaphysical tradition would have been avoided had this mystery been solved. The echo of the letter to Herz in this passage shows that the earlier 'principle' is now identified as the synthetic, a priori judgement. But the task of the *Critique* is not only to reveal the secret principle, but to draft a detailed map for the orientation of future judgement, to produce a system:

> A certain secret is hidden here, one whose disclosure alone could ensure that progress in the immeasurable field of pure knowledge of the understanding be made certain and reliable. It is to unveil with proper universality the ground of the possibility of synthetic judgements a priori, to see into the conditions which would make such a judgement possible, and to mark out this complete knowledge (which constitutes its own genus) according to its original sources, sections, extent

and borders, not through a sketchy outline, but thoroughly
and sufficient for any application.

(All, cf. B27)

Kant's attempt at the cartography of the understanding in the Analytic
followed the traditional table of logical judgements. It was criticized
almost immediately in Hamann and Herder's metacritiques, and
subsequently by Hegel and more recent commentators, for assuming
that the capacity of the human mind is exhausted by the operations
of traditional logic. This is reasonable, but emphasizes the place of
the 'Analytic of Concepts' over the 'Analytic of Principles'. It is in
the latter, especially in the first chapter, 'The Schematism of the
Pure Concepts of Understanding', that the aporia of judgement
threatening the table of categories is allowed to surface.

The *schema* is introduced through the distinction of concept and
intuition, and the necessity of bringing them together in a judgement.
However it exceeds this function, and eventually becomes a 'monogram
of pure a priori imagination', a witness to the activity of restriction
and realization which constitutes culture. In terms of the distinction
of concept and intuition, the *schema* is the 'third thing, which must
be conformable with the category on one side and the appearance
on the other, and make possible the application of the former to the
latter' (A138/B177). But in order to facilitate this mediation, the
schema must in some sense exceed the original distinction. So Kant
continues: 'This mediating representation must be pure (void of
everything empirical) and on one side intellectual, the other sensible.'
The work of schematism, like the 'fundamental judgements' of the
pre-critical philosophy, is beyond the distinction which constitutes
judgement, and cannot be contained by it. Kant indeed echoes his
pre-critical descriptions of the 'secret principle' underlying judgement
when he describes it as 'an art concealed in the depths of the human
soul, whose true working [*wahre Handgriff*] nature ever painfully keeps
us from having unveiled before our eyes' (A141/B180).

'But so much we can say . . .' The operation of schematism is
based on an alignment of activity and passivity which is prior to any
philosophical judgement. The schematism realizes through restriction,
just as do orientation in its reflective encounter with the world, and
culture in the development of human history. In an interesting
slippage toward the end of the schematism section, Kant discloses
that the work of the *schemata* in realizing and restricting the discrete
categories bears witness to a far more fundamental experience. In
the first case, it is evident 'that although the schemata of sensibility
above all realize the categories, they at the same time restrict them,

that is, limit them to conditions which lie outside the understanding (namely in the sensibility)' (A146/B186). However, this mediation between concept and intuition is later, in the final words of the section, stated in terms of the *sensibility as a whole* (*Sinnlichkeit*) 'which realizes the understanding in that it simultaneously restricts it' (A147/B187). The realization through restriction of the understanding by the sensibility as a whole is prior to the realization through restriction of discrete concepts and intuitions.

The figure of realization through restriction occurs throughout Kant's philosophy, and underlies theoretical, practical, and aesthetic judgements. We have seen in this section that it corresponds to the self-ordering of imagination in its encounter with things. It marks an alignment of activity and passivity, one which is not static but is continually being reproduced. Kant gives it various names: orientation, life, and culture; it marks a relation of production and legislation which exceeds the oppositions of philosophy, and yet makes them possible. The conformity of concept and intuition follows from a more fundamental relation, but can this relation itself be admitted in its purity, or does it mark an aporia whose sources lie elsewhere than in philosophy? And if we are positioned within this relation, how can we possibly attain a place from which to judge it, or even to know of its (secret) working? In order to answer these questions it is necessary to examine the other two bodies of judgement – practical and aesthetic – which, together with theoretical, compose the philosophical system.

Practical Judgement

> I want to sleep so he wakes me up. I want to rest or play, and he forces me to work. The raging wind forces me to shelter in a cave, but here or at least somewhere it leaves me in peace; but my master seeks me out, and because the cause of my unhappiness has reason, he is more adept at tormenting me than all the elements.
>
> Kant, *Marginalia to the Observations on the Feeling of the Beautiful and Sublime*

Kant's nightmare about his master is taken from a fragment 'On Freedom' which he jotted in the margin of his book *Observations on the Feeling of the Beautiful and the Sublime*. In this and other marginalia

Kant confronts the darker side of the orientation of judgement described in the previous section. There the representative power was seen to specify objects as appearances and then dispose them according to rules; here human freedom constitutes other human being as persons and establishes its own principles of practical judgement. Practical judgement both legislates and executes the laws of freedom, a potentially dangerous combination if the legislation through reason and the execution through affect become confused. The functions must be distinguished transcendentally, but as in theoretical judgement, for practical judgement to be at all possible, the distinction must also be suspended.

Kant consistently drew analogies between his theoretical and practical philosophies. These were usually made at the level of architectonic, although occasionally he hints at a more substantial relation between the two. On one occasion, in the *Groundwork to a Metaphysic of Ethics* (1785), he distinguishes his practical philosophy from Wolff's in terms of the difference between transcendental and formal logic; on another, in the *Critique of Practical Reason* (1788), he compares the 'typic' of pure practical with the 'schema' of theoretical reason. These analogies express the conviction that theoretical and practical reason are unified in a 'common principle, since in the end there can only be one and the same reason, which must be differentiated solely in its application' (1785; p. 391; p. 8; see also 1788; p. 92; p. 125). In the *Groundwork* Kant admits his inability to demonstrate the unity of reason 'without introducing considerations of quite another sort'. The nature of these considerations becomes apparent in the third *Critique*, where the unity of theoretical, practical and aesthetic 'applications' of reason is thematized in terms of judgement in general.

In the second *Critique* the distinction between the 'applications' of theoretical and practical reason is made in terms of their object. Theoretical philosophy is concerned with 'knowledge of objects' and moves from intuition through concepts to principles, while practical reason is concerned with the 'capacity to make objects real' and proceeds from principles through concepts to intuition. The same problems underly both applications of reason: both are distributed according to transcendental logic and aesthetic, and both seek to justify their fusion in synthetic, a priori judgements. Furthermore, both justifications follow the same procedural steps: they first distinguish between the sensible and intelligible aspects of experience, and then show the conditions under which this distinction may legitimately be suspended in a synthetic, a priori judgement.

The two steps in the development of Kant's theoretical philosophy were chronologically distinct: the transcendental distinction was established by 1770, and the conditions of its legitimate suspension set out in 1781. The development of the practical philosophy followed a similar course. In both cases the transcendental distinction was derived from the bias of reason disclosed within the philosophical tradition. In theoretical philosophy the main protagonists were Wolff and Crusius, with reference to the 'noology' of Locke. In practical philosophy the differences in the tradition were even more clearly marked, permitting Kant to discern the transcendental distinction in the conflict of tradition in practical sooner than in theoretical philosophy. As early as the announcement of his lecture programme for the winter semester of 1764, Kant distinguished the affective practical philosophy of Shaftesbury, Hutcheson, and Hume from the perfectionist Wolffian school represented by Baumgarten.

However clear Kant may have been about the importance of the transcendental distinction in practical philosophy, he remained troubled over the conditions for its legitimate suspension. In theoretical philosophy the 'difficulty' was 'escaped' by joining the discriminative activity of intuition with the subsumptive work of the understanding: they came together in schematism as aspects of the 'realization and restriction' of judgement-power. Practical judgements, though, are subject to 'special difficulties' because their principle is rigorously distinguished from sensibility, so making it difficult to see how its principle could possibly ever conform with intuition.

Kant cannot permit the distinction of sensible and intelligible aspects of a practical judgement to hold absolutely, for the maxim of theoretical philosophy that concepts without intuitions are empty and intuitions without concepts are blind also holds for practical judgements. On several occasions he designates the Wolffian and British accounts of practical judgements 'empty' and 'blind', rejecting both, as we have seen in the cases of Wolff and Hutcheson, as 'unphilosophical'. They together register the disproportioned working of the bias of reason that critical philosophy undertakes to realign. When at the end of the *Groundwork* – at the 'extreme limit of reason' – Kant justifies suspending the distinction and establishing an interest of practical reason – 'which human reason is incapable of demonstrating' (1785; p. 461; p. 99) – he does so by citing the avoidable bias of reason. Reason may be prevented from 'on the one side searching around in the world of sense for the highest motive ... a comprehensible but empirical interest, but also on the other side, from feebly flapping its wings in what is for it the empty space of transcendental concepts ... without leaving the spot and losing itself in daydreams' (p. 462; p. 100).

The bias had appeared earlier in the *Groundwork* in the 'Division of the Possible Principles of Morality According to the Concepts of Heteronomy'. Here the content of the scales is specified. On the one side, labelled 'moral feeling, this so-called special sense', sits Hutcheson and 'those unable to think' who hope, when it comes to the question of law, to be 'helped out by this feeling'. On the other side is the 'ontological concept of *perfection* (however empty, however indefinite, however useless it is . . .)' associated with the 'celebrated Wolff' and his school, which 'turns itself in a circle, tacitly presupposing the ethics it set out to demonstrate' (see pp. 442–3; pp. 73–4). Neither of the principles examines the difficulty of relating sensible and intelligible realms; one appeals to a special sense with the properties of universality, while the other smuggles in its condition of application. Neither the British nor the German school of practical philosophy is fully conscious of the difficulty involved in establishing the conditions for synthetic practical judgements.

The *Groundwork*'s task of exposing the bias of reason manifest in the two traditions is reflected in the structure of the book, which first establishes the transcendental distinction in sections 1 and 2, and then gestures in section 3 towards a 'possible synthetic use of pure practical reason' (p. 445; p. 77). But Kant can only claim the negative achievement of disclosing the sources for the distortions of practical judgements; the *Groundwork* remains at the level of an *ars docimastica*, and does not justify synthetic practical judgements. This is ventured in the *Critique of Practical Reason*, where Kant's achievement underlines the ambiguity already manifest in the theoretical philosophy.

One of the first difficulties facing the synthesis of an affective discrimination with a rational subsumption in practical judgement involves the proper object of practical philosophy. Kant was confident that practical judgements were productive, but did not specify whether they produced actions or things. The distinction between producing actions and things echoes the division in classical political philosophy between *praxis* and *poieisis*, politics and production. We have seen that this distinction determined political philosophy in Britain and Germany in the early modern period, and was overcome by Smith in the *Wealth of Nations*, as by Leibniz and Herder in their theories of culture. In Kant's practical philosophy differences of emphasis are apparent between those accounts stressing *praxis* and those stressing *poiesis*. In the practical philosophy of the *Groundwork* and the *Critique* the outcome of practical judgement is an action, while in the shorter writings, practical judgement issues in the production of a thing.

The equivocation over the object of practical philosophy is manifest in the distinct ways in which the transcendental distinction is overcome in *praxis* and *poiesis*. In the production of action Kant privileges the subsumptive moment of reason over the discriminative moment of sensibility; in the production of things he emphasizes the discriminative work of sensibility. His discussion of culture in the *Critique of Judgement* attempts to unite both aspects of practical judgement, although the difference persists in the distinction between 'culture through discipline' and 'culture through skill'. In spite of this Kant clearly recognizes the aporetic character of practical judgement, in the difficulty of determining a motive from an intelligible principle in the production of actions and of establishing a universal and necessary principle for the workings of sensibility in the production of things. The two are brought together in those privileged productions which overcome the distinction, such as the production of the 'form of volition' in the *Groundwork* or the 'artificial *habitus*' in the *Lectures on Ethics*, both of which are associated with the beautiful.

When discussing the production of actions, Kant allots the principle of judgement to reason, and its motivation to sensibility. But the precise relation of the two elements in a synthetic, a priori, practical judgement remains problematic. In the *Groundwork* he was satisfied to finish the book with the 'comprehension of the incomprehensibility' of the unconditional necessity of the moral imperative, admitting that while it is undeniable that 'reason should have a power of *infusing a feeling of pleasure* or well-being into the fulfilment of duty ... Yet it is completely impossible to see, to make a priori comprehensible, how a mere thought with nothing sensible in it, can produce a sensation of pleasure or displeasure' (p. 460; p. 97). Once again the threat of the 'empty concept' looms on the horizon: what are the conditions under which reason can 'infuse' a feeling of pleasure, or a concept discriminate between pleasure and displeasure? In the *Critique* Kant finds the required infusion in 'respect for the law' – 'a peculiar sort of sensation' which does not precede legislation, but is its by-product (1788b; p. 93; p. 95).

The problem of deriving a feeling from a concept follows from assuming that practical judgements are oriented from reason to sense, that judgement descends from the intelligible to the sensible. This orientation of the transcendental distinction follows Kant's mapping of the active and passive aspects of experience onto the distinction of intelligible and sensible, as in the *Critique of Practical Reason* where the 'absolute spontaneity of freedom' (p. 100; p. 102) contrasts with the passive heteronomy of sensibility. The origins of the active/passive dichotomy lie in Kant's distancing his practical philosophy from what he regarded as the deterministic consequences of the Wolffian principle of sufficient reason. However, even here it becomes apparent that his practical philosophy, like the theoretical, exceeds the very distinction it is founded upon.

In Kant's early outline of the philosophical system which was to be called the 'Bounds of Sense and Reason', practical philosophy had two parts: one on the 'universal principles of feeling, taste, and sensuous desire' the other on the 'basic principles of morality' (1967, p. 71). The scope of practical philosophy was wider than the rational determination of sensibility in the 'basic principles of morality' since it included the quasi-rationality of sensibility in the 'universal principles of feeling'. Alongside the determination of actions according to a spontaneous intelligible principle was another practical philosophy which discerned analogues of universality and necessity in sensibility. This branch of practical philosophy thematized *poiesis*, or the productive relation to an object, and was largely an account of pleasure which did not see it as 'infused' by reason, but as having its own laws. Just as in the theoretical philosophy, sensibility was not the passive receptivity of the subject, but marked a disposition of the representative power, so sensibility and its feeling of pleasure in practical philosophy was not just the toy of heteronomy, but a disposition of the representative power.

The more comprehensive vision of practical philosophy informs the *New Exposition*, which is far from the supposed 'rigorism' of the later practical philosophy. Kant has not yet developed the transcendental distinction, but has discovered its analogue in the opposed traditions of Wolffian determinism and Crusian voluntarism. Kant presents Crusius's two fundamental objections to Wolff's principle of sufficient reason. The first is the equivocation of real and logical ground; the second is an objection to the practical implications of the principle. Kant distinguishes his position from both Wolff's practical philosophy and Crusius's objections to it. Crusius presented Wolff's arguments in terms similar to those which had earlier led to his expulsion from Prussia. In Kant's report:

> The determining reason brings it about not only that this action and no other should take place, but that it is impossible for anything else to happen in its stead. God has so foreseen the occurrence of whatever happens in us that it is obviously impossible that anything else should take place. Our deeds cannot, therefore, be imputed to us, but God is the one cause of all things, and he has so bound us by those laws that we must in some way fulfil our destined lot.
>
> (p. 399; p. 78)

Such a position, as was earlier insinuated to Frederick William II, posed an evident threat to morality or, what was worse, to military discipline.

After travestying Wolff's practical philosophy in this way, Crusius develops a 'thelemetology', a justification of the radical voluntarism widespread among Pietist intellectuals. In Kant's version of this position:

> Titius does something of his own free will. I ask: Why did he do this rather than not do it? Crusius replies: Because he willed it. [I ask:] But why did he will it? It is, Crusius asserts, absurd to ask this. If you ask: Why did he not do something else? Crusius replies: Because he is now doing this. So Crusius thinks a free volition is actually determined by its own existence, not antecedently determined by reasons prior to its existence.
>
> (p. 397; pp. 73–4)

Kant brings out the practical implications both of Wolff's theoretical philosophy and Crusius's critique of it, but subscribes to neither position. He refuses what he regards as Wolff's passive determinism as well as Crusius's voluntarist critique. He proposes instead to reconcile determinism and voluntarism through viewing practical activity as the negotiated balance of activity and passivity.

Although Kant would bring together spontaneity of the will and receptivity of presentations, at this stage he only restates the problem. He describes their mediation as an 'inner principle', or a 'conscious impulse', or 'free judgement': 'But things which happen through the will of beings endowed with intelligence and the power of determining themselves through their own accord obviously proceed from a sound inner principle, from conscious impulses, and from the choice of one or another course of conduct according to their free judgement' (p. 404; p. 85). Although the notion of beings possessing the power to determine themselves in response to given presentations anticipates his later practical philosophy, the relation of spontaneity and determination itself is not fully explored at this stage. While Kant's account of moral judgement in the *New Exposition* avoids the extremes of determinism and voluntarism, it does not successfully mediate between them. The notion of determined choice only redescribes the problem without offering a satisfactory solution. The character of the difficulty involved here only became clear to Kant with the articulation of the transcendental distinction.

If the problem of the rational motivation of the will is not fully explored in the *New Exposition*, it is ignored in the *Negative Quantities* essay. Here Kant develops a notion of real opposition against the logical opposition maintained by the Wolffians. The use of logical opposition in practical philosophy entails defining vice as the negation of virtue; a vicious act is one which does not belong to the class of good acts. For Kant this form of practical judgement applies only to animals, for:

> An unreasoning beast exercises no virtue. But this omission is not vicious, since no inner law has been transgressed. It was not driven by an inner moral sense to a good act, nor was this resisted, so the omission or zero was indifferent and not determined as a consequence. It is a negation merely through the lack of a positive ground, and not through its deprivation.
>
> (1763a; p. 183)

But human beings are conscious of law, and this consciousness determines good and evil. But the problem of the relation between the law and the motive of the will is passed over in a hasty reference to 'moral feeling':

> Vice is not merely a negation, but a negative virtue. For vice can only take place in so far as a being has an inner law (either the conscience or the consciousness of a positive law) which is transgressed. This inner law is a positive ground of a good act, and the consequence can only be zero because that which flows from the consciousness of the law is surpassed [*aufgehoben*]
>
> (p. 182)

Vice is the actual supercession of virtue, not simply its logical negation; but the mediations through which a law becomes a 'positive ground' of a good action, and how it might possibly be cancelled remain unconsidered.

At this stage in the development of his practical philosophy Kant does not thematize the relation between consciousness of a law and the motivation of the will. In the passage from *Negative Quantities* on the indifference of animals to good and evil, Kant regards following an 'inner law' and being prompted by an 'inner moral feeling' as synonymous. A year later, in the *Enquiry*, Kant rigorously distinguishes them in terms of the formal and material grounds of practical judgement. As in the *New Exposition*, the distinction is expressed according to the bias of reason manifest in tradition, but it is now broader than the opposition of Wolffian determinism and Crusian voluntarism. Now the formal/real ground distinction is used to distinguish Wolff's 'formal' from the British philosophers' 'material' principles of practical judgement. Kant criticizes Wolff's formal perfectionism by citing the material principle of moral action:

> I am convinced that the rule: do the most perfect possible by you, is the primary *formal ground* of all obligation *to act*, as also the proposition: do not do that which would hinder the greatest possible perfection realisable through you; in respect of duty *it may not be done*. And just as nothing flowed from the first formal principle of our judgement of the true [the principle of contradiction], where no material first grounds are given, so no particularly definite obligation flows from these two rules of the good, where no unprovable material principles of practical knowledge are bound with them.
>
> (1764a; p. 299; p. 33)

Wolff's principle of maximizing perfection could not motivate an action. Like the principle of contradiction in theoretical philosophy, it was 'empty', and in need of the content offered by the 'material grounds'.

Kant finds the necessary supplement to the formal principle of morality in material principles. The material principles of practical judgement may not be resolved into the concept of perfection; they are directly analogous to the 'fundamental judgements' of theoretical judgement:

> if an action is immediately represented as good – without the action containing, in a concealed way, a certain other good, apprehensible in it by analysis, and explaining the perfection of the action – the necessity of this action is an indemonstrable material principle of obligation [*unerweislicher materialer Grundsatz der Verbindlichkeit*].
>
> (pp. 299–300; p. 33)

Regarding these material principles, 'Hutcheson and others have provided, under the name of moral feeling, a beginning to beautiful observations [*schönen Bemerkungen*]' (p. 300; p. 34). Kant suggests that the Wolffian principle of formal perfection be aligned with the material principles of the British theory of moral sense, but he is uncertain how to do so. He anticipates the transcendental distinction in warning that the knowledge and the feeling of the good 'may not be confused with each other' and that further work in practical philosophy is necessary to 'more surely determine' the 'fundamental concepts of obligation [*Grundbegriffe der Verbindlichkeit*]'. He goes on to say, 'In this respect, the deficiency of practical philosophy is even greater than that of speculative philosophy; for it has still to be discovered in the first place whether the faculty of knowledge or feeling (the first inner ground of the faculty of appetite) exclusively decides the primary principles of practical philosophy' (p. 300; p. 34). Kant remains undecided on this point, but has reasoned the need for distinguishing between formal and material principles and their sources. He prosecutes his exploration of the relation of formal and material principles through a comparison of the British and German traditions of practical philosophy. The comparative project was announced in what may be described as his first 'System's Programme', the *Nachricht von der Hinrichtung seiner Vorlesungen in dem Winterhalben-jahre von 1765–1766*. After introducing the 'tendency' of his proposed *Lectures in Metaphysics* and *Logic*, Kant turns to *Ethics*:

> I will currently lecture on general practical philosophy and ethics, both following Baumgarten. The investigations of Shaftesbury, Hutcheson, and Hume, although imperfect and deficient, have nevertheless gone furthest in search of the first grounds of ethical life [*Sittlichkeit*], and will be given that precision and scope which they currently lack.
>
> (1765; p. 311)

The search for the synthesis of material and formal grounds for morality prosecuted through the comparison of the British moral sense with the Wolffian concept of perfection characterizes Kant's lectures on ethics well into the 1770s and 1780s. In surviving transcripts of these lectures dating from around 1780, Kant distinguishes the material and formal grounds of practical judgement in terms of the 'blindness' and 'emptiness' of the British and German accounts. He goes so far as to describe the solution of how legitimately to unite them as the 'philosopher's stone'. The problem involves the reconciliation of law and sentiment, a unity Kant describes as the 'Kingdom of God on Earth' wherein human freedom happily legislates for itself.

The theological basis of Kant's idea of freedom is underlined in a panegyric to human freedom which recalls Leibniz's peroration in *Of Natural Law*. In it Kant distinguishes human freedom from natural necessity, and accords it the vocation of justifying creation:

> Freedom is, on the one hand, that faculty which gives unlimited usefulness to all other faculties. It is the highest order of life, which serves as the foundation of all perfections, and is their

necessary condition . . . If the will of all beings were so bound
to sensuous impulse, the world would possess no value. The
inherent value of the world, the *summum bonum*, is freedom
in accordance with a will which is not necessitated to action.
Freedom is thus the inner value of the world.

(1930, pp. 121–2)

Without freedom the world has no value; freedom is the *summum
bonum* in the sense of the 'highest order of life'; but it is also
potentially the source of the destruction of all life. The nightmare
which horrified Kant in his marginal jottings to the *Observations*
recurs: the same power which could justify creation might also destroy
it:

But on the other hand, freedom unrestrained by rules of its
conditional employment is the most terrible of all things . . .
If the freedom of man were not kept within bounds by objective
rules, the result would be the completest savage disorder.
There could then be no certainty that man might not use his
powers to destroy himself, his fellows, and the whole of nature.
I can conceive freedom as the complete absence of orderliness,
if it is not subject to an objective determination. The grounds
of this objective determination must be in the understanding,
and constitute the restrictions to freedom.

(p. 122)

Human freedom is not governed by natural necessity and may be the
source of utter disorder if it remains unregulated. But the only source
of regulation is freedom itself; freedom must then restrict itself in
order both to realize itself and justify creation:

In all nature there is nothing to injure man in the satisfaction
of his desires; all injurious things are his own invention, the
outcome of his freedom . . . his freedom makes it possible for
him to turn nature inside out in order to satisfy himself. Let
him desire what he pleases for satisfying his desires, so long
as he regulates the use of them; if he does not, his freedom
is his greatest misfortune. It must therefore be restricted, but
not by other properties or faculties, but by itself.

(p. 123)

Freedom's giving the law to itself – being 'in harmony' and not 'in
collision' with itself – opposes to the nightmare of human freedom

the dream of a nature justified through human enjoyment. As in Leibniz's rational jurisprudence, the productive relation to the world has to confirm with the self-legislation of human freedom. But the main problem, the 'philosopher's stone', lies in reconciling the pleasures of sensibility with the rigour of law. Freedom has both to be enjoyed and disciplined, its realization requires restriction. But in the search for this balance there is always the risk that too much weight will be given to pleasure or discipline at the expense of their equilibrium.

Kant's practical philosophy is not exhausted by the apparent rigorism of the categorical imperative, but would unify law and the feeling of pleasure. This unification is set within a notion of providence in which God gives mankind the capacities and the materials to create the Kingdom of God on earth. Providence does not direct human action through sense or reason, but gives freedom the capacity to realize or destroy itself:

> God might have made men perfect and given to each his portion of happiness. But happiness would not then have been derived from the inner principle of the world, for the inner principle of the world is freedom. The end, therefore, for which man is destined is to achieve his fullest perfection through his own freedom. God's will is not merely that we should be happy, but that we should make ourselves happy, and this is the true morality.
>
> (p. 252)

As with Pico's account of culture, human beings are given the vocation to *make* their own happiness. The true morality lies in attaining the unity of law and pleasure through harmonizing our relations with others under law with our relation to the rest of animate and inanimate creation. This is the Kingdom of God wherein the externality of law has been overcome: 'The realization of the full destiny, the highest possible perfection of human nature – this is the Kingdom of God on earth. Justice and equity, the authority not of governments, but of conscience within us, will then rule the world. This is the destined final end, the highest moral perfection to which the human race can attain' (p. 253). Happiness, or the proper unification of what is transcendentally distinguished, is the ultimate end of creation. It is attained when human beings cooperate in raising inclinations and sensibility to the level of intelligible pleasure; as the harmony of *poiesis* and *praxis*, it reveals the 'secret of a true politics' which will justify nature through legislation and enjoyment.

But realization entails restriction, and although Kant envisages the ultimate harmony of the feeling of pleasure and law, they are currently 'in collision'. The inclinations must be ruled by law if they are not to become destructive; yet the record of human judgement has not been exemplary in this respect: 'God has placed us on the stage of this world, provided us with all the materials for our welfare and with freedom to use them as we please, and everything depends on how men divide these benefits among themselves. Of this task men doubtless make a sorry mess' (p. 145). Freedom's confusion of law and pleasure has to be clarified by the legislation of freedom and judgement. In order to achieve its final end, freedom must order its judgements through a 'supreme principle of morality'; but this presupposes the recognition of the transcendental distinction between the inclinations of sensibility and the laws of the understanding. Only after making this distinction can their proper harmony be envisaged, for happiness consists in the unity of principle and discrimination – legislation and execution – but one which acknowledges their separation:

> The supreme principle of all moral judgement lies in the understanding: that of the moral incentive to action lies in the heart. This motive is moral feeling. We must guard against confusing the principle of the judgement with the principle of the motive. The first is the norm; the second the incentive. The motive cannot take the place of the rule.
>
> (pp. 36–7)

The motive without rule is blind, it cannot distinguish good and bad actions; but the rule without the motive is empty, since it cannot give content to its rule by inspiring the performance of an action.

It is from this standpoint that Kant dismisses as 'unphilosophical' first the British argument that the moral sense has been providentially infused with intellectual properties, and then the Wolffian notion that a rational principle could be immediately practical:

> But an intellectual inclination is a contradiction in terms; for a feeling for objects of the understanding is in itself an absurdity, so that a moral feeling resulting from an intellectual inclination is also an absurdity and is, therefore, impossible. A feeling cannot be regarded as something ideal; it cannot belong both to our intellectual and our sensuous nature; and even if

it were possible for us to feel morality, it would still not be possible to establish a system of rules on this principle.

(p. 37)

With the final sentence Kant rejects Hutcheson's systematization of natural rights on the basis of the moral sense. The moral sense cannot claim universality since 'Every feeling has only a private validity, and no man's feeling can be apprehended by another' (p. 38). Kant concludes that the supreme principle of moral judgement must be intellectual, but 'this pure intellectual principle must not be tautologous. It must not consist in the tautology of pure reason as does, for example, Wolff's rule, "do good and eschew evil", which, as we have already shown, is empty and unphilosophic' (p. 39). So Wolff's systematization of rights on the basis of pure reason is also disqualified by Kant. But having resisted the bias of reason in the name of the transcendental distinction, Kant has to recalibrate the two poles in a legitimate judgement: here the rule and the affection are both distinguished and combined.

In what manner can the affections be legitimately informed by the understanding, or the understanding be given content by the affections? Kant admits he is perplexed by this question, conceding that it is the fundamental question of practical philosophy. He states the problem with great clarity:

> My understanding may judge that an action is morally good, but it need not follow that I shall do that action which I judge morally good: from understanding to performance is still a far cry. If this judgement were to move me to do the deed, it would be moral feeling; but it is quite incomprehensible that the mind should have a motive force to judge. The understanding, obviously, can judge, but to give to this judgement of the understanding a compelling force, to make it an incentive that can move the will to perform the action – this is the philosopher's stone!

(pp. 44–5)

Kant struggles valiantly with the aporia of practical judgement, but always comes up against the necessity of making the transcendental distinction. He offers an argument for the understanding 'accepting' and 'refusing' to perform possible actions which can or cannot be made into a universal rule. This anticipation of the categorical imperative rests on the 'universal form of the understanding' in which the action 'can at all times become a universal rule' (p. 45). Yet the acceptance and refusal which Kant hopefully claims as 'in a sense a motive force embedded in the understanding in virtue of its own nature' is acknowledged to presuppose a feeling: 'The understanding sees that a thing is disgusting and is hostile to it, but it cannot be disgusted: it is only the sensibility which is disgusted' (p. 46). The understanding can distinguish between things which are and are not disgusting, but this discrimination is derived from the feeling of the sensibility.

The question as to how the understanding can determine action remains open. After making the transcendental distinction Kant faces three options for reconciling its terms. The first is to bring understanding and sensibility together violently, to privilege one term of the distinction over the other; the second is to mediate the terms of the distinction through a 'third thing' as in theoretical schematism; and the third is to set the distinction within a wider horizon. The first option is taken up in Kant's notion of 'discipline' explored in the *Ethics* and *Anthropology*, the second in the discussion of conscience in the *Ethics* and the 'typic' of the *Critique of Practical Reason*, while the third is gestured toward in the 'artificial *habitus*' of the *Ethics*, and fully developed in the revaluation of pleasure and law in the third *Critique*.

Kant takes up the first option in the section of the *Ethics* on 'Self-Mastery', where, after warning his students against staying too long in bed, he characterizes sensibility as 'a kind of rabble without law or rule' (1930, p. 140) which must be violently disciplined:

> There is in man a certain rabble of acts of sensibility which has to be vigilantly disciplined, and kept under strict rule, even to the point of applying force to make it submit to the ordinances of government. This rabble does not naturally conform to the rule of the understanding, yet it is good only in so far as it does so conform.
>
> (p. 138)

The rabble's refusal to conform to the understanding means that discipline has to be thought in terms of 'stamping out' the tendency 'of our sensuous nature'. Self-mastery, in other words, quickly submits to the naked mastery of the understanding over the sensibility. But although the power of reason is absolute, it is also benevolent; like the absolute monarch of *Polizeiwissenschaft*, the sensibility is guided from above for its own welfare. The similarity between the benevolent despotism of the understanding over sensibility and that of the *Landesvater* over his subjects is most evident in the 'Apology for

Sensibility' in the *Anthropology* where Kant describes the senses' inability to make judgements through a telling simile: 'they are like the common people who – unless they are rabble – readily submit to the superior understanding, but still want to be heard' (1798b; p. 25). The proviso that 'sensibility' wants to be heard points beyond the repressive model for the relation of the two faculties informing the *Ethics*. This is largely due to the re-evaluation of imagination in the *Anthropology*. In the *Ethics* imagination is cast as a threat to judgement: 'If he surrenders authority over himself, his imagination has free play; he cannot discipline himself, but his imagination carries him away by the laws of association; he yields willingly to his senses, and, unable to curb them, he becomes their toy and they sway his judgement' (1930, p. 140). In the *Anthropology*, far from swaying judgement, the imagination is what enables it to take place; it is the means by which human freedom cultivates itself through production and legislation. This position, however, points beyond the distinction of sensibility and understanding to the horizon of their distinction and conformity. They are no longer violently subsumed under the 'autocracy' of the understanding.

The second option for reconciling sensibility and law calls on a 'third thing' to mediate between them. The *schema* of theoretical judgement had to be 'homogeneous' with the category and with the appearance, and to be so it had in one respect to be 'intellectual' and in another 'sensible'. Conscience in the *Ethics* is similarly placed in respect to practical judgement: it is both a judgement and an 'instinct':

> Conscience is an instinct to pass judgement upon ourselves in accordance with moral laws. ... It is an instinct and not merely a faculty of judgement, and it is an instinct to judge not in the logical but in the judicial sense. A judge passes judgement; he does not merely form a judgement.
>
> (1930, p. 129)

Behind the judgements of the understanding stand another mode of judgement which gives them effect. Conscience stands between the senses and the understanding and mediates between them in a way which is beyond the judgement of the understanding; the conviction of the judgement exceeds the terms of judgement: 'the judgement has force of law, and is a sentence. The judge must either condemn or acquit, not merely form a judgement' (p. 129). Just as the *schema* rests on an alignment of the sensibility and the understanding which exceeds the terms of their distinction, so the decision of conscience points beyond the opposition of feeling and law.

The place of conscience between and beyond the distinction of intelligible law and sensible affect is analogous to that of the typic of pure practical judgement in the second *Critique*. The typic is introduced as the practical equivalent of the theoretical *schema* – 'sketched by the transcendental imagination' (1788; p. 69; p. 71) – and is the application to the sensuous world of a 'type of an intelligible nature'. The type is the 'form of lawfulness in general' (p. 71; p. 73), which founds the 'equivalence' of all laws as such 'regardless of whence they derive their determining grounds'. The 'form of lawfulness' underlies all laws, and offers a horizon for their 'equivalence'; but as their condition, the 'form of lawfulness' must exceed law.

With the reference to form Kant anticipates the reflections on form made in the third *Critique*. With it he goes beyond judgement to a realignment of sensibility and understanding in respect to their prior *conformity*. He anticipates this position in the *Ethics* when he speaks of our ability 'to produce a *habitus* which is not natural, but takes the place of nature, and is produced by imitation and oft-repeated practice' (1930, p. 46). The *habitus* then is a work of art, produced by imitation and practice. This mode of production corresponds to the production of form discussed in the third *Critique*, where form is produced, but underlies all production, is legislated but presupposed by law. It marks the productive legislation which produces law and objects – unites *praxis* and *poiesis* – and is experienced as the pleasure of realization and restriction. With this the transcendental distinction is placed within a wider horizon, one in which the harmony of law and the feeling of pleasure is reoriented.

Judgement and Pleasure

We are well pleased with things which touch our senses because they affect us harmoniously and permit us to feel our unhindered life or a revitalization.

Kant, *Lectures on Philosophical Theology*

Kant divided the workings of the human mind into the 'three powers' of knowledge, desire, and the feeling of pleasure and pain. Knowledge and desire became the objects of theoretical and practical philosophy; but the feeling of pleasure and pain did not constitute a discrete philosophical domain. It is not central to the third *Critique* in the same way that knowing and desiring are to the first and second. The reason for the displacement of the philosophy of pleasure into the analysis of the 'aesthetic judgement of taste' is not its intrinsic marginality but, on the contrary, its centrality. It is notable that although the feeling of pleasure and pain is fundamental, its philosophical discourse is relegated to the periphery of the critical philosophy.

This is reflected in the peculiar status of the feeling of pleasure and pain in Kant's theoretical and practical philosophy. It is cast as both a deadly threat to judgement and its essential supplement. In theoretical philosophy, 'aesthetic' or the 'critique of taste' is rigorously distinguished from logic at the same time as it is conceded to be its complement. In practical philosophy, the unity of law and the feeling of pleasure is both the abhorred heteronomous contamination of autonomous spontaneity, and the 'philosopher's stone' of human happiness. The paradoxical place given to pleasure as the feared other and the desired supplement to theoretical and practical philosophy evokes the similar paradoxes and exclusions surrounding the transcendental distinction. The distinction had to be both rigorously policed and transgressed. Pleasure too was to be procedurally excluded from theoretical and practical philosophy, only to be subsequently re-admitted. The place of the feeling of pleasure and pain, both within and without the critical philosophy, is indicated by the third *Critique*, which is both the completion of the triumphal arch of criticism and the gate to the ghetto of aesthetics.

One way to locate the feeling of pleasure and pain in the critical philosophy is to trace its relation to judgement. The third *Critique* is, after all, a *Critique of Judgement-Power*, and pleasure is explicitly aligned with judgement in the introduction. Yet Kant's understanding of this relation will remain obscure if judgement is understood in the narrow sense of logical predication. While the exposition of the 'aesthetic judgement of taste' in the third *Critique* follows the table of logical judgements, it systematically exceeds its limits. For just as in the *Only Possible Proof* existence was not a predicate, but the *position* of predicates, so in the *Critique*, pleasure is not a predicate in a judgement, but the position of judgement. Pleasure forms the pre-logical horizon which enables theoretical and practical judgements to be made.

In both theoretical and practical philosophy, Kant regards the discriminative and subsumptive work of judgement as an alignment of activity and passivity. This alignment, presented in terms of 'orientation' or 'culture', underlies the formal manoeuvres of separation and conjunction among concepts and intuitions. It is expressed in contraries such as passive and active, spontaneous and receptive, production and consumption, as well as in such internally differentiated unities as 'life' and the feeling of pleasure and pain. These contraries map onto his theological contrast of the simultaneous realization and restriciton of human activity with the restriction of non-rational beings, and the pure realization of divine activity.

Whenever Kant discusses pleasure, whether in the pre- or post-critical writings, it is always in terms of an alignment or 'proportion' between activity and passivity. In the *New Exposition* he criticizes the view that pleasure determines practical judgement by showing that pleasure is itself the outcome of an encounter between the inclination of the will and the inducement of the object: 'For what is "being pleased" if not the inclining of the will to do this rather than to do that in accordance with the inducement exercised by the object? Your "it pleases" or "it is pleasant" signifies therefore an action determined by inner reasons' (1755; p. 401; p. 80). The discrimination between 'this' and 'that' action may be determined by pleasure, but pleasure itself already designates an alignment or proportion of the passive 'inducement' of the object and the active 'determination' of the will. Later, on the basis of the transcendental distinction, Kant will reject this view of practical discrimination; yet the difficulty of determining the relation of activity and passivity in judgement persists as the 'knot' or the 'riddle' of metaphysics.

Kant rarely speaks of pleasure without its contrary, pain. The two feelings express both the alignment of activity and passivity and constitute a fundamental distinction. However, it is not a logical, but an actual distinction, one which precedes the discriminations and subsumptions of logical judgement. This point is first made in *Negative Quantities*, where Kant insists that pain is not the *logical* negation of pleasure – not merely that which is not pleasure – but its *actual* contrary: 'displeasure is in itself something positive, and not simply the absence of pleasure, but is understood to be opposed in a real sense, and so might be termed a negative pleasure' (1763a; p. 180). Pleasure and pain offer a fundamental distinction which cannot be captured by logic; they stand to each other as the inseparable + and − poles of an originary difference. Since it is fundamental, this distinction cannot fall under a logical subsumption; its grounds do not lie in membership or non-membership of the class of pleasurable or non-pleasurable objects since such classification already follows this distinction.

In the first paragraph of the *Observations on the Feeling of the Beautiful and the Sublime* (1764) Kant refers the distinction of pleasure and displeasure to the balance between 'external things' and inner 'disposition'. In the course of his observations he finds this balance to be unstable, and sees in its instability the cause for the disputes about taste: 'The various feelings of enjoyment or of displeasure rest not so much upon the nature of the external things which arouse them as upon each person's own disposition to be moved by these to pleasure and pain. This accounts for the joy of some people over things that cause aversion in others' (1764c; p. 207; p. 45). This fact offers Kant a wide 'field of observations of these peculiarities of human nature' in the diversity of responses to the same objects. Yet it is necessary to be alert to the style of this text, and not take the persona of the observer at his word. For in this text Kant not only observes, but also searches for unity in the diversity, specifically, a determining ground for the feelings of pleasure and displeasure. He makes this clear in his marginalia where he laments the 'changing tastes and various shapes of men' and desires 'fixed points in nature which cannot be moved by man' and 'markers on the shore to which we ought to adhere'.

In searching for a 'principle' with which to discriminate between pleasure and displeasure – a search which culminated in the *Critique of Judgement-Power* – Kant follows his established procedure of presenting the bias of reason. Once again the bias lies between the Wolffian and the British accounts of pleasure developed in the theories of aesthetic and taste.[14] The first half of the *Critique of Judgement-Power* searches for a principle of the 'aesthetic judgement of taste' through the presentation of the differences between the traditions of aesthetic and taste. The difficulty of this project lies in determining the proper relation of discrimination and subsumption in the 'aesthetic judgement of taste', and may be summed up in the question: are the concepts of pleasure and displeasure prior to their distinction, or is their distinction prior to the concepts?

In the aporetic procedure of the *Critique* Kant rejects both accounts; this rejection, and the 'principle' which he discerns through the bias of tradition, are visible against the background of his earlier thinking on the pleasure principle. We have already seen him reject one version of the Wolffian account of the distinction of pleasure and displeasure in the *Negative Quantities*. Against Wolff's determination of the displeasurable as any experience not included in the class of the pleasurable, Kant argues that pleasure and displeasure determine each other. In other words, Wolff's logical exclusion masks an actual discrimination. Kant also rejects Baumgarten's more sophisticated account of pleasure proposed in his aesthetic, where pleasure and displeasure are distinguished in terms of perfection. The degree of perfection present in an object dictates the pleasure or displeasure taken in it. This is a better account of the difference between pleasure and pain than Wolff's model of logical exclusion, but Kant still finds it unsatisfactory: 'Well-pleasedness [*Wohlgefallenheit*] cannot consist in the consciousness of perfection, as Baumgarten defines it, because perfection is the harmony of a manifold in a unity. But here I do not want to know what it is that I take pleasure in, I rather want to know what pleasure itself is' (1978, pp. 95–6). Baumgarten reduces pleasure to the rational discrimination arising from the 'consciousness of perfection', ignoring what is proper to it. While conceding that there is pleasure to be had in the consciousness of a perfection, Kant complains that this tells us little about pleasure itself. The rational principle for discriminating between pleasurable and displeasurable or painful objects leaves the distinction itself undetermined. The question of the relation of rational perfection to feeling remains unanswered.

In the marginalia to the *Observations* Kant criticizes Sulzer's account of pleasure for begging the question in a similar way. As we saw in chapter 3, Sulzer defines pleasure as whatever contributes to the free play of the cognitive faculties. Kant finds this definition circular: 'Sulzer says whatever facilitates and furthers the natural operation of the soul is pleasurable. This only says that it furthers natural striving after pleasure.' 'Defining' pleasure in terms of the natural operation of the soul substitutes for definition a description of an effect. Kant appears to make the same elision of definition and description in his *Anthropology* when he determines the distinction of pleasure and pain in terms of life: 'Pleasure is the feeling of life being promoted, pain of its being hindered' (p. 100). However, the apparent similarity between promoting the free working of the cognitive faculties and promoting 'life' conceals a fundamental difference between the two positions; for Kant's notion of life is more philosophically determined than Sulzer's free play of the cognitive faculties.

The distinction of pleasure and displeasure cannot be determined by the principle of perfection or by the promotion or hindrance of the play of the cognitive faculties. But in making these distinctions Kant is careful to deny that pleasure is simply a blind feeling. In practical philosophy Kant reproached Shaftesbury and Hutcheson for basing moral judgements on the feeling of pleasure and pain, but not determining the source of this distinction and its implications for universal and necessary judgements. Pleasure for the theorists of taste and moral sense is an 'I know not what' which cannot be further determined. Kant tries to recalibrate the Wolffian and British accounts of pleasure by seeing the feeling of pleasure and displeasure as a pre-logical discriminatory horizon, not only for the aesthetic judgement of taste, but for theoretical and practical judgement in general.

The bias of reason veers between conceptual and affective accounts of the distinction between pleasure and displeasure: in the one it is constituted by perfection, in the other by an 'I know not what'. Kant, however, seeks a further determination in which pleasure expresses both active and passive aspects of the experience of orientation. The distinction of pleasure and displeasure constitutes and is constituted through orientation. This is intimated in the marginalia where Kant moves from a perfectionist account of pleasure to one based on the exercise of freedom: 'We take pleasure in certain of our perfections, but much more when we are their cause. Most of all though when we are their free-working cause. The subordination of everything under the free will is the greatest perfection.' Pleasure arises from the exercise of freedom, but freedom's greatest perfection is to give laws to nature and to itself. It must dispose itself both actively and passively, in the words of a later fragment which echoes Leibniz's definition of pleasure, freedom 'must determine and must be dependent upon the determination of nature'. We have seen that freedom's self-limitation has two aspects, one with regard to objects in theoretical philosophy, the other with regard to other human beings in practical. In the determination of pleasure, however, both *poiesis* and *praxis* are significant. The feeling of pleasure and displeasure results from the exercise of freedom with respect both to objects and to others. It offers an originary relation to things and others prior to the distinction of theoretical and practical philosophy.

It is this characteristic which causes the paradoxical status of pleasure in both theoretical and practical philosophy. It marks the orientation of human being-in-the-world, and registers an alignment of activity and passivity in relation to the world and to others. In other words, pleasure offers an access to a pre-philosophical experience, an experience prior to the transcendental distinction, one which enables that distinction to be made, but also to be transgressed.

The relation of pleasure to *poiesis* is most clearly revealed in the comparison of divine and human pleasure made in the *Lectures on Philosophical Theology*. Here Kant defines pleasure as the determination of the desire to produce an object, and insists that the feeling of pleasure precedes determination:

> Now pleasure itself does not consist in the relation of my representations to their objects, it consists rather in the relation of representations to the subject insofar as these representations determine the subject to actualize the object. Insofar as a

representation is the cause of the actuality of its object, it is called a *faculty of desire*. But insofar as it first determines the subject to the desire, it is called *pleasure*. Thus it can obviously be seen that pleasure precedes desire.

(1978, p. 96)

The subject is disposed through pleasure to desire an object, but not to bring it forth into actuality. The only exception to this rule is God, whose pleasure is immediately productive: He actualizes His pleasure without any resort to desire, while for finite beings:

> the desire for something always presupposes a need, and it is because of this need that I desire it. But why is this? It is simply because no creature is all sufficient, and so each one always has need of many things. Just for this reason it always reaches a higher degree of self-contentment when what it desires is produced. But in a being which is independent and thus self-sufficient as well, the ground of its volition and desire that things external to itself should exist is just that it knows its own faculty for actualizing things external to itself.
>
> (p. 99)

Finite beings have to produce objects to satisfy their needs, although human beings differ from animals in so far as their needs are defined by pleasure and the imagination. Their pleasures are bound to by a relation of representation and production: 'I can be well-pleased with a house, even if I can only see the plans. But well-pleasedness in the *existence* of an object is called *interest*' (p. 102). Human pleasure is determined by a rift between representation and existence which is bridged by desire, need, and the production of objects. For God, on the other hand, there is no break between representation and actuality: 'He has the greatest power combined with the highest understanding. Since his understanding knows his capacity to actualize the objects of his representation he is *eo ipso* determined to activity and to the production of the good ... For God, the mere representation of a good is all that is required to actualize it' (p. 103). God does not suffer the transcendental distinction of concept and intuition, for His understanding is intuitive, bringing its representations into actuality without the deferrals of representation and desire.

Finite beings without intuitive understanding encounter resistance when attempting to actualize their representations. The encounter of their imaginative projections with the resistance of things may be pleasurable or painful, and it is this encounter which Kant sees as proper to human existence. Philosophy distributes the encounter of imaginative projection and resistance between the differentiations of intuition and the subsumptions of the understanding. But underlying the distinction is the realization through restriction experienced as the distinction between pleasure and pain; the alternation of the two poles being taken by Kant to characterize the 'life' of finite beings.

Book II of the *Anthropology* relates the distinction of the 'Feeling of Pleasure and Displeasure' to life. Life consists in the alternation of states of pleasure and pain; for without one, the other could not exist. This alternation results in the process of realization through restriction:

> no enjoyment can follow directly upon another: between one and the other, pain must intervene. Slight inhibitions of vital force alternate with slight advancements of it, and this constitutes the state of health. We mistakenly think that in a state of health we feel continuous well being; but, in fact, it consists in agreeable feelings whose succession is only intermittent (with pain always intervening between them). Pain is the spur of activity, and it is in activity, above all, that we feel our life; without pain, lifelessness would set in.
>
> (1798b; p. 100)

Life would cease without the alternation of pleasure and displeasure, 'For if the vital force were continually promoted, though it cannot be raised above a certain level, what could follow but swift death in the face of joy' (p. 100). Life, as opposed to death, 'is the same as to feel ourselves constantly impelled to leave our present state' (p. 101), so pain is nature's incitement to activity and life: 'Nature has put pain in man as the unavoidable spur to activity, so that he may continually progress to something better' (p. 103). Pleasure and displeasure may not be directly mapped onto activity and passivity; rather they are dispositions of an activity which is spurred and enjoyed. The regularity in the oscillation of pain and pleasure registers a proportion or 'principle' in the disposition of activity, but in what does this proportion consist, and how can it be spoken?

Free imagination forms things according to its pleasure, bringing them before it in representation. The determination of pleasure is not exhausted by this relation to objects, for the play of free projection and resistance in *poiesis* is accompanied by a similar play in *praxis*, where the relation to the other is more important than the relation to objects. In the *Anthropology* Kant discusses this aspect of the distinction of pleasure and displeasure under the heading of taste.

In taste the distinction of pleasure and displeasure is articulated according to its validity for others, it is a 'sensuous power of estimation' which 'proclaims necessity and therefore validity for everyone as to how the idea of an object is to be judged with respect to the feeling of pleasure and displeasure (so reason is secretly cooperating here, though one cannot derive the judgement from rational principles, and so cannot prove it)' (p. 108). The 'secret cooperation' of reason in the judgement of taste occurs when the imagination actively posits the 'passively' perceived material of sensation. Reason is covertly involved in the disposition of the material of sensation, a disposition which Kant terms 'form':

> in taste (taste that chooses) – that is, in aesthetic judgement
> – what produces our pleasure in the object is not the sensation
> immediately (the material elements in our idea of the object).
> It is rather the way in which free (productive) imagination
> arranges this material inventively – this is the form; for only
> form can lay claim to a universal rule for the feeling of pleasure.
> (p. 108)

The form through which objects are given to us, the source of pleasure, is both the arrangement or disposition of objects and their production or invention. Just as the 'forms of intuition' should not be thought as spatio-temporal receptacles for sensibility, but as principles of differentiation, so aesthetic form is not a frame within which objects are arranged, but the 'way' in which they are produced *and* arranged. In the *Critique of Judgement-Power* the radical view of form as both judgemental and inventive is related to the 'realization and restriction' of the self-legislation of freedom.

If form is understood procedurally as the disposition or *habitus* of the imagination it becomes possible to see how Kant is able to bring together the freedom of imagination, the feeling of pleasure and displeasure, and the lawfulness of law under the aegis of form. In the theoretical philosophy, concepts are precipitated by the procedures of imagination provoked by the presence of an object; similarly, the law of pleasure manifests itself in the procedure followed by the free imagination when it is confronted by an object. Pleasure arises from a disposition of freedom, which Kant significantly, if rather obscurely, relates to freedom in social relations:

> Taste is, accordingly, a power of making social judgements
> about external objects as we imagine them. Here the *Gemüt*
> feels its freedom in the play of images (and so of sensibility);

for social relations with other men presuppose freedom – and this feeling is pleasure – but the *universal validity* of this pleasure for everyone, which distinguishes tasteful choice (of the beautiful) from choice in terms of mere sensation ... involves the concept of a law; for only according to a law can the validity of the pleasure for the man who judges it be universal.

(p. 109)

In making 'social judgements' the *Gemüt* feels pleasure in the play of images; but in order for this feeling to be 'valid for everyone' the concept of a law must be 'involved'. So much is clear, but what is not immediately apparent is the place and relevance of the phrase, 'for social relations with other men presuppose freedom'. Taken in isolation this phrase is comprehensible enough, but its place within this particular sentence is baffling.

Some clarification is offered later when Kant introduces the notion of communication, supplementing the feeling of pleasure and displeasure with the feeling of satisfaction which follows the communication of this feeling:

in order to be considered universally valid, this satisfaction must have an a priori principle. Consequently, it is a satisfaction in the agreement of the subject's pleasure with the feeling of everyone else according to a universal law, which must spring from the subject's giving of universal law and so from reason. In other words, choice in terms of this satisfaction comes, according to its form, under the principle of duty.

(p. 111)

In this passage Kant inverts the difficulty which he met in his account of practical judgement. There the difficulty arose in moving from a law to an incentive or feeling; now however, the difficulty lies in moving from an affective choice (*sinnliche Beurteilung*) to its principle, from the feeling of pleasure and displeasure to the law implicated in it. Here, as in the practical philosophy where he postulated a 'form' of lawfulness to conform law and affection, the universality of pleasure 'springs' from the *form* through which universal law 'is given'.

Kant's notion of life as the negotiation of pleasure and displeasure arising from the encounter between the projections of human imagination and the resistance of objects relates directly to his theoretical and practical philosophies. We have seen that in the theoretical philosophy, the subsumptions of logic follow an original relation between imagination and objects. The encounter or orientation of the body to the world is distributed, according to the transcendental distinction, between the fundamental differences or intuitive judgements of space and time and the discursive judgements of the understanding. The originary experience of activity and passivity which founds this distinction is expressed in the feeling of pleasure and displeasure, whose priority is effaced in theoretical philosophy. Similarly, in practical philosophy, the encounter of the free subject with the other is not dictated by law or force, but by an inchoate mixture of pleasure and displeasure which is subsequently distributed according to the transcendental distinction between the faculties of free will and affection.

In both cases the relation between human activity and passivity is originally disposed in terms of pleasure and displeasure, and is only subsequently articulated into philosophical distinctions. The feeling of pleasure and displeasure becomes the bad conscience of these distinctions, being first erased, and then re-inscribed in their terms. This is evident in the poetic relation to the object in theoretical philosophy, and the practical relation to the other in practical philosophy; in both cases the feeling of pleasure and displeasure is simultaneously relegated to sensibility as a 'contamination' of reason, and elevated to the 'philosopher's stone' of the harmony of sensibility and reason. A third manoeuvre of exclusion is to limit the field of objects and judgements of pleasure and displeasure to beautiful objects. But as intimated in the brief discussion of taste above, this marginalization of pleasure generates its own difficulties.

The third option is taken up most rigorously in the cognitive aesthetic Kant developed in his *Lectures on Logic*. Since the organization of this aesthetic is structurally similar to the 'Analytic of the Beautiful' in the third *Critique*, it is worth looking at in some detail.

The aesthetic which Kant presents in the lectures is a peculiar amalgam of Baumgarten and Kames. The basic characteristic of the aesthetic judgement is, following Baumgarten, the distinction of the perfect and the less perfect. The judgement of a work of art is less concerned with whether it pleases or displeases, than whether it is perfect or imperfect. Furthermore such judgements cannot be legitimated in the same way as logical judgements, since their rules are a posteriori:

The philosopher Baumgarten in Frankfort has made the plan for a science of aesthetics. More correctly, Home [Kames] has called aesthetics a *Criticism*, since it does not give as logic does, rules *a priori* that sufficiently determine the judgement but takes up its rules *a posteriori* and generalizes, through comparisons, the empirical laws by which we cognize the less perfect and the perfect (the beautiful).

(1800; pp. 17–18)

Kant later distinguishes between aesthetic and logical perfection in terms of the laws of sensibility and understanding:

> A cognition can be perfect either according to laws of sensibility or according to laws of the understanding ... The logical perfection of cognition rests on its agreement with the object, therefore on *universally valid* laws, and can be judged by norms a priori. Aesthetic perfection consists in the agreement of cognition with the subject and is based on the special sensibility of man.
>
> (pp. 40–1)

The agreement of cognition with the 'special sensibility of man' is the ground of a subjective-general pleasure. This perfection is beauty: that which pleases the senses in intuition and for that very reason can be the object of a general pleasure, because the laws of intuition are general laws of sensibility' (p. 41). Unfortunately this derivation of pleasure from perfection doesn't bear too close examination. We know that the laws of intuition concern space and time, but how is it possible to distinguish between perfect and imperfect temporality and spatiality, and why should the perfection of either evoke pleasure?

In fact, if we continue with Kant's exposition we learn that sensibility entails more than the spatial and temporal laws of intuition. He is interested in the ground of the *agreement* of cognition with the subject's sensibility, and this agreement is beyond the distinction of intuition and understanding; it is formal:

> Through this agreement with the general laws of sensibility, the *actually, independently beautiful* whose essence consists in the *mere form* is distinguished, as to kind, from the *agreeable*, which pleases solely in sensation by stimulus or emotion and for that reason can be the ground of private pleasure only.
>
> (p. 41)

The pleasure in the beautiful is here, as later in the *Critique*, distinguished from the agreeable in terms of form. But the notion of form employed here and in the later work differ radically. While it is defined here as the 'agreement of a cognition with the laws of intuition', this is not an anticipation of the famous 'free play of the cognitive powers'. The two notions of form differ in the 'how' of relating concept and intuition, the character of their agreement or conformity. The difference is clarified by Kant's distinction between the matter and the form of cognition:

> In every cognition there is to be distinguished *matter*, i.e. the object, and *form*, i.e. the manner *how* we cognize the object. For example, when a savage sees a house in the distance, the use of which he does not know, he has the same object before him as another who knows it as a dwelling furnished for men. But as to form, this cognition of the one and the same object is different in both. In the one it is *mere intuition*, in the other *intuition* and *concept* at the same time.
>
> (p. 38)

Form, then, is the relation of concept and intuition; but it is precisely this relation that we are trying to determine. The nature of the accord between them remains unstated, although Kant's example and other hints that it is a 'norm' and not a 'rule' suggest a prior orientation in terms of form and tradition. Concept and intuition, in other words, are already oriented with regard to one another before judgement; the 'savage' wandering through East Prussia lacks a relation to tradition which would orient his judgements and give his intuitions form.

Kant unfolds the nexus of form and tradition in the *Critique of Judgement-Power*. In the *Logic* he only hints at its existence, limiting himself to determining the extent of logic by contrasting it with aesthetic. However, one further aspect of this comparison is of interest. This is Kant's use of the table of the categories – quantity, quality, relation, and modality – in a completely different way from the *Critique*. There the classification refers to dispositions of judgement of pleasure and displeasure; here, however, they correspond to the 'judging of perfection'. In the *Lectures* the quantity of an aesthetic perfection is general – the application of the cognition to a multitude of examples. Its quality is distinct, the distinctness with which a concept is exhibited *in concreto*, while its relation 'consists only in the agreement of the cognition with the subject and the laws of semblance in the senses' (p. 43). Lastly, its modality is certain; 'necessary according to the testimony of the senses'. We shall see below that the same logical *schema* was put to radically different uses in the *Critique of Judgement-Power*.

Although Kant attempts to relegate pleasure from the aesthetic outlined in the *Logic*, it returns to its central position. Pleasure is related to the fundamental issue of the accord of concept and intuition. The nature of this accord – its form – remains largely unthematized here, although there are some fascinating hints about it. It is related to issues of orientation, communication, and tradition, and also to sensibility, that which distinguishes humans from other rational beings. But the profound inquiry into these relations was not accomplished until the third *Critique*.

The Riddle of the 'Self-Alienating Understanding'

> In sensibility there is a matter which is called perception, in respect of whose differences we are passive ... But the appearances also have a form, a ground found in our subject, through which we order the impressions themselves, or that which corresponds to them, and give them their place. This can be nothing else than an activity which is naturally aroused by the impressions, but which may certainly be known for itself.
>
> Kant, *Reflection* 4634

By way of conclusion to this chapter I will examine a few shards from the *Handschriftliche Nachlass*. These will underline the relation of life and orientation found in each of the three forms of judgement explored in the critical philosophy. Read in the context of the riddles of the 'self-alienating understanding', they prepare for an appreciation of the enormity of the task Kant undertook in writing the third *Critique*.

The first fragment, uttered during a reading of Baumgarten's *Metaphysica*, concerns the insoluble difficulties or puzzles of metaphysics.

> The only insoluble metaphysical difficulty is to unite the highest condition of the practical with the condition of speculative unity; that is freedom with nature ... The spontaneity of the understanding in the series of appearances is the puzzle.

Following which, absolute necessity is the second puzzle, one which is not offered by nature, but by the pure understanding.

(Ref. 5121)

The difficulty does not only involve bringing together freedom and nature as theoretical and practical philosophy, but also relating the spontaneity of the understanding to the necessity of appearances. Things are complicated by the consideration that necessity itself is constituted by the understanding alienating itself, not recognizing its own activity. What Kant designates as passivity – the perception of appearances – is in an important sense the self-alienated product of the understanding's activity. The difficulty of metaphysics arises from thinking the disposition of spontaneity into opposed active and passive modes.

In another fragment, Reflection 4220, Kant identifies the self-alienation of the understanding as the fate of freedom. It is freedom which disposes itself actively and passively with regard to the things it encounters:

Freedom is really only the self-activity [*Selbstthätigkeit*] of which one is aware. When one allows oneself to enjoy, this is a mode [*actus*] of self-activity, but here one is not conscious of activity, but only of its effect. The expression; I think (this object) already shows that I am not passive with regard to representation, but it may be attributed to me.

(Ref. 4220)

In this passage Kant deploys the active and passive disposition of spontaneity across the three areas of practical, aesthetic, and theoretical philosophy. First of all freedom is stated in practical terms as conscious self-activity. Then it is considered with regard to enjoyment, which is also activity, but one which does not fully recognize itself. Finally, the theoretical relation of thought and object is shown to be active. Consequently the disposition of spontaneity into active and passive modes, here mapped onto consciousness and self-consciousness, underlies the three areas of philosophy discussed in this section. The work of the self-alienating understanding as an activity which disowns its freedom to produce and to legislate, is constitutive for judgement in its theoretical, practical and aesthetic employments.

At this stage it would still be exorbitant to claim conclusively that this self-alienation forms the main difficulty of metaphysics. Although Kant had already said as much in the *Dreams of a Spirit Seer*, we should try and further determine it. In a fragment from the *Nachlass* on moral philosophy, Kant brings everything down to life: 'Everything in the end comes down to life – whatever vivifies (or the feeling for the furtherance of life) is agreeable. Life is unity; accordingly all taste has as its principle the unity of vivifying sensations' (Ref. 6862). Whatever contributes to life, or to the feeling for the promotion of life, is pleasurable. Taste then is related to life, has as its principle the promotion of life. But what is the unity which Kant names life? It is not the unity of the understanding, for he goes on to say:

> freedom is the original life [*Freyheit ist das ursprüngliche Leben*] and its composition is the condition for the harmony of everything living; accordingly, that which furthers the feeling of life in general, or the feeling for the furtherance of life in general, is the cause of pleasure. Do we feel at home in universal life? The universality ensures that all our feelings agree, although this universality is not a particular kind of perception. It is the form of consensus.
>
> (Ref. 6862)

Freedom is life, and the condition for the harmony of everything living. And once again feeling for the furtherance of life in general raises pleasure. The nature of the unity of this universal is further determined; it is an '*Allgemeinheit*' or universality which brings our feelings into harmony, although it cannot itself be perceived. This transcendental unity is an imperceptible *form* of consensus.

It is possible to draw some conclusions from the above passages about life. It is a disposition of activity and passivity which is experienced as pleasure. It is also a transcendental form of unity which is not itself a particular sort of perception but the form of the consensus necessary for perception. The disposition of activity and passivity, in other words, is proportioned. Life is a proportioning activity prior to the special dispositions of theoretical and practical judgement, a realization and restriction before the unities and manifolds of judgement. The proportioning activity cannot be thought by judgement, but is experienced in pleasure. The attempt to pass the aporia of metaphysics by identifying the self-alienation of the understanding, whose freedom is the source of necessity, leads back to pleasure.

The *Critique of Judgement-Power* explicitly addresses the difficulty of reconciling freedom and necessity. It also inquires into the determination of pleasure. These two tasks, often seen as irrelevant to each other, may now be suspected as being fundamentally the same.[15] In the *Critique* we encounter a series of attempts to name the proportioned activity which founds the discrete areas of philosophy. In all of them the central concept is life as a disposition of activity and passivity: it is a concept essential to the 'technic of judgement' proposed in the Introductions, the 'Aesthetic Judgement of Taste' of the first part, and the philosophy of life, or transcendental biology, of the second part of the *Critique*. We have witnessed the intimations of Kant's concept of life in this chapter, but should now go on to the *Critique* itself.

5

The Critique of Judgement-Power

The Critical Text

There is no employment of our powers, no matter how free, not even of reason itself (which must create all its judgements from the common *a priori* source) which, if each individual had always to start afresh with the crude equipment of his natural state, would not get itself involved in blundering attempts, did not those of others lie before it as a warning. Not that predecessors make those who follow in their steps mere imitators, but by their methods they set others upon the track of seeking in themselves for the principles, and so of adopting their own, often better course.

Kant, Critique of Judgement-Power

In the previous chapter it became apparent that Kant's rhetorical distinction between 'books and systems' and the 'faculty of reason in general' belies his more considered position on the activity of criticism. In order to examine the evidence of his 'own reason' he had first of all to be 'set upon the track' through a dialogue with tradition. The necessity of orienting oneself toward tradition follows from the bias of reason not being immediately apparent; it only becomes visible through the differences within philosophical tradition. Critique weighs the claims of tradition and so orients itself for judgement. The judge on the bench of the 'critical tribunal' follows the inquisitorial procedure of examining and assessing the competing claims brought before the court in the persons of tradition. However, the judge in this tribunal is always prey to doubt about the legitimacy of his/her own judgements, since they too might not be free from the bias of reason. The judgements are provisional rulings, legitimated by principles discovered in the course of the examination of the claims. Philosophical criticism in this sense is the activity of self-orientation, the judges 'seeking in themselves for principles' through the medium of tradition.

In the critical philosophy the careful sifting of the evidence of tradition sits uneasily beside the ambition to reconstitute metaphysics according to an abstract principle. In order to achieve the revolution in metaphysics, a new principle has to be discovered, one with sufficient authority to unknot the tangled claims of tradition; but how may such a principle be sought, let alone found, without the complicity of tradition? In the record of Kant's case against traditional metaphysics – the *Critique of Pure Reason* – there is a continual tension between *discovering* the principle of synthetic a priori judgements, and *using* it to establish a system of judgements; or, following Kant's metaphor, between surveying the foundations and erecting the building. The tension between discovery and demonstration is evident throughout the three *Critiques*. The 'Analytic' of each of the *Critiques* both discovers the principle of judgement through an analysis of given modes of judgement, and legitimates its judgements according to this principle.

The tension between the discovery of a principle through an analysis of the tradition of judgements and the constitution of a system of judgements from a principle is sharply exposed in the *Critique of Judgement-Power*. The equivocation in philosophical strategy is acknowledged in the Preface of the work, where Kant begs his reader's indulgence for the shortcomings of his performance, and hopes 'that the difficulty of unravelling a problem by nature so entangled may serve as an excuse for a certain amount of hardly avoidable obscurity in its solution'. He goes on to distinguish between the 'accuracy of our statement of the principle' – the 'unravelling of the problem' – from the 'mode of deriving the phenomena of judgement from that principle' or its 'solution' which, he reiterates, 'has not all the lucidity which is rightly demanded elsewhere'. The principle which he has discovered in the third *Critique* is not one that can be used to justify judgements.

The inability to derive a system of legitimate judgements from the 'entangled principle' stems from its aporetic character. It is possible to trace the contours of this aporia through analysis and so 'state' its principle; but its principle has no further systematic employment. Kant acknowledges that it is of crucial importance for the critical philosophy that judgement be brought under judgement, but has no illusions about the difficulties of the enterprise. First he reasons the need for a judgement of judgement: 'A Critique of Pure Reason, i.e.

of our faculty of judging on *a priori* principles, would be incomplete if the critical examination of judgement, which is a faculty of knowledge, and, as such, lays claim to independent principles, were not dealt with separately' (1790a; Preface). The case presented in the *Critique of Pure Reason* cannot be closed without the scrutiny of judgement itself, but how can judgement be made to appear before itself for judgement? This question exceeds the procedure of the critical tribunal, whose preliminary investigations into the principle of such a judgement of judgement only show that it exceeds its jurisdiction. The issue of the principle by which to judge judgement raises the aporia which haunted Kant's earlier writings:

> For this principle is one which must not be derived from *a priori* concepts, seeing that these are the property of understanding, and judgement is only directed to their application. It has therefore, itself to furnish a concept, and one from which, properly, we get no cognition of a thing, but which it can itself employ as a rule only – but not as an objective rule to which it can adapt its judgement, because, for that, another faculty of judgement would again be required to enable us to decide whether the case was one for the application of the rule or not.
>
> (Preface)

The difficulty revealed in judging judgement brings to light some properties of judgement which remained concealed in the enquiry into its subsumptive employment in the first *Critique*. For judgement to be possible there must exist an adequation to a rule which is not of judgement, but furnishes its condition. The specification of the adequation to a rule through an 'art' or 'technic' of judgement is the topic of the third *Critique*.[1]

The 'technic of judgement', variously described as the 'peculiar principle', the 'entangled principle', the 'riddle of the principle of judgement', is closely allied with the feeling of pleasure and displeasure. The feeling of pleasure and displeasure (Kant always considers them as one feeling) assumes paradigmatic status in the examination of the faculty of judgement. Indeed, just as the philosophy of art was for Baumgarten the paradigm of aesthetic in general, so for Kant, 'It is chiefly in those estimates that are called aesthetic, and which relate to the beautiful and the sublime, whether of nature or of art, that one meets with the above difficulty about a principle (be it subjective or objective)' (Preface). In these judgements the existence of a disposition to judgement beyond judgement reveals itself. It is because of the manifest 'difficulty' in stating the principle of such judgements that 'the critical search for a principle of judgement in their case is the most important item in a Critique of this faculty'. The properties of judgement which remain concealed in its subsumptive mode are exposed in aesthetic judgements.

The *Critique of Judgement-Power* remains with the search for and statement of the principle. In this search it quickly becomes apparent that there is a close relation between the feeling of pleasure and displeasure and the 'technic of judgement', one which Kant suggests has been forgotten in subsumptive judgement. Aesthetic judgements reveal an aspect of judgement which has been concealed, and remains beyond the jurisdiction of judgement. But how is it possible to state this aspect of judgement in the language of judgement? Kant attempts to do so by following the *schemata* of the first two *Critiques*, providing an analysis of the logical moments of the judgement of taste, but his procedure repeatedly fails him.

At one point in the *Critique*, § 36 'The Problem of the Deduction of the Judgement of Taste', it would seem that the task of the third *Critique* is restricted to justifying the synthetic, a priori judgement of taste. According to this, the *Critique* must demonstrate how the feeling of pleasure and displeasure attends 'the representation of the Object and serves it instead of a predicate' (§ 36). In the deduction Kant subordinates pleasure to the *schema* of logical predication, inverting the subordination of logical predication to a general 'technic of judgement' involving pleasure outlined in the Preface. The task of the deduction is to legitimate those judgements, given in the 'Analytic' of the *Critique* which describe the modes in which the feeling of pleasure may be affirmed of a representation. Following the logical table of the first *Critique*, we might affirm the predicate pleasure according to its quantity, quality, relation, and modality. We might, but Kant does not. Instead, the exposition follows the logical *schema* only to undo it.

If Kant followed the *schema* of predication faithfully we should expect an exposition of the various modes by which a feeling of pleasure is asserted of a representation, and then their legitimation through a deduction. And we should be disappointed, as many have been, since this is not at all his procedure. Instead Kant uses the *schema* of judgements as a framework within which to explore the traditions of the aesthetic judgement of taste in the hope of uncovering their hidden principle. In spite of its logical form, the content of the Analytic is a search for an adequate statement of the principle of the aesthetic judgement of taste through a dialogue with tradition. Within the steel-cased logical framework of the 'Analytic' is discovered a fractured and hesitant attempt to clarify the principle of judgement through dialogue. The outcome of this conversation will be considered below. Let us stay for the moment with the formal aspects of Kant's philosophical narrative.

One of the consequences of the re-evaluation of the role of tradition in the critical philosophy is a change in the way in which it is read. The critical text in general, and that of the third *Critique* in particular, should not be approached with the prejudice that its author had an 'argument' which he presented and defended with more or less success. The philosophical 'author' should be laid to rest with his literary colleague, buried beside the notion that behind the text lies an 'essence' or 'argument' which is somehow imperfectly realized through the act of writing. Kant's philosophical position is a far more fragile and unstable thing than many commentators like to admit. It developed through its encounter and dialogue with tradition; it did not exist ensouled in some textual limbo prior to gestation in dialogue: the criteria for judging tradition emerged in the process of assessing tradition. His *Critique* should be taken as the record of a dialogue rather than the text of a prepared speech.

This is clearly the case with the 'aesthetic judgement of taste' introduced in § 1, whose very title indicates the presence of competing traditions. We should not bring to the reading of the *Critique* the notion that Kant had conceived of something called the 'aesthetic judgement of taste' which he then set out in his book. The situation is more ambiguous. It would be more accurate, if still inadequate, to say that the exposition proceeds along the *via negationis* of stating what the aesthetic judgement of taste is not, and cannot be. The passage from the negation of tradition to the statement of a position is extremely difficult, if not untraversable. Kant admits as much at the end of the 'Critique of Aesthetic Judgement' when he concedes that the sought after subjective principle of the aesthetic judgement of taste 'can only be pointed to [*gezeigt*] as the unique key to the riddle of this faculty, itself concealed from us in its sources; and there is no means of making it any more intelligible' (§ 57). Kant could only 'point to' a possible solution to the aporia of judgement, he could not give it an exhaustive philosophical description.

So we should not read the 'Analytic' as if Kant were magisterially setting out to analyse the elements of the aesthetic judgement of taste, and then legitimating them through a deduction. We should read it rather as the record of an attempt to decipher the 'riddle' of judgement, a description of a performance. Our paradigmatic texts should not be the philosophical treatises of the schools, but the travel literature of which Kant was inordinately fond. This would locate the philosophical interest and excitement of the text in the journey rather than the destination, in the struggle to find words for an unstatable principle. The presentation points beyond itself; it is an invitation to explore the aporia of judgement rather than a packaged solution to it.

One route into the 'Analytic' of the third *Critique*, one of the most perplexing texts in the philosophical literature, starts out from the 'Dialectic'. There Kant wrote that the dialectic afflicting the aesthetic judgement of taste originates in the way the principle is stated. The antinomy of taste reads: '1. Thesis. The judgement of taste is not based upon concepts ... 2. Antithesis. The judgement of taste is based on concepts' (§ 56). This antinomy points to the basic difficulty of the Analytic, namely, how it is possible to account for the quasi-logical properties of the aesthetic judgement of taste.

The recognition of the antinomy already presupposes an orientation toward tradition. The terms of the antinomy were not a gift of pure reflection, but were bequeathed to Kant by tradition. This is obliquely acknowledged in the 'Dialectic' where Kant translates the abstract positions of the 'Analytic' – agreeableness and perfection – into discrete traditions of thought:

> If ... owing to the fact that the representation lying at the basis of the judgement of taste is singular, the determining ground of taste is taken, as by some it is [*wie von einigen geschieht*], to be *agreeableness*, or, as others [*wie andere*], looking to its universal validity, would have it, the principle of *perfection*, and if the definition of taste is framed accordingly, the result is an antinomy which is absolutely irrevocable unless we show *the falsity of both propositions* as contraries (not as simple contradictories).
>
> (§ 57)

Here Kant employs the substance of his earlier critique of the Wolffian principle of contradiction as a paradigm for reading an internally divided tradition. The two positions should not be read as contradictories defining the possibility and extent of a discourse, but as contraries falling within an unthematized horizon. If we re-orient our reading with respect not only to the contradiction, but also to a horizon which discloses the contradictory as a contrary, new areas will open before us. In this way it may be possible to point out regions inaccessible to the tradition.

The identity of the 'some' and the 'others' of the divided tradition is revealed at various points in the text. The first, the 'some' who find the principle of taste to lie in the agreeable, are the theorists of taste discussed in chapter 2. This identification is supported not only by Kant's report of their position in the *Critique* and the agreement of this with his critique of Shaftesbury, Hutcheson, Kames, Hume, Burke and Smith in the pre-critical writings and reflections, but also by internal evidence in the text. The relationship of the agreeable and the theory of civil society through sympathy proposed by Hume and Smith is criticized as early as § 4:

> But that there is any intrinsic worth in the real existence of a man who merely lives for *enjoyment*, however busy he may be in this respect, even when in so doing he serves others – all equally with himself intent on an enjoyment – as an excellent means to that one end, and does so, moreover, because through sympathy he shares all their gratifications, – this is a view to which reason will never let itself be brought round.

The critique of the proliferation of senses later in the *Critique* sums up Kant's pre-critical dissatisfaction with Hutcheson and Kames:

> The name of sense is often given to judgement where what attracts attention is not so much its reflective act as merely its result. So we speak of a sense of truth, a sense of propriety, or of justice, &c. And yet, of course, we know, or at least ought well enough to know, that a sense cannot be the true abode of these concepts, not to speak of it being competent, even in the slightest degree, to pronounce universal rules. On the contrary, we recognize that a representation of this kind, be it of truth, propriety, beauty, or justice, could never enter our thoughts were we not able to raise ourselves above the level of the senses to that of higher faculties of cognition.
>
> (§ 40)

There are furthermore several references to Epicurus' view of pleasure, and as shown above in the discussion of the *Inaugural Dissertation*, Kant firmly identified Shaftesbury with Epicurus. There are also more explicit references to the representatives of this tradition in the *First Introduction* (§ X) and at § 29 where Kant compares at length his 'transcendental exposition' with the 'physiological' version 'as worked out by Burke and many acute men among us', referring to Burke as the 'foremost author in this method of treatment'. Kant follows the drift of Mendelssohn's review of the *Observations*, missing the systematic character of the *Observations* and remarking that 'As psychological observations these analyses of our mental phenomena are extremely fine, and supply a wealth of material for the favourite investigations of empirical anthropology' (§ 29). They do not tackle, according to Kant, the main problem of a transcendental exposition, which is to account for the obligatory character of judgements of taste.

As to the identity of the 'others', the 'philosophers of reputation' mentioned in § 15, it is clear from the reference to the principle of perfection that Kant is referring to the tradition of aesthetics established by Baumgarten and promoted by Meier and Mendelssohn among others. The terms in which Kant describes this position leaves no room for doubt as to whom is intended:

> But in an objective internal finality, i.e. perfection, we have what is more akin to the predicate of beauty, and so this has been held even by philosophers of reputation to be convertible with beauty, though subject to the qualification *where it is thought in a confused way*. In a Critique of taste it is of the utmost importance to decide whether beauty is really reducible to the concept of perfection.
>
> (§ 15)

In the *Critique* Kant is quite convinced that beauty cannot be reduced to perfection, a complete denial of the perfectionist account of aesthetic developed in the *Lectures on Logic*, where he allied himself with the 'philosophers of reputation'.

Finally there is the evidence of the footnote in the *Critique of Pure Reason* to show that Kant considered aesthetic and taste to be aspects of the same enterprise. It is worth citing the passage again in this context:

> The Germans are the only people who currently make use of the word 'aesthetic' to signify what others call the critique of taste. This usage originated in the abortive attempt made by Baumgarten, that admirable analytical thinker, to bring the critical treatment of the beautiful under rational principles and so raise it to the rank of a science.
>
> (A21/B36)

Even in the first *Critique* Kant was accustomed to read aesthetics and taste as the contraries of a divided tradition.

The opposed principles informing tradition uncovered in the 'Dialectic' of the third *Critique* extends to the 'Analytic'. The analysis of the aesthetic judgement of taste consists in the search for a principle of taste which transcends the contrary posed by aesthetic and taste. In the 'Analytic' Kant finds that he cannot accept either account of the principle of judgement, but neither can he state the desired principle except in a provisional and hesitant way, indicating it through the way in which the contraries of the tradition must necessarily be exceeded. This is a risky enterprise since there is a temptation to produce a new principle out of a factitious synthesis of characteristics of the two traditional accounts. This is a temptation to which Kant on occasion succumbs. Indeed, it is possible to detect the hesitation in stating the transcendental principle of taste not only in the repeated efforts to secure for it a convincing deduction – and the existence of more than one definitive deduction suggests that something is amiss – but even within the formal structure of the logical moments of the aesthetic judgement of taste.

The first moment of the 'Analytic' of the aesthetic judgement of taste immediately presents one of the many perplexing statements characteristic of the *Critique*. This is the proposition that the judgement of taste consists in the estimate 'of an object or a mode of representation by means of a delight or aversion *apart from any interest*' (§ 5). The difficulties posed by this proposition are enhanced by the reading which assumes that Kant started from the thought that beauty was without interest. His argument is positional, it is forced upon him by the necessity of transcending the opposition within tradition. Both the theorists of taste and aesthetic assume that delight in beauty is interested; they differ on the nature of the interest. Now, it is tactically possible to reorient this argument by proposing that beauty is disinterested, and thereby exploring the consequences. The search for a transcendental principle of judgement must first of all deny the horizon within which the traditions are situated; its positive content remains uncertain, for the object of the exposition is to 'state' the difficulty.

Such a reading is supported by the form of the first moment. Kant insists that his proposition be read in terms of contrast: 'This proposition, which is of the utmost importance, cannot be better explained than by contrasting the pure disinterested delight which appears in the judgement of taste with that allied to an interest – especially if we can also assure ourselves that there are no other kinds of interest beyond those presently to be mentioned' (§ 2). Kant begins with the conviction that quality in a judgement of taste is not covered by the accounts given in tradition which depend on an interest; but there is no other kind of interest conceivable, therefore beauty must be without interest. The two forms of interest, the 'agreeable' and the 'good' or 'perfect' are respectively negated in §§ 3 and 4, the one for being exclusively affective, the other for being exclusively rational. The significance of Kant's mapping of the traditions onto a form of transcendental distinction will be explored below; meanwhile the important point here is that both 'agree in being invariably coupled with an interest in their object' (§ 4). The characteristics of a disinterested judgement may only be 'pointed to' in terms of the negation of the traditions. Consequently, in § 5 on the 'Comparison of the Three Specifically Different Forms of Delight' the disinterested is indicated as that delight which is neither the interested delight in the agreeable nor the contrary, but equally interested, delight in the good. The positive content of this property remains undetermined; all that can be said is that it is negatively 'without interest'.

The second moment of the quantity of the judgement of taste observes a similar structure of argument. Once again, the outcome of the moment – the beautiful is that which apart from a concept pleases universally – must not be read as if it were a thesis which stood apart from its implication in tradition. For in this moment too Kant merely points to a property of the beautiful by demarcating it from the accounts of the agreeable and the good, this time respecting the universality of the judgement of taste. His strategy differs from that employed in the first moment: there he rejected the horizon of interest within which the traditions fell; here he refuses the terms of the opposition in which the traditions couch their claims. In § 7 – 'Comparison of the Beautiful with the Agreeable and the Good by Means of the Above Characteristic', Kant distinguishes the universality of the aesthetic judgement of taste from the absence of universality in the agreeable and the quasi-conceptual universality of the good. So on the one hand, 'as regards the *agreeable* every one concedes that his judgement, which he bases on a private feeling, and in which he declares that an object pleases him, is restricted merely to himself personally' (§ 7); while on the other hand, 'In respect of the good it is true that judgements also rightly assert a claim to validity for every one; but the good is only represented as an Object of universal delight *by means of concepts*, which is the case neither with the agreeable nor with the beautiful' (§ 7).

While the critical scale dips from one side to the other, Kant discerns a third possibility in which the beautiful is a feeling like the agreeable, but with the properties of a concept. It shares characteristics of both, but is nevertheless distinguished from each. But when Kant stops to describe this universality he puts down the scales and raises a glass of the agreeable canary wine mentioned in § 7. As the transcendental philosopher sips, we overhear his thoughts: it calls for 'no small effort' to discover the origin of this universality, and 'first one must get firmly into one's mind' that the beautiful holds for everybody without a concept. The eventual statement of the universality of such a judgement is extremely relaxed, moving from a 'universal voice' in § 8 to 'universal communicability' in § 9. The statement of the difficulty is accomplished with great precision through the oppositions of the tradition; but the solution of the difficulty is provisional, and is evoked with almost languorous diffidence.

At the end of the second moment, in § 9 where Kant mentions universal communicability as the ground for the aesthetic judgement of taste, he proposes to investigate – not to answer, but to investigate – the 'question of the relative priority in a judgement of taste of the feeling of pleasure and the estimating of the object'. He regards the 'solution' as the 'key to the critique of taste', that is, the key to the critique which is the keystone of the critical arch, which forms the porch to a door hanging on one hinge which is metaphysics . . . We shall inquire below whether the missing key was ever found, but this seems an apt point to draw out what is at stake in the search.

There are three basic issues in § 9 which define the fundamental difficulty of the *Critique*, and also justify it as one of the most profound and comprehensive works of philosophical modernity. The first concerns the nature of pleasure, the second the estimate of an object, and the third the role of communicability. Pleasure is brought into deliberate alignment with the question of the relative priority of (i) the human relation to an object, (ii) its estimate; and (iii) its relation to other humans in communicability. At stake is the relative importance of production and communication, of making and speaking, *poiesis* and *praxis*. The two relations, the productive and the communicative, are brought together under the aegis of pleasure and orientation in the philosophy of life and culture developed in the second part of the *Critique*. Here production and communication are brought into an ideal proportion, one which is anticipated in the pleasure of the judgement of taste. In this brief instance the question of the aesthetic judgement of taste is revealed in its full scope, one which far exceeds the seemingly arid and restricted anatomizing of a branch of the faculty of judgement.

Returning to the form of the 'Analytic', we arrive at the perplexing conclusion regarding the third moment of the relation of a judgement of taste that '*Beauty* is the form of *finality* in an object, so far as perceived in it *apart from the representation of an end*' (§ 17). This once more has the marks of an awkward compromise, since the celebrated *Zweckmässigkeit ohne Zweck* is only comprehensible (and then barely comprehensible) by comparison with both the absence of a *Zweck* and a *Zweckmässigkeit mit Zweck*. The character of the relation can only be indicated through the traditions. In the moment of relation Kant concentrates on refuting Baumgarten's grounding of beauty in the confused perception of a perfection. The latter, maintains Kant, does not account for the feeling of pleasure evoked in relating to an object; and yet, he insists, pleasure *does* have the law-like characteristics of a concept. Kant confidently negates the traditions:

> Now this relation, present when an object is characterized as beautiful, is coupled with the feeling of pleasure. This pleasure is the judgement of taste pronounced valid for everyone; hence an agreeableness attending the representation is just as incapable of containing the determining ground of the judgement as the representation of the perfection of the object or the concept of the good.
>
> (§ 11)

But when it comes to stating the principle he loses confidence: 'We are thus left with the subjective finality in the representation of an object, exclusive of any end (objective or subjective) – consequently the bare form of the finality in the representation whereby an object is *given* to us' (§ 11). Although we shall see that the notions of form and finality carry a great deal of weight, it is evident that this characterization of their relation states no more than the conditions for a principle in terms of a negation of tradition. Furthermore, the principle of relation in question is not what Kant set out to prove but all that he was left with after interrogating tradition: it couldn't be anything else.

Now to the fourth moment, the vital exposition of the necessity of the aesthetic judgement of taste. This moment too is defined against the claims of tradition, it does not stand up on its own: 'The beautiful is that which, apart from a concept, is cognized as an object of a *necessary* delight' (§ 22). The necessity of the judgement of taste is different from that of a concept, that is, it is not what one of the traditions claimed it to be. Once again, Kant weighs the traditions in the balance, and finds them wanting:

> Were judgements of taste (like cognitive judgements) in possession of a definitive objective principle, then one who in his judgement followed such a principle would claim unconditioned necessity for it. Again, were they devoid of any

principle, as are those of the mere taste of sense, then no thought of any necessity on their part would enter one's head.

(§ 20)

Having ruled out the options offered by tradition, Kant wearily insists on an unconvinced, and unconvincing, conclusion to his negative premisses: 'Therefore they must have a subjective principle, and one which determines what pleases or displeases, by means of feeling only and not through concepts, but yet with universal validity' (§ 20). The form of inference – neither A nor B, therefore both – is unpersuasive. The 'universal voice' of the second moment has been silenced; now we are introduced to a new characterization of the principle as 'common sense' which becomes the condition for the necessity of the judgement.[2]

The formal analysis of the moments of the 'Analytic' shows how far Kant's statement of the properties of the judgement of taste is couched in terms of the negation of the claims of tradition. His efforts to give a positive content to this negation appear to be inconsistent. This holds also for his effort to justify the universality and necessity of the judgement of taste in the deduction, situated somewhat oddly to the rear of the 'Analytic of the Sublime'. Here too Kant's statements are cautious and provisional, giving the distinct impression of someone thinking aloud. The universal validity is to rest, 'as it were', 'upon an autonomy of the Subject passing judgement on the feeling of pleasure ... upon his own taste, and yet is not to be derived from concepts' (§ 31). The nature of this universality and necessity are peculiar, and the problems of framing a deduction of the operations 'of this strange faculty' are quite entangled and tortuous. Its peculiarity consists in its claiming a universal and necessary validity for the feeling of pleasure 'as it would if it were an objective judgement, resting on grounds of cognition and capable of being proved by demonstration' (§ 33).

So far the emphasis has been on the form of the 'statement' of the 'entangled principle' of judgement exemplified in the aesthetic judgement of taste. Kant's gestures toward solving the difficulties of the principle of the aesthetic judgement of taste will be considered more closely in the following sections. But before going further it seems advisable to reflect once more on the reasons for Kant's mode of presentation in the 'Analytic of the Beautiful'. It seems clear that the positions adopted here were not derived from Kant's reflections upon his own aesthetic judgements. Indeed, the reproach of provincial philistinism sometimes levelled against his preference for flowery wallpaper over fine art misses the point entirely. Kant's reflections were not prompted by a personal predilection for birdsong and woodland glades, but by the apparently contradictory accounts of judgement presented by the tradition. We have to do with 'books and systems', and not with the idiosyncrasies of Kant's own faculty of taste. The proposals for the principle of the judgement of taste are contributions to a conversation with tradition; they are not firmly held 'arguments' but topoi or aids for orientation. Of course an outline of a position does emerge, but it becomes visible only against the backdrop of the bias of reason in tradition.

The grounds for this kind of procedure were explored in the previous chapter. The ineluctable bias of reason can only be disclosed through a performative method which, like the reversal of the biased scales, exposes it to view. In the same way, the bias of reason expressed in the traditions of aesthetic and taste presents itself as a simple opposition, one of whose extremes is correct. By running through what the opposed traditions share, their opposition is reoriented, opening the possibility for perceiving a position beyond the contradiction. However this perception is fragmentary, appearing in sudden intensities, and is by no means fully developed.

In the case of the traditions of taste and aesthetic there are additional complicating factors. The bias evinced by their opposition is not confined to reason: the differences between the two traditions have cultural presuppositions which span politics, religion, as well as philosophy. In the theory of taste, the affective emphasis reflects a wider view of the providential disposition of social relations through the moral sense. The theory of aesthetic judgement presupposed a radically different view of political organization, one which saw social relations as governed by the rational judgement of the police-state, and reason as the means for achieving the ends of providence. Both accounts of judgement were considerably overdetermined by differing perspectives on political and religious culture, so when Kant negates them he is also negating the political and cultural freight which they carry. His negation of the accounts of judgement intimates a thinking and a politics beyond judgement.

In fact further difficulties in reading the *Critique of Judgement-Power* emerge from Kant's sensitivity to the various levels of argument present in the traditions of taste and aesthetic. The distinction between them is not only equated with the distinction between a society based on 'enjoyment' and one based on 'discipline' but also with the transcendental distinction. Examples of the latter alignment throng through the text, but the most explicit is found in, § vii of the *First Introduction*. Here Kant insists that a 'specific difference' be respected between sensibility and the understanding in order to avoid the confusion or 'amphiboly' of attributing the properties of the understanding to sensibility (as in taste), or properties of sensibility to the understanding (as in aesthetic).

At one point the distinction between the traditions is superimposed onto that of rational and irrational beings. After characterizing 'human being' as an amalgam of both, Kant positions beauty between sense and reason:

> Agreeableness is a significant factor even with irrational animals; beauty has purport and significance only for human beings, i.e. for beings at once animal and rational (but not merely for them as rational – intelligent beings – but only for them as at once animal and rational); whereas the good is good for every rational being in general.
>
> (§ 5)

With this anthropological turn Kant places his account of beauty and judgement firmly within the Renaissance tradition. Human judgement is strung between reason and the senses; their alignment is effected in every act of judgement, but exemplified by the judgement of the beautiful. This particular judgement is unusual in pointing to a relation of sense and reason beyond the unity and manifold of judgement in its normal use.

The allusion to human beings as both animal and rational agrees with the anthropological foundation of the transcendental distinction and the need for its orderly transgression discussed in the previous chapter. There, after establishing the distinction, Kant faced the problem of legitimately synthesizing the two sides in a principled judgement. The problem recurs throughout the *Critique of Judgement-Power* where Kant advances various 'solutions' or principles for the inexplicable conformity of freedom and necessity. The principle of judgement which exceeds judgement manifests itself in the proportion or harmony of freedom and law. Freedom itself though is equivocal. In the sense of *Willkür* or arbitrariness it is aligned with sensibility in the transcendental distinction; but there is a more fundamental freedom which transcends the distinction. This freedom is described in the language of schematism in the first *Critique*, that is, in terms of 'realization and restriction'. And with this the problem of establishing a principle of judgement discloses itself as the problem of formation and culture.

Kant's statements of the 'principle of judgement' rely on a proportionality which exceeds and underlies the opposition of sensibility and reason in the transcendental distinction. The proportionality of the powers which Kant proposes as his 'solution' to the question of the principle of the aesthetic judgement of taste and of the teleological judgement is shown to rest on a theory of formation, which is given political significance in his analysis of culture. And common to both the principle of judgement and culture is the technic of judgement, which is the self-orientation of judgement as a formation which realizes and restricts itself, and which achieves through culture a proportioned harmony of productive and communicative activities.

Pleasure and the Technic of Judgement

> How does it come about that to that which is but a product of our self-isolated *Gemüt* there correspond objects and that these objects are subject to those laws which we prescribe to them.
>
> Kant, *Reflection* 4478

In the previous chapter I remarked upon the equivocal status of pleasure within Kant's pre-critical writings: it was both marginal, belonging to the third faculty after cognition and desire, yet central, related to the activity of orientation fundamental to all the faculties. If anything, the equivocation is intensified in the *Critique of Judgement-Power*. Here pleasure is treated both as a predicate which may be assigned to an object according to the rules of logical subsumption, and as a constitutive experience which founds the possibility of such subsumption. The aporia of aesthetic judgement manifest in Kant's refusal to make more than negative characterizations of its principle not only registers the inability of the table of logical functions to contain the experience of pleasure, but also points to a more fundamental relation of pleasure and judgement. In this, pleasure and law are united in a notion of formative activity or 'life' which Kant described elsewhere as the *summum bonum* or 'Kingdom of God on Earth'.

Kant's deployment of the table of judgements in an exposure of the bias of reason within the traditions could not contain the aesthetic judgement of taste except by negation. Such judgements are in respect of quality *without* interest; they are universally valid *without* a concept; their relation is final but *without* an end; and their modality, necessary but *without* a concept. These rigorously negative determinations illustrate the impossibility of treating pleasure as a predicate which might be affirmed of an object according to a definite quantity, quality, relation, or modality. However, it would be too quick to condemn Kant's enterprise as a failure on these grounds, for his *via negationis* points to a new relation of pleasure and judgement in which pleasure is not subordinated to logic but logic is subordinated to pleasure.

The inversion of the relation of pleasure and logic is prepared in the extremely problematic Introductions to the *Critique*. The Introductions are problematic not only in themselves, but also in there being two of them, one written before the completion of the *Critique* and rejected because of its length, and the other written after it. The Introductions span the interval between project and peformance, between what Kant wished to achieve, and what he felt he had achieved. In them he not only sketches the extremely complex relationship between pleasure, finality, and the technic of judgement with which he inverts the relation of logic and pleasure, but also reflects on the implications of this inversion for the 'greatest difficulty' of reconciling freedom and necessity.

The grounds for the failure of a logic of pleasure lie in the general aporia of judgement outlined previously. The *predication* of pleasure and displeasure of objects presupposes that objects can be distinguished according to whether they fall within the class of the pleasurable or displeasurable. But what is the principle of this distinction? The strong argument for a subsumptive account of pleasure mounted in the deduction of § 36 crumbles before this objection. Here Kant compares the aesthetic judgement of taste with theoretical judgement through the idea that both are synthetic, a priori judgements: 'It is easy to see that judgements of taste are synthetic, for they go beyond the concept and even the intuition of the Object, and join as predicate to that intuition something which is not even a cognition at all, namely the feeling of pleasure (or displeasure)' (§ 36). The parenthetical 'or displeasure' suggests that things are more complicated; and indeed, in the light of the aporia of judgement it is difficult to see how an intuition may be subsumed under the predicate pleasurable/displeasurable, since the distinction of whether an object is pleasurable or displeasurable precedes the subsumption. The subsumptive account of pleasure already assumes a fundamental distinction of pleasurable and displeasurable objects, which is beyond the opposition of concept and intuition.

In § 38 Kant maintains the subsumptive position even while admitting that 'predicates' of pleasure and displeasure differ essentially from logical predicates. Aesthetic judgements of taste, he writes,

> face unavoidable difficulties which do not affect the logical judgement. (For there the subsumption is under concepts; whereas in the aesthetic judgement it is under a mere

sensible relation of the imagination and understanding mutually harmonizing with one another in the represented form of the Object, in which case the representation may easily prove fallacious.)

(§ 38)

At this stage of composition Kant is still reluctant to draw the conclusion that the 'unavoidable difficulties' entail a fundamental revision of the differences between logical and aesthetic judgement. In a sentence which seems to unravel as it proceeds, Kant defends the subsumptive model of aesthetic judgement:

> For as to the difficulty and uncertainty concerning the correctness of the subsumption under that principle, it no more casts doubt upon the legitimacy of the claim to this validity on the part of the aesthetic judgement generally, or, therefore, upon the principle itself, than the mistakes (though not so often or easily incurred), to which the subsumption of the logical judgement under its principle is similarly liable, can render the latter principle, which is objective, open to doubt.

(§ 38)

The insistence on the affinity of the subsumptions of aesthetic and logical judgement is atypical of the third *Critique*. More characteristic is the view that the 'unavoidable difficulties' of the aesthetic judgement, and the 'unavoidable difficulty and uncertainty' around correct subsumption indicate that pleasure cannot be predicated, but refers to more fundamental synthesis than subsumption's unification of a manifold. Yet it should not be overlooked that at the first stage of composition represented by the deduction, Kant saw the insistence on the subsumptive character of the aesthetic judgement of taste as the only way of keeping such judgements within transcendental philosophy.[3]

There was another, more radical possibility which Kant takes up in the Introductions. If the peculiar difficulties of the aesthetic judgement of taste threaten to exceed the bounds of transcendental philosophy, then perhaps those bounds should be extended? This move requires a complete reconsideration of the relation between pleasure and judgement. Instead of including the aesthetic judgement of taste among subsumptive judgements, whatever the difficulties, why not extend the notion of judgement to include both forms of judgement? The negative lessons of the analytic and the deduction bring into definition the wider notion of pleasure and judgement anticipated in some of the pre-critical writings. This more generous notion of judgement shifts the emphasis of the transcendental philosophy from the twin problematic of justifying predication and unifying manifolds, to that of outlining a general technic or art of judgement in which judgement is considered as a procedure for establishing proportionality between the objects judged. This proportionality is not simply the relation of the one and the many, the individual and universal required for subsumption, but indicates a wider relation. With this move the paradigmatic status of determinate judgement, established in the 'silent decade' and codified in the first *Critique*, is extended into a notion of reflective judgement which replaces the unification of a manifold with the search for analogy and proportion within the manifold.

In both versions of the Introduction to the *Critique of Judgement-Power* the broader notion of judgement predominates over the narrower one advanced in the 'Deduction'. The notion of the 'technic of judgement' worked through in them looks back to some pre-critical positions on orientation, and forward to themes in the *Opus Postumum*.[4] The 'technic of judgement', developed especially in the first version, includes within it both determinate and reflective species of judgement. Both are procedural expressions of an orientational activity. The two introductions also grapple with the problem of the relation of this activity to the phenomena of pleasure/displeasure and finality which distinguish the two species of reflective judgement, aesthetic and teleological, examined in the two parts of the *Critique*. Before going further it may be helpful to anticipate some of Kant's conclusions.

The two forms of reflective judgement are related through their common anthropological foundation. Pleasure and finality exceed the transcendental distinction of sensibility and understanding, and point to their unity in concrete human existence. Judgement consists in the negotiation of these faculties. 'Absolutely speaking', as Aquinas would say, it is prior to the distinction; but philosophy can only speak relatively, so judgement appears, is represented as, subsequent to the negotiation. Having bracketed the status of judgement it becomes possible to see that the yes/no distinction of pleasure/displeasure is fundamental, since its distinctions found the possibility of classification and predication.[5] Without this power of differentiation there could be no decision regarding the assignment of an object to a class. But this decision seems to presuppose the existence of classes to which objects may be assigned, and the aporia of judgement manifests itself again.

Kant, however, avoids the aporia by situating the decision pleasure/displeasure within the horizon of discrimination constituted by a non-conceptual finality of judgement. The two aspects of reflective judgement, the differential activity pleasure/displeasure of the 'Critique of Aesthetic Judgement' and the dispositional activity of finality in the 'Critique of Teleological Judgement' are united in a notion of formative activity or 'life'. This comprises the negotiation of the active and passive aspects of human being in the world which appear in the ordering and disposition of nature, self and others.

We saw in the previous chapter that Kant's account of schematism in the first *Critique* employed both absolute and relative notions of judgement. Schematism appeared in two guises: it was both the 'third thing' called upon to reconcile concept and intuition, and an activity of synthesis – 'realization and restriction' – prior to their distinction. This equivocation persists in the Introductions to the third *Critique* where judgement itself appears both as a 'third thing' and an originary activity. In fact Kant contrasts schematism and reflective judgement as different modalities of a single technic of judgement whose operation is later described as hypotyposis.[6]

Although Kant distinguishes between schematism and reflective judgement, he is quite certain that they are modes of the same activity of judgement, In § v of the *First Introduction* he overturns the preference for determinate over reflective judgement evinced in the 'Deduction'. In considering the relation of genus and species and the possibility of a system of individual laws, Kant arrived at the following contrast:

> The reflective judgement thus works with given appearances so as to bring them under empirical concepts of determinate natural things not schematically, but *technically* [*technisch*], not just mechanically like a tool controlled by the understanding and the senses, but *artistically* [*künstlich*], according to the universal but at the same time undefined principle of a purposive ordering of nature into a system [*einer zweckmässigen Anordnung der Natur in einem System*].
>
> (1790b; § v)

Both forms of judgement are technical procedures, but the schematism is 'merely mechanical', an instrumental technique for applying the already formed concepts of the understanding. Reflective judgement, on the other hand, proceeds according to the indeterminate regularity of a '*zweckmässigen Anordnung der Natur*', and is an art of judgement. Both forms of judgement then are technical – '*Also ist die Urteilskraft eigentlich technisch*' – but what does Kant mean by technique, and what distinguishes a *mechanical* from an *artistic* technique?

Some approximation to an answer may be gathered from Kant's

discussion of geometrical instruments earlier in the *First Introduction*. Mechanical tools are situated within a wider body of technical procedures; and in an anticipation of Heidegger's notion of technology as a *Gestell*, or 'framing', the use of tools is shown to presuppose a context of instrumentality.[7] The instrumental use of judgement as a tool or 'third thing', for example, presupposes the context of a technic or art of judgement. Kant worries while reflecting on the example of geometrical instruments whether 'This pure and therefore noble science seems to compromise something of its worth when it admits that in its elementary form it uses instruments for the construction of its concepts, albeit only two, namely, the compass and straight-edge' (§ 1). He concludes that it doesn't because these instruments 'signify' modalities of the imagination, fundamental dispositions which are only approximated by the crude tools which it employs:

> in elementary geometry one must not think of the actual instruments [*circinus et regula*], which are incapable of rendering any figure with mathematical precision, but one should let them stand for the simplest modes of presentation [*die einfachste Darstellungsarten der Einbildungskraft*] of which the imagination is capable a priori, which no instrument can equal.
>
> (§ 1)

What is properly technical is the modality of the imagination, its power of inscription and disposition in general; however, this power has two 'modes of presentation'; the first is instrumental, the other establishes the conditions for instrumentality. Staying with geometry, Kant says that both modes of presentation underlie mechanical constructions however advanced their instruments – 'constructions of higher geometry are called "mechanical" because to construct the concepts of the latter, more complex machines are needed.' The 'mechanical' work of schematism is of this sort; the instrumentation of the concepts of the understanding which it applies is extremely intricate, and the results may be so complex a construction as Newtonian physics, but it is all the same a realization and a restriction of a fundamental modality. Without the context of instrumentality its tools would be useless; without an art or technic of judgement, there could be no judgement.

The distinction between the technique of schematism and that of reflective judgement is later presented in terms of autonomy and legislation. Schematism proceeds under the tutelage (*Leitung*) of the understanding, while reflective judgement legislates for itself through its encounters with individual things. This distinction is considered more extensively in the second Introduction, especially in the distinction between determinate and reflective judgement given in § iv on 'Judgement as a Faculty by which Laws are Prescribed A Priori' where Kant writes: 'If the universal (the rule, principle, or law) is given, then the judgement which subsumes the particular under it is *determinant* . . . If, however, only the particular is given and the universal has to be found for it, then the judgement is simply *reflective*' (1790; § iv). Both judgements are technical, that is follow a definite procedure, but for the schematism of determinate judgement 'the law is marked out for it *a priori*, and it has no need to devise a law for its own guidance to enable it to subordinate the particular in nature to the universal' (§ iv). For schematism a law is already given and is applied to the particular, but what enables it to be so given? The 'givenness' or inscription of a universal law has itself to be given, just as its object has to be present in a way appropriate to the law. Reflective judgement concerns both the giving of law itself, and the giving of law to its objects; it has to legislate for itself, 'mark out' its own law for itself and so order its own activities. The act of legislation is itself reflection, being given by the judgement 'to and from' itself: 'such a transcendental principle, therefore, the reflective judgement can only give as a law to and from itself' (§ iv). Reflection as both the giving and application of law is extended in the course of the *Critique* into a broad notion of formative activity.

The distinction between the two modes of judgement is later refined in § 59 'Beauty as a Symbol of Morality'. This section is vital for appreciating what is at stake in the technic of judgement. With regard to the presentation of the concept the activity of judgement is described as a 'hypotyposis' – the specification of how a concept may be 'given' – which is divided according to the two modes of judgement:

> All *hypotyposis* (presentation, *subjectio sub adspectum*) as a rendering in terms of sense is twofold. Either it is *schematic*, as where the intuition corresponding to a concept comprehended by the understanding is given *a priori*, or else it is *symbolic*, as where the concept is one which only reason can think, and to which no sensible intuition can be adequate.
>
> (§ 59)

Both renditions of the concept in terms of sense are distinguished by their dynamic, procedural character from marks or concepts – they are presentations, a 'bringing before' or 'giving' of the concept: 'Both are hypotyposes, i.e., presentations [*exhibitiones*], not mere *marks*'

(§ 59). The two modes of hypotyposis are themselves distinguished by their mode of presentation:

> Schemata contain direct, symbols indirect, presentations of the concept. Schemata effect this presentation demonstratively, symbols by the aid of an analogy (for which recourse is had even to empirical intuitions), in which analogy judgement performs a double function: first in applying the concept to the object of a sensible intuition, and then, secondly, in applying the mere rule of its reflection upon that intuition to quite another object, of which the former is but the symbol.
>
> (§ 59)

In schematism, intuition is subsumed under the concept, and the modality is one of unification; in symbolization, a rule of reflection is applied to a similar intuition, and the modality is one of analogy. The unification of the schema is contrasted with the proportionality of the symbol; the rule in the latter is one of reflection, not of subsumption. In the first case judgement arranges its materials instrumentally according to unification under a universal; in the other it proceeds artistically through analogy, or the discernment of a proportionate likeness which does not extinguish the differences of the particular in the uniformity of the universal.[8] In the first, the horizon within which the law and its objects are given is fixed, while in the second, the activity of giving law and bringing forth objects is itself the horizon.

Two important consequences may be drawn from the distinction of the modes of hypotyposis. The first is that a general procedure (hypotyposis) underlies its two forms; and secondly, that this procedure can be experienced (by human beings) in terms either of unification or analogy. Hypotyposis not only points to a procedure or technic of judgement underlying reflective judgement, but also suggests that the rules of this procedure are not necessarily exhausted by the unification of a manifold. Furthermore, judgement as a hypotypotic procedure or technique, whether determinate or reflective, is closely tied to the distinction of pleasure/displeasure and the inscription of finality. As indicated, the character of this relation emerges from the anthropological foundation of judgement and its relation to formative activity. Having now distinguished the general technic of judgement from its disposition in determinate and reflective judgement we may proceed to an examination of its anthropological foundation.

In §§ 76 and 77 of the 'Dialectic of Teleological Judgement' Kant offers an 'explanatory digression' on why the notion of a 'physical end', central to the teleological explanation of nature, can only be accepted as a principle of reflective judgement. The digression compares the human separation of concept and intuition with an intuitive understanding. In some remarkable paragraphs which anticipate Nietzsche's early critique of philosophical terms in 'Truth and Lies in a Non-Moral Sense', Kant deduces many of the fundamental distinctions of philosophy from the transcendental distinction. In the process he unequivocally subordinates the instrumentalities of determinate judgement to the more original legislative and productive activities of reflective judgement, for the same reason as his earlier subordination of 'higher' to 'elementary' geometry. Without the original activity of the reflective judgement in establishing uniformities and horizons of discrimination, the derived activity of determinate judgement would not be possible. But in order to establish the precedence of reflective judgement it is first necessary to develop an anthropological characterization of human activity.

Kant claims to follow the same counterfactual procedure in the digression as he used in the first *Critique*, which is to re-orient human understanding by comparing it to divine, a procedure already employed by Aquinas. In order to appreciate the 'peculiarity' of human understanding, which is an essential preliminary to self-knowledge,

> we must have an underlying idea of a possible understanding
> different from the human. (And there was a similar implication
> in the *Critique of Pure Reason*. We were bound to have present
> to our minds the thought of another possible form of intuition,
> if ours was to be deemed one of a special kind, one namely,
> for which objects were only to rank as phenomena.)
>
> (1790a; § 77)

Such a standpoint is necessary to perceive the limitations of human understanding – to recognize the 'element of contingency in its constitution' – and so criticize its activities. Otherwise there would be a constant danger of treating the 'peculiarities belonging to our own faculty of cognition' as 'objective predicates to be transferred to the things themselves' (§ 77). This danger had not been fully appreciated by previous metaphysicians, whose categories and distinctions were, to use Nietzsche's maxim, human, all too human.

The main peculiarity of human cognition is the scission of understanding and intuition. From this division, or rather from its recognition in the transcendental distinction, Kant derives many of the central dichotomies of philosophy, beginning with the most fundamental – possibility and actuality:

Human understanding cannot avoid the necessity of drawing a distinction between the possibility and the actuality of things. The reason of this lies in our own selves and the nature of our cognitive faculties. For were it not that two entirely heterogeneous factors, understanding for conceptions and sensuous intuition for the corresponding Objects, are required for the exercise of these faculties, there would be no distinction between the possible and the actual.

(§ 76)

The possibility and actuality of things exist only for the human understanding; an intuitive understanding would not suffer the distinction. Kant's exposition of the dichotomy uses the vocabulary of his earlier critique of Wolff: possibility and actuality correspond to his earlier distinction of relative and absolute position (*Setzung*). The earlier argument, which Kant preserves in its essentials, maintained that actuality was not simply a logical complement to possibility but differed from it absolutely. Kant restates the significance of this position for the critical philosophy in the following terms:

Now the whole distinction which we draw between the merely possible and the actual rests upon the fact that possibility signifies the position of the representation of a thing relative to our conception, and, in general, to our capacity of thinking, whereas actuality signifies the positing of the thing in its immediate self-existence apart from this conception.

(§ 76)

For an intuitive understanding everything would be actual, there would be no place for the distinction of actuality and possibility, and no need to worry about how to relate the two. But human thinking, judgement, is afflicted with the distinction and must negotiate it.

Kant modulates the distinction of possibility and actuality into that of necessity and contingency by way of the conception of a being who suffers neither distinction:

An understanding into whose mode of cognition this distinction did not enter would express itself by saying: All Objects that I know *are*, that is, exist; and the possibility of some that did not exist, in other words, their contingency supposing them to exist, and, therefore, the necessity that would be placed in contradistinction to this contingency, would never enter into the imagination of such a being.

(§ 76)

The distinctions of possibility and actuality, necessity and contingency are relative to our mode of perception. They may not be taken as objective without further question; but since they are rooted in our way of organizing experience, this organization should become our object of inquiry.

Several more philosophical oppositions cluster around the transcendental distinction. A further development in § 76 is the metamorphosis of the theoretical distinction of necessity and contingency into the practical distinction of obligation and act. Once again, this distinction only arises because of the division of intuition and understanding:

> it is clear that it only springs from the subjective character of our practical faculty that the moral laws must be represented as commands, and the actions conformable to them as duties ... This would not occur if reason and its causality were considered as independent of sensibility, that is, as free from the subjective condition of its application to objects in nature.
>
> (§ 76)

If this distinction did not exist, the consequence would be the same as in the case of possibility and actuality: there everything possible became actual; here 'there would be no difference between obligation and act' (§ 76). Once again, the negotiation of this difference is the work of a judgement which mediates between 'what is possible through our agency' and 'what we make actual'. Judgement is situated at the crossing of the understanding and intuition, but in order to be there it has also to be in some sense outside the distinction.

The paradigm of the transcendental distinction manifest in these contraries receives another incarnation in the opposition of universal and particular. This is one of the major loci for Kant's development of a wider notion of judgement. In order to mediate the transcendental distinction and its corollaries, judgement must exceed them; and in order to do so it is accorded a projective moment of positing a finality of particulars. This consists in an appropriateness for subsumption – a proportionality of particular and universal prior to subsumption. Here is Kant's argument, which proceeds from a description of subsumptive judgement to the derivation of the more extensive technic of judgement which it presupposes. First of all 'Our understanding must move from the universal to the particular. In respect of the particular, therefore, judgement can recognize no finality, or, consequently, pass any determinate judgements, unless it is possessed of a universal law under which it can subsume that particular' (§ 76). But Kant summons the irreducible contingency of the particular as an objection to subsumption; the representation of a universal demands contingency on the part of the particular, for without it there would be no place for a universal. An intuitive understanding, for example, does not oppose universal to particular. But for us the contingency of the particular resists the subsumption of the universal, and the transcendental distinction in the shape of universal and particular seems to undo itself: 'But the particular by its very nature contains something contingent in respect of the universal. Yet reason demands that there shall also be unity in the synthesis of the particular laws of nature, and, consequently, conformity to law' (§ 76). The contingency of the particular is defined according to its resistance to the universal, it would not be a particular without it; yet this resistance means that the particular can never be fully subsumed under the universal. In order to achieve subsumption reason demands (*erfordert*) a conformity to law which is prior to the universal, prior to law.

Before looking more closely at this conformity to law which enables the law to be applied, it would do to follow this principle along the chain of contraries in which philosophy has tried to represent it. The particular is predisposed to agree with the universal, the contingent with the necessary, the actual with the possible, the act with the obligation, the self-posited existence with its relative position, and finally the intuition with the concept. Kant now states that this 'conformity to law on the part of the contingent is termed finality. Hence it follows that the conception of a finality of nature in its products, while it does not touch the determination of Objects, is a necessary conception for the human power of judgement, in respect of nature' (§ 76). Judgement must postulate a proportion between intuition and concept which is prior to it, but can only be imperfectly understood in terms of the distinction which it exceeds.[9] Such a proportionality, with similar properties, was described by Aquinas as the transcendental 'Truth' which along with 'Unity', 'Goodness', and 'Beauty' both exceed and enable the work of the categories.

Kant develops this thought in § 77, maintaining the strategy of comparing the human and the divine understanding in order to determine what is proper to the former. Here the fundamental difference of the transcendental distinction is extended to the contraries of parts and wholes and spontaneity and passivity. From the standpoint of the understanding, the manifold of intuition is contingent; the individuality of the object of perception cannot be legislated by the understanding, and even resists its subsumption:

> For the particular is not determined by the universal of our
> [human] understanding. Though different things may agree in
> a common characteristic, the variety of forms in which they
> may be presented to our perception is contingent. Our
> understanding is a faculty of conceptions. This means that it
> is a discursive understanding for which the character and
> variety to be found in the particular given to it in nature and
> capable of being brought under its conceptions must certainly
> be contingent.
>
> (§ 77)

The 'forms' and the 'differences' of, and between, things exceed the
procedure of subsumptive judgement; they 'transcend' its categories.
As such they are represented by the understanding as 'contingent',
that is, contingent in respect of the necessity of the understanding.
But this ascription does not do the forms and differences of things
justice, and is based on a subjective estimate. When compared with
an intuitive understanding, one with 'complete spontaneity of intuition',
the assignment of contingency and necessity seems very provincial.
The subsumptive activity of the human understanding, its orderings
and exclusions, requires a negotiation of the transcendental distinction
and its corollaries, while the divine understanding 'has no such work
to perform' (§ 77). But the human understanding has work to do in
conforming the manifold of its intuition with the laws of its
understanding. But on its own the understanding cannot possibly
achieve this without presupposing a different *ratio* to its own, a prior
'harmony' or 'accord' (*Übereinstimmung*) of 'natural features with our
faculty of conception', an accord which that faculty can only represent
to itself as 'contingent'.

The previous chapter showed that the view of an active understanding working on the passive materials of sensibility cannot be sustained
in a reading of Kant's pre-critical writings. Nor, it may now be
added, does it hold for the critical philosophy. The distinction of a
passive intuition and an active understanding is an illusion of the
human understanding, and entails the suppression of a prior *ratio*
(which Kant calls 'proportion', 'harmony', 'accord', and 'conformity')
which differs from the unificatory *ratio* of the subsumptive understanding. Intuition is active, it differentiates its materials and appropriates
them for subsumption. This *ratio* exceeds the understanding, and is
'contingent' for it: 'under the circumstances mentioned this accord
must be very contingent and must exist without any determinate

principle to guide our judgement' (§ 77). According to subsumptive judgement, there is no alternative way of conceiving the 'accord of things in nature with the power of judgement' except as contingent, as 'an accord which we represent [*vorstellen*] as contingent' (§ 77). However we are not entirely barred access to this accord; we are able to conceive of it (*wenigstens denken zu können*) when, as in the current case, we orient our limited understanding by comparing it with an unlimited one. In order to *think* the *ratio* which we *represent* as contingent, we have to violate the procedures of our understanding by imagining those 'of an understanding different from our own' (§ 77).

Such a re-orientation forces Kant to compare the procedures of our judgement under the tutelage of the understanding with divine judgement. When this is done it becomes apparent that the understanding's account of itself is full of lacunae and contradictions which are otherwise invisible. For human understanding is already oriented, it 'moves from the *analytic universal* to the particular, or, in other words, from conceptions to given empirical intuitions. In this process, therefore, it determines nothing in respect of the multiplicity of the particular' (§ 77). What is specific about the orientation of human understanding becomes apparent when it is compared with one which 'not being discursive like ours, but intuitive, moves from the *synthetic universal*, or intuition of a whole as a whole, to the particular – that is to say from the whole to the parts' (§ 77). The latter procedure is not available to human understanding; but imagining it reveals that our discursive procedures are highly particular. It also reveals that there is more to them than previously imagined. Subsumptive judgement is not possible without presupposing an implicate order of intuition. It is not possible for a discursive understanding to subsume a manifold without the assumption of a 'conformity' between parts and wholes. Yet how may this conformity be represented except in terms of the understanding? In Kant's words 'How then may we avoid having to represent the possibility of the whole as dependent upon the parts in a manner conformable to our discursive understanding?' (§ 77). We may not follow the synthetic understanding in deriving particulars from the whole, but we may project or represent an idea of the whole from within which to discriminate the parts while preserving them in an order: 'the *representation* of a whole may contain the ground [*Grund*] of the possibility of the form of that whole and of the nexus of the parts which that form involves' (§ 77). Intuition is ordered prior to subsumption, and this order is designated 'form', which is both the accord of part and whole and the nexus of the parts. Form is not the whole itself, but the relation of parts to each other and to a representation of a possible whole. In terms of the *Only Possible Proof* it refers both to the relative position of existents and to the absolute position of existence.

In the digression of §§ 76 and 77 form is introduced to mediate the transcendental distinction and to reconcile the philosophical oppositions arising from it. Form is not an instrument or tool of mediation, but the activity of mediation itself; form is formative. The proportion or conformity of nature and the understanding is considered dynamically as a process of formation. As a preliminary definition we may say that formative activity consists in the assignment of differences and the configuration of a manifold. It inscribes finality in nature, but can only recognize its activity in the objective finality which it disowns. The unstatable accord between concept and intuition signifies a constant reminder to the self-alienating understanding of the formative activity which it has forgotten. Without this trace of formative activity in the unthematized accord of concept and intuition – the finality of nature for judgement – there could be no discursive judgement. But there is more. This smothered accord, the bad conscience of subsumption, is the source of pleasure/displeasure. The examination of pleasure/displeasure offers another means of access to the formative activity which founds theoretical and practical judgement.

Many of the more enigmatic sections of the Introductions are clarified by the digression of §§ 76 and 77, especially §§ vi and vii of the second Introduction – 'The Association of the Feeling of Pleasure with the Concept of the Finality of Nature' and 'The Aesthetic Representation of the Finality of Nature'. The first sentence of § vi laconically restates the thought of § 77:

> The conceived harmony of nature in the manifold of its particular laws with our need of finding universality of principles must, so far as our insight goes, be deemed contingent, but withal indispensable for the requirements of our understanding, and, consequently, a finality by which nature is in accord with our aim, but only so far as this is directed to knowledge.
>
> (1790a; § vi)

The harmony of nature and the power of judgement is prior to the subsumptive procedures of discursive judgement, and literally cannot be thought by them, 'since no law can here be prescribed to it by the understanding'. But discursive judgement cannot be accomplished without it; it is the harmony which makes the legislation of discursive judgement possible, but the harmony itself is disowned, outlawed to contingency. Yet although thus relegated by the understanding, it can still make itself *felt*.

We have access to this 'indispensible' yet 'contingent' harmony through the feeling of pleasure. Pleasure is closely bound with the formative activity of the judgement: 'The attainment of every aim is coupled with a feeling of pleasure. Now where such attainment has for its condition a representation *a priori* – as here a principle for the reflective judgement in general – the feeling of pleasure also is determined by a ground which is *a priori* and valid for all men' (§ vi). The establishment of finality and the orientation of judgement according to it is the ground of pleasure. From this it may be assumed that even subsumptive judgement, which although a highly ritualized form of orientation still requires a finality, must be pleasurable. Kant seems to deny this when he says 'As a matter of fact, we do not, and cannot, find in ourselves the slightest effect on the feeling of pleasure from the coincidence of perceptions with the laws in accordance with the universal concepts of nature (the Categories)' (§ vi). But he goes on to qualify the meaning of the word 'find' (*antreffen*) used in this passage. The reason we cannot 'find' it in ourselves is that we have forgotten where and how to look for it. Kant continues, 'Still it is certain that the pleasure appeared in due course, and only by reason of the most ordinary experience being impossible without it, has it become gradually fused with simple cognition, and no longer arrests particular attention' (§ vi). Discursive judgement has not only forgotten the formative activity expressed in the accord which founds it, it has also forgotten the pleasure that attends such activity. Here pleasure is considerably more than an accidental relation to an object, since without it 'the most ordinary experience' would be 'impossible'. The pleasure associated with finality, essential for even the most ordinary experience, has been forgotten; but it may be recalled through the special case where the relation still holds, that of pleasure in the beautiful. By examining this experience we open a window onto an experience which, like the schematism, is 'concealed in the depths of the human soul' but which unlike it, 'nature' *has* 'allowed us to discover, and to have open to our gaze'.

In § vii Kant brings the feeling of pleasure and the projection of finality together in the experience of the beautiful. In this way he gains access to the 'concealed art' or the formative activity of realization and restriction. Neither the feeling of pleasure/displeasure nor the establishment of finality are capable of being conceived, since they precede and exceed the procedures of determinate judgement. The feeling of pleasure/displeasure for instance 'is incapable of becoming an element of cognition' because 'through it I cognize nothing in the object of the representation, although it may easily be the result of the operation of some cognition or other' (§ vii). Pleasure is associated with an operation or work (*Wirkung*) and not with an object; and operations cannot be subsumed (they are only open to analogical determination). Finality too is not a quality 'that can be perceived'. It is both (*gleichwohl*) 'prior to the cognition of an object' and 'yet immediately connected with it'; as the 'subjectivity of cognition itself' it is 'incapable of becoming an object of knowledge [*Erkenntnisstuck*]' (§ vii). However, finality may be 'inferred from a cognition of things', and the path of inference leads through the equally inexplicable pleasure. Indeed, as mentioned above, Kant comes to unite pleasure and finality: 'Hence we only apply the term "final" to the object on account of its representation being immediately bound [*verbunden*] with the feeling of pleasure: and this representation itself is an aesthetic representation of the finality' (§ vii). The representation is only final if it is bound with the feeling of pleasure; but does pleasure merely indicate the presence of finality, or is it the horizon for the 'givenness' of finality? To settle this question we should examine more closely the grounds for 'binding together' (*Verbindung*) pleasure and finality, paying particular attention to the relation of the feeling of pleasure/displeasure and the active/passive dispositions of judgement-power. It should always be borne in mind that the *Verbindung* is 'transcendental', beyond the understanding, and so can only be stated indirectly.

Kant does not distinguish between the feeling of pleasure and the feeling of pleasure/displeasure. On balance he uses the latter term more often, referring to it as a single feeling – *das Gefühl der Lust und Unlust*. When he does refer to the feeling of 'pleasure' alone, he implies that the feeling includes its opposite. This is consonant with the position argued in his *Lectures on Anthropology*, *Ethics*, and *Onto-Theology* that pleasure and displeasure are positive and negative quantities, whose relation is more important than any positive characteristics the two quantities may possess. Pleasure/displeasure is an elementary distinction which cannot be further determined; it is a phenomenon of the realization and restriction of activity in formative judgement. The relation of realization and restriction, of activity and passivity, determines the feeling of pleasure/displeasure in a way to be analysed below. For now it is enough to warn that pleasure and displeasure should not be read as class descriptions which may be predicated of objects.

The relation of activity and passivity implied in the feeling of pleasure/displeasure is presented in the second Introduction in terms of apprehension and exhibition. With this choice of terminology, Kant aligns the feeling of pleasure/displeasure with two of the three dispositions of the imagination set out in the *Lectures on Anthropology*, and developed in § vii of the *First Introduction*.[10] The question then arises of the relation not only between imagination and pleasure, but also of each to finality and judgement in general.

In the account offered in the *First Introduction* Kant answers some of these questions. In his discussion of the technic of judgement – the procedure by which judgement orients itself – Kant distributes the *selbsttätigen Erkenntnisvermögen* – self-activating power of knowledge – into three activities (*Handlungen*):

> (1) the apprehension [*Auffassung*] (apprehensio) of the manifold of intuition; (2) the synthesis [*Zusammenfassung*], i.e., the synthetic unity of consciousness of this manifold in the concept of an object (apperceptio comprehensiva); (3) the presentation [*Darstellung*] (exhibitio) in intuition of the object corresponding to this concept.
>
> (1790b; § vii)

The three activities correspond to the rhetorical schema of invention, disposition, and elocution employed by Baumgarten in his aesthetic. The first activity demands imagination (*Einbildungskraft*); the second understanding (*Verstand*), and the third judgement – power (*Urteilskraft*). Imagination is inventive, it takes up the manifold of intuition, while understanding disposes it into a synthetic unity, and judgement presents the concept, adapting it to a form in which it may be exhibited in intuition.

It is important when considering these procedures not to assume that Kant has simply attributed functions to faculties. He is discussing the activity of creating experience, one which consists in a complex articulation of taking up, disposing, and presenting. Nor should the three activities be read as successive stages in some internal division of labour; as if the imagination takes up the manifold of intuition, passes it over to the understanding which places it under a concept already presented for the purpose by judgement. The activities of the *selbsttätigen Erkenntnisvermögen* presuppose each other, but are articulated around judgement. For example, the imagination cannot apprehend the manifold unless it has already been configured by the judgement as the sort of manifold that may be apprehended; the concept in its turn may not be applied if it has not been presented by the judgement as one suitable for application. These activities of unifying and distinguishing are structural and not sequential divisions, for it is as necessary to establish a provisional horizon of discrimination prior to the discrimination of the manifold, as it is to unify it under the concept.

Although Kant wishes to distinguish his fundamental activity from Wolff's faculty of representations, he does not simply adopt the reactive position of proliferating the number of faculties.[11] The original activity of the *selbsttätigen Erkenntnisvermögen* is disposed into distinct modes whose relation to each other and to the original activity which posits them cannot be described in terms of unity and manifold. However, the activity of the self-activating power of knowledge expressed in the mutual implication of apprehension, synthesis, and presentation is experienced as the feeling of pleasure. Returning now to the second Introduction, Kant sees pleasure as arising from the complex alignment of the three modes of activity. The apprehension of forms, he writes, 'can never take place without the reflective judgement, even when it has no intention of so doing, comparing them at least with its faculty of referring intuitions to concepts' (1790; § vii). This cryptic statement, characteristic of the second Introduction, simply states that apprehension always involves the activities of disposition and presentation, even if the relation of these activities is different from one which can be thought by the understanding. The activity always involves pleasure, but this is only noticeable when a determinate concept is absent. Such activity arouses pleasure because it realizes an accord of the three modes of power, a finality of the power of judgement, which is prior to unification in the concept:

> If, now, in this comparison, imagination (as the faculty of intuitions *a priori*) is undesignedly brought into accord with understanding (as the faculty of concepts) by means of a given representation, and a feeling of pleasure is thereby aroused, then the object must be regarded as final for the reflective judgement. A judgement of this kind is an aesthetic judgement upon the finality of the Object, which does not depend upon any present concept of the object, and does not provide one.
>
> (§ vii)

The accord between the modalities of the self-activating power of knowledge constitutes the principle of the judgement of taste. This accord has universal and necessary validity because it underlies all perception; but since it cannot be stated in terms of the understanding, and since we have no other terms, Kant must find another form of presentation. This is the negative statement of the principle through the disputing claims of the tradition.

In § viii Kant makes an observation consequential for the structure of the *Critique*. The accord between the modes of the self-activating power of knowledge – apprehension, synthesis, and presentation/configuration – can be approached from different directions. This permits the distinction of reflective judgement between its aesthetic and teleological varieties. In aesthetic judgement the moment of apprehension is privileged over those of synthesis and presentation; while teleological judgement emphasizes the moment of presentation. The teleological judgement is 'objective' and concerned with the 'harmony of the form of the object with the possibility of the thing itself according to an antecedent concept of it containing the ground of this form' (§ viii). Teleological judgement achieves harmony by 'reading into' the object of an estimate 'our own concept of an end' (§ viii). We configure the presentation of the object according to a notion of an end approximating to our own causality, so bestowing finality upon it. With aesthetic judgement the object is estimated according to whether it raises pleasure, considering the object 'in respect of its form as present in *apprehension* prior to any concept' (§ viii). The two judgements refer to different analogues of form which escape conceptual determination: one is a symbol, finality represented in our notion of an end; the other a feeling, finality indicated through pleasure/displeasure.

In this, as in so many of Kant's definitions, the distinction is made only to be broken. In the reconciliation of the beautiful and the sublime, and the attempt to establish a system of the fine arts, the boundaries between the aesthetic and the teleological judgement begins to blur. Both modes of reflective judgement indicate a proportioning of human activity according to a technic of judgement. Such access to fundamental proportion gives judgement the capacity to mediate between theoretical and practical philosophy: 'This faculty, with its concept of a *finality* of nature, provides us with the mediating concept between concepts of nature and the concept of freedom – a concept that makes possible the transition from the pure theoretical to the pure practical and from conformity to law in accordance with the former to final ends according to the latter' (§ ix). The technic of judgement underlying all judgements, the ground for the unification of judgement which Kant hinted at in the second *Critique*, brings together nature and human ends through a formative activity described by Kant as 'life'.

Kant's gesture toward unifying theoretical and practical reason should alert us to an important issue in the *Critique*, which is the understanding of the good life, the *summum bonum* or welfare. For Kant, as we have seen, this does not consist in contemplating creation theoretically, but in forming it according to human purposes. The good life is active. In this light aesthetic and teleological judgement are renewals of the covenant of humanity and God, since they witness an accord between human freedom and nature which is otherwise forgotten. Amid the multiplicity of natural objects and laws they indicate a proportionality according to which human judgement may 'take its bearings [*in ihr orientieren zu können*]' (§ viii). This principle of the finality of nature and its accord with human cognition is 'a principle without which understanding could not feel itself at home in nature' (§ viii). The accord, or feeling at home in nature, is described by Kant, once again, as 'life' or the promise of a good life.[12]

Kant's notion of life is constitutive for the division of the *Critique's* 'Analytic of Aesthetic Judgement' into the Analytics of the 'Beautiful' and the 'Sublime'. The two forms of aesthetic judgement are distinguished according to their manner of promoting life. The beautiful 'is directly attended with a feeling of the furtherance of life' (§ 23) while the sublime 'is a pleasure that only arises indirectly, being brought about by the feeling of a momentary check to the vital forces' (§ 23). Both judgements further life or the 'vital forces' but in different ways. This is not a careless reference on Kant's part, for we shall see throughout the Analytics of the 'Beautiful' and the 'Sublime' that the main principle of aesthetic judgement is the furtherance of life.

Kant identifies pleasure with the furtherance of life; life though is both an activity and a 'feeling at home in nature'. We have already seen how in the *Lectures on Anthropology* and *Philosophical Theology* Kant identifies life with activity, death with inertia; however, this activity is not aimless, but disposes itself proportionately. The difficult notion of an activity which proportions itself, and yet remains in accord with the finality of nature, is the basis of Kant's description of formation or culture as the negotiation of activity and passivity. This formative activity, distributed among the moments of apprehension, synthesis, and presentation, is attended by the feeling of pleasure – life and pleasure, in other words, are inseparable. The good life, or the *summum bonum*, is the proportioned activity described by Kant as the harmony of imagination and understanding beyond the subsumption of a concept.

The notion of the good life and the *summum bonum* returns us to the accounts of judgement proposed by theories of taste and aesthetic. The association of the judgement of beauty with political judgement is carried through in Kant. But whereas in the traditions the good life is achieved through enjoyment and reason, in Kant it is achieved through formative activity. Kant's welfare principle, the promotion of life, does not abstract political from productive activity – it does not separate *praxis* and *poiesis*. The question is no longer one of how God disposes, whether through the reason or the affects, but of how human beings propose to order their own self-activating power of activity.

The issues of pleasure, finality, and the technic of judgement come together in the transcendentals of the One, the True, the Good, and the Beautiful. The One, through the notion of *Verbindung*, which attends all human activity but which exceeds our notion of unity; the True through the proportionality underlying the subsumptions of theoretical philosophy; the Good through the proportionality underlying human ends; and the Beautiful through the proportionality experienced in pleasure. The four are aspects of human formative activity or life. The reunion of the mediaeval transcendentals in the pages of the third *Critique* is a profound philosophical recuperation of tradition. For although Kant's metaphysics is unmistakably modern in its emphasis on activity and judgement, his founding of them in an unstateable proportion underlying perception, action, and contemplation of the beautiful redeems the themes of mediaeval philosophy, and realizes its author's ambition to restore metaphysics to modernity.

Analytic of the Beautiful

> For, of itself alone, the *Gemüt* is all life (the life principle itself), and hindrance or furtherance has to be sought outside it, and yet in the man himself, consequently in connexion with his body.
>
> Kant, *Critique of Judgement-Power*

The theories of pleasure and judgement developed in Britain and Germany during the eighteenth century presupposed distinct notions of the common good. Kant's version of pleasure defined against the theories of taste and aesthetic points to an account of welfare and the common good distinct from them both. The tie between pleasure and welfare is apparent in the 'Analytic of the Beautiful', superficially in the reference to *Wohlgefallen* in its section headings, but more profoundly in its alignment of pleasure and life. What is theologically and politically distinctive about Kant's position emerges in the course of the critique of the traditions. What also emerges is the immense difficulty which Kant faced in stating his position in these terms.

This is because his position, while articulated against the traditions, remains to some extent confined within their language.

The difficulty Kant faced in stating his position apart from the traditions is already apparent in the first section of the 'Analytic of the Beautiful'. The first moment of the 'Analytic' considers the quality of the aesthetic judgement of taste. This consists in the estimation of an object or a mode of representation apart from any interest. The main criterion used by Kant to recognize 'interest' is the passivity of the subject making the judgement. In the aesthetic tradition the subject is disposed passively toward a determinate concept; while in the theory of taste it is passively disposed toward an object. In both cases the autonomous activity of the judge is compromised by his or her interest. Against both forms of interest Kant proposes a position which would maximize the activity, and thus the life of the subject, without abandoning the regularity of *Gesetzmässigkeit*, that is, the activity should regulate itself with all the properties of a law, but without the interest which would follow from the existence or 'givenness' of one.

Kant's outline of a possible position remains within the terms of the traditions. The quality of the pleasure relates both to an object and to a law, but not in the ways suggested by taste and aesthetic. But when Kant moves from a negative to a positive characterization of this pleasure, the thread of the argument becomes extremely tangled.[13] This transition in all its difficulty already appears in the second paragraph of the first section. Kant presents the identification of the feeling of pleasure/displeasure with life through a critique of the aesthetic tradition's derivation of pleasure from consciousness; but when he goes on to sketch out how a given representation promotes life through the feeling of pleasure/displeasure, he becomes almost incomprehensible. This is not an isolated occurrence, but a structural characteristic of the *Critique*. Since it is one which is encountered at the very outset of a reading of the *Critique*, it is worth analysing in detail.

The locus in question is the first two sentences of the second paragraph of the 'Analytic of the Beautiful'. The German reads:

> *Ein regelmässiges, zweckmässiges Gebäude mit seinem Erkenntnis-vermögen (es sei in deutlicher oder verworrener Vorstellungsart) zu befassen, ist ganz etwas anderes, als sich dieser Vorstellung mit der Empfindung des Wohlgefallens bewusst zu sein. Hier wird die Vorstellung gänzlich auf das Subjekt und zwar auf das Lebensgefühl desselben, unter dem Namen des Gefühls der Lust oder Unlust, bezogen; welches ein ganz besonderes Unterscheidungs– und*

*Beurteilungsvermögen gründet, das zum Erkenntnis nicht beiträgt,
sondern nur die gegebene Vorstellung in Subjekte gegen das ganze
Vermögen der Vorstellungen hält, dessen sich das Gemüt im Gefühl
seines Zustandes bewusst wird.*

(§ 1790a; 1)

The thought Kant is trying to express is given as much in the form
as in the content of the sentence. So if the syntax is simplified in
translation, the thought is lost. Here is an attempt at a translation
which I will follow with an unravelling of its argument.

> To take up a regular and appropriate building with one's
> capacity for knowledge (whether it be in a clear or confused
> mode of representation), is something quite different from
> being conscious of this representation with a sensation of
> delight. Here the representation is tied wholly to the Subject,
> indeed to its feeling of life – under the name of the feeling
> of pleasure or displeasure – which founds a quite particular
> capacity for distinguishing and estimating which contributes
> nothing to knowledge, but which compares the given represen-
> tation in the subject with that whole capacity for representation
> of which the *Gemüt*, in feeling its condition, becomes conscious.

In the first sentence Kant rejects Baumgarten's identification
of pleasure and consciousness: the consciousness involved in a
representation taken up by capacity of knowledge (clear or confused)
is distinct from being conscious of it with a sensation of pleasure.
Kant thus distinguishes two modes of consciousness, one expressed
in clear and confused representations, the other in pleasurable and
displeasurable ones, and insists that they must not be confused. He
analyses the feeling of pleasure in the next serpentine sentence. Along
with the shift in the object of the sentence, from representation to
the feeling of pleasure or displeasure back to the representation, goes
a change in the status of the representation. To begin with, the
representation is tied to life under the name of the feeling of pleasure/
displeasure; it then submerges as the feeling is taken to found a
capacity for discrimination and estimation which makes no contribution
to knowledge. On surfacing again in the next clause, the representation
now finds itself being compared *by* this capacity of distinction and
estimation with the complete capacity for representation. With a final
turn of the screw this capacity is then characterized as that of which
the *Gemüt* becomes conscious in feeling its condition.

The reflexive subtlety with which Kant attempts to define his position against Baumgarten's verges on incomprehensibility. Why is the representation referred twice; first *to* the feeling of life, under the name of the feeling of pleasure/displeasure, and then *by* the feeling of pleasure/displeasure to the entire capacity for representation? As a representation, would it not have been referred to the feeling of life by the capacity for representation in the first place? But then why should its traces be covered and it be re-represented under the sign of faculty of distinction and estimation to this faculty? Why should this be the source of pleasure when the representation has already been tied to the feeling of life under the name of the feeling of pleasure/displeasure? Finally, why is the capacity for representation described as that which the *Gemüt* becomes conscious of in feeling its condition?

The reader who has just turned over the first page of the 'Analytic' has not been prepared by the author even to recognize such questions. The problem only becomes visible in the definition of life made later in the *Critique*, which I cited at the head of this section. There the *Gemüt* is identified with 'the life principle itself', allowing us to identify the 'feeling of life' at the beginning of the second sentence with the *Gemüt*'s feeling of its condition at the end. We should also note that in § 29 the feeling of life is hindered and furthered from within and without the subject. This clarifies the change in the status of the representation in our passage from being referred *to* the feeling of life to being referred *by* it. From *without*, our representation is tied to the feeling of life in order to establish whether it hinders or furthers it; if it hinders, it is displeasurable; if it furthers, it is pleasurable. But this feeling of life is not constant, but is affected by the representations which it encounters; it is the feeling of its condition. Therefore our representation contributes *within* life to what it means to further and hinder life. The representation is situated reflexively as both contributing to the consciousness of the furtherance of life, while also being estimated according to it. All of which proves that the relation of pleasure and consciousness is far more involved than was imagined by Baumgarten's aesthetics.

The initial negation of Baumgarten's position on consciousness and pleasure is fairly straightforward, as is Kant's distinction between clarity of consciousness and pleasure. But the extremely convoluted effort to state an alternative relation of pleasure and consciousness violates any norm of orderly philosophical procedure. But is the third *Critique* concerned with the orderly unfolding of concepts? We should heed Kant's warning in the Preface and read his *Critique* less as the unwinding of a thread of argument than as the attempt to unknot difficulty. It is not that he anticipates in the second paragraph of his treatise an extremely intricate argument which he unfolds in the course of exposition; rather his own position is always in anticipation, emerging momentarily among the fragments thrown up by the clash of the traditions.

The defining characteristic of the quality of the judgement of taste – that it is without interest – follows from Kant's philosophy of 'life'. Life is defined as the maximization of activity, and the distinction of pleasure/displeasure aligned with that of activity/passivity. In the two traditions of taste and aesthetic the activity of the subject is restricted, albeit in different ways. In the theory of taste the activity of the subject is restricted through its relation to an object; while in aesthetic theory it is restricted by its relation to a determinate concept or law. In both cases the existence of an interest, whether in the object or the law, compromises the activity of the subject and restricts its pleasure: 'An object of inclination, and one which a law of reason imposes on our desire, leaves us no freedom to turn anything into an object of pleasure. All interest presupposes a want, or calls one forth; and, being a ground determining approval, deprives the judgement on the object of its freedom' (§ 5). The interest in an object or law restricts the productive capacity of the subject; its freedom to transform an object into an object of pleasure. Against the interested accounts of the quality of the judgement of taste, Kant points to a different relation to an object which consists in its transformation into an object of pleasure; this relation is characterized as the maximization of regular activity, or the proportion of freedom and conformity to law.

We have seen the difficulty involved in expressing this relation in the context of the quality of the judgement of taste. It is also apparent when Kant turns to the quantity of the judgement. The aesthetic judgement of taste appears to be universal, unlike feelings which are 'private'; but this universality is quite unlike the familiar universality of the concept. The universal issues from neither feeling nor law, but from communication. The relation to an object expressed in the feeling of pleasure includes a reference to other human beings as a constitutive moment. But this reference, this inclusion, this constitution, while obligatory is not legislated. The path toward expressing the relation of pleasure and the other passes through the absence of interest:

> For, since the delight is not based on any inclination of the Subject (or any other deliberate interest), but the Subject feels himself completely *free* in respect of the liking which he accords to the object, he can find as reason for his delight no personal

conditions to which his own subjective self might alone be party. Hence he must regard it as resting on what he may also presuppose in every other person; and therefore he must believe that he has reason for demanding a similar delight from every one.

(§ 6)

The subject finds itself free, and wishes to share this freedom by presupposing it in everyone else; but this largesse is not disinterested, since it establishes an obligation: the subject *demands* agreement.

The judgement has 'general validity' which 'denotes the validity of the reference of a representation, not to the cognitive faculties, but to the feeling of pleasure or displeasure of every Subject' (§ 8). The representation is referred to the feeling of pleasure and displeasure, and the capacity to experience this feeling imputed to everyone else. But the bestowal of the capacity founds the validity of the judgement, a validity which is unlegislated but nonetheless legitimate. The legitimacy or validity rests on communication, or speaking with a universal voice. When we call an object beautiful we make a call to the other and 'believe ourselves to be speaking with a universal voice and lay claim to the concurrence of every one' (§ 8). The bestowal of the capacity to experience pleasure and displeasure can only take place in speech, although the obligation which this capacity establishes is outside language.

The problem of the relation between the feeling of pleasure and displeasure and its enunciation in the language of judgement develops into the question of the priority, in a judgement of taste, of the feeling of pleasure/displeasure and the estimation of the object. The discussion in § 9 on the relative priority of pleasure and judgement in a judgement of taste is conducted in terms of pleasure and communication. Kant describes the question of priority as the 'key to the critique of taste' and strives in his answer to avoid both the solipsism of feeling and the legislative violence of the concept.

Kant approaches the question by claiming that communication precedes the feeling of pleasure, but he then veers off by subordinating both of them to the '*Gemütszustand* that presents itself in the mutual relation of the powers of representation so far as they tie [*beziehen*] a given representation to *cognition in general*' (§ 9). The *Gemütszustand* that arises from the tying of representation and knowledge in general is pleasure: it 'must be one of a feeling of the free play of the powers of representation in a given representation for cognition in general'. The mutual alignment of the powers of representation evokes pleasure, but it also establishes the possibility of communication, since 'the

subjective universal communicability of the mode of representation
. . . can be nothing else than the *Gemütszustand* in the free play of
imagination and understanding (so far as these mutually accord, as
is requisite for *cognition* in general)' (§ 9).

Both the feeling of pleasure/displeasure and communicability come
down to a *Gemütszustand* which is the 'agreement' or 'accord' of the
cognitive powers. But this does not exactly address the problem of
the relative priority of communication and the feeling of pleasure.
Rather it restates the question by pointing to their shared origin in
a *Gemütszustand*, which accords or proportions the cognitive powers.
The 'key question' of the relative priority of estimation and feeling
in the judgement of taste now becomes the 'lesser question of the
way in which we become conscious, in a judgement of taste, of a
reciprocal subjective common accord of the powers of cognition'
(§ 9). Kant suggests we must be conscious of this accord before we
can communicate it; but what is the status of this consciousness, is
it a feeling or a concept?

After rephrasing his question Kant returns from the discourse of
communication and feeling to that of estimation and feeling which
was announced in his heading. What is at stake in the question is
the access to the accord of the faculties which exceeds judgement.
The experience of this accord consists neither in passive sensation
nor in the concept. Kant describes this experience through a
comparison of schematism and the judgement of taste. Both refer to
the fundamental accord of the cognitive powers, with the difference
that schematism is formalized and rigid, obeying a restricted economy,
while pleasure in the beautiful is supple and issues in an augmentation
of activity. Now it seems as if the accord or 'subjective unity of the
relation' can only be known through the sensation of pleasure, which
Kant, consistent with his earlier alignment of pleasure and life, sees
in 'The quickening [*Belebung*] of both faculties (imagination and
understanding) to an indefinite, but yet, thanks to the given
representation, harmonious activity, such as belongs to cognition in
general, [which] is the sensation whose universal communicability is
postulated by the judgement of taste' (§ 9). So here, in contrast to
the earlier statement that the communicability of the feeling of
pleasure is prior to the feeling of pleasure, communicability follows
the sensation of the quickening of the faculties. But the sensation in
question remains aloof from sensibility as the consciousness of life
which 'can be no other consciousness than that which consists in the
sensation of the effect of the relieved play of the mutually
harmonizing enlivened powers [*Gemütskräfte*] (the imagination and the
understanding)' (§ 9). Furthermore, this consciousness of life arises

from the same 'proportionate accord' of the powers 'which we require for all cognition' (§ 9).

The passages on the universality of the judgement of taste point toward an analysis of the phenomenon of universality in general, especially its relation to the accord of the imagination and the understanding. Fundamental to this analysis is an approximation to accord which is not a rigid alignment or mechanical rule, as in the schematism, but is a self-augmenting activity. The consciousness of this active proportion which underlies all knowledge is experienced as pleasure and founds not only the universality of the judgement of taste, but judgement in general. The difficulty of this section arises from stating the consciousness of this proportion in the language of judgement. Kant can only point to such a consciousness through the negation of the accounts of the relation of pleasure and consciousness in taste and aesthetic. Pleasure in the beautiful does not consist in the relation to an object or to the law, but is the consciousness of the active accord of the cognitive powers. As such it includes elements of objectivity and the law, but their relation remains unstated and perhaps unstatable.

The third moment of the relation of the judgement of taste directly faces the problem of relating the subject's pleasure and the object of representation. Relation in transcendental logic is the specific relation of the subject and the object of knowledge, or in the case of the aesthetic judgement of taste, the relation of the subjective pleasure and the representation which provokes it. Once again, Kant states the problem and the conditions of its solution in terms of the transcendental distinction and the two traditions, arriving at what appears to be a negative characterization of the relation of the aesthetic judgement of taste: '*Beauty* is the form of *finality* in an object, so far as perceived in it *apart from the representation of an end*' (§ 17). In this section, which is crucial for any attempt to legitimate the aesthetic judgement of taste, Kant remains with the negation of the two traditions, although he does intimate the notion of form which becomes increasingly important in the course of the *Critique*.

The difficulty of the third moment lies in legitimating the relation between the form of the representation and the feeling of pleasure in the subject. The establishment of this relation is complicated by the disqualification of the main relation known to human beings – causality. As a concept of the understanding, causality is inadequate to express the more fundamental relation evinced by the feeling of pleasure:

> To determine *a priori* the connexion of the feeling of pleasure
> or displeasure as an effect, with some representation or other

(sensation or concept) as its cause, is utterly impossible; for that would be a causal relation which (with objects of experience) is always one that can only be cognized *a posteriori* and with the help of experience.

(§ 12)

Kant immediately qualifies this comment by adverting to the causality of freedom proposed in the *Critique of Practical Reason*, but then qualifies the qualification by saying that the feeling of respect was not 'caused' by the determination of the will, but simply expressed such determination. The notion of causality is inappropriate for describing practical relations, since it is inseparable from the form of temporality. Similarly with the judgement of taste. There can be no question of the causality of beauty, although Kant does introduce an index of this relation which might, by analogy, be described as causal.

The analogy of cause is introduced in the definition of pleasure proposed in § 10. This definition initially strikes the reader as an unexpected innovation, until its purpose is revealed in § 12. It reads:

The consciousness of the causality of a representation in respect of the state of the Subject as one tending *to preserve a given continuance* of that state, may here be said to denote in a general way what is called pleasure; whereas displeasure is that representation which contains the ground for converting the state of the representations into their opposite (for hindering or removing them).

(§ 10)

The consciousness of the unstatable causality (causal only by analogy) is registered in the desire to perpetuate a given state, while displeasure is indicated by the desire to change the state. This consciousness is an index of an otherwise unstatable relation in the same way as the feeling of respect was indicative of the causality of the moral law.

The preservation of a given condition requires that the subject augments its activity, 'The consciousness of mere formal finality in the play of the cognitive faculties of the Subject attending a representation whereby an object is given, is the pleasure itself, because it involves a determining ground of the Subject's activity in respect of the quickening of its cognitive powers' (§ 120). The consciousness of such activity is pleasure itself, but the cause of augmentation – the character of the relation between subject and object – must be rigorously distinguished from the causality of the understanding. Although we may only speak of causality by analogy, the augmentation of activity or consciousness of life as pleasure, 'still involves an inherent causality, that, namely, of *preserving a continuance* of the state of the representation itself and the active engagement of the cognitive powers without ulterior aim. We *dwell* on the contemplation of the beautiful because this contemplation strengthens and reproduces itself.' (§ 12). The causality of pleasure can only be perceived in the desire to preserve a given condition; and this preservation requires the augmentation of activity.

Kant distinguishes tarrying with beauty from lingering with charm; they are 'analogous' but the former is active and augmentative, while the latter 'keeps arresting the attention' because the *'Gemüt* is passive' (§ 12). Kant maintains this distinction throughout his elucidation of the form of causality and its object in the aesthetic judgement of taste. The distinction is couched in terms of the traditions of taste and aesthetic. In §§ 13–14 he distinguishes the roles of design and charm in a judgement of taste in terms of pleasure as *consciousness of life* and pleasure as *sensation*. In a rigorous deployment of the transcendental distinction Kant insists 'A judgement of taste, therefore, is only pure in so far as its determining ground is tainted with no merely empirical delight' (§ 12). Design has precedence over the content of a judgement, although this distinction is taken in an unexpected direction.

While distinguishing the pleasure in the beautiful from the agreeableness of an object, Kant avoids privileging the concept over the content of a judgement. In § 15 he again rejects the Baumgartian account of aesthetic perfection for eliding the transcendental distinction:

> Beauty, therefore, as a formal subjective finality, involves no thought whatsoever of a perfection of the object, as a would-be formal finality which yet, for all that, is objective: and the distinction between the concepts of the beautiful and the good, which represents both as differing only in their logical form, the first being merely a confused, the second a clearly defined, concept of perfection, while otherwise alike in content and origin, all goes for nothing: for then there would be no *specific* difference between them.
>
> (§ 15)

Such an elision evokes the amphiboly already exposed in the first *Critique*, one in which 'we shall find ourselves with an understanding judging by sense, or a sense representing its objects by concepts – a mere choice of contradictions' (§ 15). It is necessary both to observe the distinction and so avoid the contradiction, and then to transgress it in a controlled way.

It is the spirit of the transcendental distinction that Kant proceeds to his notorious distinction of free and dependent beauty: 'The first presupposes no concept of what the object should be; the second does presuppose such a concept and, with it, an answering perfection of the object' (§ 16). The establishment of free beauty rests on the distinction of charm and design which follows that of the agreeable and the perfect. But as we saw above, the transcendental distinction is made to be broken, but legitimately, under controlled conditions. In this light it is incorrect to regard the emphasis on design and free beauty as Kant's last word on beauty, for as he admits, the distinction is only a methodological device for assessing the biased claims of tradition: 'This distinction enables us to settle many disputes about beauty on the part of critics; for we may show them how one side is dealing with free beauty, and the other with that which is dependent: the former passing a pure judgement of taste, the latter one that is applied intentionally' (§ 16). The distinction itself, however, does not constitute a statement of the principle of the aesthetic judgement of taste, but merely offers an aid to orientation.

A statement of the principle, or legitimate transgression of the transcendental distinction, is nevertheless ventured in the discussion of the 'Ideal of Beauty' in §§ 14 and 17. After distinguishing the pure judgement of taste from the agreeable and the charming, Kant goes on to a more dialectical understanding of the relation of charm and design. Charm may bring design to light, foreground or surround it with a nimbus. The design, or as Kant calls it at the end of the section, the *form* of the object, whether in space or time, is illuminated by charm or the parerga. The parerga do not contribute directly to the beauty of the form, 'The real meaning rather is that they make this form more clearly, definitely, and completely intuitable, and besides stimulate the representation by their charm, as they excite and sustain the attention directed to the object itself' (§ 14). This understanding of the relation of sense and form in the judgement of taste exceeds the transcendental distinction by showing that form may be highlighted through sensation, and together with it excite the activity of the subject.

From the standpoint of taste, the agreeable is allowed to transgress the transcendental distinction for as long as it facilitates the revelation of form. But what is this form? It is not Baumgarten's perfection; it does not please because it is a confused perception of a perfection, but because it agrees with the transcendental proportion of the imagination and the understanding which precedes the subsumptions of the understanding. Perfection, Kant claims, differing with both Baumgarten and the medieval tradition, is not transcendental but a concept of the understanding, and so cannot be used to describe the transcendental accord of the cognitive powers.

The pleasure taken in form arises from its reference to the transcendental proportion which underlies the operations of the cognitive powers. This proportion cannot be determined causally, but may be discerned indirectly through such registers as the augmentation of activity. Using the language of the Introductions, Kant writes that the 'subjective finality of the representations in the *Gemüt* of the subject intuiting', 'gives a certain finality of the representative state of the Subject, in which the Subject feels itself quite at home in its effort to grasp a given form in the imagination, but no perfection of any Object, the latter not being here thought through any concept' (§ 15). The feeling of being at home precedes determination by concepts, and cannot be reduced to the terms of such determination. The feeling of being at home – pleasure or the consciousness of life – exceeds the transcendental distinction of concept and feeling, and refers to an experience prior to the division, 'the feeling (of the internal sense) of the concert in the play of the Gemütskräfte [is] a thing only capable of being felt'. This concert or harmony of the Gemütskräfte takes place before the understanding distinguishes between their elements.

The transgression of the transcendental distinction from the standpoint of the concept is presented in § 17. The question involves the qualification of perfection, its suitability to serve as the principle of the aesthetic judgement of taste. The only permissible perfection is one which is not a concept, and Kant warns: 'It is only throwing away labour to look for a principle of taste that affords a universal criterion of the beautiful by definite concepts; because what is sought is a thing impossible and inherently contradictory' (§ 17). However, the communicability of the 'sensation of delight and aversion' exists without a concept, and offers a 'weak' criterion for the existence 'of grounds deep-seated and shared alike by all men, underlying their agreement in estimating the forms under which objects are given to them' (§ 17). Kant carefully refers to the forms under which objects are given and not the objects themselves, and form, according to § 14, registers the fundamental proportion of the cognitive powers.

In § 17, form's agreement with the fundamental accord is realized through a non-conceptual perfection named the 'ideal'. The ideal is the perfect individual embodiment of the forms through which individuals appear. It cannot be deemed to exist apart from its incarnation, since this would equate it with a concept of the understanding; however, it may be used to judge or estimate individual approximations to form, but not discursively.[14] The ideal is not 'capable of being represented by means of concepts, but only in an individual representation' (§ 17). However, since human judgement can only approximate to a presentation of the ideal, a new, extended notion of judgement is brought into play. This is the view of judgement as orientation, in which the definition of the ideal is sharpened by its use in estimating forms and objects. This model of judgement avoids the difficulties of relating estimation and subsumption which afflict determinate judgement, and offers a non-conceptual mode of estimation. This model rests on the play of 'idea' as a 'concept of reason' and 'ideal' as the 'representation of an individual existence as adequate to an idea'. The process of 'adequating' ideal to idea, the relation of universal and individual which it involves, differs entirely from the conforming of intuition to concept in judgement.

Kant explores this process of adequation through a distinction between the normal and the rational ideas. In the normal idea the issues of judging beauty and estimating teleology come together. The normal idea expresses the form through which individuals come into appearance, and is constituted by the comparison of individual differences and similarities. Here, the possibility of estimation follows from the recognition of a proportionality according to which differences may be distinguished:

> The normal idea must draw from experience the constituents which it requires for the form of an animal of a particular kind. But the greatest finality in the construction of this form – that which would serve as a universal norm for forming an estimate of each individual of the species in question – the image that, as it were, forms an intentional basis underlying the technic of nature, to which no separate individual, but only the race as a whole is adequate, has its seat merely in the idea of the judging Subject.
>
> (§ 17)

What characterizes the normal idea, and distinguishes it from a concept, is its proportionality – it is neither individual nor universal but between the two – and also its capacity for 'being fully in concreto in a model image' without merely being the exemplification of a concept, nor attaining the individual incarnation of the 'ideal'.

Kant asks how it is possible to judge according to the normal idea, a reference to the aporia involved in deriving an 'image' from the comparison of differences without first postulating a principle of distinction. He claims only 'to render the process to some extent intelligible (for who can wrest nature's whole secret from her?)' and describes the process in terms of the production of a 'mean contour' through an unconscious superimposition: 'if the mind is engaged upon comparisons, we may well suppose that it can in actual fact, though the process is unconscious, superimpose as it were one image upon another, and from the coincidence of a number of the same kind arrive at a mean contour which serves as a common standard for all' (§ 17). This statement is developed into a full scale optical metaphor. The superimposition of the images by the 'power of imagination' is said to lead to an intensification of light around the 'normal contour'. The individual images 'fall one upon the other' and 'in the space where they come most together, and within the contour where the place is illuminated by the greatest concentration of colour, one gets a perception of the *average size* . . . and this is the stature of the beautiful man' (§ 17). The epiphany of the norm marks the revelation through light of form. This view of perception as the intensification of the light within each individual is the closest Kant came to Aquinas's theory of perception. Perception according to the normal idea consists in the illumination of pure form through the intensification of the light in individual things. The active accord here shines out as beauty and life.

In the case of charm, the form is revealed by contrast with the parerga; in a philosophical chiaroscuro, the light of form is emphasized by the shadows surrounding it. With the normal idea, by contrast, the intensity of light and colour limns the form, which shines through not by contrast with the parerga, but through the coincidence of intensities. The normal idea is a presentation of form through the intensification of the light which shines dimly in each individual. It provides a canon for beauty, 'the form which constitutes the essential condition of all beauty' but cannot be used as an organon. It 'is not derived from proportions taken from experience as *definite rules*' because it is 'according to this idea that rules for forming estimates first become possible' (§ 17); but neither is it constitutive. It has the peculiar ontological status of a 'floating' or 'hovering' image of a genus.

an intermediate between all singular intuitions of individuals, with their manifold variations – a floating image for the whole genus [*das zwischen allen einzelnen . . . schwebende Bild für die ganze Gattung*], which nature has set as an archetype underlying those of her products that belong to the same species, but which in no single case she seems to have completely attained.

(§ 17)

The 'floating image' is neither subjective nor objective, it enables judgement as orientation to take place, but may not itself be used in subsumption. In Kant's words, it is 'far from giving the complete *archetype of beauty* in the genus' (§ 17) since it only gives the 'form that constitutes the indispensable condition of all beauty' (§ 17). It provides the light in which beauty may appear, but it is not a sufficient condition for its appearance.

The normal idea does not contain 'anything specifically characteristic', that is, it does not specify what may appear within it: it is a horizon. The ideal of the beautiful, by contrast, is also characteristic, since it specifies the form through which the moral ends of humanity may come to appearance. The creation or even the estimation of a characteristic form, which includes both the general formal condition of the normal idea, and its individual embodiment, is the work of genius, and 'involves a union of the pure ideas of reason and great imaginative power, in one who would even form an estimate of it, not to speak of being the author of its presentation' (§ 17). With the ideal of the beautiful, the individual incarnation of the idea, Kant anticipates the doctrine of genius developed later in the *Critique*.

This anticipation offers some important clues for understanding the full development of the doctrine. Genius is not simply subjective expression, but consists in embodying the 'floating image' in an individual ideal. We shall return to this below. What is of interest now is that the discussions of the relation of the normal idea and ideal of the beautiful are used to conclude the moment of the relation of the judgement of taste. This relation or 'adequation' of idea and ideal is not causal in any uncomplicated sense, since it transcends the transcendental distinction. In this section Kant tries to redetermine the relation of the beautiful object to the subject. This relation must not be thought across the terms of sensibility and the understanding, or object and subject, but is a different alignment, one which consists in the revelation of a form which corresponds to the fundamental proportion of imagination and understanding.

The importance of the fundamental proportion is underlined in the final and key moment of the modality of the judgement of taste. The beautiful representation is one which 'apart from a concept, is cognized as an object of *necessary* delight' (§ 22). In the exposition of this moment Kant follows the recognizable procedure of distinguishing between the absence of the required necessity in those accounts which emphasize the sensibility and rationality of the judgement of taste. The presupposition (and the result!) of this distinction is the existence of a fundamental accord of sensibility and understanding which underlies their empirical agreement in determinate judgement. In § 20 Kant points out that were judgements of taste 'in possession of a definite objective principle' they would claim unconditioned necessity, and that 'were they devoid of any principle' there would be no question of necessity. The judgement of taste obeys neither alternative, so it 'must have a subjective principle, and one which determines what pleases or displeases, by means of feeling only and not through concepts, but yet with universal validity (§ 20). But what is the nature of this peculiar principle and why must it be necessary?

Kant labels this principle the 'common sense' (*sensus communis*), a term he uses descriptively and prescriptively. The first, descriptive usage, stems from the Aristotelean tradition, while the second, prescriptive, is taken from Shaftesbury. It both describes and explains the necessity of the judgement of taste as arising from a common sense by which we claim the concurrence of others with our judgement. It is not to be thought of as a sense or a faculty 'but the effect arising from the free play of our powers of cognition' (§ 20). It is the outcome of the play of the cognitive powers, and not its source.

In § 21 Kant inquires further into the character of this 'effect'. He deduces from the communicability of our judgements and their attendant conviction the necessity of a 'harmony' (*Übereinstimmung*) between our 'cognitions and judgements' and the object. He then claims that this attunement or proportion of the cognitive powers is common to all subjects:

> if cognitions are to admit of communication, then our *Gemütszustand*, that is, the way in which the cognitive powers are attuned for cognition generally, and in fact that proportionality [*diejenige Proportion*] which is required for representation (through which an object is given to us), from which knowledge is made [*daraus Erkenntnis zu machen*], must also admit of being universally communicated, as, without this, which is the subjective condition of the act of knowing, knowledge, as an effect, would not arise.
>
> (§ 21)

In this passage Kant confirms that the proportionality of the powers precedes the giving of objects through representation. Experience presupposes this proportionality, each act of representation marking a certain ratio of knowledge powers (*Erkenntniskräfte*). A given object, then,

> through the intervention of sense, sets the imagination at work in arranging the manifold, and the imagination, in turn, the understanding in giving to this arrangement the unity of concepts. But this attunement of the cognitive powers has different proportion according to the differences of objects that are given [*Aber diese Stimmung der Erkenntniskräfte hat, nach Verschiedenheit der Objekte, die gegeben werden, eine verschiedene Proportion*].
>
> (§ 21)

This is not only one of Kant's clearest statements of the active proportion of the knowledge powers which is disposed for each act of representation; it also justifies the necessity of the aesthetic judgement of taste.

We saw above that the beautiful form excites the activity of the subject's representative powers by reference to a proportion which underlies the normal deployment of those powers: 'there must be [a particular proportion] in which this internal ratio suitable for enlivening [*Belebung*] (one power by the other) is best adapted for both powers [*Gemütskräfte*] in respect of cognition (of given objects) generally; and this attunement [*Stimmung*] can only be determined through feeling (not through concepts)' (§ 21). The fundamental proportion inspires the mutual vivification of the knowledge powers, a vivification which occurs in every experience but which is only recognized in the case of beautiful objects. It can only be determined in terms of feeling, since it founds and exceeds cognition, but this feeling is not one of the sensibility, but is the *sensus communis*.

Kant proposes to make the accord or proportionality of the knowledge powers – the *sensus communis* – into a normative idea of the judgement of taste. From this norm he will establish the necessity of the aesthetic judgement of taste. Although it is a feeling, the common sense is not a private, but a 'public sense'. The subject proposes his feeling as exemplary: 'Here I put forward my judgement of taste as an example of the judgement of common sense, and attribute to it on that account *exemplary* validity. Hence common sense is a mere ideal norm' (§ 22). In other words, common sense, like the 'normal idea' of the third moment, is a 'floating image of a genus'. But if this is so, what is the obligation claimed in the 'ought' of common sense, and where lies the objectivity in the 'objective necessity of the coincidence of the feeling of all with the particular feeling of each' (§ 22)? If the common sense is not constitutive – and it cannot be without becoming a determinate judgement – then what is the source of its necessity? Where is the con in the sensus? Kant at this point postpones his investigations – 'These are questions which as yet we are neither willing nor in a position to investigate' (§ 22). They will be investigated later in considering the relation of genius and tradition.

The answer to these fundamental questions clearly involves the proportion of the powers which constitute common sense, and whose working is both descriptive and prescriptive. Kant hazards some guesses about the nature of this proportion in the 'General Remark' with which he closes the first part of the 'Analytic of the Beautiful'. Everything points, he says, to taste being a critical faculty which estimates an object according to the 'free conformity to law of the imagination'. However, instead of relating this paradoxical 'free conformity' to the fundamental accord which is unstatable in the language of judgement, Kant tries to bring it under judgement by representing it in terms of the distinction of imagination and understanding.

This representation distributes the active proportion of the powers – the self-augmenting realization and restriction of life – between the productivity of the imagination and the legislation of the understanding. The productive capacity of imagination is its freedom, but one which seems arbitrary: 'If now, imagination must in the judgement of taste be regarded in its freedom, then, to begin with, it is not taken as reproductive, as in its subjection to the laws of association, but as productive and asserting an activity of its own (as originator of arbitrary forms of possible intuitions)' (§ 22). But the understanding does not trust this productive activity to legislate itself; it takes upon itself to give it law. Kant allies himself with the understanding when he refuses the paradox of 'free conformity to law' for the productive activity of the imagination: 'But that the *imagination* should be both *free and of itself conformable to law*, i.e. carry autonomy with it, is a contradiction. The understanding alone gives a law' (§ 22). However, the contradiction exists only in the eyes of the understanding, and its legislative enactments do not exhaust the ways in which the fundamental proportion may be realized. There always remains the possibility of a different economy, a different ratio of production and legislation.

Kant however restricts his choice to the subjective and objective attunement of the imagination and understanding, both of which borrow their accord from the same source. And this source is one which exceeds the understanding, and can only appear paradoxical in its eyes. Kant gives it some air in the formulations of the subjective attunement, but only as a contrary to the objective:

> Hence it is only a conformity to law without a law, and a subjective harmonizing of the imagination and the understanding without an objective one – which latter would mean that the representation was referred to a definite concept of the object – that can consist with the free conformity to law of the understanding (which has also been called finality apart from an end) and with the specific character of a judgement of taste.
>
> (§ 22)

But some positive characterizations do emerge from the paradoxes of the subjective attunement which were suffocated in the earlier demand for law. The subjective harmony augments activity while the objective harmony restricts it; the former is supple and analogical while the latter is rigid and subsumptive. The objective harmony with its 'stiff regularity' is 'repugnant to taste'; 'it imposes an irksome constraint upon the imagination' (§ 22). The subjective harmony, on the contrary, augments the activity of the knowledge powers and would perpetuate itself, for 'Anything that gives the imagination scope for unstudied and final play is always fresh to us' (§ 22).

Since Herder's metacritique in *Kalligone* and Hegel's *Aesthetics* the 'Analytic of the Beautiful' has been reproached for reducing beauty to judgement. But this reading – even under the aegis of Heidegger and Derrida – underestimates the ways in which Kant's text repeatedly undoes itself. Against the rituals of judgement, Kant consistently affirms pleasure as consciousness of life, as the unrestricted economy of a self-augmenting proportion, one which unites production and legislation. The text weaves in and out of tradition, using both it and the 'second-hand frame' of the table of judgements as a relief on which to trace some of the characteristics of pleasure, thought as the consciousness of life.

But there is a darker side to the play in the light of life. With the 'Analytic of the Sublime' Kant turns to another way of augmenting activity. Instead of being at home in the world – instead of the vivifying proportion of the knowledge powers – he turns to the augmentation of activity through estrangement and the deliberate violation of harmony and proportion.

Analytic of the Sublime

The point of excess for the imagination (towards which it is driven in the apprehension of the intuition) is like an abyss in which it fears to lose itself; yet again for the rational idea of the supersensible it is not excessive, but comformable to law, and directed to drawing out such an effort on the part of the imagination: and so in turn as much a source of attraction as it was repellent to mere sensibility.

Kant, *Critique of Judgement-Power*

In the previous chapter Kant's doctrine of judgement as orientation was seen to have its darker side in the limitless degradation of the senses by an imagination driven toward totality by reason. Correspondingly, in the *Critique of Judgement-Power*, the exposition of the aesthetic judgement of taste according to a fundamental proportion attained by a subject in its contemplation of a beautiful form is complemented by a treatment of the transgression of this proportion in the sublime. The proportion of the knowledge powers signifies an orientation prior to determinate judgement (itself a limited trope of orientation, moving from the universal to the individual). By virtue of its foundational role, this proportion cannot be enunciated in the language of judgement, but only in the feeling of pleasure/displeasure. But is this experience as fundamental as it appears in the 'Analytic of the Beautiful'? In the 'Analytic of the Sublime' the reader experiences not only the transgression of this proportion, the sacrifice of beauty, but is also initiated into the knowledge that beauty, proportion, and life may themselves rest on sacrifice.

In the 'Analytic of the Sublime' Kant examines the relation of proportionality and activity/passivity. This relation was implied in the identification of life and activity in the 'Analytic of the Beautiful', although now it is explicitly thematized in the organization of material in terms of the 'mathematical' and 'dynamic' sublime. In one of the most violent gestures in philosophy Kant 'sacrifices' beauty, breaking the proportionality which made human beings 'at home in nature' and exposing human activity as violence against nature and an 'outrage' upon itself. Human beings are not 'at home in nature' as the existence of a fundamental proportion would suggest, but are violently opposed to it.

In spite of their apparently opposed characters, the beautiful and the sublime share a suspicious number of family resemblances. Both involve orientation, in the one a movement toward proportionality, in the other, a movement toward disproportionality. Although seemingly opposed, both movements contribute to 'life'; both 'judgements' are reflective and distinguished from determinate judgements. Their tropes each involve an alignment of the powers: the beautiful aligns the power of presentation with the understanding, the sublime aligns it with the reason. The differences between the beautiful and the sublime appear as the implicated opposition of positive and negative quantities. The beautiful is, as we have seen, 'a question of the form of the object, and this consists in limitation', while the sublime is 'devoid of form' (§ 23). The beautiful 'is directly attended with a feeling of the furtherance of life', while the sublime is 'brought about by the feeling of a momentary check [*Hemmung*] to the vital forces [*Lebenskräfte*] followed at once by a discharge [*Ergiessung*] all the more powerful' (§ 23). The pleasure in the beautiful is figured as positive, that taken in the sublime negative; but as we saw in the previous chapter, positive and negative quantities involve relation, and it turns out that the feeling of the sublime also contributes to the furtherance of activity and life, although indirectly, through a mediation.

The mutual implication of the beautiful and the sublime is also manifest in their 'most important and vital distinction'. The beautiful object 'conveys a finality in its form making the object appear, as it were, pre-adapted to our power of judgement', while the sublime 'may appear to contravene the ends of our power of judgement, and to be ill-adapted to our faculty of presentation, and to be as it were an outrage on the imagination' (§ 23). Both the beautiful and the sublime involve a disposition of the power of judgement; in the first objects *appear* in agreement with its finality, while in the case of the sublime, objects *appear* to violate (*gewalten*) the finality of judgement.

Even outrages have their logic, and Kant orders his according to quantity, quality, relation, and modality. The sublime outrage on the imagination is universal, without interest (a disinterested outrage!), subjectively final, and necessary. But in contrast to the 'Analytic of the Beautiful', the four topics are disposed into the two groupings of the 'Mathematical' and the 'Dynamic' Sublime. The 'Mathematical Sublime' is concerned with the transgression of proportion, while the 'Dynamic Sublime' concentrates upon the negotiation of activity and passivity. Yet, in spite of the logical armature, there is no sense in which the sublime may be considered a feeling predicated of an object; indeed, the logical table is used to present the impossibility of predication.

The moment of the quantity of the sublime presented in §§ 25–6 has two main aspects. The first is a description of the experience of the sublime, the second an account of why the 'pleasure' provoked by this experience may be considered universally valid. The description of the experience of the sublime takes in the degradation of proportion, the outrage on the imagination, and the pleasure arising from the feeling of superiority which accompanies these apparently degrading and outrageous acts.

The sublime is defined as the absolutely great; but what is greatness, and can it be absolute? Kant states that greatness is comparative; it is not a discrete quantity, but always implies a ratio or proportion:

> What, then, is the meaning of the assertion that anything is great, or small, or of medium size? What is indicated is not a pure concept of understanding, still less an intuition of sense; and just as little is it a concept of reason, for it does not import any principle of cognition. It must, therefore, be a concept of judgement, or have its source in one, and must introduce as basis of the judgement a subjective finality of the representation with reference to the power of judgement.
>
> (§ 25)

The constitution of size by subjective finality has three main aspects. The first is 'multiplicity (number of units)' followed by 'the magnitude of the unit (the measure)'. But then an additional factor is required, a decision on the measure, which is always comparative:

> since the magnitude of this unit [of measure] in turn always requires something else as its measure and as the standard of its comparison, and so on, we see that the computation of the magnitude of phenomena is, in all cases, utterly incapable of affording us any absolute concept of a magnitude, and can, instead, only afford one that is always based on comparison.
>
> (§ 25)

Here, not only is the sublime's absolutely great reduced to an act of comparison, but the fundamental proportion of the beautiful has gone as well. Instead we return to a new version of the aporia of judgement in which an ascription of greatness involves a prior act of orientation which establishes a horizon of comparison 'and so on'. The problem now arises of the nature of the act of comparison, and its relation to the act which founds the measure or horizon of comparison.

In tackling this problem Kant opts for a move anticipated in his pre-critical philosophy; this entails an original appropriation, an 'intuitive immediate grasp' (*in einer Anschauung unmittelbar fassen*) of the fundamental unit of measure (*Grundmass*):

> The estimation of the magnitude of the fundamental measure
> must, therefore, consist merely in the intuitive immediate grasp,
> and the use to which our imagination can put this in presenting
> the numerical concepts: i.e. all estimation of the magnitude of
> objects of nature is in the last resort aesthetic (i.e. subjectively
> and not objectively determined).
>
> > (§ 26)

All estimation is founded in an immediate grasp which cannot be
further determined or explicated. It is an act of appropriation which
orients the activity of comparison. But once proportion is established
in this way, it becomes vulnerable to disruption, as the original
appropriation fails before the exorbitance of comparison.

Kant describes the instability of the fundamental unit in a phrase
reminiscent of the pre-critical phenomenology of discrimination in
the *Differentiation* and the passage on the bias of reason in the
'Methodology' of the first *Critique*:

> A tree judged by the height of man gives, at all events, a
> standard for a mountain; and, supposing this is, say, a mile
> high, it can serve as unit for the number expressing the earth's
> diameter, so as to make it intuitable; similarly the earth's
> diameter for the known planetary system; this again for the
> system of the Milky Way, and the immeasurable host of such
> systems, which go by the name of nebulae, and most likely in
> turn themselves form such a system; [this progression] holds
> out no prospect of a limit. Now in the aesthetic estimate of
> such an immeasurable whole, the sublime does not lie so much
> in the greatness of the number, as in the fact that in our
> onward advance we always arrive at proportionately greater
> units.
>
> > (§ 26)

Although orientation through the proportionality of the knowledge
powers may conduce to a feeling of being at home in the world, the
same procedure of orientation may lead to a disruption of this
proportion, and a feeling of estrangement from the universe.

The self-degradation before the immensity of the universe also
contains its opposite. The ability to disrupt proportion, to re-orient
judgement, also degrades the world, subordinating it to human
imagination, for:

we readily see that nothing can be given in nature, no matter how great we may judge it to be, which, regarded in some other relation, may not be degraded to the level of the infinitely little, and nothing so small which in comparison with some still smaller standard may not for our imagination be enlarged to the greatness of a world.

(§ 25)

Size is recognized as a product of human imagination and comparison, which finds in itself a faculty which transcends natural greatness and smallness. The possession of the power to form comparisons raises imagination above the objects which it compares. The breakdown of the intuitively established fundamental unit awakens

a feeling of the supersensible faculty within us; and it is the use to which judgement naturally puts particular objects on behalf of this latter feeling, and not the object of sense, that is absolutely great, and every other contrasted employment small. Consequently it is the disposition of soul evoked by a particular representation engaging the attention of the reflective judgement, and not the object, that is to be called sublime.

(§ 25)

The sublime arises from the activity of comparison, and not from the object which is deemed great, and to make such comparisons is deemed by Kant the human vocation (*Bestimmung*) which is alienated in objects of nature.

The exceeding of nature by judgement makes it feel superior, but also degrades the natural and sensuous side of human existence. Far beyond nature, the reflective judgement no longer 'finds itself set to a key that is final in respect of cognition generally' (§ 25). The feeling awakened by the sublime oscillates between pleasure and displeasure; it is

at once a feeling of displeasure, arising from the inadequacy of imagination in the aesthetic estimation of magnitude to attain to its estimation by reason, and a simultaneously awakened pleasure arising from this very judgement of the inadequacy of the greatest faculty of sense being in accord with ideas of reason, so far as the effort to attain to these is for us a law.

(§ 27)

The perverse pleasure in the sublime does not arise from the agreement of the form of the object with the accord of the knowledge powers, as with beauty, but from the simultaneous degradation and mastery of the subject. While the pleasure in the sublime intensifies the feeling of life by enhancing activity, the form of its activity is quite different: 'This movement, especially in its inception, may be compared with a vibration, i.e. with a rapidly alternating repulsion and attraction produced by one and the same Object' (§ 27). The perversity of this pleasure consists in the violence done by the subject to itself in sacrificing the proportion of the powers which allow it to be at home in nature.

Kant describes this violence in terms of fixing the activity of apprehension in comprehension, so abolishing the temporal condition of experience:

> the comprehension of the manifold in the unity, not of thought, but of intuition, and consequently the comprehension of the successively apprehended parts at one glance, is a retrogression that removes the time-condition in the progression of the imagination and renders *co-existence* intuitable. Therefore, since the time-series is a condition of the internal sense and of an intuition, it is a subjective movement of the imagination by which it does violence to the internal sense – a violence which must be proportionately more striking the greater the quantum which the imagination comprehends in one intuition.
>
> (§ 27)

But this act of violence characterizes all perception, all setting of proportion. Furthermore, Kant described this originary violence in the *Lectures on Philosophical Theology* as 'freedom'. Freedom is the violent appropriation which sets boundaries and establishes proportion between things; it legislates the fundamental unit of comparison to which all future comparisons must conform.

The pleasure/displeasure of the sublime foregrounds the origin of measure and law in violence, it also redeems it for perception:

> The effort, therefore, to receive in a single intuition a measure for magnitudes which it takes an appreciable time to apprehend, is a mode of representation which, subjectively considered, is contra-final, but, objectively, is requisite for the estimation of magnitude, and is consequently final. Here the very same violence which is wrought on the Subject through the

imagination is estimated as final *for the whole province* of the *Gemüt*.

(§ 27)

The proportion of normal experience originates in the abnormal experience of the sublime; the regularity of proportion has its source in the irregular violence of the sublime; and the life-enhancing form of beauty is traced back to the violent outrage which the imagination visited upon itself. The pleasure of the sublime is the consciousness of the violence of legislation, a cathartic pleasure provoked when 'the subject's very incapacity betrays the consciousness of an unlimited power of the same subject' (§ 27).

The relation of pleasure/displeasure with activity/passivity is disclosed in Kant's definition of the sublime as a 'pleasure that is only possible through the mediation of a displeasure' (§ 27). The mediating term between pleasure and displeasure – resistance – is unfolded in the sections on the 'Dynamic Sublime'. We have already come across this concept in the pre-critical phenomenology of activity and passivity. There we saw that resistance indicates the encounter between active and passive aspects of human experience. Kant expresses the resistance involved in the sublime in terms of the distinction of might and dominion: '*Might* is a power which is superior to great hindrances. It is termed *dominion* if it is also superior to that which itself possesses might' (§ 28). Kant uses this distinction to characterize the sublime: nature has might over human beings; while they possess dominion over nature. The oscillation of activity and passivity which characterizes the sublime, passive in the face of the might of nature, active in its dominion over it, is normalized in the notion of resistance.

As the locus of activity and passivity, resistance is both subjective and objective. It refers both to the might of nature and the dominion of human beings. In the following passage the first sentence refers to resistance as might, the second as dominion: 'For in forming an aesthetic estimate (no concept being present) the superiority to hindrances can only be estimated according to the greatness of resistance. Now that which we strive to resist is an evil, and, if we do not find our powers commensurate to the task, an object of fear' (§ 28). Resistance plays the same role in the sublime as form in the beautiful. It registers a relation which cannot be expressed in the language of judgement, but may be used to form estimates. In the pleasure/displeasure of the sublime, the resistance of nature, its might, is trumped by our resistance, and it is the encounter of the two resistances which provokes movement, so enhancing activity and life. This movement of resistance between subject and object is constitutive of the sublime; the might of nature alone would only evoke fear and passivity. We must overcome might, re-establish our dominion. Kant distinguishes between the dread and terror which accompanies the sight of the terrible and the joy which follows the escape from it. The sublime brings both experiences together. From a safe vantage point we dispose ourselves at once fearfully – subject to the might of the spectacle – and at the same time with joy as we realize that we are not under its dominion.

The disposition of activity and passivity in resistance is the same phenomenon as the violence of the mathematical sublime. When encountering objects in time we are subject to their might; but we bring them under dominion when we arrest them in space and determine them according to our proportions. Kant shrewdly observes that the principle of simultaneous subjection and mastery may appear 'far-fetched and subtle', but is in fact 'the foundation of the commonest judgements, although one is not always conscious of its presence' (§ 28). One is certainly unaware of its presence in the experience of beauty, since the pleasure is referred directly to the proportion. But in the pleasure of the sublime, this enhancement of activity takes place through the negotiation of subjection and mastery experienced as resistance.

In the final moment of the modality of the sublime, Kant refers to the emergence of freedom from nature's dominion as culture. He writes, 'In fact, without the development of moral ideas, that which, thanks to preparatory culture, we call sublime merely strikes the untutored man as terrifying' (§ 29). Culture consists in the ability to achieve dominion over nature, to resist its resistance. Kant sees the development of culture as accompanied by the emergence of a sublime God, an idea of divinity resting not on the might of nature, but on the dominion of the supernatural. The subjection of nature through culture rests on human beings having an object of fear, or rather respect, higher than the powers of nature, the existence of which is vouched for by the ability of the human judgement to make the great small and the small great.

The relation hinted by Kant between the pleasure of the sublime and monotheism, points to the religious vocation underlying the feelings of the beautiful and sublime. Both are concerned with the relation of pleasure and law, with attributing to the feeling of pleasure the properties of law. But this union of pleasure and law is what Kant calls the 'Kingdom of God', or final aim of human culture in the *Ethics* and *Philosophical Theology* lectures. It is not accidental that Kant's most extended discussion of the concept of culture occurs in the context of the treatment of onto-theology in the second part of the *Critique* – 'The Critique of Teleological Judgement'.

Kant returns at the end of the discussion of the judgement of the sublime to what distinguished it from the judgement of the beautiful. In the 'General Remark upon the Exposition of Aesthetic Reflective Judgements' he strings the distinction of the beautiful and the sublime together with other distinctions such as positive and negative pleasure, immediate and mediated pleasure, and love and sacrifice. The relation between the two poles of the distinction is extremely complicated. The proportion underlying beauty presupposes sacrifice, for the proportion is established through violence. The beautiful again must be sacrificed, as its origin in violence has to be exposed and brought to recognition. Pleasure must always be accompanied by displeasure, the 'vibration' or convulsion (*Erschütterung*) between pleasure and displeasure commemorating the sacrifice and the life which it purchases:

> delight in the sublime in nature is only *negative* (whereas that in the beautiful is *positive*): that is to say it is a feeling of imagination by its own act depriving itself of its freedom by receiving a final determination in accordance with a law other than of its empirical employment. In this way it gains an extension and a might greater than that which it sacrifices. But the ground of this is concealed from it, and in its place it *feels* the sacrifice or deprivation [*Aufopferung oder Beraubung*] as well as its cause, to which it is subjected.
>
> (§ 29)

The constant sacrifice and reward of an extension of power cannot be expressed in the language of the understanding, which sees in it only a 'contradiction', even though this lies at the foundation of its laws.

The pleasure taken in the sublime evokes the sacrifice involved in prostrating ourselves before nature, and so raising ourselves above it. It corresponds, in the language of the first *Critique*, to the 'restriction' and 'realization' of human freedom. To be at home in nature we first have to master it, to bring it under dominion, and then to efface our violence. The sublime is the proportion of the beautiful without this effacement, the fear and trembling of violent appropriation. It is the promotion of life through the recognition of death.

Tradition in the Deduction

> and the halo in the grotto of Antiparos is merely the work of
> water percolating through strata of gypsum.
>
>   Kant, *Critique of Judgement-Power*

After the exposition of the judgements of the beautiful and the
sublime Kant turns to their deduction, or rather, to the deduction
of the judgement of the beautiful alone, since the exposition of the
sublime suffices for a deduction. A deduction involves the citation
of the grounds for the legitimacy of a judgement, and since the
appeal to reason in the exposition of the sublime suffices to justify
its universal and necessary validity, there is no need for a discrete
deduction. The beautiful, however, since it hangs on the form of an
object, requires the ascription of an a priori principle to legitimate
its claims. But what is the nature and the source of this principle?
We shall see that Kant rests his case on an appeal to the universality
and necessity of tradition. In other words, tradition is the a priori
principle of the aesthetic judgement of taste; but further, it is a
constituent element in the production of fine art by genius.

We may start to legitimate such claims by reconsidering the dual
character of pleasure. It was shown that the issue of pleasure is both
at the centre and in the margins of the transcendental philosophy.
At first glance pleasure only involves a 'strange faculty' with the
peculiar bent of making universal and necessary 'singular judgements'
(§ 31). But on closer inspection, the deduction of such peculiar
judgements is found to involve such fundamental issues as communicability, culture, and the proportion of the powers. Such judgements
of pleasure point to a special and fundamental disposition of
judgement, one which is described as an 'estimate prior to a concept'
(§ 37) or a fundamental activity which

> Without any guiding-line of end or principle ... attends the
> ordinary apprehension of an object by means of the imagination,
> as the faculty of intuition, but which is related to the
> understanding as a faculty of concepts through a procedure of
> judgement which has also to be invoked in order to obtain the
> commonest experience.
>
>   (§ 39)

In the judgement of taste the difficulty of determining the source of this pleasure in the relation of the knowledge powers is revealed with especial clarity.

In his deduction Kant tries to contain the difficulty raised by the judgement of taste by limiting his treatment to the logical functions and peculiarities of such judgements. He insists that we 'abstract at the outset from all content of the judgement, viz. from the feeling of pleasure, and merely compare the aesthetic form with the form of objective judgements as prescribed by logic' (§ 31). The ambition to treat pleasure in the beautiful as a predicate which may be ascribed with universal and necessary validity by a subject to an object underlies the deduction. But judging in this way throws up two awkward peculiarities which threaten the whole enterprise of deduction:

> *first*, it has universal validity *a priori*, yet without having a logical universality according to concepts, but only the universality of a singular judgement. *Secondly*, it has a necessity (which must invariably rest upon *a priori* grounds) but one which depends upon no *a priori* proofs by the representation of which it would be competent to enforce the assent which the judgement of taste demands of everyone.
>
> (§ 31)

These peculiarities appear to subvert the logical analogy of the judgement of taste, as Kant concedes when he restricts the deduction to the 'solution of these logical peculiarities' (§ 31).

In the course of his solution Kant exceeds the limitations of not only the particular problem of the judgement of taste, but also the general problem of the critical philosophy regarding the possibility of synthetic, a priori judgements. From within the aporias of the judgement of taste and judgement in general, Kant appeals to tradition.

A paradox shimmers beneath the surface of the first logical peculiarity of the judgement of taste examined in § 32. We are required to treat the universality of the judgement 'as if it were objective', but not a conceptual objectivity since 'Taste lays claim simply to autonomy' (§ 32). Let's avoid 'groping about among other people's judgements and getting previous instruction from their delight in or aversion to the same object' (§ 32); don't take a vote, that's heteronomy. But what is this 'as it were' objectivity? To explain it Kant turns to a third option which is neither the heteronomy of the concept nor an empirical vote but a 'working through' (*Ausübung*) of tradition.

With the recommendation of *Ausübung* Kant returns to the

distinction of the passive and active modes of appropriating tradition outlined in the pre-critical writings. The universality of taste is formed and cultured in the active appropriation of tradition. The predecessors in tradition set an example for the 'blundering attempts' of the tyro 'with the crude equipment of his natural state' (§ 32) to measure himself against. The tyro should 'follow' tradition, that is, actively appropriate it through a 'Following [*Nachfolge*] which has reference to a precedent, and not imitation, [this] is the proper expression for all influence which the products of an exemplary author may exert upon others' (§ 32). Such influence, which enables the autonomy of the individual taste to be cultured without sacrificing it to heteronomy, establishes the universality of the judgement of taste. Kant spells it out for us: 'Taste, just because its judgements cannot be determined by concepts or precepts, is among all faculties and talents the very one that stands most in need of examples of what has in the course of culture maintained itself longest in esteem. Thus it avoids an early lapse into crudity, and a return to the rudeness of its earliest efforts' (§ 32). The universality of the judgement of taste is legitimated, surprisingly, by the active appropriation of tradition, a remembrance which surpasses both autonomy and heteronomy.

The solution of the first peculiarity of the judgement of taste, the first stage of the deduction, appeals to the active appropriation of tradition. The second peculiarity also adverts to tradition by inquiring into the mode of proof which it requires. The necessity of tradition is not mechanical, we are not on the 'treadmill of the Wolffian or some other edifice of learning' as Kant put it earlier. The proof of the necessity of the judgement does not appeal to the authority of tradition at the expense of the subject's autonomy, nor does it employ the logical proofs of the syllogism. The authority of tradition is exercised in orienting the judgement of the subject within it, educating its judgement. If the individual judgement disagrees with tradition, the judge does not abandon his position and his autonomy, but instead begins to 'harbour doubts as to whether he has formed his taste upon an acquaintance with a sufficient number of objects of a particular kind (just as one who in the distance recognizes, as he believes, something as a wood, which everyone else regards as a town, becomes doubtful of the judgement of his own eyesight)' (§ 33). Not being able to see the town for the trees makes us suspect our judgement, but it does not convince us that we are in error. However, in the development of tradition an objective principle manifests itself to which all can agree without compromising their autonomy; and this consists in the proportion of the knowledge powers. The bias of the individual judgements corrects itself in the time of tradition, and it is this ability to correct which gives the judgement of taste its necessity.

Kant promised that the solution of the two difficulties of the judgement of taste would serve as a deduction, but this solution involves the relation of the singular judgement and the tradition of judgements. The character of the 'principle' of the judgement of taste is determined by the relation of the singular judgement to tradition. Stated externally, the alignment of the singular judgement to tradition approximates to the proportion or accord of the knowledge-powers informing all judgement. The principle consists in this accord, one which cannot be stated directly, but whose outline may be traced in the movement of the bias of reason through tradition.

When Kant states the 'principle' apart from its implication in tradition, his formulation appears tautologous. The principle consists in the accord of the powers, or 'the subjective formal condition of a judgement in general' which can only be described as 'the judging faculty itself, or judgement'. But the reference to tradition rescues the principle of the aesthetic judgement from tautology. We have seen that judgement, or more precisely, the formal condition of judgement – its technic – consists in the accord of the powers, an accord which is presupposed by the set of empirical judgements requiring justification. There is an important distinction between judgement and judgements which Kant states clearly in the following passage:

> The subjective condition of all judgements is the capacity to judge itself, or judgement-power [*Urteilskraft*]. Employed in respect of a representation whereby an object is given, this requires the harmonious accordance of two powers of representation. These are, the imagination (for the intuition and the arrangement of the manifold of intuition), and the understanding (for the concept as a representation of the unity of this arrangement).
>
> (§ 35)

When this accord is experienced apart from any concept of an object, apart, that is, from the procedures of subsumption and its hierarchical subordination of a manifold under a unity, there arises the feeling of pleasure. And with pleasure, in some complex way, is granted the enhancement of power and life, for the experience of the free accord of the powers evokes the 'sensation of the mutually quickening activity of the imagination in its *freedom*, and of the understanding with its *conformity to law*' (§ 35). The enhancement of life through the accord of the powers is present, although repressed, even in the hierarchical disposition of the powers in determinate judgement.

The judgement of taste is legitimated by the alignment of the powers prior to any discrete judgement. There is an art by which judgement-power disposes itself; in other words, it 'contains a principle of subsumption, not of intuitions under *concepts*, but of the *faculty* of intuitions or presentations, i.e. of the imagination, under the *faculty* of concepts, i.e. the understanding, so far as the former *in its freedom* accords with the latter *in its conformity to law*' (§ 35). With the reference to the powers as a whole, anticipated in the second statement of the schematism in the first *Critique*, Kant looks beyond the hierarchy of subsumption to a different relation, one of the accord of the faculties or powers.

Once having established the principle of the aesthetic judgement of taste as consisting in the accord of the powers, some serious problems arise. Along with the difficulty of expressing this accord outside of the hierarchical discourse of judgement, with its unity and its manifold and its law and its freedom, there is also the legitimation of the principle itself. How is it possible to appeal to the principle as a legitimating condition of judgement if we only have access to it through judgements? The deduction is not 'so easy' as Kant thought, since it is necessary to justify how 'the same subjective conditions of judgement which we find in ourselves are universally present in every man, and further that we have correctly [*richtig*] subsumed the given Object under these conditions' (§ 38). In order to achieve this justification (of the universality and necessity of judgements) Kant finds it necessary to amplify his appeal to tradition. In tradition it is possible to perceive the legitimatory condition apart from the bias expressed in the individual judgements.

In the 'Remark' to § 38 Kant gets sidetracked into the issue of the correct subsumption of a judgement of taste (what constitutes 'correctness' anyway, that is the question). But in a footnote he offers a deduction of the principle of the deduction. The accord of the knowledge-powers must be common to every human being, since 'otherwise men would be incapable of communicating their representations or even their knowledge' (footnote, § 38). The deduction is justified by the character of tradition, which consists in the communication or transmission (*Mitteilung*) of knowledge. But the ability to communicate indicates both the alignment of the knowledge-powers and the medium or 'postal network' through which this becomes manifest. The mode of communication called tradition is distinguished in § 39 from both the autism of the agreeable, which is restricted to the object of enjoyment, and the dictates of the concept spoken through the 'instrumentality of reason' (§ 39). This form of communication is fundamental, it is directed toward neither an object nor a concept, but to the accord of the powers presupposed by these activities, one which is also the source of pleasure:

> This pleasure must of necessity depend for every one upon the same conditions, seeing that they are the subjective conditions of the possibility of a cognition in general, and the proportion of these cognitive faculties which is requisite for taste is requisite also for ordinary sound understanding, the presence of which we are entitled to presuppose in every one.
>
> (§ 39)

Tradition, Kant goes on to say, is the medium in which the *sensus communis* finds its proportion, and the record of the body of judgements through which this takes place.

The presupposition of both taste and sound understanding is the accord of the knowledge-powers entitled *sensus communis*. But we have seen that *sensus communis* is also Kant's name for the active appropriation of tradition. Kant defines it as the 'collective reason of mankind', and describes its work in terms of the mode of necessity proper to tradition: it is

> the idea of a *public* sense, i.e. a critical faculty which in its reflective act takes account (*a priori*) of the mode of represen- tation of every one else, in order, *as it were*, to weigh its judgement with the collective reason of mankind, and thereby avoid the illusion arising from subjective and personal conditions which could readily be taken for objective, an illusion that would exert a prejudicial influence upon its judgement.
>
> (§ 40)

The bias of individual judgements is corrected within the collective reason; in other words, the body of prejudice given in tradition is a prophylactic against prejudice in individual judgement. The maxims of common human understanding, 'think for oneself', 'think from the standpoint of everyone else', and 'always think consistently', are maxims of the active appropriation rather than passive imitation or hasty dismissal of tradition. The transcendence of the bias of reason takes place through this active appropriation of tradition, for in order to think for oneself, one must, in words which echo the journey through the horizons of the first *Critique*, 'reflect upon one's own judgement from a *universal standpoint* (which can only be determined by shifting ground to the standpoint of others)' (§ 40). The *sensus communis* is this critical relation to tradition, the principle of its active appropriation, but it also refers to the fundamental proportion which evokes pleasure.

The *sensus communis* is more than a navigational aid for intellectual orientation, more than a critical faculty for estimating one's position according to the horizon of tradition. It is also, as common sense, the 'effect that mere reflection has upon the mind; for then by sense we mean the feeling of pleasure' (§ 40). Here the two senses of judgement discussed above return to consideration. Judgement is critical and estimative, yet also the source of pleasure; but now we are in a position to determine the relation of the two – the 'key to the critique of taste' – with more precision. The *sensus communis* overcomes the bias of reason, the passive disproportion of the cognitive faculties afflicted by prejudice, and through its activity approximates to a proportioned understanding. But this approximation to proportion is also the source of pleasure.

The two aspects of judgement as a critical faculty and as the source of pleasure come together in tradition. The active appropriation of tradition, finding a universal standpoint that is both without and within, autonomous and heteronomous, consists in communication or transmission. Being in communication with the collective reason of mankind in tradition, presupposes an accord of the knowledge-powers which it also develops through pleasure:

> The aptitude of men for communicating their thoughts requires, also, a relation between the imagination and the understanding, in order to connect intuitions with concepts, and concepts, in turn, with intuitions, which both unite in cognition. But there the accord [*Zusammenstimmung*] of both powers [*Gemütskräfte*] is according to law, and under the constraint [*Zwange*] of determinate [*bestimmter*] concepts. Only when the imagination in its freedom arouses [*erweckt*] the understanding, and the understanding apart from concepts transposes [*versetzt*] the power of imagination into regular play, does the representation communicate itself not as thought, but as an internal feeling of an appropriate [*Zweckmässigen*] condition of the Gemüt.
>
> (§ 40)

Communication both presumes the accord of the powers, in knowledge, but also points to a different stance with regard to this accord, one without constraint, in pleasure.

To judge an object beautiful requires a principle, and this Kant found in the proportion of the knowledge-powers. This proportion may be transposed, under constraint, into determinate judgement, or into the regular play of pleasure. Both transpositions involve communication, but communication concerns the 'collective reason' of mankind, that is, it is not communication with contemporaries, but also with predecessors. The understanding of communication as remembrance exposes the important role of tradition in the aesthetic judgement of taste. Through the experience of the beautiful, the forgotten accord of the powers, erased under constraint by the concept, is brought to remembrance. The quickening activity of this remembrance, the equation of what cannot be equated (freedom and conformity to law) is stimulated by the encounter of the individual judgement with the tradition of judgements.

Kant's understanding of tradition is accordingly far broader than a collection of judgements amassed in books and systems. For the records of communication concern the relation of humans both to each other and to their environment. The beginning of civilization lies in 'the estimate formed of one who has the bent and turn for communicating his pleasure to others, and who is not quite satisfied with an Object unless his feeling of delight in it can be shared in communion with others' (§ 41). Indeed, for Kant the highest point of civilization is reached when a society

> makes this work of communication almost the main business of refined inclination, and the entire value of sensations is placed in the degree to which they permit of universal communication. At this stage, then, even where the pleasure which each one has in an object is but insignificant and possesses of itself no conspicuous interest, still the idea of its universal communicability almost indefinitely augments its value.
>
> (§ 41)

At this stage the relation of freedom and conformity to law no longer requires an object as the external stimulus for the work of communication; *praxis*, in other words, overcomes *poiesis*. The imagination is no longer forced to arouse the understanding, and the understanding no longer has to dispose the imagination into regular play, since now both augment each other. This blaze of activity which transcends the object and the occasion is, once again, Kant's vision of the Kingdom of God developed in the *Lectures on Philosophical Theology* and *Ethics*.

The discussion of communication falls in § 43 on the 'empirical interest' in the beautiful. But the main point of this section is to establish a contrast which is of great importance for the remainder of the 'Analytic of the Beautiful'. This is the distinction of the 'empirical' and 'intellectual' interests in the beautiful. The empirical interest consists in sensation of the object of beauty, while the intellectual interest involves the relation of the beautiful and the concept. However, we have seen that the concept cannot be a determining ground of our delight in beauty, a point Kant supports with a series of bizarre examples ranging from the planting of artificial flowers to the employment of a 'young rogue' to imitate the song of the nightingale on a summer's night. The lover of the beautiful is disenchanted when the artifice is uncovered. Yet this relegation of the concept from the beautiful leads to great difficulties in the case of fine art, which is always produced in accord with some concept or *Zweck* in view. Once again, the solution of this 'difficulty' involves recourse to tradition.

Kant proceeds through § § 43–5 to establish the parameters of the problem of fine art, to 'state the difficulty'. In § 43 he offers a definition of art in general, in § 44 a definition of fine art in particular, then situates both within the context of the aesthetic judgement of taste by setting out their differences and essaying a reconciliation in § 45.

The main difficulty lies in the definition of art as 'everything formed in such a way that its actuality must have been preceded by a representation of the thing in its cause' (§ 43). This sort of production is specific to human work, where 'rational deliberation forms the basis of labour' (§ 43). However, the two elements of art, the representation of an end and the performance of the labour may be separated. In this context Kant offers two distinctions which are developed further in his critique of culture. To start with, '*Art*, as human skill, is distinguished also from *science* (as *ability* from *knowledge*), as a practical from a theoretical faculty, as technic from theory' (§ 43). Following on the distinction of theory and practice is the separation of labour from the representation of the end, as in the distinction of free and industrial art. In the latter, 'labour [is] a business, which on its own account is disagreeable (drudgery), and is only attractive by means of what it results in (e.g. the pay), and which is consequently capable of being a compulsory imposition [*zwangmässig auferlegt*]' (§ 43). Here is another example of the disproportion between concept and intuition resulting first in the emptiness of the concept as the end represented to be achieved, and then in the blindness of intuition, or compulsory labour which realizes the end without any insight into the end or purpose of the work.

Free art falls between the two extremes of the transcendental distinction. As the proportionality of concept and intuition, it transcends both the empty autonomy of the concept and the blind heteronomy of intuition. Fine art must be free, it must both restrict and realize: 'in all free arts something of a compulsory character is still required, or as it is called, a *mechanism*, without which the *soul*, which in art must be *free*, and which alone gives life to the work, would be bodiless and evanescent' (§ 43). But the question arises of how to achieve this kind of production without violating the determining grounds of the judgement of taste. This causes special problems with the case of the fine arts.

Both the agreeable and the fine arts appear to have been disqualified as objects of the aesthetic judgement of taste: agreeable art is unacceptable because of the sensation of pleasure it involves, and fine art because of its reference to an end. Exception may be made for fine art, as long as it is 'a mode of representation which is intrinsically final, and which, although devoid of an end, has the effect of advancing the culture of the *Gemütskräfte* in the interests of social communication' (§ 44). But wait, 'art has always got a definite intention of producing something' (§ 45). The only way of reconciling these contradictory demands is to formulate a definition of fine art which will keep both sides happy. On his first try Kant is paradoxical:

A product of fine art must be recognized to be art and not nature. Nevertheless the finality in its form must appear just as free from the constraint of arbitrary rules as if it were a product of mere nature ... Nature proved beautiful when it wore the appearance of art, and art can only be termed beautiful, where we are conscious of its being art, while yet it has the appearance of nature.

(§ 45)

In order to achieve definition Kant must have recourse to a notion of illusion – nature must appear as art, art must appear as nature – both share the property of appearing. In the case of nature, it wears the appearance of art, while in the case of art, we are 'conscious' of it being art even though it appears to be nature. Clearly a complicated notion of appearance is at work here, one in which appearance lays bare its artifice.

The notion of appearance is developed in the discussion of the appearance proper to fine art. The key to the natural appearance of fine art consists in the *Zweckmässigkeit ohne Zweck* involved in the production of the work:

> Hence the finality in the product of fine art, intentional though it be, must not have the appearance of being intentional; i.e. fine art must be clothed *with the aspect* of nature, although we recognize it to be art. But the way in which a product of art seems like nature, is by the presence of perfect *exactness* in the agreement with rules prescribing how alone the product can be what it is intended to be, but with an absence of *laboured effect* (without academic form betraying itself) i.e. without a trace appearing of the artist having always had the rule present to him and of it having fettered his *Gemütskräfte*.
>
> (§ 45)

The question of the natural appearance of art is resolved into the manner in which the rule is present for the *Gemütskräfte*, and the trace left by this presence in the product. What is most important is that the artist does not appear to have laboured under the constraint of the rule, even though it was present. Kant's paradigm for the manner in which the rule is present and effaced in fine art is, again, the active appropriation of tradition where restriction is a realization. The bringing to presence and effacing of the trace, whose production appears to be natural and artificial, is the work of genius.

Everything in the discussion of genius hangs on the relation of productive activity to law. The difficulty of determining this relation emerges in the vexed question of the 'originality' of genius, or its relation to tradition. Genius does not obey normal temporality; it follows and anticipates tradition: it is 'a talent for producing that for which no definite rule can be given' whose 'products must at the same time be models, be exemplary (§ 46). The 'possibility of this is difficult to explain' admits Kant, for the rule

> cannot be one set down in a formula and serving as a precept – for then the judgement upon the beautiful would be determinable according to concepts. Rather must the rule be gathered from the performance, i.e. from the product, which others may use to put their own talent to the test, so as to let it serve as a model, not for imitation but for following.
>
> (§ 47)

Genius stands to the rule as the heir to tradition who did not bury his talent in mere imitation, but followed, that is, put himself 'to the test' before tradition. And the nature of the test consists in imitating not the products, but the proportion embodied in them: 'The artist's ideas arouse like ideas on the part of his pupil, presuming nature to have visited him with a like proportion of the *Gemütskräfte*' (§ 47). Once again, it is the active appropriation of tradition which enables the experience of the fundamental accord of the knowledge powers.

Since taste is estimative and genius productive there is clearly a distinction between their respective orientations within tradition. The nature of this difference is explored at length in the remainder of the 'Analytic'. The sections following § 49 have perplexed and disappointed commentators, who cannot see any order in Kant's discussion of aesthetic ideas, the relation of genius and taste, and the system of the individual arts. It is seen as a ragbag, the place where Kant threw together a few odd thoughts he couldn't put anywhere else. But there is an order to these sections, hidden, perhaps, even to Kant himself. It consists in another reworking of the rhetorical schema of *inventio*, *dispositio*, and *elocutio* which recurs so often in enlightenment philosophy. The discussion of aesthetic ideas at § 49 corresponds to the invention of the materials of a work of art; the relation of taste and genius correspond to the disposition of the materials into a form, and the system of individual arts, divided according to expression, corresponds to *elocutio*. Within this rhetorical *schema* Kant extends his exploration of the relation of beauty, proportion and culture which he began in the logical *schema* of the four moments.

In the discussion of aesthetic invention in § 49, Kant presents his views on the origin and effect of aesthetic ideas in terms of a series of related oppositions. Alongside such familiar contraries as 'imagination and understanding', he sets those of 'spirit and soul', and 'the spirit and the letter'. The aesthetic idea is produced by the imagination/spirit exceeding the understanding/soul/word through its access to an original accord of the opposition which vivifies them both. The aesthetic idea 'sets the *Gemütskräfte* into a swing that is final, i.e. into a play which is self-maintaining and strengthens the powers for such activity' (§ 49). The aesthetic idea which provokes this activity is not exhausted by the understanding; on the contrary, it cannot even be expressed by it: it is 'that representation of the imagination which induces much thought, yet without the possibility of any definite thought whatever, i.e. concept, being adequate to it, and which language, consequently, can never get quite on level terms with or render completely intelligible' (§ 49). The aesthetic idea originates in the imagination producing a 'second nature out of the material supplied to it by actual nature', a mode of production which works nature up 'into something else, namely, what surpasses nature' (§ 49). The new product – or aesthetic idea – undermines the concept by using it to point beyond natural appearance to the fundamental accord underlying it. It is:

> a representation of the imagination, annexed to a given concept, with which, in the free employment of imagination, such a multiplicity of partial representations are bound up, that no expression indicating a definite concept can be found for it – one which on that account allows a concept to be supplemented in thought by much that is indefinable in words, and the feeling of which quickens the cognitive faculties, and with language, as a mere thing of the letter, binds up the spirit (soul) also.
>
> (§ 49)

The production of aesthetic ideas exceeds the letter/law of the understanding, using it to point to what is indefinable, but quickens the powers.

In this productive activity the imagination gains access to a proportion of the knowledge-powers hidden from the understanding. Genius consists in the 'union in a certain relation' of the imagination and understanding, a 'relation' discovered and produced by the imagination. Although the relation in question is not discovered through rules, it must be represented in a communicable form: the study of the invention of aesthetic ideas must be complemented by one of their disposition. Because imagination is not confined to the restricted accord of the concept, which consists in subsuming a manifold under a unity, it is 'free to discover other [relations] which manifest themselves in pleasure', or the 'subjective quickening of the cognitive faculties', but these must be disposed into a communicable form. Genius then becomes

> the happy relation, which science cannot teach nor industry learn, enabling one to find out ideas for a given concept, and, besides, to hit upon the *expression* for them – the expression by means of which the subjective attunement of the powers [*Gemütsstimmung*] induced by the ideas as the concomitant of a concept may be communicated to others.
>
> (§ 49)

In other words, genius consists both in invention, the 'finding' and production of aesthetic ideas, and their disposition or expression in communicable form. Kant thematizes this 'happy relation' of invention and disposition in terms of the relation between genius and taste.

The presentation of the fundamental proportion evoked in the aesthetic idea is achieved through taste, which appears as both a constituent and an auxiliary of genius. Returning to the problem of form and taste, Kant observes that form is inseparable from tradition: 'this form is not, as it were, a matter of inspiration, or of a free swing of the *Gemütskräfte*, but rather of a slow and even painful process of improvement, directed to making the form adequate to thought without prejudice to the freedom in the play of those powers' (§ 48). Form is the disposition of the imaginative power, its 'vehicle of communication and a mode, as it were, of execution'. It is the means by which the products of genius are adapted for transmission through tradition: 'it introduces a clearness and order into the plenitude of thought, and in so doing gives stability to the ideas, and qualifies them at once for permanent and universal approval, for being followed by others, and for a continually progressive culture' (§ 50). In tradition, the proportion of the faculties evoked by genius becomes manifest; it is communicated, not by being brought under a concept, but through the 'collective reason' of tradition.

The third division of the rhetorical *schema* employed in the system of the fine arts is *elocutio*, or expression proper. If taste disposes the inventions of genius into communicable form in general, the division of the arts in *elocutio* attends to specific expression in space and time. Kant follows the classical elocutionary *schema* in his division of the fine arts into those of speech, gesture and tone. The main determinant of his classification is the relation of the object to the mode of communication. Poetry and rhetoric are the arts of speech, the formative arts of sculpture, painting, and architecture are the arts of gesture, and music and the 'art of colour' form the arts of tone. As in Lessing's *Laocoon*, each of the arts stands in a particular relation to the forms of intuition and uses the spatial and temporal aspects of its object as a *schema* for the expression of aesthetic ideas. The formative arts of gesture employ the spatial form, while the arts of tone exploit the temporal aspect of their material; the art of poetry, however, points beyond the object thought in its spatial and temporal determinations.

Beginning with the formative arts of painting and sculpture, 'both', says Kant,

> use figures in space for the expression of ideas: the former makes figures discernible to two senses, sight and touch (though, so far as the latter sense is concerned, without regard

to beauty), the latter makes them so to the former sense alone. The aesthetic idea (archetype, original) is the fundamental basis of both in the imagination; but the figure which constitutes its expression (the ectype, the copy) is given either in its bodily extension (the way the object itself exists) or else in accordance with the picture which it forms of itself in the eye (according to its appearance when projected on a flat surface).

(§ 51)

Expression consists largely in the relation of arche- and ectype, the former comprising the aesthetic idea, the latter its expression in space. Kant develops this thought in his subsequent justification of bringing formative art under the heading of gesture. There is a peculiar relation between the arche- and the ectype, not one of cause and effect, but one of mimicry and vivification through genius; spirit is given body through the body being brought to speech:

> through these figures the spirit [*Geist*] of the artist furnishes a bodily expression for the what and how [*was und wie*] of his thought, and makes the thing itself speak, as it were, in mimic language – a very common play of our fancy, that attributes to lifeless things a spirit in accord with their form, and that speaks out of them [*welche leblosen Dingen ihrer form gemäss einen Geist unterlegt, der aus ihnen spricht*].

(§ 51)

Here the happy relation of idea and form, arche- and ectype, is represented as a kind of mimicry in which things are brought to life by becoming the medium of the spirit, being made to speak. This relation of spirit and thing is not the violent subsumption we are accustomed to from theoretical philosophy, but one in which things are given voice mimetically, in accord with their form. However, the natural appearance of this mimicry is always qualified by an 'as it were' or trace of artifice in appearance; without this trace we surrender the happy illusion of the speaking thing for the depressing deception of the whistling young rogue.

Apropos of music, the arts of tone also communicate ideas through sensation, but over time. Here form consists in a proportion which may be perceived in the relations of sensible tones as they are played across time. The pleasure which is taken in it consists in 'the effect of an estimate of form in the play of a number of sensations' (§ 51).

The arts of gesture and tone use spatial and temporal relations as *schemata* for the expression of aesthetic ideas. Poetry, however, uses speech as its medium. Speech is an equivocal phenomenon for Kant, since it is both of the idea and of sense. Rhetoric employs speech technically, as an instrument deployed to realize pre-established ends. In poetry, however, a different relation to speech emerges, one in which speech is both intuition and idea, one in which their distinction is overcome. It anticipates the pure communication which is the 'height' of civilization for Kant, the unity of the spirit and the letter in the Kingdom of God on Earth. Instead of the object mimicking language, language speaks itself. It is for this reason that poetry is for Kant the supreme art: it promotes life by embodying and not just representing the fundamental proportion of the powers.

The affinity of poetry and pure communication alerts us to the relation between Kant's hierarchy of the arts and the other themes explored so far. His hierarchy rests on the relation to the accord of the powers, and the definition of culture as the expansion and quickening of the faculties necessary for cognition. It is the relation of imagination and understanding, one which cannot be conceived in terms of subsumption under a rule, but rests on a different paradigm of judgement, one derived from the relation of a judgement to a tradition of judgements. These points become even more prominent in the 'Dialectic' of the aesthetic judgement of taste.

Kant's solutions to the deduction of the judgement of taste ground the universality of the judgement in the cultivation of individual discriminations through tradition, and its necessity in the persuasive force of tradition. The issue of the universality and necessity proper to the judgement of taste is taken up again in the 'Dialectic', where the dispute as to whether or not the judgement is based on concepts returns to the 'two peculiarities of the judgement of taste previously set out in the Analytic' (§ 57). Here too, the issue is presented in terms of the disputes and contentions of tradition.

In the 'Dialectic' Kant shows that the option of whether the judgement of taste is 'open to dispute (decision by means of proofs)' or whether there could be 'room even for contention in the matter' (§ 57) does not exhaust the range of possibilities. He attempts to re-orient the contrary, to 'look beyond the horizon of the sensible', in order to expose the mutual implication of the two positions. But his third option requires the active appropriation of tradition: it requires the exposition of the bias of reason manifest in the arguments over the determining grounds of the judgement of taste, which is taken 'by some' as agreeableness and by 'others' as perfection. We have seen that this exposition of tradition structured the 'Analytic's' re-orientation of the bias of reason and its intimations of a more proportioned principle of judgement.

However, it was also seen that this proportioned position could only be expressed allusively. It could not be directly stated or proven since it exceeded the language of philosophical proof. The 'point of union of all our faculties a priori' is asymptotically approached, lying beyond the reach of the understanding. Kant is unequivocal when he says:

> The subjective principle – that is to say, the indeterminate idea of the supersensible within us – can only be pointed to as the unique key for unpuzzling this faculty whose sources are hidden from us, and which cannot be made any more comprehensible [*kann nur als der einzige Schlüssel der Enträtselung dieses uns selbst seinen Quellen nach verborgenen Vermögens angezeigt, aber durch nichts weiter begreiflich gemacht werden*].
>
> (§ 57)

The jurisdiction of the rules and precepts of the understanding does not reach the harmony of the powers which secretly ensures the universality and necessity of the judgement of taste. The beautiful may only be estimated according to the 'final attunement of imagination-power to a harmony with the faculty of concepts in general' (§ 57). This 'attunement to a harmony' of the power and faculty,

> cannot be comprehended under rules or concepts, that is to say, the super-sensible substrate of all the Subject's faculties (unattainable by any concept of understanding), and consequently in that which forms the point of reference for the harmonious accord of all our faculties of cognition – the production of which accord is the ultimate end set by the intelligible basis of our nature.
>
> (§ 57)

This harmonious accord cannot be considered as a unity of a manifold, since the moments of unity and manifold are subsequent to it; it is the general proportionality or ratio which enables other limited ratios such as unification and analogy to be effected.

In the final section of the 'Dialectic' on 'Beauty as a Symbol of Ethical Life' Kant reflects on the manner of 'indicating' the harmonious accord of the powers. This accord points to a different relation between the judging subject and the world from that offered by the understanding. The main issue in this section is the procedure of hypotyposis already mentioned above. This, we saw, is an ordering activity based on the comparison of patterns, and not the unification of the manifold discovered by subsumptive judgement. The possibility of such patterns lies in the existence of a proportionality of the judging subject and the world which exceeds the concept. In symbolic knowledge, the achievement of subsumption is subordinated to the activity of discovering relations, proportions between the unlike which do not efface their differences.

The paradigm of symbolic knowledge is knowledge of God. Since the object of such knowledge exceeds our comprehension, we may only follow procedures for knowing Him without presuming ever to attain adequate knowledge of his Being. However, there is a tendency for the understanding to reify the activity of comparison, to convert the analogies it discovers into objects of knowledge. Kant illustrates this point with a critique of philosophical terminology, not only the dichotomies which we considered earlier, but such fundamental terms as: 'the word *ground* (support, basis), *to depend* (to be held up from above), to *flow* from (instead of to follow), *substance* (as Locke puts it: the support of accidents), and numberless others, [which] are not schematic, but rather symbolic hypotyposes' (§ 59). These terms are the precipitates of an activity of comparison which are treated as if they corresponded to objects in intuition. However, they are properly seen less as concepts to be applied than designations of the procedures for orienting experience.

In the procedure of symbolic knowledge – 'applying the mere rule of reflection upon an intuition to quite another object', a proportionate ordering of perception is achieved which is not the unification of a manifold. The activity of proportioning the knowledge-powers and the world is a paradoxical orientation, paradoxical because it transgresses the distinctions of unity/manifold, inner/outer on which the understanding depends. Kant embraces the paradox:

> both on account of this inner possibility in the Subject, and on account of the external possibility of a nature harmonizing therewith, it [judgement-power] finds itself referred to something within the subject and outside it, [something] which is not nature nor freedom, although it is tied with the ground of the latter, namely the supersensible, and in which the theoretical faculty would be bound up into unity with the practical in a common but unfamiliar way [*auf gemeinschaftliche und unbekannte Art zur Einheit verbunden wird* - cf. Meredith's 'intimate and obscure manner'].

(§ 59)

Judgement then, orients itself according to something both within and without it, something which is neither nature nor freedom, in which the theoretical and practical are bound together in a way that is common, but unfamiliar. The activity of orientation according to fundamental proportion can only be indicated from the standpoint of the distinctions of unity/manifold, inner/outer, nature/freedom, theory/practice, but it cannot be properly stated in these terms. It can be disclosed in the traditions where these distinctions display their instability, whose bias points to a more fundamental relation upon which they 'depend' and which is 'common' to them, but which they also obscure and make unfamiliar.

The oppositions within tradition are of far wider significance than the outcome of disputing factions within the academy. We saw in part I that the differences between the traditions of taste and aesthetic had considerable theological and political significance. Kant takes this up symptomatically in the 'Methodology of the Critique of Aesthetic Judgement' when he considers the communication of tradition in terms of 'the freedom of the imagination in its very conformity to law – a freedom without which a fine art is not possible, nor even as much as a correct taste of one's own for estimating it' (§ 60). But following this familiar statement of the reconciliation of freedom and conformity to law in tradition, Kant makes a sudden, violent leap to the political aspects of this relation:

> There was an age and there were nations in which the active impulse towards a social life *regulated by laws* – what converts a people into a permanent community – grappled with the huge difficulties presented by the trying problem of bringing freedom (and therefore equality also) into union with constraining force (more that of respect and dutiful submission than of fear).
>
> (§ 60)

Then equally suddenly, the relation of freedom and constraining force is transformed into the relation between the 'cultured and the ruder sections of the community', between the 'amplitude and refinement of the former and the natural simplicity and originality of the latter'. The question arises of how this political relation should be thought. What is the character of the 'force' which unites freedom and law, through what means are they brought to conform? At this point the political metaphysics underlying the philosophy of art openly announces itself, and remains at centre stage for the remainder of the *Critique*.

Life and Finality

the part must be a tool *producing* the other parts – each, consequently, reciprocally producing the others. No artificial tool [*Werkzeug der Kunst*] can answer to this description, but only that tool from whose resources the materials for all other tools (including artificial ones) is drawn. And only then and in this way can such a product be designated an organized and self-organizing being.

Kant, *Critique of Judgement-Power*

From his dialogue with the traditions of taste and aesthetic Kant came to see the principle of the aesthetic judgement of taste as a 'fundamental proportion' which could not be expressed in the language of judgement. It was manifest in the feeling of pleasure, or the enhancement of life. In the 'Critique of Teleological Judgement' Kant develops the theological and political themes underlying this conclusion. It was seen in the first part of this book that the traditions of taste and aesthetic were implicated in distinct understandings of providence, production and legislation. And just as Kant's statement of the aesthetic judgement of taste exceeds the traditions, so do the wider theological and political implications of his theory of judgement. The alignment of pleasure, life and finality in the first part of the *Critique* is given its full theological and political weight in the second part.

This is accomplished through the intensification of the analysis of the technic of judgement presupposed by the judgement of taste. Kant generalizes the account of hypotyposis developed in the penultimate section of Part I of the *Critique*. What there was used to introduce the notion of beauty as a symbol of morality, now describes the interpretative predicament of human existence. Since humans possess neither the comprehensive vision of God nor the limited perception of the animals, they are condemned to interpret – to judge. Hypotyposis as an art or technic of judgement is the procedure for organizing the materials of perception. Its orientational activity however is determined by a fundamental proportion which it cannot experience except in terms of pleasure. In the second part of the *Critique*, the orientational activity of hypotyposis becomes the end of human life; Kant finds in this activity the *summum bonum* or justification of creation.

In Aquinas the contemplation of proportion is also the highest good, the justification of human life and of the whole of creation.

But there is a crucial difference between his and Kant's positions. For Kant, the orientation with regard to the world and to others in the world is not a contemplative, but a practical activity. Proportion is not revealed through contemplation, but is produced through culture. In this way he synthesizes the Aristotelean understanding of proportionality and the limits of unificational activity of judgement with the Renaissance emphasis on production and culture. Proportion is revealed through culture, understood as orientation with respect both to an object in production, and to others in communication. Culture consists both in acknowledging the disproportion of concept and intuition, between communication and labour, and working towards a just proportion. On many occasions Kant nevertheless describes this proportion in terms of unifying a manifold, but he also points beyond these terms, especially when the recognition of its aporias had become unavoidable.

The project of establishing proportion by working through the disproportions of culture is allied to that of discovering intellectual proportion by following the bias of reason through tradition. In the technical procedures of the one, and the estimative activity of the other, horizons are established within which discrimination may take place. This orientational activity of the technic of judgement, like that of the aesthetic judgement of taste, is determined by a principle which has its own space, time, and necessity in tradition.

The theological basis of the notion of human activity as self-orientation is explored in the second part of the *Critique*. The ability to reveal the proportion buried in matter through production and communication in culture – human life – is seen by Kant as a divine gift for the glorification of creation. It requires a finality of nature and the human powers, but not those proposed by the theorists of taste and aesthetic. The approximation to proportion is not achieved through providential 'leading strings' whether those of a rational sense or sensible reason, but through experiment and self-orientation. Human culture establishes provisional horizons of discrimination, which in the course of development become increasingly refined and accurate.

The relation between human activity and the technic of judgement is presented in the discussion of hypotyposis. The technic of judgement is either schematic or symbolic: the first procedure unifies a manifold under a universal, while the second applies the rule of reflection from one intuition to another. Kant considers the latter, analogical procedure to be fundamental to human perception, since it establishes similarities which offer horizons for the perception of differences. He warns against reading this activity of identifying and differing into the things themselves; it is only a reflective or 'estimative' principle of subjective finality, 'a finality relative to comprehensibility – man's power of judgement being such as it is – and to the possibility of uniting particular experiences into a connected system of nature' (§ 61). This finality, insists Kant, is relative to the human faculty of judgement; it is not objective or a 'physical end' as was thought by Herder and Forster.[15] Kant sees the objectification of finality as leading to 'mental jugglery', some fine examples of which we have seen among the theorists of taste and aesthetic.

The reason why Kant insists on the subjectivity of finality is his reluctance to subscribe to a providential theology: the notion of a physical end brings a theodicy with it. For Kant, the teleological estimate is a principle of orientation, and is only admitted 'with a view to bringing (nature) under principles of observation and research by *analogy* to the causality that looks to ends, while not pretending to *explain* it by these means. Thus it is an estimate of the reflective, not of the determinant, judgement' (§ 61). The causality which looks to ends is human productive activity, which first sets an end and then disposes the means to realize it. If this form of causality were ascribed to nature, then a new form of physical causality would have to be admitted, one which could not be thought within the form of the causal relation known to mechanics. But if it were not admitted, then it is difficult to see how any perception could be possible. Kant's solution is to say that there is a finality between perception and nature, but we can only perceive it through an analogy with the form of causality known to us. The ability to draw such an analogy rests on the fundamental disposition of the power of judgement which we saw at work in the experience of the beautiful. And there we saw that judgement can dispose itself finally without presupposing an end (*Zweckmässigkeit ohne Zweck*) because it is the disposition that constitutes ends.

The exposition of the teleological estimate is conducted within Kant's habitual *schema* of Analytic, Dialectic, and Methodology. The 'Analytic' is more loosely organized than usual, following the division of the 'Analytic of the Sublime' into mathematical and dynamical principles. The 'Analytic of Teleological Judgement' begins with a reference to tradition, this time to Plato and Anaxagoras, in an exposition of the extremely complex phenomenon of the construction of a geometrical figure. The finality of the geometrical figure 'expresses the way [it] lends itself to the production of the many proposed figures, and is cognized through reason' (§ 62). The finality of the figure is not material – it does not issue from the object it represents – but is intelligible and derived from the reason alone.

Kant supports this claim by pointing to the invention of geometrical forms in classical geometry which were without any physical application. He uses this to underline the peculiar temporality of tradition; the constructions of the geometers were 'exemplary' in anticipating and making possible the later discoveries of the physicists. The ancient geometers

> investigated the properties of the ellipse without a suspicion that a gravitation was also discoverable in the celestial bodies, and without knowing that the law that governs it as the distance from the point of attraction varies, and this makes the bodies describe this curve in free motion. While in all these labours they were working unwittingly for those who were to come after them, they delighted themselves with a finality which, although belonging to the nature of the things, they were able to present completely *a priori* as necessary.
>
> (§ 62)

Kant sees the need for metaphysics as arising from such disjunctures between the discovery of the intellectual finality of geometrical figures and their physical approximation. He distributes geometrical intuition and physical empiricism between Plato and Anaxagoras; the former thought 'that from the pure intuition residing in the depths of the human soul he could derive all that Anaxagoras inferred from the objects of experience and their purposive combination' (§ 62). And true to his appropriative stance toward tradition, Kant uses the difference in tradition to orient himself between an intuitive a priorism and empiricism.

He does so by mobilizing the notion of appearance presented in a different context in the first part of the *Critique*. Returning to the geometrical figure, he finds that the necessity of such figures is two-fold, equivocal, for 'while appearing to be an original attribute belonging to the essential nature of things regardless of service to us, [it] is yet final and formed as if purposely designed for our use' (§ 62). This 'appearance' of objectivity and the 'as if' of usefulness is the source of the 'admiration of nature' which is both external to us, and yet seated in our reason. In fact it is our activity of ascribing finality which provokes admiration. In the construction of a geometrical figure, intuition is inscribed with a finality which is then 'read off' as if it were objective. The inscription is a demarcation of space and an ordering of its contents which appears as objective, and which allows objects to come into appearance:

space, by the limitation of which (by means of the imagination acting in accordance with a conception) the Object was alone possible, is not a quality of the thing outside me, but a mere mode of representation existing in myself. Hence, when I draw a figure *in accordance with a conception*, or, in other words, when I form my own representation of what is given to me externally, be its own intrinsic nature what it may, what really happens is that I *introduce the finality* into that figure or representation.

(§ 62)

Here Kant draws an analogy between perception and the inscription of a figure. The self-alienating understanding inscribes finality on nature, and then subjects itself to its laws as if they were objective; in other words, it disowns responsibility for inscription, allowing its spirit to become letter. The inscription of finality rests on a hypotypotic procedure which applies to objects in intuition the experience of a finality peculiar to human agency. This is subsequently 'read off' in perception as if it were objective.

But this understanding of the inscription of finality does not mean that Kant abandoned objective proportion. Although he throws out the idea that it may be intuited or known, he does allow that its very excess over intuition and understanding may be felt. Thus, in a distinction between admiration and astonishment which echoes that of the beautiful and the sublime, Kant maintains that

> *astonishment* is a shock that the mind receives from a representation and the rule given through it being incompatible with the mind's existing fund of root principles, and that accordingly makes one doubt one's own eyesight or question ones judgement; but *admiration* is an astonishment that keeps continually recurring despite the disappearance of this doubt. Admiration is consequently quite a natural effect of observing the above-mentioned finality in the essence of things.

(§ 62)

The passage also echoes the description of the *Vernunftglaube* in the orientation essay as the discriminative ability underlying the assessment of metaphysical judgements. That, it will be remembered, operated through a feeling of approval or disapproval of metaphysical judgement. Here, the shock of a disproportion between the object and the procedures of judgement, earlier named the sublime, is countered by the admiration of the agreement of objective and subjective finality, earlier named the beautiful. Like these feelings, and the response of the *Vernunftglaube*, the agreement or disagreement of finalities is foundational, and cannot be explained in terms of the procedures of judgement. It founds the possibility of inscription, but cannot itself be inscribed. In Kant's terms, the agreement of concept and intuition cannot be explained in terms of concept and intuition.

However, this agreement may be approximated in a process of orientation, and, as in the feeling of the beautiful, the concordance of the finalities so discovered leads to an enhancement of life:

> For the agreement of the above form of sensuous intuition, which is called space, with the faculty of conceptions, namely understanding, not only leaves it inexplicable why it is this particular form of agreement and not some other, but, in addition, produces an expansion of the *Gemüt*, in which it gets, so to speak, a secret feeling of the existence of something lying beyond the confines of such sensuous representations, in which, perhaps, although unknown to us, the ultimate source of that accordance could be found.
>
> (§ 62)

Once again, now in the 'Analytic of Teleological Judgement', the 'inexplicable' fundamental proportion expressed in the agreement of the understanding and intuition, manifests itself in pleasure – an excessive 'secret feeling' – and the augmentation of the *Gemüt*. And now as earlier, it is the harmony of the faculties in general, and not a particular representation which constitutes the pleasure.

The relation between human and natural finality is first produced, and then ascribed to objects themselves. This movement plays an important role in Kant's agreement of nature and freedom in the *summum bonum*. But returning to the agreement of the finality of the geometrical figure with the laws of nature, it is now the production and relegation of the agreement which is important. The inability to recognize its own activity leaves this agreement as a 'hidden proportion' or disowned ratio of the understanding and the intuition, one which underlies both the inscription of a geometrical figure in space and the appearance of an object. From this Kant proceeds to look more closely at the dynamic quality of the teleological judgement, the force which ascribes causality.

The inexplicability of the fundamental proportion extends into the section on the dynamic teleological estimate. Here Kant extends the notion of a proportion which can only be captured by a hypotyposis. At issue is the exposition of organic life according to the hypotyposis of human causality according to ends. The inability of mechanical explanations of nature fully to account for the organization or form of a living organism encourages us to estimate this phenomenon according to the concept of objective purpose. Accordingly, the relation of part and whole in organic life is estimated in terms of human production according to art or technique. Human production, we have seen, consists in the projection of an end, the *Zweck*, and the selection and mobilization of means for realizing that end. In this activity, 'the freedom of man's causality enables him to adapt physical things to the purposes he has in view' (§ 63).

Unfortunately this model of causality breaks down when employed to estimate nature. According to such an estimation, 'A thing is possible only as an end where the causality to which it owes its origin must not be sought in the mechanism of nature, but in a cause whose capacity for acting is determined by conceptions' (§ 64). We recognize that the form of organized life cannot be explained on mechanical grounds, and so have to supplement our account with a hypotyposis of productive activity. The causality according to conceptions 'becomes the faculty of acting according to ends – that is to say, a will; and the Object which is represented as only deriving its possibility from such a will, will be represented as possible only as an end' (§ 64). But the notion of a physical end, the hypotyposis of productive activity, fails before the formative activity of nature: 'We do not say half enough of nature and her capacity in organized products when we speak of this capacity as being the *analogue of art*' (§ 65). For we would then have to consider nature as the material expression of the will of a master artist who works from without.

Kant does not find this sort of causality in nature and its products: he hesitantly concedes a paradox: 'As a provisional statement I would say that a thing exists as a physical end *if it is* (though in a double sense) *both cause and effect of itself*' (§ 64). This paradoxical statement transgresses not only the law of contradiction, as Kant himself recognizes, but also the analogy of art. Kant is being deliberately provocative, for the insistence that something be both cause and effect of itself shows our hypotyposis of causality through art breaking down before the intricate interpolation of cause and effect in organic nature, or as he comes to describe it, before life. For example, in the reproduction of a tree, 'the genus, now as effect, now as cause, is continually produced and in the same measure produces itself [*unaufhörlich hervorgebracht und ebenso sich selbst oft hervorbringend*] and so preserves itself generically' (§ 64). A 'formative' activity of continual producing and being produced underlies and exceeds the causal relation. This activity is specified in the description of the life of a plant, which generates itself through the forming of its constituents, and where we find a similar pattern of formation as in 'realization and restriction':

> The plant first prepares the matter that it assimilates, and bestows upon it a specifically distinctive quality which the mechanism of nature outside it cannot supply, and it develops itself by means of a material which, in its composite character, is its own product. For, although in respect of the constituents that it derives from nature outside, it must be regarded as only an educt, yet in the separation and recombination of this raw material we find an original capacity of selection and construction on the part of natural beings of this kind such as infinitely outdistances all the efforts of art.
>
> (§ 64)

A similar process, which violates the distinction of cause and effect, is also apparent in life's relation of part and whole cited in the epigraph to this section. The phenomenon perpetually exceeds the horizons within which we are able to situate it – 'a condition which has to be removed to an ever-retreating horizon' – and leaves us with the conclusion that 'This condition is the unconditional condition' (§ 67).

This process of 'selection' and 'construction' points to another analogy. This is the analogy of life as the mutual dependence of discrimination and unification. Kant admits this explicitly after rejecting the analogy of art and proposing in its stead the analogy of life:

> But nature, on the contrary, organizes itself, and does so in each species of its organized products – following a single pattern, certainly, as to general features, but nevertheless admitting deviations calculated to secure self-preservation under particular circumstances. We might perhaps come nearer to the description of this inpenetrable property if we were to call it an *analogue of life*.
>
> (§ 65)

But if this analogy were to be pursued rigorously, then we would have to introduce a soul into nature, which is unacceptable. We are then left with the negative conclusion that 'Strictly speaking, therefore, the organization of nature has nothing analogous to any causality known to us' (§ 65). Kant is completely consistent in this claim since he has already, in Part I of the *Critique*, maintained that life exceeds our notion of causality and cannot be determined by the understanding. It is not possible to bring life under judgement, since its separations and constructions, its discriminations and unifications, even its restrictions and realizations, exceed judgement's horizon.

This activity called life, the orientation of human beings and the adaptation of plants, is literally transcendental, beyond the categories, and distinguishes life from art. The categories of the understanding recognize only mechanical causality, and within this horizon of perception, nature is regarded as a machine. But Kant insists that the organization of nature is not mechanical but formative:

an organized being is, therefore, not a mere machine. For a machine has solely *motive* power, whereas an organized being possesses inherent formative power, and such, moreover, as it can impart to material devoid of it – material which it organizes. This, therefore, is a self-augmenting formative power [*eine sich fortpflanzende bildende Kraft*], which cannot be explained by the capacity of movement alone, that is to say, by mechanism.

(§ 65)

Kant names this formative power, which is more than mere motion, 'life'. It is a movement which is self-augmenting – one which does not spend itself – and formative, able to give form to itself and its material, if these can be separated. As it exceeds motion, it also exceeds the categories of the understanding. Where, then, does this formative power stand with regard to the other transcendental areas of Kant's thought?

The notion of life proposed in the first part of the *Critique of Judgement-Power* was also formative, it being the adaptation of power to a fundamental proportion. The proportion governs the form of the formative power, and is expressed not only in the mechanism of schematism, but also in the *Zweckmässigkeit ohne Zweck* of the aesthetic judgement of taste. The power has a selective moment, in which it discriminates its material, and a constructive one in which it forms them. It disposes itself into intuition and concept. These two modes of formation also underpin Kant's definition of culture as the proportion between production – the selection and preparation of materials – and the laws of political organization. It is a relation fundamental to German thought, subsequently evoked in Marx's famous disproportion of productive forces and productive relations.[16] The political implication of the distinction is revealed by Kant in a footnote to the passage on the inscrutability of self-organizing, formative power of life.[17] There the inseparability of cause and effect is applied analogously to the French Revolution. This is seen as the formative power of a people organizing themselves into a state. He returns to an image of the body politic which, infused like Leviathan with a formative energy, gives itself a constitution, or constitutes itself as an organized polity.[18] Kant informs his readers of the

> case of a complete transformation [*Umbildung*], recently undertaken, of a great people into a state, [where] the word organization has frequently and with much propriety, been used for the constitution of the legal authorities and even of the entire body politic. For in a whole of this kind certainly no member should be a mere means, but should also be an end, and seeing that he contributes to the possibility of the entire body, should have his position and function in turn defined by the idea of the whole.
>
> (footnote, § 65)

Before pursuing the hint in this passage that the formative activity of culture promises the advent of the Kingdom of Ends, in which each part produces and gives laws to itself and others, we should return to judgement, and consider its relation to reflection and to analogy.

The notion of physical causality according to an end cannot be comprehended by human judgement. It is not, Kant insists against Herder and others, 'a constitutive conception either of understanding or of reason, but yet it may be used by reflective judgement as a regulative conception for guiding our investigation of objects of this kind by a remote analogy with our own causality according to ends generally, and as a basis of reflection upon their supreme source' (§ 65). He refuses to introduce any new causality into the understanding of life, allowing only a regulative employment of the hypotyposis of causality according to ends. We can use the teleological estimate only by analogy to the formative power. We may only speak of the forms thrown up by the activity of the formative power, but not of the power which disposes itself in these forms. This formative activity is beyond the purview of judgement, and we may approximate to an understanding of it only through analogy.

Yet although Kant continually points to the procedural aspects of the technic of judgement, the employment of hypotyposes as horizons of interpretation, he returns to privileging the relation of the one and the many over the forms of proportionable relation. The horizon of interpretation established by the reflective judgement is treated as if it were a unity, instead of an orientational horizon within which

unities may be constituted. This is apparent in the way Kant thinks
the relation of idea and matter: 'idea is an absolute unity of the
representation, whereas the material is a plurality of things that of
itself can afford no definite unity of composition' (§ 66). There is
no notion in this particular passage of any relation outside unity and
plurality; there is a distinct lack of proportion. Kant does not fully
grasp his own point that unity is just another hypotyposis that has
usurped its sovereignty. To be consistent, he would have to privilege
proportion in general over unity and plurality. Formative activity
disposes itself into separation and construction, and it is illegitimate
to translate the proportions of this activity into judgement's language
of unity and manifold.

The hesitation in unequivocally privileging the analogical activity
of reflection over the subsumptive activity of bringing a manifold
under a unity becomes increasingly exposed in the second part of
the *Critique*. It is most apparent in the distinction between the
teleological and mechanical estimates in the 'Antinomy', and then
again in the 'Methodology'. There it seriously affects Kant's
understanding of the political aspects of culture anticipated in the
footnote on the self-constitution of the French people. Kant's reading
of tradition in terms of excessive unification and discrimination may
have permitted him to discover a more fundamental relation in the
formative activity of productive legislation, but it was under perpetual
threat of lapsing into the language of judgement.

The dialectic of teleological judgement arises from the internal
conflict of the maxims of reflection. When confronted with the
heterogeneity of particular laws it is necessary to organize our
experience through a principle of reflection; but this principle cannot
be derived from understanding or intuition; consequently, 'judgement
must be a principle to itself, even for the mere purpose of searching
for a law and tracking one out in the phenomenon of nature. For it
needs such a principle as a guiding thread' (§ 70). The principle of
reflection is a disposition of judgement which helps it orient itself
among the multiplicity of nature. But the disposition is unstable, and
can give rise to conflicting maxims: it may establish one horizon in
which everything is estimated according to mechanical causality; or
another in which everything is estimated according to final causality.
The antinomy arises when the determinate laws of mechanical
causality and the reflective laws of final explanation are taken as
objective and not as maxims for the guidance of judgement. As
reflective maxims, or horizons of interpretation, both principles are
compatible; but if they are accorded objective status they become
antinomic.

Kant surveys various examples of the confusion of the maxims of reflection, ranging from Epicurus to Spinoza, and concludes that it is impossible to determine an objective finality or physical end. The inscription of finality upon nature is a hypotyposis following from the structure of our judgement. Against the claim that nature is only possible through a final cause pursuing a determinate design, Kant insists that this is only a hypotyposis, for '*by the peculiar constitution of my cognitive faculties* the only way I can judge of the possibility of those things and of their production is by conceiving for that purpose a cause working designedly, and, consequently, a being whose productivity is analogous to the causality of an understanding' (§ 75). The hypotyposis must be read as a subjective maxim for reflective judgement and not as an objective principle. Although we may read finality in nature, we cannot assume that it is actually there because we have probably written it in ourselves: 'strictly speaking, we do not *observe* the ends in nature as designed. We only *read* this conception *into* the facts as a guide to judgement in its reflection upon the products of nature' (§ 75). We orient ourselves in nature by mapping it according to the hypotyposis of our own productive activity. Our self-alienating understanding inscribes a finality, which is then read off as objective. Instead of recognizing that we write our own laws and then judge ourselves by them – as in the 'critical tribunal which is the *Critique of Pure Reason*' – and then embracing the necessity of the delay between inscription and judgement 'steadfastly' and with responsibility, we put ourselves under the tutelage of our own law by objectifying it. Furthermore, we then attribute this legislation to providence, who does not suffer finitude, and whose laws are immediately judgements.

The question of whether there is a providential design in nature yields to that of the 'peculiar constitution of human nature' which needs to postulate one. The remainder of the 'Antinomy' is devoted to this question, and leads through the 'remark' or survey of the transcendental philosophy discussed above. Here the philosophical distinctions of possibility/actuality, contingency/necessity, part/whole, obligation/action are traced back to the hypotyposis of human judgement. This is related to finitude through the transcendental distinction of the sensibility and the understanding. When viewed from the standpoint of an infinite being with intellectual intuition, the distinctions appear distinctly provincial. An intuitive understanding does not suffer the distinction of concept and intuition and its correlates; human understanding does, and has to mediate them. But Kant then allows that the possibility of mediation demands an accord between the concept and intuition which is prior to their distinction.

There then arises a view of finality as fundamental, a 'conformity to law on the part of the contingent [which] is termed finality' (§ 76). Without this conformity there could be no mediation of concept and intuition; it underlies all experience as the 'harmonizing of natural features without the faculty of conceptions' (§ 77). But the accord itself cannot be determined (since it founds determination), and so 'must exist without any determinate principle to guide our judgement' (§ 77).

Teleological judgement is a more comprehensive approximation to this accord than determinate judgement since it works with a wider notion of causality. This is both its strength and its weakness; for while it is open to a more generous notion of the attunement of understanding and sensibility than determinate judgement, it cannot determine their relation. It does however point to the ground of agreement necessary for the performance of determinant judgement according to mechanical principles. The intelligibility of nature's plurality of laws given in teleological judgement is broader, but less defined than their explanation according to determinate laws. We may orient ourselves toward the manifold of natural laws, attune our judgement – power to nature through its reflective employment, before we make the more visibly legitimate, but narrower determinations according to mechanical principles:

> We may and should explain all products and events of nature, even the most purposive, so far as in our power lies, on mechanical lines – and it is impossible for us to assign the limits of our powers when confined to the pursuit of inquiries of this kind. But in so doing we must never lose sight of the fact that among such products there are those which we cannot even subject to investigation except under the conception of an end of reason.
>
> (§ 78)

But this does not give us a licence to confuse the two interpretative horizons. They must be kept analytically separate in any explanation, even if it is conceded that they share a 'single principle' or 'supersensible ground' beyond judgement.

Reflective judgement is essentially procedural; it is not directed toward making a definitive judgement but is continually approximating to a fundamental accord or proportion. This procedural aspect of judgement, judgement as a disposition, as care, means that the methodological side of the judgement should be given more attention than its analytic and dialectic. Consequently twelve out of thirty sections in the 'Critique of Teleological Judgement' are devoted to the method of judgement. And it is in these that the latent theological themes of the *Critique* become most prominent.

The 'Methodology' reveals the hidden agenda of the entire *Critique* to be the justification of creation by a being which has been ordained to legislate its own freedom. The self-cultivation of such a being is shown to be the cultivation of the entire creation. It was observed how in the *Lectures on Philosophical Theology* Kant emphasized activity and work as God's gift to humanity. It is through work that the approximation to proportion is achieved, that is, through a practical and not a theoretical vocation. In the 'Methodology', life as the unity of production and legislation is considered in terms of human self-cultivation and the cultivation of the entire creation.

Yet while Kant's view of orientation and life points to an experimental setting of horizons and temporary discriminations, to a generous notion of proportionality, he can often only think this in terms of unity and manifold. He delivers the immanent finality of nature to unity, and thus to plurality. While his view of the *summum bonum* goes beyond the unification of a manifold to the revelation of the analogy of being, the play of analogy is often brought violently back to the forced unification of a resistant manifold. Instead of freedom's productive legislation bringing forth the fundamental proportion of freedom and nature, it delivers itself to the task of subjugating nature.

Life and the *Summum Bonum*

> Faith as *habitus*, not as *actus* . . . is the steadfast principle of the *Gemüt*, according to which the truth of what must necessarily be presupposed as the condition of the supreme final end being possible is assumed as true in consideration of the fact that we are under an obligation [*Verbindlichkeit*] to pursue that end – and assumed notwithstanding that we have no insight into its possibility, though likewise none into its impossibility.
>
> Kant, *Critique of Judgement-Power*

The analysis of finality pursued across the two parts of the *Critique of Judgement-Power* reveals itself in the end as a restatement of the *summum bonum* for modernity. All the scattered arguments of the *Critique* are gathered together in the restatement of the fundamental problem of metaphysics. The emendation of the concept of the highest good involves a synthesis of the objective proportionality of the Aristotelean tradition with the productive legislation of modernity. The highest good is the proportioned activity remembered in beauty – reason's 'uncertain voice' – and which we are bound resolutely to pursue even though we can never know whether it is possible, or impossible, to realize.

It may be claimed that Kant's position is closer to that of Aquinas than to the Renaissance humanists and their heirs in the British and German theories of taste and aesthetic. He regards nature as irradiated with proportionality or 'finality' – even if it has only been put there by human agency – it is not the grey adversary of human freedom. Nevertheless, his position inserts itself in the humanist tradition with the insistence that this proportionality is revealed through formative activity. This formative activity both produces and discovers this proportionality or finality in nature; in other words, it is inventive. This inventive formation, moreover, is in the strict sense of the word 'transcendental', since it is 'beyond' the concepts and intuitions of judgement, and is the condition for its subsumptions. The proportion of nature and freedom constitutes the *summum bonum*, which Kant presents both in the terms of the modern distinction of freedom and natural necessity, and in those of a proportionality which transcends this distinction. The *summum bonum* is only thinkable in terms of an accord between natural finality and the ends produced by human legislation. In terms of the architectonic of the third *Critique*, the 'Methodology' is required to show how the realms of physical theology and ethical theology may be brought to an accord through culture.

This understanding of the *summum bonum* leads to a different principle of welfare than those of the British and German traditions of civil society and the police-state. Kant's imputation of finality to nature and his view of culture as realizing the accord of natural finality and human ends through work, contrasts starkly with the denegration of nature and work in the other traditions. Kant accords labour a key role in realizing the proportion of the *summum bonum*, while for the others it is a degrading activity performed under compulsion. However, Kant also concedes disproportion, detecting the emergence of an imbalance between the productive and legislative moments of formative culture which can only be corrected through violence. This vacillation between placing the accord of freedom and nature violently within judgement or inventively beyond it rends the remainder of the text.

After surveying the extrinsic finality of nature in § 82, Kant asks 'What is the end and purpose of these and all preceding animal kingdoms?' His answer to this question regarding the ultimate end and purpose of creation, is human activity. These kingdoms are

For man, we say, and the multifarious uses to which his intelligence teaches him to put all these forms of life. He is the ultimate end of creation here upon earth, because he is the one and only being upon it that is able to form a conception of ends, and from an aggregate of things purposively fashioned to construct by the aid of his reason a system of ends.

(§ 82; see also §§ 83, 87)

Here, as for the humanists Ficino and Pico, the vocation of humanity is identified as the mediation between nature and God. But how does Kant understand this mediation? A familiar movement is apparent in the above passage, one that corresponds to that of the 'realization and restriction' or 'separation and construction' of life. Formative activity configures natural things as final, disposing them into a pre-conceptual order adapted to construction by the reason. This activity is analogous to the plant's adaptive separation of materials, and their construction into a new form, and the discrimination and subsumption of orientation. But in human formation the accord of the activities of separation/discrimination and construction/subsumption is unstable, opening the possibility of a disproportion between the work of configuring nature, and the activity of disposing the products of this activity into new forms.

The twofold activity of setting ends and disposing the materials for their realization is unstable and prone to bias. Therefore, the two activities should be analytically separated: culture too must obey the transcendental distinction. Kant observes this in his exposition of the *summum bonum* as well as in his description of human existence as involving

> the highest end – the end to which, as far as in him lies, he may subject the whole of nature, or contrary to which at least he must not deem himself subjected to any influence on its part. – Now assuming that things in the world are beings that are dependent in point of their real existence, and, as such, stand in need of a supreme cause acting according to ends, then man is the final end of creation.

(§ 84)

Human setting of ends has to be abstracted from the influence of nature, but this is not the existential truth of the relationship, for 'without man the chain of mutually subordinated ends would have no ultimate point of attachment.' It is, paradoxically, human freedom which grounds the rest of creation; its ability to legislate apart from nature is what 'alone qualifies [mankind] to be a final end to which entire nature is teleologically subordinated' (§ 84). But if this ability to legislate apart from nature remains totally aloof from its object, then it can no longer serve to ground or justify it. There must be a point at which the causality of nature and the causality of human will meet and find themselves in accord.

The *summum bonum* requires unconditioned causality, but must also relate to nature. Kant works up to showing how this is accomplished by way of negation. Without humanity 'the whole of creation would be a mere wilderness, a thing in vain, and have no final end' (§ 86). But then how does humanity cultivate this wilderness and give it some point? Not, as in traditional metaphysics, through contemplating it: 'it is not man's cognitive faculty, that is, theoretical reason, that forms the point of reference which alone gives its worth to the existence of all else in the world – as if the meaning of his presence in the world was that there might be some one in it that could make it an object of *contemplation*' (§ 86). This is because contemplation follows from the inscription of finality, 'a final end of the world must be presupposed as that in relation to which the contemplation of the world may itself possess a worth' (§ 86). Contemplation alone does not suffice to justify itself, let alone underwrite the rest of creation.

Continuing along the *via negationis*, Kant next dismisses pleasure as a candidate for the justification of creation:

> Neither is it in relation to the feeling of pleasure or the sum of such feelings that we can think that there is a given final end of creation, that is to say, it is not by *well-being*, not by enjoyment, whether bodily or mental, not, in a word, by happiness, that we value that absolute worth. For the fact that mankind, when it exists, makes happiness its final purpose, affords us no conception of any reason why he should exist at all, or of any worth he himself possesses, for which his real existence should be made agreeable to him.
>
> (§ 86)

This criterion too presupposes that there is already a finality in creation by which mankind may consider its happiness as justified: 'mankind must already be presupposed to be the final end of creation, in order that we may have a rational ground to explain why nature, when regarded as an absolute whole according to principles of ends, must be in accord with the conditions of his happiness' (§ 86). The principle which might justify creation does not consist in happiness, although we shall see that, whatever it is, it must accord or harmonize with the conditions of happiness. It must consist in some kind of relation between finality and its contemplation and enjoyment.

If the final principle of creation is neither theoretical contemplation nor the pleasurable enjoyment of creation, then perhaps it consists in the practical stance toward it. This requires that practical philosophy be understood in the broad sense as the inscription of finality and the forming of an estimate in accordance with this inscription. Creation is then justified in terms of human freedom and self-estimation:

> it is the worth which it alone can give to itself, and which consists in what it does – in the manner in which and the principles upon which it acts in the *freedom* of its faculty of desire, and not as a link in the chain of nature. In other words a good will is that whereby man's existence can alone possess an absolute worth, and in relation to which the existence of the world can have a *final end*.
>
> (§ 86)

At first sight this position seems paradoxical, insofar as the principle of legislation can only justify the world, in Kant's words, be 'in relation' to it, as long as it does not stand in a relation to it. The apparent suppression of this paradox in the categorical imperative provoked the reading of Kant's moral philosophy which finds that its 'rigorism' negates nature by subjecting it to despotic decrees.

Kant's definition of the *summum bonum*, however, stresses the mediation of the distinction between nature and freedom's autonomy. In § 87 the autonomy of legislation is presented as only the 'formal condition' which 'binds us' to striving after the *summum bonum*:

> The moral law is the formal rational condition of the employment of our freedom, and, as such, of itself alone binds us [*verbindet uns*], independently of any end as its material condition. But it also defines for us a final end, and does so *a priori*, and determines us [*bestimmt uns*] to strive towards its attainment. This end is the *summum bonum*, as the highest good *in the world* possible through freedom.
>
> (§ 87)

Not only does the law define a 'final end' for humanity in the highest good, but it also 'binds' and 'determines' us to strive for its realization. But then we are left with the difficulty of characterizing this binding and determination – this *restriction* – of the law through which we are enjoined to *realize* the highest good.

The condition through which the intelligible is mediated with the physical is pleasure, and the *schema*, so to speak, of human freedom – the *summum bonum* – is happiness. The furtherance of happiness becomes Kant's welfare principle, one he rigorously distinguishes from both Wolff's eudaemonistic perfectionism and empirical happiness. He describes his principle at the beginning of § 88 as the alignment of the highest good with the greatest welfare:

> We are called [*bestimmt*] *a priori* through reason to further the *summum bonum* [*Weltbeste*] as far as in us lies. This *summum bonum* consists in the binding [*in der Verbindung besteht*] of the greatest welfare [*grössten Wohls*] of the rational beings in the world with the supreme condition of their good, or, in other words, by the union of universal happiness with the most law-abiding ethical life [*gesetzmässigsten Sittlichkeit*].
>
> (§ 88)

This particular articulation of the *summum bonum* juxtaposes the traditions of the moral sense and perfection – happiness and legality. But the conditions for this synthesis – the call to bind them – still remain open.

The characterization of the *summum bonum* as the *Verbindung* of happiness and a law-governed ethical life begs the question of the manner and the place of their binding. Kant says that the binding itself cannot be named, since it lies beyond our naming, is transcendental. It is impossible to think this accord, this 'necessary harmonizing' of natural and ethical finality in terms of our narrow notions of relation. It not only lies beyond determinate judgement, but also transcends reflective judgement. The situation seems hopeless, philosophy has let everyone down: 'This is the least that could be demanded of speculative philosophy, which undertakes to connect the ethical end with physical ends by means of the idea of a single end. Yet even this little is still far more than it can ever accomplish' (§ 88). We can only assume this principle of the accord of physical and ethical ends, and act with the steadfast faith that such an accord is neither possible nor impossible to realize.

There is consolation in the fact that while the existence of an accord between physical and ethical ends can never be objectively verified, it would not be possible to think or act without assuming its existence. We could not live without this assumption, for:

by virtue of the moral law which enjoins this final end upon us, we have reason for assuming from a practical point of view, that is for the direction of our energies towards the realization of that end, that it is possible, or in other words, practicable. Consequently we are also justified in assuming a nature of things harmonizing with such a possibility – for this possibility is subject to a condition which does not lie in our power, and unless nature played into our hands the realization of the final end would be impossible.

(§ 88)

So in order to direct our energies, to live, it is necessary to assume that our ends are adaptable to the finality of nature, that the two finalities are proportionable. This accord, once more, is unstatable; it cannot be figured in terms of mechanical causation, and so, on the hypotyposis of our own agency, it is assumed to be the product of a final end, a creator God who simultaneously produces and legislates beyond both physical and human finalities.

Kant's admission of the inexplicability of the accord of natural finality and human ends gestures toward life as proportioned action. In the formative synthesis of production and legislation Kant comes close to naming his absolute. He sees in this synthesis the source of the call to bind together freedom and necessity; indeed this synthesis is prior to judgement, being something extremely primitive, 'for it was there in human reason before its earliest quickening [*Aufkeimung*], and with the progressive culture of that faculty was only further developed' (§ 88). This original synthesis was also an original differentiation between right and wrong. The call of reason, in other words, was originally a cry for justice. Kant imagines a time before law when 'men's eyes as yet cast but a heedless regard at the finality of nature, and when they took advantage of it without imagining the presence of anything but nature's accustomed course.' But even before law there was judgement, but one which founded and did not apply the law:

> one undeniable judgement must have come into presence among them [*unvermeidlich einfinden*]. It could never be that the issue is all alike, whether a man has acted fairly or falsely, with equity or with violence, albeit to his life's end, as far at least as human eye can see, his virtues have brought him no reward, his transgressions no punishment.

(§ 88)

The original judgement which came among them, appeared, made itself present (in Meredith's translation 'forced itself upon them'), was spoken as a difference which followed an unspeakable proportion or accord: reward and punishment must be apportioned, even if there is no law for doing so. In telling the story of how this judgement first came among us, Kant employs Leibnizian terminology to describe the voice calling us to strive for justice as a *dunkle Vorstellung*:

> It was as if they perceived in themselves a voice, it must go otherwise; they must have felt an obscure perception of something to which they were bound to strive, and with which such a result wouldn't make any sense [*sich garnicht zusammenreimen lasse*], or with which, once they regarded the way of the world as the only order of things, they would not be able to reconcile the attunement of their powers [*Zweckbestimmung ihres Gemüts*] [Meredith – 'significant bent of their minds'].
>
> (§ 88)

The voice announced to them that their obscure representation of a just proportion had been violated. This was felt as the difference between right and wrong. Moreover, this violation of the *Weltlauf* – the 'way of things' – made them feel no longer at home in the world.[19]

Kant sees both metaphysics and religion arising as narratives which try to make sense of this violation of proportion. They sought to bring the way of the world into harmony with the sense of proportion. These narratives, 'crude as are their curious notions', concern 'the way in which such an irregularity [*Unregelmässigkeit*] (of which nothing is more repugnant to the human powers . . .) could be put straight' (§ 88). The normalizing of the irregularity consists in bringing natural finality into accord with human activity, in postulating a supreme cause as the 'one principle upon which they could even conceive it possible for nature to harmonize with the moral law dwelling within them' (§ 88). It is the notion of divinity which permits the agreement of human action and proportion, an agreement which we have already heard Kant describe as life.

What does it mean to cultivate this 'original germ' of the sense of violation – the source of the feeling for the sublime – and to develop its distinction of good and evil? Culture brings the course of the world and the sense of justice into proportion; it straightens irregularities and realizes the proportion between finality and human freedom. Culture brings the fundamental proportion into view by forming nature in accordance with human ends. But the relation of activity and proportion develops through time, in history, and it too 'hatches many absurdities' and disproportions. In this history, culture is driven to bind together happiness as the relation to an object or the way of the world, and freedom's autonomy. Its activity relates to nature, but is not part of its causality; it actualizes a proportion of nature and human ends, but in a way that is prone to distortion. Instead of the achievement of the *summum bonum*, the harmony between the finality of nature and human legislation, it is possible that freedom will violate this proportion.

The justification of creation through the *summum bonum* is attained through culture. Central to the theory of culture, sketched out in § 83 and in several of Kant's paralipomena, is the theological idea that human activity is the ultimate end of creation. Human activity justifies nature by moulding it according to a finality which is not natural, but this is conditional on the responsible setting of ends in accordance with justice and natural finality. An important step towards a responsible disposition is the analytical separation of the legislation of ends and natural finality.

For this reason the proper relation of human activity and natural things cannot be found exclusively in happiness. Happiness is indeed 'the material substance of all [human] earthly ends' but it does not suffice to determine the relation between human ends and natural finality; it 'renders [human beings] incapable of positing a final end for their own real existence and of harmonizing therewith' (§ 83). For a subreption has taken place if the actualization of ends is made into a principle of their determination. The determination of ends must be analytically separated from their actualization, a distinction consonant with Kant's earlier separation of possibility and actuality. For if happiness became determinate, actuality would vanquish possibility, and human beings would no longer be free, that is, no longer find themselves in the predicament of having to act responsibly with respect to possibility.

The disposition to strive for *summum bonum*, or the faith in the possibility of a just world in which human and natural finalities would be in proportion, informs all human activity and thought. Such a conformity of free activity and law, described earlier as 'feeling at home in the world', or life, is anticipated in beauty. The notion of a beautiful relation between humans and between them and nature is always threatened by the disproportion of the might and dominion of the sublime. This is because the aptitude to legislate ends may become detached from their productive realization: 'we are left only with a formal, subjective condition, that, namely, of the aptitude [of mankind] for setting ends before themselves at all, and, independent of nature in their power of determining ends, of employing nature as a means in accordance with the maxims of his free ends generally' (§ 83). However, once again, although this disposition follows from the idea of a proportioned activity it becomes afflicted by bias when the setting of ends is not conformable with their material realization.

Culture is burdened by this disproportion. Properly proportioned, it consists in the harmony of legislation and execution, between the setting of ends and their actualization. It is the disposition or *habitus* through which the *summum bonum* is realized: 'The production in a rational being of an aptitude for any ends whatever of its own choosing, consequently of the aptitude of a being in its freedom, is *culture [Kultur]*' (§ 83). But the production of the disposition for setting ends and realizing them can only be achieved through violence. The potential for beauty in the habitus is surrendered to the sublime.

The bias of culture manifests itself in a disproportion between the legislative and executive functions which can only be corrected through violence and discipline. The mode of executing ends is skill, and in a remarkable passage Kant aligns the disproportion of executive and legislative activities with class conflict, anticipating Hegel's master and slave dialectic. To begin with, 'Skill can hardly be developed in the human race otherwise than by means of inequality among men. For the majority, in a mechanical kind of way that calls for no special art, provide the necessaries of life for the ease and convenience of others who apply themselves to the less necessary branches of culture in science and art' (§ 83). But this disproportion is unstable, the productive activity of the majority can only be maintained through violence, injustice and eventually mutual destruction. The unproductive minority,

> keep the masses in a state of oppression, with hard work and little enjoyment, though in the course of time much of the culture of the higher classes spreads to them also. But with the advance of this culture – the culminating point of which, where devotion to what is superfluous begins to be prejudicial to what is indispensable, is called luxury – misfortunes increase equally on both sides. With the lower classes they arise by external violence [*fremde Gewalttätigkeit*] with the upper from seeds of discontent within.

> (§ 83)

However, this intensification of the bias of culture could be regarded, within a certain horizon, as a tendency toward harmony. For 'this splendid misery is connected with the development of natural tendencies in the human race, and the end pursued by nature itself, though it be not our end, is thereby attained' (§ 83).

The process of culture has formal similarities to orientation; in it things are discriminated according to an unknown principle, and then subsumed. It is necessary to present intuitions to the understanding suitably conformed for subsumption. This entails a complex activity of projecting horizons of discrimination which are themselves neither discriminative nor universal. They permit things to appear as differentiated, as well as adapted to finality. This activity of differentiating and proportioning does not fall within the transcendental distinction of concept and intuition, but is spoken through the discourse of 'realization and restriction'. This also follows Kant's discourse of life, which, in the case of organic adaptation, separates materials according to a 'principle' which also conforms them for construction according to the ends of the organism. Culture disposes itself according to analogous laws.

Everything depends on the way in which 'realization and restriction' is thought in culture. On the one hand Kant thinks it in terms of the proportioning of activity, the bringing to appearance of natural finality through human projection, and the construction of a world in which human ends find themselves realized in the *summum bonum*. But the proportion underlying this disposition is difficult to represent. And when Kant tries to do so, he translates it into the language of judgement. Instead of recognizing a proportion within human freedom which may be realized and restricted through an ethical life, he sees in it only the spectacle of a lawless manifold which must be subsumed under unity.[20] The notion of a self-proportioning constitution which he observed in his note on the French Revolution falls to a subsumption of a manifold; now it seems that we do indeed need a master: 'The formal condition under which nature can alone attain this its real end is the existence of a constitution so regulating the mutual relations of men that the abuse of freedom by individuals striving one against another is opposed by a lawful authority centred in a whole, called a civil society [*bürgerliche Gesellschaft*]' (§ 83). It is conceded here that the freedom of individuals cannot proportion itself, but must submit to unification through the law of the centralized state.

With this, the discourse of proportion and realization, which exceeds the transcendental distinction, is reduced to its terms. An unconfigured and internally destructive manifold is opposed by a centralized unity. The proportioned ethical life is presented in terms of civil society and the police-state. The perspectives of the tradition are thus brought together: a civil society with no inherent principle is ordered by a police-state which possesses reason. The bias within the tradition is corrected, but from within the tradition, the language of the beautiful – *Übereinstimmung* – is surrendered to that of the sublime – *Entgegensetzung*.

The accord of freedom with conformity to law so crucial in the first part of the *Critique*, where it is thought in terms of a proportioned activity which exceeded the bias of the traditions, is now rendered in terms of their violent unification. Instead of the active proportionality of life there is now the unification of individual freedom under law. But we have already seen that such judgement yields to aporia, that subsumption requires a prior conformity in discrimination; that the law must be appropriate to those which it legislates.[21]

These aporias surface in the *Metaphysik der Sitten* as the difficulty of establishing proportionality in private and public law. The notions of proportioned activity developed in the first part of the *Critique* are forgotten, and the relation of citizen and law treated in terms of intuition and concept. Yet even here a more complex account of recognition underlies the dry exposition of legal and moral relations. Humans cannot relate in terms of unity and dispersion, there is a more fundamental activity of differentiating and establishing proportion taking place through their recognition of each other. Such an accord of recognition is announced in the *Zweckmässigkeit ohne Zweck* of beauty, with its hint of the agreement of the way of the world with justice, and its intimation of the *summum bonum* in which each restricts and realizes the other in living the good life.

Beyond Judgement

> So far this activity has been rarely disputed, even though it deserves in-depth investigation; but this is not the place to linger on it.
>
> Kant, *Critique of Judgement-Power*

If after all this we are still left with judgement in a tangle, the knot yet untied, how can there be any question of 'beyond judgement'? One understanding of 'beyond' would require that all the knots be untied, all the secrets revealed, and the conflicting traditions of judgement raised into a higher unity. But is this the 'beyond' or 'transcendence' of the transcendental philosophy? According to some readers, pre-eminently Derrida, such unification is its desire if not its accomplishment. For him transcendental philosophy remains within judgement, its transcendence the more or less deferred unity of the subject. And, indeed, there are several places in the third *Critique* where Kant does appeal to such transcendence; but the structure of his argument points in a different direction. Where or when, then, is the 'beyond' of the *Critique of Judgement-Power*?

First of all, being beyond judgement might mean having transcended the traditions of judgement, discovering a legitimate place from which to judge it. This was the ambition of the first *Critique*, but was abandoned in the third where judgement is less a faculty than a knot in tradition. And Kant knows that he cannot imitate Alexander and cut the knot, but neither is he willing to submit to its constriction; instead he inquires into how he is bound. His judgement of tradition is inventive: it reproduces tradition not passively as imitation, but actively as discovery. By confronting the tradition with its own contradictions and tangles, Kant is able to free his arm sufficiently to point beyond it. The tangles of tradition register the limits of judgement and, if approached artfully, these limits may be transcended. But such moments of transcendence are intermittent, and only bear witness to a different relation or law. Transcendental philosophy, in other words, can only happen on occasion.

While it is not possible to transcend judgement from within its limits, it can be shown to be partial in restricting itself to the unifications of manifolds, or the identifications of differences. Even in such unifications and identifications it can be shown to encounter its limit in an order, or pre-figuration of the 'unity' and the 'manifold' prior to judgement. Without this anticipation of synthesis, judgement could not judge and the unity and manifold could not be brought to conform. There is a relation within the relation but also beyond it, one which is erased and forgotten. It appeared whenever the traditions of judgement fell into difficulty legislating their discriminations or discriminating their legislation; it appeared in the appeal to a forgotten order which was designated as providence or relegated to 'beauty', one whose traces were violently repressed. Nevertheless, these difficulties mark the limit of judgement and were used by Kant to point beyond it. But while judgement-power always exceeds itself it is not without relation: but this relation is not a unification, but a binding or obligation (*Verbindung*). Kant repeatedly points to a *nexus* which is not one of unity and manifold, not one of subject and object, neither free nor necessary, but common and unfamiliar. It is a binding which is before judgement, and so beyond it. It cannot be written, but it can be witnessed, testified to, pointed at, remembered, by saying what it is not, and cannot be.

Throughout the third *Critique* Kant evokes the procedure of hypotyposis which is implicated and erased in judgement. It indicates a proportioned order which cannot be thought as unity and manifold, but only in analogy. With this Kant evokes the metaphysical tradition of analogy, with its reference to a transcendental proportionality inaccessible to categorial thought, but refuses to 'linger' with it. However the question of the nature of this transcendence is unavoidable: does it remain within judgement or does it truly transcend its categories? For Derrida transcendental philosophy rises for judgement at the moment it appeals to analogy,[1] and here, in the *Critique*, analogy serves to legitimate the violence of framing: 'it *gathers together* without-concept and concept, universality *without* concept and universality *with* concept, the *without* and the *with*; it thus legitimates the violence, the occupation of a nonconceptual field by the grid of a conceptual force' (p. 76). For Derrida, Kant's appeal to analogy is a legitimation of the violence of the *logos* against that which is different.

But is analogy really the 'legitimation' of a violent 'gathering together' or the 'occupation' of a nonconceptual field? Before whom must Kant legitimate such an occupation; who has called him to account and by what law? The question of legitimation is wrongly addressed, for there is no 'nonconceptual field'; Kant's analogy and proportional order is a de-legitimation of judgement, a questioning of the claims by which judgement-power has legitimated its prior occupations. With analogy and the *via negationis* Kant remembers the usurpatory act as the foundation of judgement, and points beyond it.

The third *Critique* rehearses judgement-power's usurpation of a binding or *nexus* which always exceeds it. It summons the 'legitimacy' of this particular appropriation before judgement, and points to other relations of law and production implied in the workings of judgement-power. The text bears witness to a binding which is prior to law – an act of binding which is also a realization – and which does not efface differences but congregates them in the furtherance of life evoked by the beautiful. But it nevertheless gives the furies their due in the sublime, where the proportioned life remembers and mourns the violence at its foundation. The text recognizes that beauty and proportion imply the sublime, that life rests on violence; but it points to an open and free acknowledgement that while realization must be restriction, the knots of judgement need not be suffered. The reciprocal bond acknowledged before judgement remembers its violence but stands in the promise of a bond beyond judgement.

Notes

The Aporia of Judgement

References in both text and notes comprise date of original publication followed, where appropriate, by the page number of the edition used. Where a date and page number are separated by a semi-colon, the page reference is to a modern edition or translation, where a comma is used the date and page are for the same edition, and where two page numbers are separated by a semi-colon the first is the German edition, the second the English translation. Full details of original works and translations are to be found in the Bibliography.

1 For an examination of the persons and procedures of the critical tribunal – its 'maze of litigation and inquisition' – see Rose 1984, chapter 1, 'From Metaphysics to Jurisprudence'.

2 Edward Booth's consummate *Aristotelean Ontological Aporia in Islamic and Christian Thinkers* (1983), explores both the substance and the hermeneutics of aporia. Booth's position is analogous to Leo Strauss's hermeneutic of secrecy in *Persecution and the Art of Writing*: 'Secret, however, has manifold meanings. It may refer to the secret hidden by a parable or word, but it may also mean the parable or word itself which hides a secret' (1952; p. 39).

3 Booth (1983) shows it to have been the case with the late classical and early medieval reception of the Aristotelean ontological aporia, which either dissolved the aporia into a wider unity or analysed it out of existence.

4 The first phase of its reception, exemplified by Schelling's *System of Transcendental Idealism*, emphasized the unification of freedom and necessity. An interesting exception is Friedrich Schlegel, whose '*Aufzeich-nungen aus dem Nachlass*' (see Kulenkampff 1974), is altogether more

unsure of the text. The reading of the *Critique* as a synthetic unity was dominant until recently in English scholarship; it is exemplified by such writers as Macmillan (1912), for whom it is the 'crowning phase' of the critical philosophy; Coleman (1974), who sees in it 'the harmony of reason'; and Crawford (1974) who reads the work in terms of five progressive stages. Recent analytical exegesis has reacted against this tendency, as is admitted by Schaper (1979). This tradition has produced, in the shape of Paul Guyer's *Kant and the Claims of Taste* (1979), one of the most rigorous readings of the *Critique*, but one based on a conscious abridgement of the text. He excludes Kant's crucial and currently widely debated and controversial analysis of the sublime, as an 'afterthought' (p. 399) without 'much interest to modern sensibilities' (p. 400), mainly because it 'does minimise the question of intersubjectivity, which is my main concern'. The location of the deduction at the end of the 'Analytic of the Sublime' is attributed to Kant's 'carelessness'; it is 'a mistake, and should be ignored' (p. 263). Both he and Schaper 'regret' (Schaper 1979; p. 131) Kant's 'lapse' (Guyer 1979; p. 64) into metaphysics. Like the synthetic readings, the analytic interpretations implicitly posit a text that will conform to their reading.

Chapter 1   Beauty under Judgement

1 Plato also cites this proverb in *Republic* at 497d.
2 On the importance of the distinction between invention and judgement see Caygill 1988, pp. 8–9.
3 The Minims were an order of friars founded in 1435, and reaching their greatest influence in the first half of the sixteenth century (*Oxford Dictionary of the Christian Church*, p. 919). The Latin title of Mersenne's fellow Minim, François Niceron's book was *Thaumaturgus Opticus*, pointing to its relation with 'artificial magic' understood as the achievement of marvellous effects through artifice. See Baltrusaitis 1977, p. 60.
4 Galileo uses the metaphor of anamorphic art in his critique of Ariosto; see Panofsky 1957.
5 De Witt Thorpe (1940) analyses at length the relation of judgement and fancy which Hobbes employs in this and in other passages.
6 The best account of the iconography of the *Leviathan* frontispiece is Corbett and Lightbown 1979, but see also Brown 1978.
7 Corbett and Lightbown (1979, pp. 6–7) characterize the baroque frontispiece as the triumphal arch for the entrance of the heroic reader to the text.
8 The theological origins of the sense of the uncanny which surrounds the 'person' are noted by Tricaud 1982, pp. 97–8.
9 Pufendorf frequently cites Cumberland in the second edition of *De Jure*.
10 Krieger's short account of Pufendorf's thought in the *German Idea of Freedom* (1957, pp. 50–6) is excellent, like much in that book. See also his later work, *The Politics of Discretion* (1965).

2   Taste and Civil Society

1 The OED and ODE differ on the Latin root of taste. The OED suggests *taxitare*, to touch, while the ODE suggests a corruption of *tangere*, to touch, and *gustare*, to savour.

2 The standard history of the Financial Revolution is Dickson 1967. The social and theological implications of the Revolution have been explored within the Arendtian paradigm by J.G.A. Pocock; see his characterization of the revolution in 1975, p. 425, and its ideological confrontation of 'the ideology of real property with the threat from the operations not of a trading market, but by a system of public credit' (1985, p. 68). The subversion of real by mobile property meant the replacement of the 'political' by the 'social' and an emphasis on fantasy over virtue.

3 Gunn 1983, however, sees the Moral Revolution more positively as unleashing 'a torrent of social and political criticism that had in some measure been suppressed by the previous regime (p. 10).

4 It is important not to overemphasize the autonomy of civil society in Augustan Britain. Krieger wrote in 1970 that 'What distinguished Great Britain from its continental competitors was not so much the obvious difference between limited and absolute sovereignty – since this difference was quite deceptive in terms of effective political power – but rather the difference between a state run by an alliance of social groups and states run by officials who mediated between social groups' (p. 105). Clark more provocatively describes early Hannoverian England as 'among the most effectively totalitarian of European states of that time' (1985, p. 150).

5 Shaftesbury's influence on the European Enlightenment was both direct and indirect. His *Characteristics* of 1711 went through several English editions and was translated into German in 1768 and French in 1769. As early as 1712 Leibniz had written a critical appreciation of the work, and by 1745 Diderot had translated the 'Inquiry Concerning Virtue or Merit' (1699, revised 1711). Shaftesbury's indirect influence was even greater. His work was the main inspiration of the 'moral sense' school which dominated English moral philosophy and was exported to Europe, where we shall see it played a major role in the formation of Kant's moral philosophy.

6 The *Philosophical Regimen* is a notebook containing entries from Holland 1698 to Naples 1712. It is described by its editor as 'one of the most remarkable unpublished contributions of modern times in the domain of philosophical thought'. Perhaps not, but it is certainly valuable for revealing the social assumptions hidden beneath the stucco of the unctuous rhapsodizing of the *Characteristics*, later criticized by Adam Smith in his *Lectures on Rhetoric*.

7 The 'Inquiry' was written before 1699 when it was published without Shaftesbury's consent from a manuscript in the possession of John

Toland; this forms the basis of Walford's edition. It was revised and appeared among other essays in the *Characteristics*. The accompanying essays are: 'A Letter concerning Enthusiasm' (1708), 'Sensus Communis: An Essay on the Freedom of Wit and Humour' (1709), 'Soliloquy, or Advice to an Author' (1710), 'The Moralists, A Philosophical Rhapsody' (1709), and finally 'Miscellaneous Reflections on the Preceding Treatises' (1711).

8 'At bottom he was saying that the real world of economy and polity rested on a myriad of fantasy worlds maintained by private egos' (Pocock 1975, p. 465).

9 Mandeville's critique of Shaftesbury was emphasized in the German translation of the *Fable* known to Kant, which was titled: *Anti-Shaftesbury oder die entlarvte Eitelkeit der Selbstliebe und Ruhmsucht in philosophischen Gesprachen nach der Englandischen*, published in 1761.

10 'It was because he posed the conflict between virtue and commerce so starkly that he had such a great influence upon the most important moral philosophers of the later part of the century – Hutcheson, Hume, and Smith – all of whom had to rejoin what Mandeville had torn asunder' (Horne 1978, p. 33).

11 Hutcheson was introduced to Pufendorf's writings by his teacher Gershom Carmichael who published a translation and commentary on *De Officis* in 1718.

12 This prompted Cassirer to observe, 'He can think of no better analogy for the immediacy with which we grasp the beautiful than that of sense perception' (1951, p. 321).

13 One overenthusiastic reviewer in the *Scot's Magazine* wrote 'We entertain no kind of doubt but that the Elements of Criticism may one day supersede the critical labours of the Stagirite' (cited in W.C. Lehmann 1971, p. 228). Adam Smith did entertain all kinds of doubts, and is reputed to have said of Kames's books in general and of the *Elements* in particular 'They are all bad, but this is the worst'.

14 Hume's political philosophy has been reconstructed by Miller 1981.

15 Lessing read the *Philosophical Enquiry* in 1757 and he and later Herder both considered translating it, although this was eventually done by Christian Garve in 1773. Mendelssohn echoed Lessing's judgement in his review of the work in the *Bibliothek der schönen Wissenschaften und der freyen Künste* (1758; p. 216). C.P. Macpherson also agrees, seeing in it 'no moral dimension, apart from some homilies about the design of the creator' (1980, p. 19).

16 Castoriadis emphasizes the metaphysical origins of the question of proportion in his seminal essay 'Value, Equality, Justice, Politics: From Marx to Aristotle and from Aristotle to Ourselves': 'Behind the constituted exchange, there is the exchange which is constitutive; and this in its turn requires and implies a commensurability or "equality" (1984, p. 263).

3　Aesthetic and the Police-State

1 Frederick the Great wrote in his *Political Testament* of 1752: 'The government rests on four great pillars: on the administration of justice, prudent taxation, the maintenance of discipline in the army, and finally, the art of co-ordinating the measures for the preservation of the interest of the state, which is called policy' (1941, p. 3; see Behrens 1985, p. 39). Ten years later Smith declared in his lectures 'We will find that there are four things which will be the design of every government: The first and chief design of every system of government is to maintain justice ... When this end, which we may call the internal peace, or peace within doors is secured, the government will next be desirous of promoting the opulence of the state. This produces what we call police. Whatever regulations are made with respect to the trade, commerce, agriculture, manufactures of the country are considered as belonging to the police ... As the government can not be supported without some expense, though the state was very opulent, it would next be considered in what manner this expense should be born ... Besides these three considerations of the security of property, the police, and the revenue of the kingdom or state, it must also be necessary to have some means of protecting the state from foreign injuries' (1978, pp. 5–6).

2 The close relation between Wolff's philosophy and the ideology of the Fredrickian state has been discussed by Bloch 1961, p. 51; Böckerstette 1982, p. 136; Dorwart 1971, p. 18; and Krieger 1957, p. 66.

3 The classic essay is 'Prussian Reform Movements before 1806', (Hintze 1975, pp. 64–87). For the political and economic history of this crucial period see Reinhart Koselleck, (1967), and the debate edited by Barbara Vogel (1980).

4 See Bleek 1972 and Treue 1951 for studies of German 'Smithianismus', and the influence of Kant and Smith's writings on the Prussian administrative class.

5 For the history of policy in general see Maier 1980, Raeff 1983, and Wessel 1978; for the influence of municipal law on the formulation of policy, Mack Walker 1971; and of Prussian police in particular, Dorwart 1971.

6 Sagarra gives a clear account of the Great Elector's strategy (1977, p. 49), while Behrens (1985, p. 46) and Dorwart (1971, *passim*) give a clear picture of the centralized state bequeathed to Frederick II by his father.

7 The police theorist von Justi insists on the unity of the three branches of policy in his *Grundsätze der Polizeiwissenschaft*: 'Other books have treated Policey in connection with principles of *Cameral-oder-Finanz-Wissenschaft*, to the disadvantage of each science, though they are nearly related. Policy is the ground of genuine cameral science, and the police expert must sow if the cameralist is to reap' (cited in Small 1909, p. 437).

8 The tenacity of the police ideology in the Prussian bureaucracy is evident from the text of an interview for a Prussian civil service job cited by Brunschwig: 'The examiners at Minden ask candidate Hash on 21 December 1801: "What is your conception of a state?" "The state is an association of citizens who have come together in order to augment the general happiness and security to the greatest possible degree." "What does a state need in order to augment the general happiness?" "A higher power which uses the state's resources wisely for the general good." "What are the various kinds of state?" "Monarchy, aristocracy and republic." "Which is to be preferred?" "Monarchy, because we ourselves are most happy in one"' (1974, p. 19).

9 The words 'reconcinnation' and 'emendation' are taken from Leibniz's works '*Ratio corporis juris reconcinnandi*' (1668) and '*De primae philosophiae emendatione, et de notione substantiae*' (1694). Luig 1975 is a superb review of Leibniz's law reform activities.

10 Some details of Leibniz's Mainz period can be found in Meyer 1952; Müller and Krönert 1969, and Aiton 1985, pp. 23–37.

11 Leibniz wrote in the Memorandum 'many members of the Estates are fishing in troubled waters, rejoicing over the disruption of the Empire, and avoiding proper justice and its prompt execution like the plague; they love the present confusion, in which everyone is free to create factions, to impede his opponent, to elude judgement and the law, to fasten himself upon his friends, and to live irresponsibly in whatever manner he likes best. Common people fear oppression, the mighty ones a curtailment of their limitless power, for in fact they recognize no authority' (cited in Meyer 1952, p. 130); Leibniz also warned of the dangers of 'a badly established trade and manufacture, an extremely debased currency; [and] in the uncertainty of law and the delay of legal actions'.

12 Leibniz's system of reflecting mirrors reappears in many contexts; it is related to pleasure in his bizarre plans for an Academy of Pleasure in 1675: '"There would be several houses or Academies of this nature through the city. These houses or halls would be built in such a way that the director of the house could see and hear everything said and done without anyone perceiving him, by means of mirrors and openings, something that would be very important for the state and a form of political confessional" ... (rest torn).' (1675; p. 590). There seems to be an analogy between the director of the house, the omniscient absolute monarch, and God 'whose government is the most perfect state one can conceive, where nothing is neglected, where every hair of our head is counted' (1703–5; p. 58).

13 My reading of the chiasmus is indebted to Greg Bright (1983).

14 By 'political laws' Leibniz meant the *Polizeiordnungen*. This is proved by Leibniz's 'Systema Iuris', a classification of law from the mid 1790s (dated by Grua 1695–7) *Textes Inedits*, Paris 1948, in which Leibniz uses '*ordinationes politicae*' and '*Polizeisachen*' synonymously. He divides the field of law into private, semi-public, and public; and includes under

the semi-public laws (otherwise all listed in Latin) '76. *Kammersachen*' and '78. *Politica, Polizeisachen ordinationes politicae*' (p. 837).

15 Arnsperger 1897 is still the best statement of the complex links between Leibniz and Wolff's philosophy. Wolff and Leibniz were seen by Manteufel literally as two sides of the same coin: he founded a 'Societas Aletheophilarum' and had a medal struck with the images of Leibniz and Wolff one on each side, and the enlightenment slogan '*sapere aude*'. His enthusiasm was not entirely disinterested, since he was a paid spy of the Saxon court trying to ingratiate himself with Frederick: see Hinrichs 1971, p. 430.

16 The move from Latin to the vernacular was an important characteristic of the reformed philosophy, so Wolff's single-handed translation of Latin philosophical vocabulary into German was another aspect of his reconciliation of tradition and modernity; see Blackall 1978, p. 26. The glossary of Latin and German philosophical terms which Wolff appended to his German metaphysics is an invaluable yet neglected resource for both historians and students of German philosophy.

17 For general discussions of Wolff's metaphysics see especially Bissinger 1970, and also Gilson 1949; Gurr 1959; and Heimsoeth 1956. Max Wundt's two books of 1939 and 1945 are invaluable for setting Wolff's work in the context of the historical development of German metaphysics; the English accounts in J.V. Burns's 1964 study of Wolff's Cosmology, and Beck 1968 are useful introductions to the splendours and the miseries of Wolffian metaphysics.

18 Wolff and his followers refer indiscriminately to the lower and higher faculties in the singular and plural. The oscillation between 'faculty' and 'faculties' is symptomatic of their division of a continuous power into discrete classes of knowledge.

19 For the classic account of Wolff's political philosophy see Frauendienst 1927 and the fundamental revision of this reading in Bachmann 1977. For a good account in English see Krieger 1957. For an aporetic reading of both Wolff's political philosophy and its place in the tradition see Böckerstette 1982.

20 The slump in his popularity following his return to Halle is nicely illustrated by Solomon Maimon's account of how he rescued his copy of Wolff's *Metaphysics* from the greasy hands of a butter dealer: 'By chance I went into a butter shop one day, and found the dealer in the act of anatomizing a somewhat old book for use in his trade. I looked at it and found, to my no small astonishment, that it was Wolff's *Metaphysics, or the Doctrine of God, of the World, and of Man's Soul*. I could not understand how in a city so enlightened as Berlin such important works could be treated in this barbarous fashion. I turned to the dealer, and asked if he would not sell the book. He was ready to part with it for two groschen. Without thinking long about it I paid the price at once, and went home delighted with my treasure' (Maimon 1975, p. 74).

21 Birke (1966b) gives a good account of the travails of Wolff's philosophy of art.

22 For accounts of the dispute see Cruger 1884 and Freier 1973.

23 The full title was: *Von dem Einfluss und Gebrauch der Einbildungs-kraft zur Ausbesserung des Geschmacks: oder genaue Untersuchung aller Arten Beschreibungen, worinnen die ausserlesenste Stelle der berühmtesten Poeten dieser Zeit beurtheilt werden.*

24 For the history of the German reception of taste in general, and Gottsched's in particular see Bäumler 1967, esp. pp. 65–82; for his fusion of Wolffianism and traditional poetic see also Birke 1966a, pp. 560–75.

25 This position, stated originally by Habermas in his *Strukturwandel der Öffentlichkeit*, was employed with great sensitivity by Hans Freier in his study of Gottsched (1973, see pp. 26, 85).

26 There are signs of revived scholarly interest in Baumgarten's philosophy. For an excellent introduction in English, consult Reill 1975, pp. 61–4; then see Franke 1972, Casula 1973, Schweizer 1973, and Jäger 1980.

27 We can get some idea of what it was like to be a Wolffian in Prussia in the 1730s from Baumgarten's own *Philosophische Briefe von Aletheophilus* (1741). He introduces the work by evoking a secret society of Aletheophilen (or Wolffians) modelled on the Freemasons. The first letter begins by answering the question as to whether he is a Wolffian or not, (p. 1) and goes on to give a taste of the treatment accorded to the suspected Wolffian. After careless words at the supper table, 'It was then spread around that I was a Wolffian. A creepy friend wrote home to my mother about it, and because a know-all neighbour told her these were bad, poisonous people, she wrote to me saying I would do my good dead father shame to fall from the truth in such a way. What was to be done?' (p. 3).

28 Barnard translates *Besonnenheit* as 'mind' in preference to 'reflection', 'because it is much closer to Herder's intended meaning' (1969, p. 132). However, Herder himself uses *reflection* as a synonym for *Besonnenheit* and Barnard's appeal to his intended meaning is not sufficiently persuasive to override this usage. At one point Herder writes '*Der Mensch in den Zustand von Besonnenheit gesetz, der ihm eigen ist, und diese Besonnenheit (Reflexion) zum erstenmal freiwurkend, hat Sprache erfunden. Denn was ist Reflexion? was ist Sprache?*' (1969, p. 754). Barnard's translation of this passage is incoherent, translating the first *Besonnenheit* as 'mind', omitting the second and mentioning only 'reflection' and maintaining the final 'reflection' without its connotation of *Besonnenheit*.

Chapter 4   Judgement before the Critique

1 Derrida's underestimation of tradition in Kant is consistent with his characterization of 'transcendental analysis' in the Introduction to Husserl's *Origin of Geometry*. The history of the emergence of geometry, Derrida argues, 'remains hidden for Kant'; in transcendental philosophy the 'spontaneous eidetic reduction' is 'always already done' (1978, p. 41)

but forgotten. Yet Kant's thematic of tradition addresses precisely the 'protohistory' which Derrida claims it invokes and forgets. Consequently, transcendental philosophy is not the 'other' of an empirical history, but refers to a different, non-Platonic notion of trancendence. See below for the discussion of Kant's view of the origins of geometry in the *First Introduction* to the *Critique of Judgement-Power*.

2 Hans-Georg Gadamer's seminal *Truth and Method* situates the hermeneutic problem of meaning in the context of self-understanding through tradition. He shows how 'method' is itself discovered in and through tradition. Yet his understanding of tradition underestimates the struggle around the concealment and recovery of meaning which shapes it, that which Kant calls the 'bias of reason' and Habermas later calls 'systematically distorted communication'. Kant's method cross-examines the divided claims of tradition as a means to making them betray their own partiality.

3 Oddly enough, both Heidegger and Derrida develop Kant's association of orientation and walking. Heidegger approaches Kant's text barefoot, using the street as 'equipment for walking' that 'slides itself, as it were, along certain portions of one's body – the soles of one's feet' (1927; pp. 141–2). He is directed by 'certain signs' to Kant's dark room in Königsberg. In Derrida's case, we are left with the equipment for walking which Heidegger forgot – boots – and with them arrive at the relation of orientation and difference. The difference presupposed by comparison, the aporia of judgement, comes down to orientation, wherein, Derrida wagers parenthetically 'Kant's whole transcendental aesthetic is at issue' (1978; p. 375).

4 See Tonelli 1975 for the institutional factors contributing to Kant's anti-Wolffianism; for philosophical assessments of the influence of Wolff on Kant, see Gilson 1949, p. 120 and Beck 1968.

5 This periodization avoids the conventional division of Kant's writings into pre-critical, critical, and post-critical phases by showing continuities across the tripartite *schema* as well as differences within it. The privileged position of the *Critiques* is inevitably questioned when Kant's works are read as an entirety, as in de Vleeschauwer's account of the transcendental deduction (1962), and Hinske's account of the origins of transcendental philosophy (1970). Such studies emphasize the complexity of Kant's relation to philosophical tradition, as in Hinske's three-stage model outlined on p. 127 of his work.

6 The most influential representative of this largely Pietist reaction was Christian August Crusius (1715–75). His critique of the principle of sufficient reason was set out in the short text of 1744, the *Ausführliche Abhandlung*, and developed at length in his anti-systematic system: see Heimsoeth's essay '*Metaphysik und Kritik bei Chr. August Crusius*' (1956) and Tonelli's exemplary inroduction to his edition of *Die philosophische Hauptwerke* (Crusius 1969).

7 Cassirer's commentary on the background and implications of this elision may be helpful:

the effort to overcome the separation between the material content of knowledge and the principles of knowledge dominates [Wolff's system], so that the attempt is made to reduce them to the logical principle of identity and prove them from it. In this sense Wolff assayed a proof of the 'principle of a ground' which was in fact circular: if there was something without a ground, he reasoned, then nothing must be the ground of something, which is self-contradictory. He even tried to deduce the necessity of the spatial order of appearances in this way, purely from the validity of the supreme logical principle: what we think as different from us, the inference ran, we must think as existing outside us, thus as spatially separated from us. The 'other than us' *praeter nos* was here directly translated into an 'outside us' the abstract concept of diversity into the concrete intuitive externality of space.

(1981, p. 73)

On the same issue, see Beck 1968, p. 452.

8 The position which de Vleeschauwer attributes to the 'post-critical' is also present in the 'pre-critical' writings: in the *Opus Postumum*, he writes, 'Affection is replaced by the term *Setzung* or position. In the self there reigns the most absolute spontaneity. The self is stripped of all ontological significance. To posit the self is an act of thought. The self is not considered as a being, not even as a source of activity. The self is pure act' (1962, p. 187).

9 *Gemüt* is one of Kant's most widely used terms, and is prevalent in the third *Critique*. It is commonly translated as 'mind' or 'mental state' although this is too restrictive a meaning: it denotes more a 'feeling'. Kant describes it on occasion as the 'feeling of the attunement of the representative powers' or as the 'life principle itself'. It is not 'mind' as composed of the powers of sensibility, imagination, understanding and reason, but the position of these powers. This agrees with its original meaning in medieval mysticism, where it refers to the 'stable disposition of the soul which conditions the exercise of all its faculties' (Gilson 1955, pp. 444, 758). It is helpful to compare *Gemüt* with the 'mood' of Heidegger's *Being and Time*; that is, not as a subjective, psychological state, but as a way of being in the world.

10 Heimsoeth (1956, p. 8) is the only authority to recognize the significance of the *Dreams* as a first statement of the method and the aim of Kant's emendation of metaphysics.

11 However, 'absolute position' does bear considerable resemblance to Newton's metaphysical description of space in the 'General Scholium' to the *Mathematical Principles*.

12 De Vleeschauwer (1962, p. 54) understands the distinction of reason and sensibility in terms of activity and passivity. Hermann Glockner, however, in a close study of the *Inaugural Dissertation* (1967) finds the evidence inconclusive. Gadamer points to the importance of differential intuition in his wonderful essay 'Intuition and Vividness' where he writes 'An epistemology that refuses to recognize the formative power of

distinction operative in all perception succumbs to a dogmatic concept of objective givenness' (1986, p. 160). Incidentally, the reading of intuition as differential again sets the transcendental aesthetic at issue, but in a different way from that imagined by Derrida above (n. 3).

13 On Kant's 'Scotism' see Gilson 1949, p. 130.

14 See Schlapp 1901, and Menzer 1952, for the textual details of Kant's reception of the two traditions. I might add that all the works discussed in Chapter 2 were known by Kant in translation.

15 Kulenkampff 1976, pp. 1 and 28 is an example of the tendency to separate Kant's aesthetic from its place in the system which is challenged in this and the following chapter.

Chapter 5   The Critique of Judgement-Power

1 Adorno insists that such a conformity or 'similarity' is also presupposed in the first *Critique*: 'By letting what he held in the beginning to be the raw material of cognition be preformed by an "art concealed in the depths of the human soul", he can declare the similarity between categorial form and sensible content without which the two "breeds" of cognition would simply not go together' (1982, p. 147). Once again, the 'transcendental aesthetic' is at stake here, 'For if in fact the Transcendental Aesthetic did function as the architecture of the system prescribed, then the transition to the Transcendental Logic would be a miracle.' It is noteworthy that both Adorno and Derrida's staking of the transcendental aesthetic arrives at a doctrine of similarity or mimesis, as becomes evident when comparing the former's *Aesthetic Theory* with the latter's *The Truth in Painting*.

2 For a study of the Aristotelean origins of the *sensus communis* and its development in Renaissance theory of art, see Summers 1987.

3 The section of the *Critique* on taste was probably written around 1787; see Tonelli's suggestive but not entirely trustworthy anatomy of the composition of the *Critique* (1954), as well as the letters of 1787 to Jakob and Reinhold (Kant 1967).

4 This continuity is the theme of Gerhardt Lehmann's series of articles representing the 'new perspective in Kant studies' (see 1969 and 1980) which combine philological insight into the development of Kant's thought with an appreciation of its aporetic dimension. In '*Voraussetzungen und Grenzen systematischer Kantinterpretation*' and '*System und Geschichte in Kants Philosophie*' (1969) he shows how the questions of system and aporia are inseparable in Kant's thought. His main contribution to Kant studies consists in showing the development of the notion of a technique of judgement from the third *Critique* through to the *opus postumum*; he regards these texts as representing Kant's move toward a 'philosophy of technique, a critique of technical reason', ('*Kants Nachlasswerk und die*

Kritik der Urteilskraft' 1969, p. 294). For other studies of this theme see his '*Das philosophische Grundproblem in Kants Nachlasswerk*' (1969) and '*Zur Problemanalyse von Kants Nachlasswerk*' (1980).

5 This anticipates Nietzche's position in *Human, All Too Human*: 'The first stage of the logical is the judgement: and the essence of the judgement consists, according to the best logicians, in belief. At the bottom of all belief there lies the *sensation of the pleasurable or painful* in respect to the subject experiencing the sensation' (1886, § 18).

6 This is set out very clearly in Mertens 1975, pp. 52–6.

7 See *Being and Time*, Part I, division iii and the later essay 'The Question Concerning Technology'.

8 For a study of the importance of analogy in Kant's metaphysics, see Marty 1980, esp. p. 200.

9 Guyer reduces Kant's account of proportion to the unity and manifold of judgement which it was trying to avoid: 'proportion would consist in the fact that the multiplicity of items in a manifold may be seen as a unity from the point of view dictated by some concept or another' (1979, p. 295). He then criticizes Kant for psychologizing proportion: 'Kant's notion of proportion would then be not a purely epistemological concept of the general unifiability of all manifolds, but a psychological concept of the ease with which given manifolds may be felt to be unified' (p. 296). Perhaps the third alternative of 'lapsing' into metaphysics should also be considered?

10 The question of the modalities of imagination is addressed in Heidegger's reading of the 'Transcendental Deduction' of the first *Critique* in *Kant und das Problem der Metaphysik* (1929). In spite of this careful and sustained justification of the importance of the modalities of imagination in Kant, there is still a tendency to regard his account of imagination as Kant's concession to contemporary psychology. See de Vleeschauwer 1962, p. 85, Guyer 1979, and Schaper 1979.

11 This was an option commonly taken up by the critics of Wolff, and has already been seen at issue in Herder's critique of Crusius and Riedel in chapter 3 above; it was systematically developed by Tetens.

12 For an indispensable study of the ethical significance of *Zweckmässigkeit* in the *Critique* see Marc-Wogau 1938. The term finality, or *Zweckmässigkeit*, was originally used to justify the activities of the police-state, as shown by Wessel 1978. The relation of finality to Kant's political philosophy is explored in Patrick Riley's extremely stimulating study which follows Arendt in seeing the third *Critique* as Kant's key text in political philosophy: 'It is in *Judgement* above all that the place of politics in Kant's philosophy is wholly clear' (1983, p. 84).

13 This agrees with Heidegger's reading of the moment of quality in his *Nietzsche* book: 'Before Kant says constructively what the determining ground is, and therefore what the beautiful itself is, he first says by way of refutation what never can and never may suppose itself to be such a ground, namely, an interest' (1979, p. 109). He believes this refutation permitted Kant to discover the essence of the beautiful: 'Precisely by

means of the "devoid of interest" the essential relation to the object itself comes into play ... now for the first time the object comes to the fore as pure object and such coming forward into appearance is the beautiful' (p. 110). While agreeing with the first argument that Kant is establishing what beauty cannot be, my reading suggests that no essential relation comes into play, but that such a coming forward into appearance can only be intimated.

14 A similar understanding of form is crucial to Cassirer's attempt to place German Idealism as a development of Renaissance Platonism (through the Cambridge Platonists and Shaftesbury); see 1981, pp. 277–83.

15 Kant argued his differences with Herder and Forster in the essay *Über den Gebrauch teleologischer Prinzipien in der Philosophie* (1788a) which anticipates some of the arguments of the second part of the *Critique*. For a discussion of this *Streit* see Riedel 1979.

16 'At a certain stage of their development the material productive forces of society come into conflict with the existing relations of production or – what is merely a legal expression for the same thing – with the property relations within the framework of which they have hitherto operated' (p. 3).

17 This anticipates Castoriadis's notion of the social imaginary which institutes itself, but whose power of institution cannot be determined.

18 Kant's discussion of organization has been developed in the sociology of institutions. Gehlen presents the institution in terms of Kant's distinction of 'blind intuitions' and 'empty concepts' (1980, p. 71). This form of argument, common among German right-wing intellectuals in the 1930s is characterized in Lacoue-Labarthe's *La Fiction du Politique* (1987). A different reading of the problem of institutionalization, which relates it to the French Revolution, is that of Hannah Arendt. She takes Kant's concern with political institutions in the third *Critique* and other later works as registering a shift in interest from the social, the forms of human sociability, to the political, 'the way a body politic should be organized and constituted' (1982, p. 16). Arendt extends this to the first part of the *Critique* which for her 'contains the greatest and most original aspects of Kant's political philosophy' (1980, p. 219) in its suggestion that judgement rests on an anticipated consensus.

19 Gillian Rose has shown the relation between the law which is not legislated and the 'way': 'Many of the ancient words now translated as "Law" originally meant "the way": the Hebrew word for law, *Halachah*, means, literally, "the going" – the way one should go; the Arabic word for law, *Shari'a*, means, literally, "the road to the watering place"; the Greek name for the Goddess of Vengeance, *Dike*, means, "the way things happen"' (1988, p. 360). The relationship of law and walking, or orientation, indicated here is central to Kant's account of fundamental judgement.

20 Kant's vacillation between liberalism and authoritarianism has been noted by critics since Krieger. Williams's account of his political philosophy

remarks 'a number of discrepancies in his political theory which are difficult always to justify' (1982, p. 161), especially those between his 'liberal individualistic premisses' and 'his support to conservative and authoritarian principles', and his notion of welfare 'which is derived from the rational individual's pursuit of his self-interest [yet] must be limited by the state in the interests of society as a whole. Nobody's welfare is directly increased by this policing, but it does prevent civil society from undermining itself' (p. 195).

21 These aporias are discussed in Böckerstette 1982 and Kersting 1984.

Beyond Judgement

1 '*Analogy*. It operates everywhere in the book, and one can systematically verify its effect' (1978, p. 76). For a critical discussion of Derrida's use of analogy see Gasché's (1986) final chapter 'The Inscription of Universality'.

Bibliography

Abbt, Thomas 1768–82: *Vermischte Werke*. Berlin and Stettin.

Adorno, T. 1970: *Aesthetic Theory*. C. Lenhardt (tr.), London 1984.

——1982: *Against Epistemology*. Willis Domingo (tr.), Oxford.

Aiton, E.J. 1985: *Leibniz: A Biography*. Bristol and Boston.

Aquinas, St Thomas 1256–9: *The Disputed Questions of Truth* (3 vols). R.W. Mulligan, J.V. Mcglynn, R.W. Schmidt (trs), Chicago 1952–4.

——1268–73: *The Summa Theologica*. Fathers of the English Dominican Province (trs), London.

Arendt, Hannah 1958: *The Human Condition*. Chicago.

——1980: *Between Past and Future*. Harmondsworth.

——1982: *Lectures on Kant's Political Philosophy*. Brighton.

Arnauld, Antoine 1662: *The Art of Thinking: Port-Royal Logic*. James Dickoff and Patricia James (trs), Indianapolis 1964.

Arnsperger, Walther 1897: *Christian Wolffs Verhältnis zu Leibniz*. Weimar.

Bachmann, Hans Martin 1977: *Die Naturrechtliche Staatslehre Christian Wolffs*. Berlin.

Bahlmann, Dudley W.R. 1957: *The Moral Revolution of 1688*. New Haven.

Baltrusaitis, Jurgis 1977: *Anamorphic Art*. Cambridge.

Baumgarten, Alexander Gottlieb 1735: *Reflections on Poetry: A.G. Baumgarten's Meditationes philosophicae de nonnullis ad poema pertinibus*. K. Aschenbrenner and W.B. Holther (trs), Berkeley/Los Angeles 1954.

——1739: *Metaphysica*. Reprint of the 7th edition (1779), Hildesheim 1963.

——1740: *Ethica Philosophica*. Halle.

——1741: *Philosophische Briefe von Aletheophilius*. Frankfurt and Leipzig.

——1742: *Handschrift der Ästhetik Baumgartens*. In Bernhard Poppe, *Alexander Gottlieb Baumgarten: Seine Bedeutung und Stellung in der Leibniz-Wolffischen Philosophie und seine Beziehungen zu Kant*. Borna-Leipzig.

——1747: *Dissertatio periodica de Disciplinus Oeconomicopolitico-Cameralibus*. Praeside Alexandro Gottlieb Baumgarten ... defendet Johann Daniel Schwechten, Halle.

——1750–8: *Aesthetica* (2 vols). Frankfurt a.d. Oder. Reprinted Hildesheim 1961.

——1765: *Acroasis Logica*. Halle. Reprinted in Wolff *Gesammelte Schriften*, vol. 27.

——1763: *Jus Naturae*. Halle.

——1770: *Philosophia Generalis*. Reprinted Hildesheim 1968.

——1983: *Texte zur Grundlegung der Ästhetik*. Hans Rudolf Schweizer (ed.), Hamburg.

Bäumler, Alfred 1923: *Das Irrationalitätsproblem in der Ästhetik und Logik des 18. Jahrhunderts bis zur Kritik der Urteilskraft*. Darmstadt 1967.

Beck, Lewis White 1969: *Early German Philosophy: Kant and his Predecessors.* Cambridge, Mass.

Behrens, C.B.A. 1985: *Society, Government and the Enlightenment: The Experience of Eighteenth Century France and Prussia.* London.

Birke, J. 1966a: '*Gottscheds Neuorientierung der deutschen Poetik an der Philosophie Wolffs*', *Zeitschrift für Deutsche Philologie* 85, 560–75.

——1966b: *Christian Wolffs Metaphysik und die zeitgenossische Literatur- und Musiktheorie.* Berlin.

Bissinger, A. 1970: *Die Struktur der Gotteserkenntnis. Studien zur Philosophie Christian Wolffs.* Bonn.

Blackall, Eric A. 1978: *The Emergence of German as a Literary Language.* Ithaca and London.

Blackwell, R.J. 1961: 'The Structure of the Wolffian Philosophy,' *The Modern Schoolman*, 203–18.

Bleek, Wilhelm 1972: *Von der Kameralausbildung zum Juristenprivileg: Studium, Prüfung und Ausbildung der höheren Beamten des allgemeinen Verwaltungsdienstes in Deutschland im 18. und 19. Jahrhundert.* Berlin.

Bloch, Ernst 1961: *Natural Law and Human Dignity.* Dennis J. Schmidt (tr.), Boston 1986.

Bodmer, Johann Jacob 1740: *Critische Abhandlung von dem Wunderbaren in der Poesie.* Stuttgart 1966.

Böckerstette, Heinrich 1982: *Aporien der Freiheit und ihre Aufklärung durch Kant.* Stuttgart-Bad Cannstatt.

Booth, Edward 1983: *Aristotelean Aporetic Ontology in Islamic and Christian Thinkers.* Cambridge.

Breitinger, Johann Jacob 1740: *Critische Dichtkunst* (2 vols). Stuttgart 1966.

Bright, Greg 1983: 'The Identification of Desire in Leibniz', unpublished Gladstone Seminar paper.

Brown, F.A. 1952: *On Education: John Locke, Christian Wolff, and the 'Moral Weeklies'*, University of California Publications in Modern Philology, vol. XXXVI, no 5, Berkeley.

Brown, Keith 1978: 'The Artist of the Leviathan Title Page', *British Library Journal*, vol. IV, 24–36.

Brunschwig, Henri 1974: *Enlightenment and Romanticism in Eighteenth Century Prussia*, Frank Jellinek (tr.), Chicago.

Burke, Edmund 1756: *A Philosophical Enquiry into the Origin of our Ideas of the Sublime and Beautiful.* James T. Boulton (ed.), London 1958.

——1790: *Reflections on the Revolution in France.* London 1955.

Burns, John V. 1964: *Dynamism in the Cosmology of Christian Wolff.* New York.

Busch, Otto 1981: *Militärsystem und Sozialleben im alten Preussen 1713–1807.* Berlin.

Bush, R.L. 1984: *The English Aristocracy: A Comparative Synthesis.* Manchester.

Cassirer, Ernst 1951: *The Philosophy of the Enlightenment.* Chicago.

——1981: *Kant's Life and Thought.* James Haden (tr.), London.

Castoriadis, Cornelius 1984: *Crossroads in the Labyrinth*. Kate Soper, Martin H. Ryle (trs), Brighton

——1987: *The Imaginary Institution of Society*. Kathleen Blumey (tr.), Oxford.

Casula, Mario 1973: *La Metafisica di A.G. Baumgarten*. Milan.

Caygill, Howard 1988: 'Post-modernism and Judgement', *Economy and Society* 17, 1–20.

Clark, J.C.D. 1985: *English Society 1688–1832: Ideology, Social Structure and Political Practice during the Ancien Regime*. Cambridge.

Coleman, Francis X.J. 1974: *The Harmony of Reason: A Study in Kant's Aesthetic*. Pittsburgh.

Corbett R. and Lightbown M. 1979: *The Comely Frontispiece; the Emblematic Title Page in England 1500–1600*. London.

Crawford, Donald W. 1974: *Kant's Aesthetic Theory*. Wisconsin.

Cruger, Johannes 1884: *Joh. Christoph Gottsched und die Schweizer*. Darmstadt 1965.

Crusius, Christian August 1744: *Ausführliche Abhandlung von dem rechten Gebrauche und der Einschrankung des sogenannten Satzes von zureichenden oder besser determiniereden Grundes*. Leipzig.

——1969: *Die Philosophische Hauptwerke*. Giorgio Tonelli (ed.), Hildesheim.

Cumberland, Richard 1672: *A Treatise of the Laws of Nature (De Legibus Naturae)*. John Maxwell (tr.), London 1727.

Derrida, Jacques 1962: *Edmund Husserl's Origin of Geometry: An Introduction*. John P. Leavey (tr.), New York 1978.

——1978: *The Truth in Painting*. Geoff Bennington and Ian McLeod (trs), Chicago 1987.

De Witt Thorpe, Clarence 1940: *The Aesthetic Theory of Thomas Hobbes*. Michigan.

Dickson, P.G.M. 1967: *The Financial Revolution in England*. London.

Dickinson, H.T. 1977: *Liberty and Property – Political Philosophy in Eighteenth Century Britain*. London.

Dorwart, Reinhold August 1971: *The Prussian Welfare State before 1740*. Cambridge, Mass.

Eisler, Rudolf 1984: *Kant Lexicon*. Hildesheim.

Franke, Ursula 1972: *Kunst als Erkenntnis – Die Rolle der Sinnlichkeit in der Ästhetik des Alexander Gottlieb Baumgartens*. Wiesbaden.

Frauendienst, Werner 1927: *Christian Wolff als Staatsdenker*. Berlin.

Frederick the Great 1941: *Die Politische Testamente*. München.

Freier, Hans 1973: *Kritische Poetik – Legitimation und Kritik der Poesie in 'Gottscheds Dichtkunst'* Stuttgart.

Fulbrook, Mary 1985: *Piety and Politics: Religion and the Rise of Absolutism in England, Wurtemburg and Prussia*. Cambridge.

Gadamer, Hans-Georg 1960: *Truth and Method*. London 1975.

——1986: *The Relevance of the Beautiful and other Essays*. Robert Bernasconi (ed.), Cambridge.

Gasché, Rodolphe 1986: *The Tain of the Mirror*. Cambridge, Mass.

Gehlen, Arnold 1980: *Man in the Age of Technology*. Patricia Lipscomb (tr.) New York.

Gilson, E. 1949: *Being and Some Philosophers*. Toronto.

——1955: *History of Christian Philosophy in the Middle Ages*. New York.

Glockner, Hermann 1967: '*Kant und die Metaphysik – 1763 bis 1772*'. *Tradition und Kritik – Festschrift für Rudolf Zocker*, Stuttgart, pp. 107–22.

Gottsched, J.G. 1730: *Versuch einer critischen Dichtkunst. Ausgewählte Schriften IV*, Berlin/New York 1973.

——1733: *Erste Gründe der gesamten Weltweisheit, Ausgewählte Schriften V*, Berlin/New York, 1983.

Gracian, Baltasar 1647: *The Oracle: A Manual of the Art of Discretion*. L.B. Walton (tr.), London 1953.

Grua, Gaston 1948: *Leibniz Textes Inedits*. Paris.

——1953: *Jurisprudence universelle et Theodicée selon Leibniz*. Paris.

——1956: *La Justice humaine selon Leibniz*. Paris.

Gunn, J.A.W. 1983: *Beyond Liberty and Property – the Process of Self-Recognition in Eighteenth Century Political Thought*. Kingston/Montreal.

Gurr, John 1959: *The Principle of Sufficient Reason in some Scholastic Systems*. Toronto.

Guyer, Paul 1979: *Kant and the Claims of Taste*. Harvard.

Haase, Carl 1966: '*Leibniz als Politiker und Diplomat*'. In Wilhelm Totok and Carl Haase (eds), *Leibniz. Sein Leben – Sein Wirken – Seine Welt*, Hannover.

Habermas, Jürgen 1969: *Strukturwandel der Öffentlichkeit*. Neuwied and Berlin.

Heidegger, Martin 1914: *Die Lehre vom Urteil im Psychologismus. Frühe Schriften*, Frankfurt am Main 1972.

——1927: *Sein und Zeit*. Tübingen 1979. *Being and Time*. John Macquarrie and Edward Robinson (trs), Oxford 1978.

——1929: *Kant und das Problem der Metaphysik*. Frankfurt am Main 1973.

——1979: *Nietzsche vol. I: The Will to Power as Art*. D.F. Krell (tr.), Los Angeles.

Heimsoeth, Heinz 1956: *Studien zur Philosophie Immanuel Kants: metaphysische Ursprunge und ontologische Grundlagen. Kantstudien Ergänzungshefte 71*, Köln.

Herder, Johann Gottfried 1766–7: *Über die neuere Deutsche Literatur*. Bernhard Suphan (ed.), *Herders Sämtliche Werke* I, Berlin 1878.

——1767a: *Entwürf zu einer Denkschrift auf A.G. Baumgarten, J.D. Heilmann und Th. Abbt. Werke* XXXII.

——1767b: *Von Baumgartens Denkart in seinen Schriften. Werke* XXXII.

——1769a: *Kritische Wälder. Oder Betrachtungen über die Wissenschaft und Kunst des Schonen. Werke* IV.

——1769b: *Journal meiner Reise im Jahr 1769. Werke* IV; *Journal of My Voyage in the Year 1769*, F.M. Barnard (tr.), Cambridge 1969.

——1771: *Abhandlung über den Ursprung der Sprache. Werke* V; *Essay on the Origin of Language*, 1969.

——1774: *Auch eine Philosophie der Geschichte zur Bildung der Menschheit. Werke* V; *Yet another Philosophy of History*, 1969.

——1775: *Vom Erkennen und Empfinden, den zwo Hauptkräften der menschlichen Seele. Werke* VIII.

——1778: *Plastik. Werke* VIII.

——1800: *Kalligone. Werke* XXII.

Hinrichs, Carl 1971: *Preussentum und Pietismus. Der Pietismus in Brandenburg-Preussen als religiös-soziales Reformbewegung*. Göttingen.

Hinske, Norbert 1970: *Kants Weg zur Transzendentalphilosophie: der dreissigjahrige Kant*. Stuttgart.

Hintze, Otto 1975: *The Historical Essays of Otto Hintze*. Felix Gilbert (ed.), Oxford.

Hirschmann, Alfred O. 1977: *The Passions and the Interests: Political Arguments for Capitalism before its Triumph*. Princeton.

Hobbes, Thomas 1640: *The Elements of Law, Natural and Politic*. Ferdinand Toennies (ed.), London 1969.

——1642a: *De Cive; English Version*. Howard Warrender (ed.), *The Clarendon Edition of the Philosophical Works of Thomas Hobbes* III, Oxford 1983.

——1642b: *Thomas White's De Mundo Examined*. Harold Whitmore Jones (tr.), Bradford 1976.

——1646. *A Minute of First Draft of the Optiques*. British Library *Harl. ms.* 3360.

——1650: *The Answer of Mr Hobbes to Sir William Davenant's Preface before Gondibert*. Sir William Molesworth (ed.), *The English Works of Thomas Hobbes vol.* IV, reprinted Aachen 1966.

——1651: *Leviathan, or The Matter, Forme, & Power of a Common-Wealth Ecclesiasticall and Civill*. C.B. Macpherson (ed.), Harmondsworth 1980.

——1655: *Concerning Body (De Corpore). The English Works of Thomas Hobbes vol.* I.

——1657: *On Man (De Homine)*. Bernard Gert (ed.), *Man and Citizen*, New York 1978.

Horne, Thomas A. 1978: *The Social Thought of Bernard Mandeville: Virtue and Commerce in the Eighteenth Century*. London.

Hume, David 1739: *A Treatise of Human Nature*. P.H. Nidditch (ed.), Oxford 1981.

——1751: *An Inquiry Concerning the Principles of Morals*. In *Essays, Literary, Moral, and Political*, London.

——1757: *Of the Standard of Taste. Essays, Literary, Moral, and Political*, London.

Hutcheson, Francis 1725: *An Inquiry into the Original of our Ideas of Beauty and Virtue. Collected Works* vol I, Hildesheim 1971.

——1728: *An Essay in the Nature and Conduct of the Passions with Illustrations of the Moral Sense. Collected Works vol.* II.

——1747: *A Short Introduction to Moral Philosophy. Collected Works vol.* IV.

——1755: *The System of Moral Philosophy. Collected works vols.* V & VI.

Jäger, Michael 1980: *Kommentierende Einführung im Baumgartens 'Ästhetica'*. Hamburg.

Kames, (Henry Home) 1751: *Essays on the Principles of Morality and Natural Religion*. Edinburgh.

——1762: *Elements of Criticism*. New York 1972.

Kant, Immanuel 1747: *Gedanken von der wahren Schätzung der lebendigen Kräfte. Kants gesammelte Schriften (Akademie Ausgabe)* (AA) Band I, Berlin 1912.

——1755: *Principiorum primorum cognitionis metaphysicae nova dilucidatio*. AA II Berlin 1912; tr. *Kant's Latin Writings*, Lewis White Beck (ed.), New York 1986.

——1758: *Neuer Lehrbegriff der Bewegung und Ruhe*. AA II, Berlin 1912.

——1762: *Die falsche Spitzfindigkeit der vier syllogistischen Figuren*. AA II.

——1763a: *Versuch, den Begriff der negativen Grössen in die Weltweisheit einzuführen*. AA II.

——1763b: *Der einzig mögliche Beweisgrund zu einer Demonstration des Daseins Gottes*. AA II; *The One Possible Proof for the Existence of God*, G. Treash (tr.), New York 1979.

——1764a: *Untersuchung über die Deutlichkeit der Grundsätze der naturlichen Theologie und der Moral*. AA II; *Kant Selected Pre-Critical Writings and Correspondence with Beck*, G.B. Kerferd and D.E. Walford (trs), Manchester 1968.

——1764b: *Versuch über die Krankheiten des Kopfes*. AA II.

——1764c: *Beobachtungen über das Gefühl des Schönen und Erhabenen*. AA II; *Observations on the Feeling of the Beautiful and the Sublime*, John T. Goldthwaite (tr.), Los Angeles 1973.

——1765: *Nachricht von der Hinrichtung seiner Vorlesungen in den Winterhalben-jahre von 1765–1766*. AA II.

——1766: *Träume eines Geistersehers, erläutert durch Träume der Metaphysik*. AA II; *Dreams of a Spirit Seer*, John Manelesco (tr.), New York 1969.

——1768: *Von dem ersten Grunde des Unterschieds der Gegenden im Raume*. AA II; *Kant Selected Pre-Critical Writings*.

——1770: *De mundi sensibilis atque intelligibilis forma et principiis*. AA II; *Kant Selected Pre-Critical Writings*.

——1781: *Kritik der reinen Vernunft* (Schmidt edition) Hamburg 1956; *Critique of Pure Reason*, Norman Kemp Smith (tr.), London 1929.

——1785a: *Rezensionen von Herders Ideen zur Philosophie der Geschichte der Menschheit*. AA VIII.

——1785b: *Grundlegung zur Metaphysik der Sitten*. AA IV;. *Fundamental Principles of the Metaphysics of Ethics*, Thomas Kingsmill Abbot (tr.), London 1965.

——1786: *Was heisst, sich im Denken orientieren?* AA VIII.

——1788a: *Über den Gebrauch teleologischer Prinzipien in der Philosophie*. AA VIII.

——1788b: *Kritik der praktischen Vernunft*. AA IV; *Critique of Practical Reason*, Lewis White Beck (tr.), Indianapolis 1956.

——1790a: *Kritik der Urteilskraft*. Hamburg 1924; *Critique of Judgement*, James Creed Meredith (tr.), Oxford 1952.

——1790b: *Erste Einleitung in die Kritik der Urteilskraft.* Hamburg 1977; *First Introduction to the Critique of Judgement,* James Haden (tr.), Indianapolis 1965.

——1790c: *Über eine Entdeckung, nach der alle neue Kritik der reinen Vernunft durch eine altere entbehrlich gemacht werden soll.* AA VIII; *On A Discovery According to which any New Critique of Pure Reason has been made Superfluous by an Earlier One,* Henry E. Allison (tr.), Baltimore 1973.

——1791: *What Real Progress Has Metaphysics Made in Germany since the Time of Leibniz and Wolff.* Ted Humphrey (tr.), New York 1983.

——1793a: *Religion Within the Limits of Reason Alone,* Theodore M. Greene and Hoyt H. Hudson (trs), New York 1960.

——1793b: *Über den Gemeinspruch; das mag in der Theorie richtig sein, taugt aber nicht für die Praxis.* AA VIII; *On the Common Saying: 'This May be True in Theory, but it does not apply in Practice'.* Hans Reiss and H.B. Nisbet (ed. & tr.), Cambridge 1987.

——1798a: *Der Streit der Fakultäten. The Conflict of the Faculties.* Mary J. Gregor (tr.), New York 1979.

——1798b: *Anthropologie in pragmatischer Hinsicht.* AA VII; *Anthropology from a Pragmatic Point of View.* Mary J. Gregor (tr.), The Hague, 1974.

——1800: *Logic.* Robert Hartman and Wolfgang Schwarz (trs), Indianapolis 1974.

——1930: *Lectures on Ethics.* Paul Menzer (ed.), Louis Infield (tr.), London 1979.

——1967: *Philosophical Correspondence 1759–1799.* Arnulf Zweig (tr.), Chicago.

——1978: *Lectures on Philosophical Theology.* Allen W. Wood and Gertrude M. Clarke (trs), Ithaca and London.

——*Reflections: Handschriftliche Nachlass,* AA xiv–xix.

Kenyon J.P. 1977: *Revolution Principles: The Politics of Party 1689–1720.* Cambridge.

Kersting, Wolfgang 1984: *Wohlgeordnete Freiheit – Immanuel Kants Rechts und Staats Philosophie.* Berlin.

Kosellek, Reinhardt 1967: *Preussen zwischen Reform und Revolution. Allgemeines Landrecht, Verwaltung und Soziale Bewegung von 1791 bis 1848.* Stuttgart.

Krieger, Leonard 1957: *The German Idea of Freedom.* Boston.

——1965: *The Politics of Discretion.* Chicago.

——1970: *Kings and Philosophers 1689–1789.* Chicago.

Kulenkampff, Jens 1974: *Materiallen zu Kants 'Kritik der Urteilskraft'.* Frankfurt am Main.

——1976: *Kants Logik des ästhetischen Urteils.* Frankfurt a. Main.

Lach D.F. 1953: 'The Sinophilism of Christian Wolff', *Journal of the History of Ideas,* XIV, 561–74.

Lacoue-Labarthe, Philippe 1987: *La Fiction du Politique.* Paris.

Lehmann, Gerhard 1969: *Beiträge zur Geschichte und Interpretation der Philosophie Kants.* Berlin.

——1980: *Kants Tugenden: Neue Beiträge zur Geschichte und Interpretation der Philosophie Kants*. Berlin.

Lehmann, William C. 1971: *Henry Home, Lord Kames, and the Scottish Enlightenment*. The Hague.

Leibniz, Gottfried Wilhelm 1666: *Dissertation on the Art of Combinations. Philosophical Papers and Letters* (PPL), Leroy E. Loemker (ed. and tr.), Dordrecht 1969.

——1668: 'Ratio corporis iuris reconcinnandi'. L. Dutans (ed.) *Leibnitii Opera Omnia*, IV, III, 235–2.

——1670: *Preface to an Edition of Nizolius*. PPL, pp. 121–30.

——1670–1: *Elements of Natural Law*. PPL, pp. 131–7.

——1675: *Essay on a New Plan for a Certain Science*. Philip P. Wiener (ed.), *Leibniz Selections*, New York 1951.

——1684: *Meditations on Knowledge, Truth and Ideas*. PPL, pp. 291–4.

——*c.* 1690a: *On the Method of Distinguishing Real from Imaginary Phenomena*. PPL, pp. 363–5.

——1693–1700a: *On Wisdom*. PPL, pp. 425–8.

——1693–1700b: *On Natural Law*. PPL, pp. 428–9.

——1693–1700c: *A Classification of Societies or Communities*. PPL, pp. 429–30.

——1693: *Codex Iuris Gentium (Praefatio). The Political Writings of Leibniz* (PWL), pp. 165–76, Patrick Riley (ed.), Cambridge 1981.

——*c.* 1694–8: *Felicity*. PWL, pp. 82–4.

——1695a: *Specimen Dynamicum*. PPL, pp. 435–50.

——1697: *On the Radical Origination of Things*. PPL, pp. 486–91.

——1703–5: *New Essays on Human Understanding*. Peter Remnant and Jonathan Bennett (trs and eds), Cambridge 1981.

Lessing, Gotthold Ephraim, 1766: *Laocoon*, William A. Steel (tr.), London 1930.

Linn, Marie-Luise 1967: 'A.G. Baumgarten's "Aesthetica" und die antike Rhetorik', *Deutsche Vierteljahrschrift für Literatur Wissenschaft*, 41, 424–43.

Locke, John 1690: *An Essay Concerning Human Understanding*. John W. Yolton (ed.), London 1977.

Luig, Klaus 1975: 'Die Rolle des deutschen Rechts in Leibniz' Kodificationsplänen'. *Ius Commune* v, pp. 56–70.

Lyotard, Jean-François: *Sensus Communis*. NOT FOR PUBLICATION.

Macmillan R.A.C. 1912: *The Crowning Phase of the Critical Philosophy, a Study in Kant's Critique of Judgement*. London.

Macpherson, C.P. 1980: *Burke*, Oxford.

Maier, Hans Hermann, 1980: *Die ältere deutsche Staats- und Verwaltungslehre*. 2nd end, München.

Maimon, Solomon 1975: *An Autobiography*. Moses Haas (ed.), New York.

Mandeville, Bernard 1924: *The Fable of the Bees: or, Private Vices, Publick Benefits* (2 vols). F.B. Kaye (ed.), Oxford.

Marc-Wogau, Konrad 1938: *Vier Studien zu Kants Kritik der Urteilskraft*. Uppsala. Martens, Wolfgang 1968: *Die Botschaft der Tugend: Die Aufklärung im Spiegel der deutschen moralischen Wochenschriften*. Stuttgart.

Marty, François, 1980: *La Naissance de la Metaphysique chez Kant.* Paris.

Marx, Karl 1976: *Preface and Introduction to a Contribution to the Critique of Political Economy.* Peking.

May, J.A. 1970: *Kant's Concept of Geography and its Relation to Recent Geographical Thought.* Toronto.

McClelland, Charles E. 1980: *State, Society, and University in Germany 1700–1914.* Cambridge.

Meier, Georg Friedrich 1747: *Beurtheilung der Gottschedischen Dichtkunst.* Halle.

——1748–50: *Anfangsgründe aller schönen Wissenschaften.* Halle

——1763: *Alexander Gottlieb Baumgartens Leben.* Halle

Mendelssohn, Moses 1757: Über die Hauptgrundsätze der schönen Künste und Wissenschaften. D.F. Best (ed.), *Aesthetische Schriften in Auswahl*, Darmstadt 1986.

——1758: 'E. Burke Enquiry into the Origin of the Sublime and Beautiful'. *Gesammelte Schriften* Band 4, Stuttgart, 1977.

Menzer, Paul 1952: *Kants Ästhetik in ihrer Entwicklung.* Berlin.

Mertens, Helga 1975: *Kommentar zur ersten Einleitung in Kants Kritik der Urteilskraft.* München.

Meyer, R.W. 1952: *Leibniz and the Seventeenth Century Revolution.* J.P. Stern (tr.), Cambridge.

Miller, David 1981: *Philosophy and Ideology in Hume's Political Thought.* Oxford.

Müller, Kurt und Krönert Gisela 1969: *Leben und Werk von G.W. Leibniz.* Frankfurt-am-Main.

Nietzsche, Friedrich 1886: *Human, All Too Human: A Book for Free Spirits.* R.J. Hollingdale (tr.), Cambridge 1986.

Ong, Walter J. 1983: *Ramus: Method and the Decay of Dialogue.* Cambridge, Mass.

Oestreich, Gerhard 1982: *Neostoicism and the Early Modern State.* David McLintock (tr.), Cambridge.

Panofsky, Erwin 1957: *Galileo as a Critic of the Arts.* The Hague.

Pico della Mirandola 1486: *Oration on Human Dignity*, (tr.) in Ernst Cassirer et al., *The Renaissance Philosophy of Man*, Chicago 1948.

——1492: *Of Being and Unity.* Victor Michael Hamm (tr.), Milwaukee 1943.

Plumb, J.H. 1967: *The Growth of Political Stability in England 1675–1725.* London.

Pocock, J.G.A. 1975: *The Machiavellian Moment.* Princeton.

——1985: *Virtue, Commerce, and History.* Cambridge.

Preu, Peter 1983: *Polizeibegriff und Staatszwecklehre.* Göttingen.

Pufendorf, Samuel 1672: *De Jure Naturae et Gentium Libri Octo.* C.H. and W.A. Oldfather (trs), New York and London 1964.

Raeff, Marc 1983: *The Well-Ordered Police State: Social and Institutional Change through Law in the Germanies and Russia 1600–1800.* New Haven.

Reill, Peter Hans 1975: *The German Enlightenment and the Rise of Historicism.* Los Angeles.

Riedel, Friedrich Justus 1767: *Theorie der schönen Künste und Wissenschaften.* Jena.

——1768: *Ueber das Publicum.* Jena.

Riedel, Manfred 1979: '*Historizismus und Kritizismus: Kants Streit mit G. Forster und J.G. Herder'. Studien zum achtzehnte Jahrhundert: Das Achtzehnte Jahrhundert als Epoche*, Neudeln, pp. 31–48.

Riley, Patrick 1983: *Kant's Political Philosophy.* New Jersey.

Rose, Gillian 1984: *Dialectic of Nihilism: Post-Structuralism and Law.* Oxford.

——1988: 'Architecture to Philosophy – The Postmodern Complicity', *Theory, Culture & Society*, vol. 5, 357–71.

Rosenberg, Hans 1958: *Bureaucracy, Aristocracy and Autocracy: The Prussian Experience 1660–1815.* Cambridge/Mass.

Sagarra, Eda 1977: *A Social History of Germany 1648–1914.* London.

Saisselin, Remy G. 1970: *The Rule of Reason and the Ruses of the Heart: A Philosophical Dictionary of Classical French Criticism, Critics, and Aesthetic Issues.* Cleveland/London.

Schaper, Eva 1979: *Studies in Kant's Aesthetics.* Edinburgh.

Schlapp, Otto 1901: *Kants Lehre von Genie und die Entstehung der Kritik der Urteilskraft.* Göttingen.

Schlipp, Paul Arthur 1938: *Kant's Pre-Critical Ethics.* Evanston and Chicago.

Schmitt, Carl 1938: *Der Leviathan in der Staatslehre des Thomas Hobbes – Sinn und Fehlschlag eines politischen Symbols.* Hamburg.

Schneider, Hans Peter 1967: *Justitia Universalis, Quellenstudien zur Geschichte 'Christlichen Naturrechts' bei Gottfried Wilhelm Leibniz.* Frankfurt.

Schneiders, Werner (*hsg.*) 1983: *Christian Wolff 1679–1754. Studien zum achtzehnten Jahrhunderts* Band 4. Hamburg.

Schöffler, Herbert 1956: *Deutsches Geistesleben zwischen Reformation und Aufklärung. Von M. Opitz zu Christian Wolff.* Frankfurt-am-Main.

Schweizer, Hans Rudolf 1973: *Ästhetik als Philosophie der sinnlichen Erkenntnis.* Basel/Stuttgart.

Shaftesbury (Anthony Ashley Cooper) 1688: *An Enquiry Concerning Virtue or Merit.* David Walford (ed.), Manchester 1977.

——1711: *Characteristics of Men, Manners, Opinions, Times.* New York 1964.

——1900: *The Life, Unpublished Letters, and Philosophical Regimen of Anthony, Earl of Shaftesbury.* Benjamin Rand (ed.), New York.

——1914: *Second Characters, or the Language of Forms.* Benjamin Rand (ed.), Cambridge.

Small, Albion W. 1909: *The Cameralists: The Pioneers of German Social Polity.* Chicago.

Smith, Adam 1759: *The Theory of Moral Sentiments.* A.C. Macfie and D.D. Raphael (eds), *The Glasgow Edition of the Works and Correspondence of Adam Smith*, vol. I, Oxford 1976.

——1776: *An Inquiry into the Nature and Causes of the Wealth of Nations.* R.H. Campbell and A.S. Skinner (eds), *Glasgow Edition*, vol. II, Oxford 1976.

——1978: *Lectures on Jurisprudence.* R.L. Meek, D.D. Raphael, P.G. Stein (eds), *Glasgow Edition*, vol. V, Oxford.

Stolnitz, Jerome 1961: 'On the significance of Lord Shaftesbury in Modern Aesthetic theory', *The Philosophical Quarterly* vol. II, 97–113.

Strauss, Leo 1952: *Persecution and the Art of Writing*. Glencoe.

Sulzer, Johann Georg 1751: *Untersuchung über den Ursprung der angenehmen und unangenehmen Empfindungen. Vermischte philosophische Schriften*, Leipzig 1773.

——1771–4: *Allgemeine Theorie der schönen Künste*. Leipzig.

Summers, David 1987: *The Judgement of Sense*. Cambridge.

Tonelli, Giorgio 1954: '*La formazione del testo della Kritik der Urteilskraft*', *Revue Internationale de Philosophie*, VIII, Bruxelles, 423–48.

——1964: '*Das Wiederaufleben der deutsch-aristotelischen Terminologie bei Kant während der Entstehung der "Kritik der reinen Vernunft"*', *Archiv für Begriffsgeschichte* 9, 233–42.

——1975: 'Conditions in Königsberg and the Making of Kant's Philosophy', in *Bewusst sein: Gerhard Funk zu eigen*, A.J. Backer (*hsg.*), Bonn.

Treue, Wilhelm 1951: '*Adam Smith in Deutschland: zum Problem des "politischen Professors" zwischen 1776 und 1810*'. Werner Conze (*hsg.*), *Deutschland und Europe – Festschrift für Hans Rothfels*, Düsseldorf.

Tricaud, Francois 1982: 'An Investigation Concerning the Usage of the Words "Person" and "Persona" in the Political Treatises of Hobbes', J.G. van der Bend (ed.), *Thomas Hobbes – His View of Man*, Amsterdam.

Vierhaus, Rudolf 1978: *Deutschland im Zeitalter des Absolutismus*. Göttingen.

Viner, Jacob 1972: *The Role of Providence in the Social Order*. Princeton.

de Vleeschauwer, Herman-J. 1962: *The Development of Kantian Thought: The History of a Doctrine*. A.R.C. Duncan (tr.), London.

Vogel, Barbara (ed.) 1980: *Preussische Reformen 1807–1820*. Königstein.

Werkmeister, W.H. 1979: *Kant's Silent Decade: A Decade of Philosophical Development*. Tallakassee.

Wessel, Helga 1978: *Zweckmässigkeit als Handlungsprinzip in der deutschen Regierungs- und Verwaltungslehre der frühen Neuzeit. Schriften zur Verfassungs-geschichte* Band. 28, Berlin.

Western, J.R. 1972: *Monarchy and Revolution: The English State in the 1680s*. London.

Wiedeburg P. 1962: *Der Junge Leibniz, Das Reich und Europa* (Part One). Wiesbaden.

Williams, Howard 1982: *Kant's Political Philosophy*. Oxford.

Wolff, Christian 1713: *Vernünfftige Gedanken von den Kräften des menschlichen Verstandes und ihrem richtigen Gebrauche in Erkenntnis der Wahrheit (German Logic)*. Halle.

——1719: *Vernünfftige Gedanken von Gott, der Welt und der Seele der Menschen, auch allen Dingen überhaupt (German Metaphysics)*. Halle.

——1720: *Vernünfftige Gedanken von der Menschen Thun und Lassen zu Beförderung ihrer Glückseligkeit*. Halle.

——1721: *Vernünfftige Gedanken von dem gesellschaftlichen Leben der Menschen und insonderheit dem gemeinen Wesen zu Beförderung der Glückseligkeit des menschlichen Geschlechts.* Halle.

——1728: *Preliminary Discourse on Philosophy in General.* Richard Blackwell (tr.), Indianapolis.

——1841: *Eigene Lebensbeschreibung.* H. Wuttke (ed.), Leipzig.

——1860: *Briefwechsel zwischen Leibniz und Christian Wolff.* C.I. Gerhardt (ed.), Halle.

Wundt, Max 1939: *Die deutsche Schulmetaphysik des 17. Jahrhunderts.* Tübingen.

——1945: *Die deutsche Schulmetaphysik im Zeitalter der Aufklärung.* Tübingen.

Index